Billy Fichrer

$ 4.25

FROM ABSOLUTISM TO REVOLUTION

1648-1848

SECOND EDITION

EDITED BY

HERBERT H. ROWEN

Rutgers University

D0141031

The Macmillan Company
Collier-Macmillan Limited, London

CB
401
.F75
1968

© Copyright, The Macmillan Company, 1968

All rights reserved. No part of this book may be reproduced or transmitted in any form or by any means, electronic or mechanical, including photo-copying, recording or by any information storage and retrieval system, without permission in writing from the Publisher.

Third Printing, 1970

Earlier edition © copyright 1963 by The Macmillan Company.

Library of Congress catalog card number: 68–10120

THE MACMILLAN COMPANY
866 THIRD AVENUE, NEW YORK, NEW YORK 10022
COLLIER-MACMILLAN CANADA, LTD., TORONTO, ONTARIO

PRINTED IN THE UNITED STATES OF AMERICA

PREFACE

In order to explain the purpose of the present volume, the Preface to the first edition bears repeating. The two centuries from 1648 to 1848 form the tract of time between a Europe still half-medieval to one distinctly modern. Such terms as "medieval" and "modern" are not plain names for simple things; they stand for complex interweavings of many historical threads in which we can detect several large, loosely connected patterns. It is these over-all patterns—which become more elusive the more closely we look at them, but nevertheless should never, if possible, be lost from sight—which define our historical "ages." In this sense the characteristic patterns of the medieval period were the coexistence of localism and universalism, the predominance of the manorial and feudal systems in a predominantly agrarian society, the guild system and the "closed" town, a social order frankly based upon hereditary privilege, an all-embracing and universally accepted Christianity, and the philosophical-theological system of Christianity-plus-Aristotelianism called scholasticism. In the modern period, on the other hand, the characteristic patterns are nationalism and the nation-state, the predominance of the city in a predominantly industrial and capitalist society, a social order divided into classes but hostile to inherent privilege, with individual equality and freedom before the law, and, in the world of thought and belief, the ascendancy of secularism and science.

The selections reproduced on these pages illustrate many of these themes at different times and places within two eventful centuries of history. A few patterns have been deliberately highlighted—not that what has been left in the shadows here is truly less important; it is only that choice and elimination were necessary. Fuller understanding arises from the examination of similar events, ideas, and men, noting both likeness and difference, illuminating "facts" by historical generalizations and other principles of analysis and judgment, and testing the generalizations against hard, specific reality. The themes emphasized here are the new natural science, the shifting world views in religion and philosophy, the state (that is, the uses men make of the instrument of public power and what it does to them), economic life, and how men seek a life that is better both economically and otherwise.

The selections are made from various kinds of materials. There are the writings of men of action and of men of thought; there are documents taken, as it were, almost out of the jaws of the events, and sober narrations and analyses made afterward; there are pamphlets and treatises, constitutions, laws, and parliamentary speeches, travel accounts, a play and the preface to a play, and studies by modern historians. Contemporary translations have been used when available and when reasonably accurate and idiomatic; otherwise, good modern translations have been selected. Some of the materials in French, German, and Italian have been specially translated for this volume.

In the second edition, I have followed the plan of the first by retaining all selections and adding seven new ones. To maintain the comprehensive coverage of the volume, the new material has been spread throughout, with each part receiving one or two additional pieces. It is hoped that the book will be more useful with this additional material.

H. H. R.

CONTENTS

I / 1648-1715:
THE AGE OF
LOUIS XIV

The late seventeenth century is traditionally, and rightly, called "the Age of Louis XIV." Absolute monarchy as he practiced it became the characteristic political form of the Old Regime in Europe. It may also be called his age because he embodied so clearly the ideas of the alliance of Church and state, altar and throne, of self-righteous orthodoxy, of pride of rank and place, power and glory, which are the very spirit of the Old Regime. We may even go further and say that Louis XIV helped shape the political and intellectual movements hostile to the Old Regime by providing them with a specific pattern to reject.

1 / SIR ISAAC NEWTON:
THE RULES OF THE
NEW SCIENCE

In an age so filled with minds of the highest power that it has been called "the century of genius," Sir Isaac Newton (1642– 1727) was a giant among giants. His greatest fame is as a physicist, but his stature as a mathematician, particularly as one of the creators of calculus, is not less. His success in embracing the motions of bodies upon earth and of the sun, planets (including the earth), and moon in the skies in a single rigorous system was the supreme intellectual achievement of the new natural science. The purpose, method, and implications of his work as a physicist are set forth by Newton in these passages from his Philosophiae Naturalis Principia Mathematica *("Mathematical Principles of Natural Philosophy"), which was presented to the Royal Society of London in 1686 and first published in Latin the next year. The contemporary transla-*

*tion into English by Andrew Motte has been revised by Florian
Cajori, a modern scholar.*[1]

NEWTON'S PREFACE TO THE FIRST EDITION

Since the Ancients (as we are told by *Pappus*) esteemed the science
of mechanics of greatest importance in the investigation of natural
things, and the moderns, rejecting substantial forms and occult qualities, have endeavored to subject the phenomena of nature to the laws
of mathematics, I have in this treatise cultivated mathematics as far
as it relates to philosophy. . . . Geometry is founded in mechanical
practice, and is nothing but that part of universal mechanics which
accurately proposes and demonstrates the art of measuring. But since
the manual arts are chiefly employed in the moving of bodies, it happens that geometry is commonly referred to their magnitude, and
mechanics to their motion. In this sense rational mechanics will be
the science of motions resulting from any forces whatsoever, and of
the forces required to produce any motions, accurately proposed and
demonstrated. This part of mechanics, as far as it extended to the five
powers which relate to manual arts, was cultivated by the Ancients,
who considered gravity (it not being a manual power) no otherwise
than in moving weights by those powers. But I consider philosophy
rather than arts and write not concerning manual but natural powers,
and consider chiefly those things which relate to gravity, levity, elastic
force, the resistance of fluids, and the like forces, whether attractive
or impulsive; and therefore I offer this work as the mathematical principles of philosophy, for the whole burden of philosophy seems to consist in this—from the phenomena of motions to investigate the forces
of nature, and then from these forces to demonstrate the other phenomena; and to this end the general propositions in the first and second
Books are directed. In the third Book I give an example of this in the
explication of the System of the World; for by the propositions mathematically demonstrated in the former Books, in the third I derive from
the celestial phenomena the forces of gravity with which bodies tend
to the sun and the several planets. Then from these forces, by other
propositions which are also mathematical, I deduce the motions of the
planets, the comets, the moon, and the sea. I wish we could derive
the rest of the phenomena of Nature by the same kind of reasoning
from mechanical principles, for I am induced by many reasons to suspect that they may all depend upon certain forces by which the par-

[1] Sir Isaac Newton, *Mathematical Principles of Natural Philosophy*, ed. Florian
Cajori, translated from the Latin by Andrew Motte, with revisions by Florian
Cajori (Berkeley: University of California Press, 1934), pp. xvii–xviii, 398–400,
543–7. Reprinted by permission of University of California Press.

ticles of bodies, by some causes hitherto unknown, are either mutually impelled towards one another, and cohere in regular figures, or are repelled and recede from one another. These forces being unknown, philosophers have hitherto attempted the search of Nature in vain; but I hope the principles here laid down will afford some light either to this or some truer method of philosophy. . . .

Rules of Reasoning in Philosophy

RULE I. *We are to admit no more causes of natural things than such as are both true and sufficient to explain their appearances.*

To this purpose the philosophers say that Nature does nothing in vain, and more is in vain when less will serve; for Nature is pleased with simplicity, and affects not the pomp of superfluous causes.

RULE II. *Therefore to the same natural effects we must, as far as possible, assign the same causes.*

As to respiration in a man and in a beast; the descent of stone in *Europe* and in *America;* the light of our culinary fire and of the sun; the reflection of light in the earth, and in the planets.

RULE III. *The qualities of bodies, which admit neither intensification nor remission of degrees, and which are found to belong to all bodies within the reach of our experiments, are to be esteemed the universal qualities of all bodies whatsoever.*

For since the qualities of bodies are only known to us by experiments, we are to hold for universal all such as universally agree with experiments; and such as are not liable to diminution can never be quite taken away. We are certainly not to relinquish the evidence of experiments for the sake of dreams and vain fictions of our own devising; nor are we to recede from the analogy of Nature, which is wont to be simple, and always consonant to itself. We no other way know the extension of bodies than by our senses, nor do these reach it in all bodies; but because we perceive extension in all that are sensible, therefore we ascribe it universally to all others also. That abundance of bodies are hard, we learn by experience; and because the hardness of the whole arise from the hardness of the parts, we therefore justly infer the hardness of the undivided particles not only of the bodies we feel but of all others. That all bodies are impenetrable, we gather not from reason, but from sensation. The bodies which we handle we find impenetrable, and thence conclude impenetrability to be a universal property of all bodies whatsoever. That all bodies are movable, and endowed with certain powers (which we call the inertia) of persevering in their motion, or in their rest, we only infer from the like properties observed in the bodies which we have seen. The extension, hardness, impenetrability, mobility, and inertia of the whole, result from the extension, hardness, impenetrability, mobility, and inertia of the parts; and hence we conclude the least particles of all bodies to be also all extended, and hard and impenetrable, and movable, and endowed with their proper inertia. And this is the foundation of all philosophy. Moreover, that the divided but contiguous particles of bodies may be separated from one another, is matter of observation; and, in the particles that remain undivided, our minds are able to distinguish yet lesser parts, as is mathematically demonstrated. But whether the parts so distinguished, and not yet divided, may, by the powers of Nature, be actually divided and separated from one another, we cannot certainly determine. Yet, had we the proof of but one experiment that any undivided particle, in breaking a hard and solid body, suffered a division, we might by virtue of this rule conclude that the undivided as well as the divided particles may be divided and actually separated to infinity.

Lastly, if it universally appears, by experiments and astronomical observations, that all bodies about the earth gravitate towards the earth, and that in proportion to the quantity of matter which they severally contain; that the moon likewise, according to the quantity of its matter, gravitates towards the earth; that, on the other hand, our sea gravitates towards the moon; and all the planets one towards another; and the comets in like manner towards the sun; we must, in consequence of this rule, universally allow that all bodies whatsoever are endowed with a principle of mutual gravitation. For the argument from the appearances concludes with more force for the universal gravitation of all bodies than for their impenetrability; of which, among those in the celestial regions, we have no experiments, nor any manner of observation. Not that I affirm gravity to be essential to bodies; by their *vis insita* I mean nothing but their inertia. This is immutable. Their gravity is diminished as they recede from the earth.

RULE IV. *In experimental philosophy we are to look upon propositions inferred by general induction from phenomena as accurately or very nearly true, notwithstanding any contrary hypotheses that may be imagined, till such time as other phenomena occur, by which they may either be made more accurate, or liable to exceptions.*

This rule we must follow, that the argument of induction may not be evaded by hypotheses. . . .

(General Scholium.) The six primary planets are revolved about the sun in circles concentric with the sun, and with motions directed towards the same parts, and almost in the same plane. Ten moons are revolved about the earth, Jupiter, and Saturn, in circles concentric with them, with the same direction of motion, and nearly in the planes of the orbits of these planets; but it is not to be conceived that mere mechanical causes could give birth to so many regular motions, since the comets range over all parts of the heavens in very eccentric orbits; for by that kind of motion they pass easily through the orbs of the planets, and with great rapidity; and in their aphelions, where they move the slowest, and are detained the longest, they recede to the greatest distances from each other, and hence suffer the least disturbance from their mutual attractions. This most beautiful system of the sun, planets, and comets, could only proceed from the counsel and dominion of an intelligent and powerful Being. And if the fixed stars are the centres of other like systems, these, being formed by the like wise counsel, must be all subject to the dominion of One; especially since the light of the fixed stars is of the same nature with the light of the sun, and from every system light passes into all the other systems: and lest the systems of the fixed stars should, by their gravity, fall on each other, he hath placed those systems at immense distances from one another. . . .

Hitherto we have explained the phenomena of the heavens and of our sea by the power of gravity, but have not yet assigned the cause of this power. This is certain, that it must proceed from a cause that penetrates to the very centres of the sun and planets, without suffering the least diminution of its force; that operates not according to the quantity of the surfaces of the particles upon which it acts (as mechanical causes used to do), but according to the quantity of solid matter which they contain, and propagates its virtue on all sides to immense distances, decreasing always as the inverse square of the distances. Gravitation towards the sun is made up out of the gravitations towards the several particles of which the body of the sun is composed; and in receding from the sun decreases accurately as the inverse square of the distances as far as the orbit of Saturn, as evidently appears from the quiescence of the aphelion of the planets; nay, and even to the remotest aphelion of the comets, if those aphelions are also quiescent. But hitherto I have not been able to discover the cause of those properties of gravity from phenomena, and I frame no hypotheses; for whatever is not deduced from the phenomena is to be called an hypothesis; and hypotheses, whether metaphysical or physical, whether of occult qualities or mechanical, have no place in experimental philosophy. In this philosophy particular propositions are inferred from the phenomena, and afterwards rendered general by induction. Thus it was that the impenetrability, the mobility, and the impulsive forces of bodies, and the laws of motion and gravitation, were discovered. And to us it is enough that gravity does really exist, and acts according to the laws which we have explained, and abundantly serves to account for all the motions of the celestial bodies, and of our sea.

And now we might add something concerning a certain most subtle spirit which pervades and lies hid in all gross bodies; by the force and action of which spirit the particles of bodies attract one another at near distances, and cohere, if contiguous; and electric bodies operate to greater distances, as well repelling as attracting the neighboring corpuscles; and light is emitted, reflected, refracted, inflected, and heats bodies; and all sensation is excited, and the members of animal bodies move at the command of the will, namely, by the vibrations of this spirit, mutually propagated along the solid filaments of the nerves, from the outward organs of sense to the brain, and from the brain into the muscles. But these are things that cannot be explained in a few words, nor are we furnished with that sufficiency of experiments which is required to an accurate determination and demonstration of the laws by which this electric and elastic spirit operates.

2 / PIERRE BAYLE: THE ASSAULT UPON SUPERSTITION BEGINS

The new scientific world outlook—and the habit of rational analysis of experience from which it arose and to which it gave encouragement—imperiled the traditional world outlook. This included a vast variety of beliefs about man's relationship to the world which lay in the indefinite area between religion and magic called superstition. These beliefs had often sifted into traditional religion but, not being part of formal doctrine, were more open to criticism. No critic of superstition in the late seventeenth century was more relentless and penetrating than Pierre Bayle (1647–1706), a French Huguenot who spent most of his productive life in exile in the Netherlands. His Pensées sur la comète, écrites à un docteur de la Sorbonne *("Thoughts Concerning the Comet, Written to a Doctor [of Theology] of the Sorbonne," 1682), from which the following passages are taken, was an early work that made his reputation.*[2]

This is still the Opinion of the Multitude. The Historians seldom take notice of Eclipses, but mention their prognosticating the Death

[2] Pierre Bayle, *Miscellaneous Reflections, Occasion'd by the Comet Which appear'd in December 1680, Chiefly tending to explode popular superstitions,* translated from the French (London: J. Morphew, 1708), Vol. I, pp. 101–5.

of such a King, the Revolt of such a Province, or some Disaster of this kind they met in their way. From the Astrologers who deal in Almanacks to those who meddle only in Horoscopes of Quality, there's not one but tells you, that Eclipses presage War, Pestilence, Famine, Inundations, Deaths of great Men, and so forth; and they meet with more credit in this particular, than when they foretel the Season only, whether wet or windy, hot or cold, &c. The Eclipse of the Sun, which happen'd the *12th of August* 1654. was in their account to turn the World upside down: some reckon'd upon a Deluge of Water at least, like that of *Noah;* and some upon a Deluge of Fire, which was to put an end to this World; others contented themselves with the Thoughts of strange Revolutions in States, or the final Destruction of *Rome.* The People were so terrify'd, that they who only shut themselves up in Cellars, or close Rooms, well air'd and well scented by the Physician's directions, to provide against the damps of the Eclipse, thought they had a right to laugh at timorous Minds, and to be reckon'd men of bold Thought. In good earnest their Conduct shew'd a great Force of Mind, in comparison of those who fear'd no less than the end of the World. The Consternation was so great, that a Country Curate not being able to confess all his Parishioners round, who were preparing for the last Hour, was oblig'd to tell 'em in his *Prone,*[3] that they need not be in such hurry to confess, the Eclipse was put off for a fortnight longer. You may meet with the Passage in a Book of Mr. *Petit,* Intendant of the Fortifications, a man of Sense, perfectly free from Superstition, and who oppos'd popular Error with a great deal of Courage.

You see the Antients and Moderns, the Christians and the Pagans, perfectly agreed about Eclipses presaging great Calamitys. And yet 'tis a notorious Error, 1. Because Eclipses can do no harm; 2. Because they can be no Signs of harm.

I say then, that an Eclipse, whether of the Moon or Sun, can have no evil effect, because the worst it can do, is to hinder the Earth's being illuminated for a little while, and this can't be of any consequence. You know what the Opinion of *Pericles* was in this point, one of the greatest Men of Antiquity; he was just ready to set sail with the Fleet under his Command on some great Expedition, when there hapned an Eclipse of the Sun, which so confounded his Pilot, he neither knew where he was, nor what he was doing: *Pericles,* freed from these Superstitions by the Philosopher *Anaxagoras,* held up his Cloke before the Pilot's Eyes, and ask'd him if he thought there was any ill luck in that; no, says the Pilot: Then says *Pericles,* there's no ill luck in the Sun's being eclips'd; for all the difference between my Cloke which shades the Light from

---

[3] The Homily or Discourse which the Priest makes every Sunday for the Instruction of his Parishioners. (Translator's note)

your Eyes, and the Body which causes the Eclipse, is, that one is some-what bigger than t'other. This Reflexion is so obvious, 'tis strange so few shou'd fall into it.

There's no Man can't easily comprehend, that one may be whole days together in places much darker than the darkest Eclipse, without prejudice to his Health; and keep a Pare or an Apple-tree in the thick-est Shade for three or four hours, without hurting the Fruit or Leaves for that Year. There's no Farmer who wou'd not lengthen the Nights some hours, if he cou'd with a Wish, that the Heat of the Sun might not come on so soon to scorch the Fruits of the Earth. People are agreed, those very thick Clouds which darken the Air, sometimes 5 or 6 days together, more than an Eclipse of the Sun of 5 or 6 digits, when it happens without any Cloud at all, are often favorable to the Harvest. And I'm apt to think, shou'd the New Moon amuse her self for a whole Day and Night with the Sun, so as not to give Light to the Earth for that time, her Absence cou'd cause no harm. 'Tis not to be doubted, one may bear the want of Meat and Drink for a day, without indanger-ing his Life or Health, or feeling the least Inconveniences two days after. And yet 'tis certain Nourishment is much more Necessary for the Support of Life than the Light of the Sun, since there are Nations which pass many Months comfortably enough without the Sun's rising above their Horizon. And yet amidst all these Discoverys of our Rea-son, we cannot or will not comprehend how the Moon or the Shadow of the Earth shou'd intercept the Sun-beams for a very small time, but infinite Disasters must ensue. Nay, they fancy the Malignity of this Darkness goes further, that it marks out the King in the midst of his Court, and distinguishing him from common Men, strikes him alone with a mortal Distemper; which is certainly very extraordinary. Is any thing more sensless than to see People, who retrench with all their Skill behind double Curtains, and Umbrella's, and Window-shutters; who dare not stir abroad but by Night, except in Mask and Parasol, tremble at the thoughts of an Eclipse, which, to express my self nicely for once, is at some Seasons of the Year no more than a kind Office the Moon does the Earth, in serving her for an Umbrella.

Let's now see, whether Eclipses ben't at least the Signs of those Evils which happen in the Earth. I say, Not, Sir: And here I expect the greatest shock, for here's the last resource of those who assert the Malignity of Eclipses and Comets. But to beat 'em out of it, I insist on two points only: 1. That Eclipses are the Effect of such a constant Law of Nature, that there's no little Astrologer who can't foretel the Day, the Hour, and the Point of the Heavens in which they happen, many Ages before they do. 2. That they happen in all Seasons and in all Countrys; sometimes more than four in a Year; sometimes at hours when nobody takes notice of 'em but those whose Trade it is; and often when the Clouds hinder People's perceiving 'em.

The first of these Reasons seems convincing in my Judgment; for in a word, if Eclipses are a natural and necessary Consequence of the Motions of the Stars, they happen independently of Man, and without any regard to his Merits or Demerits, and consequently wou'd happen as they do, whether God resolv'd to punish Sinners or no; insomuch that they can't be construed the forerunning Signs of Divine Justice. Besides, we must forfeit all claim to common Sense, and allow that a natural Effect can't be said to be the Sign of any thing, unless when it produces such a thing, or is it self produc'd by it, or where both depend on the same Cause. We shall examine the other ways of one thing's becoming the Sign of another, in a proper place. At present I only take notice, Eclipses don't denote Evils to come, in any of the three ways here mention'd, because I have shown they're not the Causes of 'em.

3 / JOHN TOLAND: THE REASONABLENESS OF CHRISTIANITY

One of the most vigorous denials of the existence of any true conflict between reason and revealed religion was made by John Toland (1670–1722) in his Christianity not Mysterious *(1696), from which the following passage was taken. Whatever Toland's intention, the work was bitterly attacked by defenders of orthodoxy. Toland, born a Roman Catholic in northern Ireland, was converted to Protestantism at the age of fifteen, and studied at Glasgow, Edinburgh, and Leiden.[4]*

What we discours'd of REASON before, and REVELATION now, being duly weigh'd, all the Doctrines and Precepts of the New Testament (if it be indeed Divine) must consequently agree with *Natural Reason,* and our own ordinary Ideas. This every considerate and wel-dispos'd Person will find by the careful perusal of it: And whoever undertakes this Task, will confess the Gospel *not to be hidden from*

[4] John Toland, *Christianity not Mysterious,* 2nd ed. (London: Sam. Buckley, 1696), pp. 46–50.

us, nor afar off, but very nigh us, in our Mouths, and in our Hearts. It affords the most illustrious Examples of close and perspicuous Ratiocination conceivable; which is incumbent on me in the Explication of its MYSTERIES, to demonstrate. And tho the Evidence of *Christ's* Doctrine might claim the Approbation of the *Gentiles,* and its Conformity with the Types and Prophecies of the *Old Testament,* with all the Marks of the *MESSIAH* concurring in his Person, might justly challenge the Assent of his Countrymen; yet to leave no room for doubt, he proves his Authority and Gospel by such Works, and Miracles as the stiff-neck'd *Jews* themselves could not deny to be Divine. *Nicodemus* says to him, *No Man can do these Miracles which thou do'st, except God be with him.* Some of the Pharisees acknowledg'd *no Sinner could do such things.* And others, that *they exceeded the Power of the Devil.*

JESUS himself appeals to his very Enemies, ready to stone him for pretended Blasphemy, saying; *If I do not the Works of my Father, believe me not: But if I do, believe not me, believe the Works; that you may know, and believe that the Father is in me, and I in him:* That is, believe not rashly on me, and so give a Testimony to my Works; but search the *Scriptures,* which testify of the *Messiah;* consider the Works I do, whether they be such as become God, and are attributed to him: If they be, then conclude and believe that I am he, &c. In effect, several of the People said, *that Christ when he should come could do no greater Wonders;* and *many of the Jews believ'd, when they saw the Miracles which he did.*

How shall we escape, says the Apostle, *if we neglect so great a Salvation, which at the first began to be spoken by the Lord, and was confirm'd unto us by them that heard him; God also bearing them witness with divers Miracles, and Gifts of the Holy Spirit, according to his own Will?* Those who heard *Christ,* the Author of our Religion, speak, and saw the Wonders which he wrought, *renounce all the hidden things of Dishonesty, all Craftiness and deceitful handling of the Word of God:* And *that they manifest nothing but Truth, they commend themselves to every Man's Conscience,* that is, they appeal to every Man's Reason, *in the Sight of God. Peter* exhorts Christians *to be ready always to give an Answer to every one that asks them a Reason of their Hope.* Now to what purpose serv'd all these Miracles, all these Appeals, if no Regard was to be had of Mens Understandings? if the Doctrines of *Christ* were incomprehensible, contradictory; or were we oblig'd to believe reveal'd Nonsense? Now if these Miracles be true, *Christianity* must consequently be intelligible; and if false, (which our Adversaries will not grant) they can be then no Arguments against us.

But to insist no longer upon such Passages, all Men will own the

Verity I defend, if they read the sacred Writings with that Equity and
Attention that is due to meer Humane Works: Nor is there any different Rule to be follow'd in the Interpretation of *Scripture* from what is
common to all other Books. Whatever unprejudic'd Person shall use
those Means, will find them notorious Deceivers, or much deceiv'd themselves, who maintain the *New Testament* is written without any Order
or certain Scope, but just as Matters came into the *Apostles* Heads,
whether transported with Enthusiastick Fits, (as some will have it) or,
according to others, for lack of good Sense and a liberal Education. I
think I may justly say, that they are Strangers to true Method, who
complain of this Confusion and Disorder. But the Proof of the Case
depends not upon Generalities: Tho, whenever it is prov'd, I will not
promise that every one shall find a Justification of the *particular Method*
he was taught, or he has chosen, to follow. *To defend any PARTY is
not my business, but to discover the TRUTH.*

4 / NICOLAS BOILEAU: THE REASONABLENESS OF POETRY

*The sway of reason was not disputed in the arts as it was
in religion. The rule book of reasonable poetry writing as it was
practiced during the late seventeenth and most of the eighteenth
centuries was the* Art poétique *("The Art of Poetry," 1674) of
Nicolas Boileau-Despréaux. He was not only a forceful critic but
also a subtle and vigorous poet in his own right. The translation
from which the following sections are taken was made by the Englishman, Sir William Soames.*[5]

What-e're you write of Pleasant or Sublime,
Always let sence accompany your Rhyme:
Falsely they seem each other to oppose;
Rhyme must be made with Reason's Laws to close:
And when to conquer her you bend your force,
The Mind will Triumph in the Noble Course;

[5] [Nicolas Boileau-Despréaux], *The Art of Poetry, Written in French by the
Sieur de Boileau, Made English* (London: R. Bentley and S. Magnes, 1683), pp.
2–3, 10–11.

To Reason's yoke she quickly will incline,
Which, far from hurting, renders her Divine:
But, if neglected, will as easily stray,
And master Reason, which she should obey.
Love Reason then: and let what e're you Write
Borrow from her its Beauty, Force, and Light.
Most Writers, mounted on a resty Muse,
Extravagant, and Senceless Objects chuse;
They Think they erre, if in their Verse they fall
On any thought that's Plain, or Natural:
Fly this excess; and let *Italians* be
Vain Authors of false glitt'ring Poetry.
All ought to aim at Sence; but most in vain
Strive the hard Pass, and slipp'ry Path to gain:
You drown, if to the right or left to stray;
Reason to go has often but one way. . . .
     Observe well the Language well in all you Write,
And swerve not from it in your loftiest flight.
The smoothest Verse, and the exactest Sence
Displease us, if ill *English* give offence:
A barb'rous Phrase no Reader can approve;
Nor Bombast, Noise, or Affectation Love.
In short, without pure Language, what you Write,
Can never yield us Profit, or Delight.
Take time for thinking; never work in hast;
And value not your self for writing fast.
A rapid Poem, with such fury writ,
Shews want of Judgment, not abounding Wit.
More pleas'd we are to see a River lead
His gentle Streams along a flow'ry Mead,
Than from high Banks to hear loud Torrents roar,
With foamy Waters on a Muddy Shore.
Gently make haste, of Labour not afraid;
A hundred times consider what you've said:
Polish, repolish, every Colour lay,
And sometimes add; but oft'ner take away.
Tis not enough, when swarming Faults are writ,
That here and there are scattered Sparks of Wit;
Each Object must be fix'd in the due place,
And diff'ring parts have Corresponding Grace:
Till, by a curious Art dispos'd, we find
One perfect whole, of all the pieces join'd.
Keep to your Subject close, in all you say;
Nor for a sounding Sentence ever stray.

The publick Censure for your Writings fear,
And to your self be Critic most severe.

5 / CHARLES I:
THE RIGHT OF KINGS—
"A GOOD CAUSE"

In the arena of politics the great combat of the Age of Reason was between absolute monarchy and its opponents and critics. An eloquent statement of the position of monarchical right was made by Charles I of England after his overthrow by the parliamentary party and just before his execution as a traitor. Though as a politician Charles had been a double-tongued equivocator, here he spoke plainly and with all the sincerity of one who knew he would never speak again. The following section is from a pamphlet published in London some months after the execution. The year 1648 in the title is Old Style, because England, unlike most continental European countries, continued to begin the new year on Lady Day, March 25, not on January 1; New Style, Charles was beheaded on January 30, 1649.[6]

The King being come upon the Scaffold, look'd very earnestly on the Block, and asked Col: *Hacker* if there were no higher; and then spake thus (directing his speech chiefly to Col: *Thomlinson*)

King.
I shall be very little heard of any body here, I shall therefore speak a word unto you here; indeed I could hold my peace very wel, if I did not think that holding my peace, would make some men think that I did submit to the guilt, as well as to the punishment; but I think it is my duty to God first, and to my countrey, for to clear my self both as an honest man, and a good King, and a good Christian. I shall begin first with my innocency. In troth I think it not very needful for me to insist long upon this, for all the world knows that I never did begin a War with the two Houses of Parliament, and I call God to witness, to whom

[6] *King Charls his Speech Made upon the Scaffold at Whitehall-Gate, Immediately before his Execution, On Tuesday the 30 of Ian. 1648. With a Relation of the maner of his going to Execution* (London: Peter Cole, 1649), pp. 5–12.

I must shortly make an account, that I never did intend for to incroach upon their Priviledges, they began upon me, it is the Militia, they began upon, they confest that the Militia was mine, but they thought it fit for to have it from me; and to be short, if any body will look to the dates of Commissions, of their Commissions and mine, and likewise to the Declarations, will see clearly that they began those unhappy troubles not I; so that as the guilt of these Enormous crimes that are laid against me, I hope in God that God will clear me of it, I will not, I am in charity; God forbid that I should lay it upon the two Houses of Parliament, there is no necessity of either, I hope that they are free of this guilt; for I do believe that ill Instruments between them and me, has been the chief cause of all this bloodshed; so that by way of speaking, as I finde my self clear of this, I hope (and pray God) that they may too: yet for all this, God forbid that I should be so ill a Christian, as not to say that Gods Judgements are just upon me: Many times he does pay Justice by an unjust Sentence, that is ordinary; I will onely say this, That an unjust Sentence [7] that I suffered for to take effect, is punished now, by an unjust Sentence upon me; that is, so far I have said, to shew you that I am an innocent man.

Now for to shew you that I am a good Christian: I hope there is [8] a good man that will bear me witness, that I have forgiven all the world; and even those in particular that have been the chief causers of my death; who they are, God knows, I do not desire to know, I pray God forgive them. But this is not all, my Charity must go farther, I wish that they may repent, for indeed they have committed a great sin in that particular; I pray God with St. *Stephen,* That this be not laid to their charge; nay, not onely so, but that they may take the right way to the Peace of the Kingdom, for my Charity commands me not onely to forgive particular men, but my Charity commands me to endeavor to the last gasp the Peace of the Kingdom: So (Sirs) I do wish with all my soul, and I do hope (there is [9] some here will carry it further) that they may endeavor the Peace of the Kingdom. Now (Sirs) I must shew you both how you are out of the way, and will put you in a way; first, you are out of the way, for certainly all the way you ever have had yet as I could finde by any thing, is in the way of Conquest; certainly this is an ill way, for Conquest (Sir) in my opinion is never just, except there be a good just Cause, either for matter of wrong or just Title, and then if you go beyond it, the first quarrel that you have to it, that makes it unjust at the end, that was just at first: But if it be only matter of Conquest, then it is a great Robbery; as a Pirat said to *Alex-*

---

[7] Strafford. (Note in original)

[8] Pointing to Dr. *Juxon.* (Note in original)

[9] Turning to some Gentlemen that wrote. (Note in original)

ander, that He was the great Robber, he was but a petty Robber; and so, Sir, I do think the way that you are in, is much out of the way. Now Sir, for to put you in the way, believe it you will never do right, nor God will never prosper you, until you give God his due, the King his due (that is, my Successors) and the People their due; I am as much for them as any of you: You must give God his due, by regulating rightly his Church (according to his Scripture) which is now out of order: For to set you in a way particularly now I cannot, but onely this, A National Synod freely called, freely debating among themselves, must settle this; when that every Opinion is freely and clearly heard.

For the King, indeed I will not, (then turning to a Gentleman that touched the Ax, said, Hurt not the Ax that may hurt me.[10] For the King:) The Laws of the Land will clearly instruct you for that; therefore, because it concerns my own particular, I onely give you a touch of it.

For the People. And truly I desire their Liberty and Freedom, as much as any Body whomsoever; but I must tell you, That their Liberty and their Freedom, consists in having of Government; those Laws, by which their life and their Goods, may be most their own. It is not for having share in Government (Sir) that is nothing pertaining to them. A Subject and a Soveraign, are clean different things; and therefore, untill they do that, I mean, That you do put the People in that Liberty as I say, certainly they will never enjoy themselves.

Sirs, It was for this, that now I am come here: If I would have given way to an Arbitrary way, for to have all Lawes changed according to the power of the Sword, I needed not to have come here; and therefore, I tell you, (and I pray God it be not laid to your charge) That I am the Martyr of the People.

In troth Sirs, I shall not hold you much longer; for I will only say this to you, That in truth, I could have desired some little time longer, because that *I* would have put this that *I* have said in a little more order, and a little better digested, then *I* have done; and therefore *I* hope you will excuse me.

I have delivered my Conscience, *I* pray God, that you do take those courses that are best for the good of the Kingdom, and your own Salvations.

Doctor *Juxon.*

Will Your Majesty (though it may be very well known Your Majesties Affections to Religion, yet it may be expected, that You should) say somewhat for the Worlds satisfaction.

---

[10] Meaning if he did blunt the edge. (Note in original)

King.

I thank you very heartily (my Lord) for that, I had almost forgotten it. In troth Sirs, My Conscience in Religion, I think, is very well known to all the World; and therefore, I declare before you all, That I die a Christian according to the Profession of the Church of ENGLAND, as I found it left Me by My Father; and this honest man [11] I think will witness it. Then turning to the Officers said, Sirs, excuse me for this same. I have a good Cause, and I have a gracious God; I will say no more.

6 / THOMAS HOBBES: SOCIAL CONTRACT AND THE RIGHT OF KINGS

Not long after the death of Charles I, a defense of monarchical right that was as heterodox as the late king's was orthodox came from the pen of the philosopher Thomas Hobbes (1588– 1679). Hobbes was a thoroughgoing rationalist who rejected the argument from tradition in favor of that from advantage and utility. He thereby modernized the ancient doctrine of the social contract and gave it the form in which it was thereafter debated. Although committed to the Stuart dynasty, indeed for a while the tutor of the future Charles II in mathematics, Hobbes made his peace with Cromwell in 1651, returning from a decade-long residence in France. The Cavaliers and their successors, the Tories, always rejected Hobbes' defense of monarchy, because it was founded on neither tradition nor religion. The following selections are taken from the first edition of Hobbes' masterpiece, Leviathan (1651).[12]

Nature (the Art whereby God hath made and governes the World) is by the *Art* of man, as in many other things, so in this also imitated, that it can make an Artificiall Animal. For seeing life is but a motion of Limbs, the beginning whereof is in some principall part within; why may we not say, that all *Automata* (Engines that move themselves by

[11] Pointing to Dr. *Juxon.* (Note in original)
[12] Thomas Hobbes, *Leviathan, or The Matter, Forme, & Power of a Commonwealth Ecclesiasticall and Civill* (London: Andrew Crooke, 1651), pp. 1, 60–5, 71, 85, 87–90, 114.

springs and wheeles as doth a watch) have an artificiall life? For what is the *Heart,* but a *Spring;* and the *Nerves,* but so many *Strings;* and the *Joynts,* but so many *Wheeles,* giving motion to the whole Body, such as was intended by the Artificer? *Art* goes yet further, imitating that Rationall and most excellent worke of Nature, *Man.* For by Art is created that great LEVIATHAN called a COMMON-WLALTH, or STATE, (in latine CIVITAS) which is but an Artificiall Man; though of greater stature and strength than the Naturall, for whose protection and defence it was intended; and in which the *Soveraignty* is an Artificiall *Soul,* as giving life and motion to the whole body; The *Magistrates,* and other *Officers* of Judicature and Execution, artificiall *Joynts; Reward* and *Punishment* (by which fastned to the seate of the Soveraignty, every joynt and member is moved to performe his duty) are the *Nerves,* that do the same in the Body Naturall; the *Wealth* and *Riches* of all the particular members, are the *Strength; Salus Populi* (the *peoples safety*) its *Businesse; Counsellors,* by whom all things needfull for it to know, are suggested into it, are the *Memory; Equity* and *Lawes,* an artificiall *Reason* and *Will; Concord, Health; Sedition, Sicknesse;* and *Civill war, Death.* Lastly, the Pacts and *Covenants,* by which the parts of this Body Politique were at first made, set together, and united, resemble that *Fiat,* or the *Let us make man,* pronounced by God in the Creation. . . .

Nature hath made men so equal, in the faculties of body, and mind; as that though there be found one man sometimes manifestly stronger in body, or of quicker mind than another; yet when all is reckoned together, the difference between man, and man, is not so considerable, as that one man can thereupon claim to himself any benefit, to which another may not pretend, as well as he. For as to the strength of body, the weakest has strength enough to kill the strongest, either by secret machination, or by confederacy with others, that are in the same danger with himself.

And as to the faculties of the mind, (setting aside the arts grounded upon words, and especially that skill of proceeding upon general, and infallible rules, called Science; which very few have, and but in few things; as being not a native faculty, born with us; nor attained, (as Prudence,) while we look after somewhat else,) I find yet a greater equality amongst men, than that of strength. . . .

From this equality of ability, ariseth equality of hope in the attaining of our Ends. And therefore if any two men desire the same thing, which neverthelesse they cannot both enjoy, they become enemies; and in the way to their End, (which is principally their owne conservation, and sometimes their delectation only,) endeavour to destroy, or subdue one another. And from hence it comes to passe, that where an Invader hath no more to feare, than an other mans single power; if one plant, sow, build, or possesse a convenient Seat, other[s] may

probably be expected to come prepared with forces united, to dis-
posesse, and deprive him, not only of the fruit of his labour, but also
of his life, or liberty. And the Invader again is in the like danger of
another. . . .

Hereby it is manifest, that during the time men live without a
common Power to keep them all in awe, they are in that condition
which is called Warre; and such a warre, as is of every man, against
every man. For WARRE, consisteth not in Battel onely, or the act of
fighting; but in a tract of time, wherein the Will to contend by Battel
is sufficiently known: and therefore the notion of *Time*, is to be considered in the nature of Warre; as it is in the nature of Weather. For
as the nature of Foule weather, lyeth not in a showre or two of rain;
but in an inclination thereto of many dayes together: So the nature of
War, consisteth not in actuall fighting; but in the known disposition
thereto, during all the time there is no assurance to the contrary. All
other time is PEACE.

Whatsoever therefore is consequent to a time of Warre, where every
man is Enemy to every man; the same is consequent to the time,
wherein men live without other security, than what their own strength,
and their own invention shall furnish them withall. In such condition,
there is no place for Industry; because the fruit thereof is uncertain:
and consequently no Culture of the Earth; no Navigation, nor use of
the commodities that may be imported by Sea; no commodious Building; no Instruments of moving, and removing, such things as require
much force; no Knowledge of the face of the Earth; no account of
Time; no Arts; no Letters; no Society; and which is worst of all, con-
tinuall feare, and danger of violent death. And the life of man, solitary,
poore, nasty, brutish, and short. . . .

To this warre of every man, against every man, this also is consequent; that nothing can be Unjust. The notions of Right and Wrong,
Justice and Injustice have there no place. Where there is no common
Power, there is no Law: where no Law, no Injustice. Force, and Fraud,
are in warre the two Cardinall vertues. Justice, and Injustice are none
of the Faculties neither of the Body, nor Mind. If they were, they
might be in a man that were alone in the world, as well as his Senses,
and Passions. They are Qualities, that relate to men in Society, not in
Solitude. It is consequent also to the same condition, that there be no
Propriety, no Dominion, no *Mine* and *Thine* distinct; but onely that to
be every mans, that he can get; and for so long, as he can keep it.
And thus much for the ill condition, which man by meer Nature is
actually placed in; though with a possibility to come out of it, consisting partly in the Passions, partly in his Reason.

The Passions that encline men to Peace, are Feare of Death; Desire
of such things as are necessary to commodious living; and a Hope by

their Industry to obtain them. And Reason suggesteth convenient Articles of Peace, upon which men may be drawn to agreement. These Articles, are they, which otherwise are called the Lawes of Nature. . . .

And consequently it is a precept, or generall rule of Reason, *That every man, ought to endeavour Peace, as farre as he has hope of obtaining it; and when he cannot obtain it, that he may seek, and use, all helps, and advantages of Warre.* The first branch of which Rule, containeth the first, and Fundamentall Law of Nature; which is, *to seek Peace, and follow it.* The Second, the summe of the Right of Nature; which is, *By all means we can, to defend our selves.*

From this Fundamentall Law of Nature, by which men are commanded to endeavour Peace, is derived this second Law; *That a man be willing, when others are so too, as farre-forth, as for Peace, and defence of himself he shall think it necessary, to lay down this right to all things; and be contented with so much liberty against other men, as he would allow other men against himself,* For as long as every man holdeth this Right, of doing any thing he liketh; so long are all men in the condition of War. But if other men will not lay down their Right, as well as he; then there is no Reason for any one, to devest himself of his: For that were to expose himself to Prey, (which no man is bound to) rather than to dispose himself to Peace. This is that Law of the Gospel; *Whatsoever you require that others should do to you, that do ye to them.* And that Law of all men, *Quod tibi fieri non vis, alteri ne feceris.*[13]. . .

From that law of Nature, by which we are obliged to transferre to another, such Rights, as being retained, hinder the peace of Mankind, there followeth a Third; which is this, *That men performe their Covenants made:* without which, Covenants are in vain, and but Empty words; and the Right of all men to all things remaining, we are still in the condition of Warre. . . .

The final Cause, End, or Design of men, (who naturally love Liberty, and Dominion over others,) in the introduction of that restraint upon themselves, (in which we see them live in Common-wealths,) is the foresight of their own preservation, and of a more contented life thereby; that is to say, of getting themselves out from that miserable condition of War, which is necessarily consequent (as hath been shewn) to the natural Passions of men, where there is no visible Power to keep them in awe, and tye them by fear of punishment to the performance of their Covenants, and observation of those Laws of Nature set down in the 14th. and 15th. Chapters. . . .

The only way to erect such a Common Power, as may be able to defend them from the invasion of Forreigners, and the injuries of one

---

[13] What you would not have others do to you, do not to them. (ed.)

another, and thereby to secure them in such sort, as that by their own industry, and by the fruits of the Earth, they may nourish themselves and live contentedly; is, to conferr all their power and strength upon one Man, or upon one Assembly of men, that may reduce all their Wills, by plurality of voices, unto one Will: which is as much as to say, to appoint one Man, or Assembly of men, to bear their Person; and every one to own, and acknowledge himself to be Author of whatsoever he that so beareth their Person, shall Act, or cause to be Acted, in those things which concern the Common Peace and Safety; and therein to submit their Wills, every one to his Will, and their Judgments, to his Judgment. This is more than Consent, or Concord; it is a real Unity of them all, in one and the same Person, made by Covenant of every man with every man, in such a manner, as if every man should say to every man, *I authorize and give up my Right of Governing my self, to this Man, or to this Assembly of men, on this condition, that thou give up thy Right to him, and Authorize all his Actions in like manner.* This done, the Multitude so united in one Person, is called a COMMON-WEALTH, in Latine CIVITAS. This is the Generation of that great LEVIATHAN, or rather (to speak more reverently) of that *Mortal God,* to which we owe under the *Immortal God,* our peace and defence. For by this Authority, given him by every particular man in the Common-wealth, he hath the use of so much Power and Strength conferred on him, that by terrour thereof, he is enabled to form the wills of them all, to Peace at home, and mutual aid against their enemies abroad. And in him consisteth the Essence of the Commonwealth; which (to define it) is *One Person, of whose Acts a great Multitude, by mutual Covenants one with another, have made themselves every one the Author, to the end he may use the strength and means of them all, as he shall think expedient, for their Peace and Common Defence.*

And he that carrieth this Person, is called SOVERAIGN, and said to have *Soveraign Power;* and every one besides, his SUBJECT.

The attaining to this Soveraign Power, is by two ways. One, by Natural force; as when a man maketh his children, to submit themselves, and their children to his government, as being able to destroy them if they refuse; or by War subdueth his enemies to his will, giving them their lives on that condition. The other, is when men agree amongst themselves, to submit to some Man, or Assembly of men, voluntarily, on confidence to be protected by him against all others. This lat[t]er, may be called a Political Common-wealth, or Common-wealth by *Institution;* and the former, a Common-wealth by *Acquisition.* And first, I shall speak of a Common-wealth by Institution. . . .

From this Institution of a Common-wealth are derived all the Rights, and Faculties, of him, or them, on whom the Soveraign Power is conferred by the consent of the People assembled.

First, because they Covenant, it is to be understood, they are not obliged by former Covenant to anything repugnant hereunto. And consequently they that have already Instituted a Common-wealth, being thereby bound by Covenant, to own the Actions, and Judgments of one, cannot lawfully make a new Covenant, amongst themselves, to be obedient to any other, in any thing whatsoever, without his permission. And therefore, they that are subjects to a Monarch, cannot without his leave cast off Monarchy, and return to the confusion of a disunited Multitude; nor transferr their Person from him that beareth it, to another Man, or other Assembly of men: for they are bound, every man to every man, to Own, and be reputed Author of all, that he that already is their Soveraign, shall do, and judge fit to be done: so that any one man dissenting, all the rest should break their Covenant made to that man, which is injustice: and they have also every man given the Soveraignty to him that beareth their Person; and therefore if they depose him, they take from him that which is his own, and so again it is injustice. Besides, if he that attempteth to depose his Soveraign, be killed, or punished by him for such attempt, he is author of his own punishment, as being by the Institution, Auther of all his Soveraign shall do: And because it is injustice for a man to do any thing, for which he may be punished by his own authority, he is also upon that title, unjust. And whereas some men have pretended for their disobedience to their Soveraign, a new Covenant, made, not with men, but with God; this also is unjust: for there is no Covenant with God, but by mediation of some body that representeth Gods Person; which none doth but Gods Lieutenant, who hath the Soveraignty under God. But this pretence of Covenant with God, is so evident a lye, even in the pretenders own consciences, that it is not only an act of an unjust, but also of a vile, and unmanly disposition.

Secondly, Because the Right of bearing the Person of them all, is given to him they make Soveraign, by Covenant only of one to another, and not of him to any of them; there can happen no breach of Covenant on the part of the Soveraign; and consequently none of his Subjects, by any pretence of forfeiture, can be freed from his Subjection. . . . If any one, or more of them, pretend a breach of the Covenant made by the Soveraign at his Institution; and others, or any other of his Subjects, or himself alone, pretend there was no such breach, there is in this case, no Judge to decide the controversie: it returns therefore to the Sword again; and every man recovereth the right of Protecting himself by his own strength, contrary to the design they had in the Institution. . . .

Thirdly, because the major part hath by consenting voices declared a Soveraign; he that dissented must now consent with the rest; that is, be contented to avow all the actions he shall do, or else justly be destroyed by the rest. For if he voluntarily entred into the Congregation of them that were assembled, he sufficiently declared thereby his will (and therefore tacitely covenanted) to stand to what the major part should ordain. . . .

Fourthly, because every Subject is by this Institution Author of all the Actions, and Judgments of the Soveraign Instituted; it follows, that whatsoever he doth, it can be no injury to any of his Subjects; nor ought he to be by any of them accused of Injustice. For he that doth any thing by authority from another, doth therein no injury to him by whose authority he acteth: But by this Institution of a Common-wealth, every particular man is Author of all the Soveraign doth; and consequently he that complaineth of injury from his Soveraign, complaineth of that whereof he himself is Author; and therefore ought not to accuse any man but himself; no nor himself of injury; because to do injury to ones self, is impossible. It is true that they that have Soveraign power, may commit Iniquity; but not Injustice, or Injury in the proper signification. . . .

Fifthly, and consequently to that which was said last, no man that hath Soveraign power can justly be put to death, or otherwise in any manner by his Subjects punished. For seeing every Subject is Author of the actions of his Soveraign; he punisheth another, for the actions committed by himself. . . .

The Obligation of Subjects to the Soveraign, is understood to last as long, and no longer, than the power lasteth, by which he is able to protect them. For the right men have by Nature to protect themselves, when none else can protect them, can by no Covenant be relinquished. The Soveraignty is the Soule of the Common-wealth; which once departed from the Body, the members doe no more receive their motion from it. The end of Obedience is Protection; which, wheresoever a man seeth it, either in his own, or in anothers sword, Nature applyeth his obedience to it, and his endeavour to maintaine it. And though Soveraignty, in the intention of them that make it, be immortall; yet is it in its own nature, not only subject to violent death, by forreign war; but also through the ignorance, and passions of men, it hath in it, from the very institution, many seeds of a naturall mortality, by Intestine Discord.

7 / LOUIS XIV:
LESSONS IN KINGSHIP

If Charles I of England may be said to represent the failure of would-be absolutism, Louis XIV may equally be called the embodiment of triumphant absolutism. In his lifetime (1638–1715) absolute monarchy became the prevailing form of government in most of Europe, and most of Europe's kings modeled themselves upon the "Grand Monarch" who ruled in France. The aims and character of Louis XIV therefore became crucial facts in the lives of the peoples. He disclosed his aims and character with fullest frankness in the so-called Memoirs for the Dauphin. These are a series of precepts and evaluations of events drawn up, either by the king in his own hand or by his secretaries at his dictation and suggestion, for the instruction of the Dauphin, the king's eldest son and heir to the throne. They were begun shortly after Louis XIV first became a father in 1661 and were continued intermittently for nearly two decades. The following selections are taken from the edition of the memoirs by Charles Dreyss, a French historian of the nineteenth century.[14]

It is beyond dispute that that subjugation which compels a sovereign to let his people lay down the law to him is the worst calamity into which a man of our rank can fall. Perhaps if we judged things rightly, we would say that a private man who can take orders is happier than the prince who cannot command, for the former is confident that the modesty of his status can be attributed only to the orders of his fate, while the latter is always in danger of having the respect in which his virtue is held diminished by a stain upon the brilliance of his character. The grandeur and majesty of kings come not so much from the scepter which they hold as from the way in which they hold it. To assign the right of decision to subjects and the duty of deference to sovereigns is to pervert the order of things. The head alone has the right to deliberate and decide, and the functions of all the other members consist only in carrying out the commands given to them.

[14] Charles Dreyss, ed., *Mémoires de Louis XIV pour l'instruction du Dauphin* (Paris: Didier, 1860), Vol. II, pp. 6–8, 14–17, 518–20. Translated from the French by Herbert H. Rowen.

If I showed you before the wretchedness of princes who entrust their peoples and their dignity to the guidance of a prime minister, I have all the more reason to demonstrate to you here how wretched are princes who have been surrendered to the heedlessness of an assembled populace; for the prime minister, after all, is a man whom you choose according to your own lights, whom you bring into government only so far as you please, and who has the principal influence in affairs only because he has first place in your heart. In appropriating your wealth and your authority for himself, at least he retains gratitude and respect for your person; and, no matter how great we make him, he cannot escape ruin whenever we have the strength simply to want to maintain him no longer. He is at most a single companion beside you upon the throne; if he despoils you of a part of your glory, at the same time he spares you from the thorniest of your problems; his interest in his own glory urges him to maintain yours; it is his pleasure to conserve your rights as property which he enjoys in your name; and if he shares your diadem with you, at least he works to leave it intact for your descendants.

But it is otherwise with the power which an assembled people takes for itself. The more you grant it, the more it claims; the more favors you bestow upon it, the more contempt it feels for you; and what it once has in its possession is held by so many arms that it cannot be wrested away without the greatest violence.

Among the multitude who comprise these great assemblages, those who act with the greatest licence are always the least intelligent; if you defer to them once, they claim forever after the right to determine your plans as the fancy strikes them; and the constant necessity to defend yourself against their assaults furnishes you with more troubles than all the other interests of your crown. Thus it is that a prince who wishes to leave an enduring peace to his people and an intact dignity to his successors, cannot be too careful in repressing such turbulent audacity.

But I have dwelled too long upon thoughts which appear useless or can serve only to help you recognize the wretchedness of our neighbors, since it is certain that in the state where you will reign after me you will find no authority which is not proud to derive its origins and its powers from you, no corporation which dares to voice its decisions in any but terms of respect, no company which does not feel the duty to seek its greatness principally in the good of your service and its sole security in humble submission. . . .

There is not the slightest doubt that we have nothing of which we should be more zealous than that pre-eminence which constitutes the principal beauty of the place we hold. Whatever marks it off or preserves it should be infinitely precious to us; what is at stake is not only our own interest, for it is a possession for which we are accountable to the public and to our successors. We cannot dispose of it as the fancy strikes us, and we should not question that it is one of the rights of the crown which cannot validly be given away.

Those who believe that such claims as these involve nothing but ceremony are gravely mistaken, for in this matter everything must be considered and everything has its importance. The people over whom we reign are unable to see into the heart of things, and hence base their judgments upon what they can see on the surface; most of the time they proportion their respect and their obedience to the spectacle and the rank which they observe. As it is important for the public that it should be governed by only one man, it is also important to it that the man who performs this function should be so far above other men that no one could be mistaken for him or compared to him, and one cannot deprive the head of the state of the least mark of superiority which distinguishes him from the other members, without doing harm to the entire body of the state.

But keep still in mind, my son, that the pre-eminence which you should most seek and which will distinguish you to greatest advantage will be that which comes from your own personal qualities.

High rank is never more solid or assured than when it is supported by singular merit; and this is what has doubtless persuaded some that it might be advantageous to the reigning prince to see those who are closest to him by birth greatly distinguished from him by their conduct. This wide interval which his virtue puts between him and them makes him appear more brightly and brilliantly before the eyes of the entire world. His lofty and solid qualities of mind obtain wholly new luster from the lack of distinction of those who come near him. The grandeur and firmness of soul which are visible in him are enhanced by the contrast with the weakness of soul observed in them; and the love of work and true glory which he displays is infinitely brighter when one discovers elsewhere nothing but ponderous sloth or love of trivialities.

Thanks to this difference, all eyes are fixed upon him alone; all requests are addressed to him alone, all respects are paid to him alone, everything is hoped for from him alone; nothing is undertaken, nothing is expected, nothing is done, except through him alone. His favor is regarded as the only source of all good things; men believe that they are rising in the world to the extent that they come near him or earn his esteem; all else is cringing, all else is powerless, all else is sterile, and it may even be said that the brilliancy he possesses in his own state passes by transference into foreign lands. The shining image of the greatness to which he has raised himself is borne everywhere on the wings of his fame. Just as his subjects admire him, so neighboring nations are soon awed by him. If only he is able to make good use of these advantages, there is nothing either under his sway or beyond it which in the course of time he cannot succeed in doing.

But although these reasons may seem quite plausible to you, and my explanations may perhaps give you cause to believe that they are not wholly unfamiliar to my feelings, do not think that if you should have brothers one day, my passion for you would be so blind that I myself would seek to give you all the advantages which I have just discussed with you; on the contrary, I would truly endeavor to give you all the same instruction and the same examples, but it would be your task to distinguish yourself from them by your particular skill in profiting by these lessons. . . .

Kings are often obliged to do things which go against their inclinations and offend their natural goodness. They should love to give pleasure and yet they must often punish and destroy persons on whom by nature they wish to confer benefits. The interest of the state must come first. One must constrain one's inclinations and not put oneself in the position of berating oneself because one could have done better in some important affair but did not because of some private interest, because one was distracted from the attention one should have for the greatness, the good and the power of the state. Often there are troublesome places where it is difficult to make out what one should do. One's ideas are confused. As long as this lasts, one can refrain from making a decision. But as soon as one has fixed one's mind upon something which seems best to do, it must be acted upon. This is what enabled me to succeed so often in what I have done. The mistakes which I made, and which gave me infinite trouble, were the result of the desire to please or of allowing myself to accept too carelessly the opinions of others. Nothing is more dangerous than weakness of any kind whatsoever. In order to command others, one must raise oneself above them and once one has heard the reports from every side one must come to a decision upon the basis of one's own judgment, without anxiety but always with the concern not to command anything which is of itself unworthy either of one's place in the world or of the greatness of the state. Princes with good intentions and some knowledge of their affairs, either from experience or from study and great diligence in making themselves capable, find numerous cases which instruct them that they must give special care and total application to everything. One must be on guard against oneself, resist one's own tendencies, and always be on guard against one's own natural bent. The craft of a king is great, noble and delightful when one feels worthy of doing well whatever one promises to do. But it is not exempt from troubles, weariness and worries. Sometimes uncertainty causes despair, and when one has spent a reasonable time in examining an affair, one must make a decision and take the step which one believes to be best. When one has the state in view, one works for one's self. The good of the one constitutes the glory of the other. When the former is fortunate, eminent and powerful, he who is the cause thereof becomes glorious and consequently should find more enjoyment than his subjects in all the pleasant things of life for himself and for them. When one has made a mistake, it must be corrected as soon as possible, and no other consideration must stand in the way, not even kindness.

8 / JACQUES BOSSUET: "BY THE GRACE OF GOD, KING"

The classical statement of the doctrine of divine-right monarchy was made by Louis XIV's court preacher, Jacques Bénigne Bossuet, bishop of Meaux. In his Politique tirée des propres paroles de l'Écriture sainte *("Politics Drawn from the Very Words of Holy Scripture," 1709), Bossuet draws together in a single coherent argument all those elements of the centuries-old divine-right theory which could be made to serve the cause of hereditary and absolute monarchy. Bossuet (1627–1704) was a noted historian and theologian as well as a political theorist. It should be mentioned that the French noun* politique *stands for the two English words "politics" (the art and science of government in general) and "policy" (the aims and methods of a particular government). The biblical passages in the translation which follows are taken from the Douai-Rheims version, the official Catholic version in English, modified to follow Bossuet's fairly free French translation.*[15]

God is the King of kings: his is the right to instruct and command them as his agents. Pay heed, my lord, pay heed to the lessons he teaches them in his Scripture, and learn from him the rules and examples on which they should shape their conduct.

Among the many benefits of Scripture is this, that it records the history of the world from its first beginnings and thereby shows us

[15] *Œuvres complètes de Bossuet*, ed. F. Lachat (Paris: Louis Vives, 1864), Vol. XXIII, pp. 476, 478, 490–3, 495, 498, 526–9, 532–3, 536–8, 558, 643, 645. Translated from the French by Herbert H. Rowen.

more clearly than any other history, the original principles on which empires were established.

No other history better reveals the good and the evil within the human heart, the things which uphold kingdoms and those which overthrow them, what religion can do to establish them and irreligion to destroy them. . . .

God, . . . by whom kings reign, overlooks no lesson by which they can learn to reign well. The ministers of princes and those who under his authority share in the government of states and the administration of justice will find in his words lessons that they can receive only from God. One part of Christian morality consists in establishing the magistracy according to his laws: God has wished to decide all things, that is, to command all orders of men and hence most of all that order upon which all others depend.

This, my lord, is the greatest of all goals that we can set before men, and they cannot pay too close heed to the rules according to which they will be judged, receiving a sentence eternal and irrevocable. Those who believe that piety weakens policy will be confuted; for the policy you will see [in these pages] is truly divine. . . .

All is disunity and partiality among men.

It is not enough for men to dwell in the same land or speak the same language, for the violence of their passions has made them obstinate and their various humors have made them incompatible, so that unity among them is impossible unless all together they submit to a single government to govern them all.

In lack whereof, Abraham and Lot could not bear to dwell together and had to part. "Neither was the land able to bear them, that they might dwell together: for their substance was great and they could not dwell together. Whereupon also there arose a strife between their herdsmen. So that they were driven to agree that one should go to the left hand and the other to the right." (Gen. 13: 6–7, 9)

If their servants caused a quarrel between Abraham and Lot, both just and such near kinsmen, what turmoil would have been the result among wicked men?

Only the authority of government is able to bridle the passions and violence which have become man's nature.

"If thou shalt see the oppressions of the poor, and violent judgments, and justice perverted in the provinces, the evil is not without remedy: for he that is high hath another higher, and there are others still higher than these: Moreover there is the king that reigneth over all the land who commands over all of them." (Eccl. 5: 7–8) Justice is maintained by authority and the subordination of powers and by naught else.

Such order puts the bridle upon license. When each can do as he wishes and possesses no rule of conduct but his own desire, all falls into confusion. A Levite broke the most holy part of the law of God. This is how Scripture explains his deed: "In those days there was no king in Israel, but every one did that which seemed right to himself." (Judges, 17: 6) . . .

Unity among men is established only by the authority of government.

This result of lawful command is marked for us by the oft repeated words of Scripture: At the command of Saul and the lawful power, "all Israel went out as one man. (I Kings 11: 7 and elsewhere) All the multitudes as one man, were forty thousand. (I Esdr. 2: 64)" Such is the unity of the people when each renounces his own will and transfers and joins it to that of the prince and the magistrates. Else there is no unity and the people wander aimlessly like a scattered flock. . . .

Under regular government each individual renounces the right to take possession by force of what he finds to his purpose.

Take government away and the earth with all its goods will be all men's in common like air and light. God told all men: "Increase and multiply, and fill the earth." (Gen. 1: 28, 9: 7) He gave to each and all without distinction "every herb bearing seed upon the earth, and all trees that grow upon it." (Gen: 1: 29) According to this primal law of nature, no one has any special right to anything whatever, and all things are every one's prey. . . .

After the conquest of the land of Canaan, Moses ordered the land to be shared out among the people by the authority of the sovereign magistrate. . . .

This is the origin of the right of property: and in general all rights must come from the public authority, and no one is permitted to break in upon another's property nor to seek anything by force. . . .

Whence it results that there is no worse condition than anarchy, which exists when there is no government nor any authority whatever. Wherever every one wishes to do as he pleases, no one can actually do as he pleases; wherever there is no master, every one is a master; wherever every one is a master, every one is a slave. . . .

The law is sacred and inviolable.

To achieve a perfect understanding of the nature of law, we must note that all who have discussed this matter well have considered its origin to lie in a pact and solemn treaty by which men agreed among themselves, through the authority of the princes, to do that which is necessary to establish their social order.

This does not mean that the authority of laws depends upon the consent and acquiescence of the people, but only that the prince (who because of his office has, in any case, no interest other than the public interest) is aided by the wisest heads among the nation and is supported by the experience of past ages. . . .

Hereditary monarchy has three principal advantages.

There are three reasons why this is the best form of government.

The first is that it is most in accord with nature and perpetuates itself by its own action. No state is more enduring than one which lasts and perpetuates itself by the same causes which make the universe last and which perpetuate the human race. . . .

In this kind of state there are neither intrigues nor cabals to make a king, for he has been made by nature: as the saying goes, the dead invests the living and the king never dies.

That government is best which is farthest from anarchy. To something as necessary as government among them, we must provide the easiest principles and a means of operation which works best by itself.

The second reason which favors this form of government is that it is the one which makes the potentates who direct the state possess the greatest interest in its preservation. The prince who works for his state works for his children; and the love which he bears the kingdom, merging with the love he bears for his family, becomes part of his nature. . . .

The third reason derives from the rank of the houses which possess hereditary rule over kingdoms. . . .

Thus it is that the peoples grow to love the royal houses. The jealousy one naturally feels for a superior here becomes transformed into love and respect. Even the magnates obey without reluctance a house which has always held mastery, one to which no other house can ever be compared.

There is no more effective way to overcome partiality and to hold to their duty those who are equal in rank and are made incompatible by ambition and envy. . . .

One should be loyal to the form of government which is already established in one's country. . . .

There is no form of government, no human institution, which does not have its drawbacks, so that one should preserve that form of state to which the people have grown accustomed over the ages. That is why

God takes under his protection all legitimate governments, in whatever form they have been established. He who seeks to overthrow them is not only a public enemy but also the enemy of God. . . .

Royal authority has four characteristics or essential qualities.

First, royal authority is sacred; second, it is paternal; third, it is absolute; fourth, it is subject to reason. . . .

Princes therefore act as the agents of God and his lieutenants upon earth. It is through them that he wields his power of command. . . . This is why we have seen that the royal throne is not the throne of a man but the throne of God himself. . . .

The respect which we pay to the prince therefore has within it something of religion. The service of God and respect for kings are things united; and Saint Peter joins these two duties together: "Fear God; honor the king." (I Peter 2: 17)

God has therefore put something of divinity in princes. "I have said: You are gods, and all of you are the sons of the most High." (Psalm LXXXI: 6) . . .

Kings should respect their own power and employ it only for the public welfare.

Since their power comes from on high, as we have said, they should not believe that they are its masters, having a right to use it however they wish. They should use it with fear and restraint as a thing which comes to them from God and for which God will call them to account. . . .

Kings should therefore tremble when using the power which God gives them, and keep in mind how horrible is the sacrilege of misusing a power which comes from God. . . .

Royal authority is absolute.

There are some who pretend that they cannot find any difference between absolute and arbitrary government, in order to make the name of "absolute government" odious and insufferable. But there is no greater difference than this between them. . . .

Without this absolute authority, he [the king] can neither do good nor repress evil; his power must be such that no one can hope to escape him, and finally, the only defense of individuals against the public power must be their innocence. . . .

Only God can judge their judgments and their persons. . . .

The prince, as prince, is not to be considered a private person; he is a public figure, the whole state is in him, the will of the whole people is contained in his. Just as all the perfections and virtues are joined in God, so is the power of all private persons joined in the prince's person. What greatness that one man should have so much power!

God's power is felt in an instant from one end of the world to the other; royal power takes the same time to act throughout the kingdom. It preserves the order of the whole kingdom, as does God with the whole world. Let God take away his hand and the world will fall back into nothingness; let authority fail in the kingdom, and total confusion will result.

Consider the king in his work-chamber. From it go forth the orders which make magistrates and captains, citizens and soldiers, provinces, navies and armies, act in unison. He is the image of God, who from his throne in highest heaven makes all the world go. . . .

Something of divinity adheres to the prince and inspires the people's fear. Let not the king therefore forget what he is himself. "I have said (it is God who speaks): You are gods and all of you the sons of the most High. But like men you shall die: and shall fall like one of the great." (Psalms LXXXI: 6–7) I have said that you are gods, that is, that you possess within your authority and carry upon your brow the character of divinity. You are the sons of the most High; it was he who established your power for the good of the human race. But, O gods of flesh and blood, O gods of mud and dust, you will die like men, you will fall as the great have fallen. For a little time greatness sets men apart; in the end a common fall makes them all equal.

Therefore, O kings, be bold in your use of power, for it is divine and beneficial to the human race, but use it with humility. It is set upon you from without. In the end it leaves you weak, it leaves you mortal, it leaves you sinful, and it places upon you the burden of answering to God for so much more.

9 / HERBERT H. ROWEN: DYNASTIC MONARCHY ANATOMIZED

Bossuet had explained and defended absolute monarchy by rhetoric and by political theory. Modern historians not only look at political institutions in the light of political theory; they also turn to the analysis of political events and practice to give specific meaning and range to political theory. Indeed, the institution of hereditary monarchy turns out to be effectively comprehended only by this latter method. The argument that dynasticism rested fundamentally upon the practice and concept of ownership of the state by the ruler, or by the ruling family (dynasty), is presented in this study of Louis XIV's ideas about his relationship to the state, written by the editor of this book, a specialist in the history of France and the Netherlands in the seventeenth century.[16]

The relationship between king and state in the French monarchy of the Ancien Régime, although generally taken to be one of the plainest pieces of historical knowledge, is actually in an essential respect one of the least understood. The customary picture of French kingship in the centuries before the Revolution may be summed up in two phrases, *"L'État c'est moi"* [17] and *"la grâce de Dieu"* [18] (usually Englished as "divine right"): *"L'État c'est moi"* here implies an administrative monarchy equated with the person of the king, and *"la grâce de Dieu"* is concerned with the justification rather than the description of the monarchy. Yet close scrutiny of the historical literature reveals a current of uneasiness—something has been increasingly pushed into the background, something which ought to be in the very foreground of any study of the monarchy of the Ancien Régime, namely, that the king was the proprietor of the state, that he felt, even if he never literally said, *"L'État c'est à moi."* [19] The practice and the words of French kings and statesmen for many centuries, and most of all during the seventeenth, the zenith century of French monarchy, can be clearly understood only if we accept the principle that the dynastic king was, *among other things,* the owner of the kingdom.

Yet it is not sufficient simply to acknowledge the principle at its face value, as has been usual among those historians who do not neglect the factor of dynasticism; for the concept of proprietary kingship itself turns out to be a source of difficulties. The kingdom was the king's property—but in what sense? It could not be his private property, for the term "private" as applied to property implies a denial of public character, and the problem concerns the ownership of the *public* power. Furthermore, it is beyond dispute that French subjects, those who were truly "private" persons, owned property in fact and in law

[16] Herbert H. Rowen, " '*L'État C'est à Moi*': Louis XIV and the State," *French Historical Studies,* Vol. II, No. 1 (Spring, 1961), pp. 83–8, 91–3, 97–8. Reprinted by permission of *French Historical Studies.*

[17] I am the state.

[18] The grace of God.

[19] The state is mine.

—how does this square with the property of the king in the state? Lastly, the French king was always seen in political and legal theory as the holder of an office, that is, as the recipient of delegated function and authority, while "property" meant inherent rights, which were one's own, not delegated. How then could *office* and *property* co-exist in the same institution? . . .

The term "property" is now used primarily to mean things—physical objects—over which the owner has rights of use and decision to serve his own advantage and purpose. This usage was frequent in the seventeenth century, but it had not wholly displaced the deeper legal meaning, by which property consists in rights held by a given person or persons to the exclusion of others, rights which are enforceable at law, that is, by the state. This is what is ordinarily meant by "private property." Implicit in both these definitions—the "objective" and the "legal"—is a wider general sense, according to which property consists of exclusive rights ("mine," not "thine") which are of advantage to their holders. These advantages are primarily and ordinarily economic, as producers of revenue; but they may also be social or political, providing glory, power, prestige, self-esteem or even the opportunity to do good and have fun. In this last meaning, "right" embodies a sense of ethical legitimacy as distinct from legal enforceability; and it is this broad meaning which historians have usually failed to see or to use.

The term "state" is no less varied and complex. By the seventeenth century it had already taken on the full panoply of meanings which it still possesses. Its most general significance was that of the community, the "nation," politically organized, with widely varying degrees of ethnic unity implied. From this broad definition derived more specific usages, as the territory over which a ruler has sovereignty, and as the subjects under that sovereignty. Lastly, it was used for the instrument of power and government—the armed forces and the administrative agencies of political authority.

The crossing over of these definitions provides the elements of our problem. The objective meaning of property can be applied only to the territorial meaning of the state; in that case, the description of the state as the king's property would mean that he was literally the owner of all the wealth within its boundaries, which was obviously not true in a society permeated by the fact and the spirit of private property. Yet, as we shall see, this position was indeed maintained, though in a very special sense. The legal definition is more troublesome. The king's claim upon the crown was clearly one of exclusive right; but we can speak of it as "enforceable at law" only if the king did not assert his absolute unshared sovereignty, for the existence of a separate legal authority to enforce his claim would have constituted a denial of his sovereignty, while the notion of the king's enforcing of his own claim at the same time that he was the source of law involves a tautology. The state as the source of economic and other advantages obviously falls within the last of the three kinds of property discussed here. It makes clear sense but does not emerge as distinctly from contemporary theoretical discussions as it does from the less self-conscious writings and actions of the monarchs and their ministers.

Approaching the problem from the side of the definitions of the state yields somewhat different results. The notion of the king's ownership of the political community was antipathetic to most seventeenth-century thought no less than to that of our own time. On the other hand, royal ownership of the territory of the state was accepted doctrine. As against other territorial sovereigns, the king was manifestly the "owner" of his state; diplomatic usage recorded this conception by its free use of the term "property" for realms, provinces and lands transferred from one sovereignty to another. As against subjects' property, the king's property in the territory was that of "eminent domain," a term which then included the supreme claims of both suzerainty and sovereignty. Normally, however, such claims outside the royal domain (where the king was proprietor of the land in the same way as, elsewhere in the realm, subjects were owners of "their land") meant only the king's right to take a portion of his subjects' wealth by taxation, or to expropriate it, usually with compensation, for the public use. Since taxation was customarily explained and justified upon the basis of the king's status as supreme office-holder, the debate over his right to levy taxes for his own interest was bitter and unending. The notion of the king's subjects as the "property" of the monarch raised similar difficulties. It was uniformly denied that French subjects were slaves, the property of the sovereign like the Janissaries and other members of the government establishment in the Ottoman Empire. Yet the king undeniably possessed a right to command his subjects, a right not easily distinguished from that of the slaveowner over his "living tools" except by the doctrine that the king commanded his subjects in the general interest, that is, for their own welfare. The state as government in the concrete sense presents less of a problem, since the administrators and military officers held their powers by delegation from the crown—they were clearly servants, not slaves.

These distinctions carry us part of the way to a solution of the problem we have posed. It was precisely the "public power," the right of legitimate command, which the king claimed as his own, as his birthright, by the gift of God through the means of inheritance or conquest (these were, it may be noted, the original meaning of the term *"la grâce de Dieu"* as applied to the crown); and it was from his ownership of the state *in this sense* that the king's property in the state *in other senses* was derived. The assent of subjects and fellow-princes to the king's birthright claim upon the crown was an acknowledgment, not a creation of it. Nonetheless the polarity between "office" and "property" persisted, for the notion of "*public* power" never ceased to have as its primary meaning that the kingship was an office, that it was the duty of the king to serve the general welfare, the common good, and not his "own" interests. But this polarity is dissolved to some extent, and to some extent intensified and made explosive, when we realize that dynastic monarchy was in fact these two elements—property and office—at one and the same time. . . . Bossuet fundamentally derived his analysis of the king's office from this conception of a grant by God, although we may note that he also described the office as a "*charge*," a term which in his day meant a venal office, one held as property, and not as a "*commission*," that is, a revocable office not held as property. (It seems to have escaped the attention of most later theorists that medieval legists had fitted freehold property, or allod, into their structure of feudal relationships, by describing it as a fief held directly of God, or *Sonnenlehn.*)

Practicing statesmen—the kings and their ministers—did not for their part falter in their adherence to the principle that the realm belonged to the king. The use of the possessive form in speaking of the state is so common in their documents and correspondence, without the least sign of embarrassment or need to explain or justify, that it would be proving the obvious to give instances; nor can it be maintained that the usage was only metaphorical or symbolic, nor that it was limited to the occasions when any of us would speak naturally of "our country" or "our government" without claiming to possess the state as property. It is true, on the other hand, that the relation of the king to the state cannot be summed up in either phrase, "*L'État c'est moi*" or "*L'État c'est à moi.*" Richelieu and Mazarin, Louis XIV and his ministers, and their successors down to the Revolution, all assumed the validity of both ideas—*L'État c'est moi* in the sense of the king as the symbol of the nation and the sole source of authority in the state; and *L'État c'est à moi* as the concept of property-kingship.

In 1666 Louis XIV put many of the elements of the problem in a nutshell in a famous assertion in his "Memoirs for the Dauphin." "Kings," he declared, "are absolute lords and by nature have complete and free disposition of all wealth owned either by churchmen or by laymen, for them to use at all times as prudent managers, that is, according to the general need of their state." "Absolute lordship" is here equated to "complete and free disposition" of the wealth of the nation, including that of churchmen (that is, the revenues of their benefices), but it should be used without waste and for "the general need of their state." "Complete and free disposition" means taxation, as the context of the passage indicates; but the right of "complete and free disposition" when held by any one other than the sovereign is exactly identical with the right of property. On the other hand, Louis XIV takes it for granted that subjects have their own individual right of property in particular "goods," but this is not an absolute right; it is subject to the higher royal right to claim a portion of these goods for "the general need." Indeed, in a preceding passage, Louis XIV specifically rejects the customary absolute distinction made by the legists between the royal domain and the rest of the national wealth. "Some princes," he wrote, "commit a major error when they take possession of certain things and certain persons as if these belonged to them in a different way than the remainder of what they rule. Everything within the boundaries of our states, no matter what its kind, belongs to us by the same title and should be equally dear to us. The moneys in our own coffers, those remaining in the hands of our treasurers, and those which we permit to remain in the trade of our peoples—all should be used by us with the same equal prudence." We may compare this royal assertion with the observation made by a Venetian ambassador in France a century earlier, to the effect that the property of subjects in France "was no more than the treasury of the prince distributed among many purses."

But, to return to Louis XIV, this latter statement of his makes even clearer his feeling that although the king and his subjects share rights of property it is the royal property which is primary and unconditional, that private property is something conceded by him; thus taxation ceases to be a claim of the sovereign upon the support of the nation for the public good and becomes merely the action of the monarch in transferring his wealth from one pocket to another. There is in this statement the same equation of sovereignty and property which most of the legists and political theorists refused to accept; there is also a refusal on the king's part to permit himself to be limited by the jurists' distinctions when these interfered with his own powers of decision and utilization over the wealth of France.

The conception that the king owned his realm played an essential part in the history of European international relations. Dynastic wars were no accident, nor were they purely and simply the guise in which conflicts arising out of the clash of quite different interests were presented to the world; they arose specifically from the peculiar uncertainties resulting from the application of the European family pattern, with its enormous complication of agnate lines, to the system of power-holding. To treat wars of dynastic succession as needless tragedies may be obvious and proper under the ideological assumptions of our own age, but to apply such conceptions to the seventeenth century without qualification is to assign to the political personages of that time a notion just beginning to emerge from their experiences, and which was not to become clear and firm for another century and more. Some of the most famous episodes of the reign of Louis XIV can be adequately explained only upon the basis that one of the primary driving motives of the monarch and his ministers was the honest belief that he possessed proprietary claims which he had the right and the duty to enforce by his armies when the occasion presented itself. . . .

A century later, a historical personage for whom a dynastic throne was a dream which after a while and for a time became reality, summed up the proprietary character of his royal predecessors. "Consider well," declared Napoleon Bonaparte while still First Consul in 1802, "that a First Consul does not resemble those kings by the grace of God who looked upon their states as a heritage."

The significance of the property-kingship issue lies not only in clarifying the character of the monarchy of the Ancien Régime. It is also an instance of the perennial problem in the political thought and practice of the West, the tension between the function assigned to the state by political theory—the service of the common welfare; and, on the other hand, the utilization of the state for their own advantage by the holders of political power, or by the individuals or groups able to influence them. For the tendency of such groups and individuals has always been to define the "common interest" in terms of their own advantage, thereby reinforcing the doctrine at the same time as they undermine it in practice. Louis XIV himself, in a rare moment of insight, wrote in 1670: "Furthermore, my son, never be mistaken about this, we have to do not with angels but with men to whom excessive power almost always gives the temptation in the end to use such power." He had, of course, the magnates and the servants of the crown in mind, but need it be said how well his own attitude and acts illustrated his warning—or that it applies with equal force in other ages and other places?

For the historian and the political thinker, there is another, separate question here. Is there actually an empirically definable "common interest" apart from that of specific groups, or groups-of-groups, as is usually assumed in both political theory and in historical writing? If there is not—and no effort to define it to date has withstood the criticism of those hostile to the particular groups doing the defining—then the definitions of historical institutions based on the conception of "common interest" in the abstract lack utility for historical analysis in the concrete. But it cannot be denied that the belief of almost all men that the state ought to serve the "common interest," however defined, has been one of the most powerful forces molding historical events that the modern world has known.

10 / THE DEADLY GAME OF REBELLION

The absolutism of Louis XIV had its origins in more than the resounding arguments of Bossuet; the monarch never forgot his bitter hatred for the strength of rebellious subjects as displayed in the famous Fronde. This was a series of uprisings and civil wars in France during the king's youth, extending from 1648 to 1653, directed against the government of the king's mother, Anne of Austria, and her prime minister, Cardinal Jules Mazarin. The story of the origin of the Fronde is told from the royalist side (A) by an Italian historiographer in the service of the king, Galeazzo Gualdo Priorato (1606–1678). The contemporary translation from which the following passages are taken was made from the Italian; a number of French terms which Gualdo Priorato adapted into Italian were left in that form by the English translator, and the original French terms have been inserted in brackets where appropriate.[20]

The Frondeurs' own side of the story of their rebellion against the authority of Mazarin was told with enormous vigor, not to say venom, in a flood of pamphlets and broadsheets which poured out over France (B). One series of a dozen pamphlets was called "The French Courier, who brings all the true news of events since the King's kidnapping, both in Paris and at Saint-Germain-en-Laye." Saint-Germain-en-Laye was the principal royal residence until the construction of the palace at Versailles. The following passages are taken from the fourth, eighth, and twelfth arrivées *(arrivals).*[21]

A. GUALDO PRIORATO

The King's Exchequer being much exhausted by so long War, the Council was forc'd to think upon ready and feasible Expedients to raise

[20] *The History of France, Written in Italian by the Count Gualdo Priorato. Containing all the Memorable Actions in France, and Other Neighbouring Kingdoms. The Translation whereof being begun by the Right Honourable Henry, late Earl of Monmouth: Was finished by William Brent, Esq.* (London: William Place *et al.*, 1676), pp. 4–9.

[21] *Le Covrier François, apportant tovtes les Nouuelles veritables de ce qui s'est passé depuis l'enleuement du Roy, tant à Paris, qu'à S. Germain en Laye* (Paris: Rolin de la Haye, 1649), "qvatriesme arrivée," pp. 6–7; "hvictiesme arrivée," p. 3; "douziesme arrivée," p. 3. Translated from the French by the editor.

Moneys; which gave occasion to the Male-contents to mask their indiscreet Zeal, and to make use of this publick necessity, so to undertake with more boldness pernitious novelties.

Divers means were proposed to raise Moneys; but all means requiring time, and being in some sort grievous to the people, and therefore not certain whether the Councils resolutions would be approved in Parliament or no; Monsieur *Emery*, Superintendant of the Finances, proposed the taking away of the *Paoletta* [Paulette], or Annual Right, upon designe either to make the Parliament more submiss, and more obedient to the will of the Court, and consequently less averse to pass the Edicts of the Council-Royal; or else to renew the Annual Right in some other form, which might be more advantagious, and more proper to raise ready Moneys. This as it had a fair appearance, and came from one who was reputed to be of a high Spirit, and of a great reach, pleased many Lords of the Council; but the Cardinal would not have this fallen upon in haste, but wisht it might be more maturely examined. So by reason of some other Emergency which arose, it was laid aside.

Antiently, and before the Reign of *Francis* the First, who was he that brought in the selling of Offices, Places were by the King conferr'd onely upon well-deserving men, and such as were capable of them. In the time of *Henry* the Fourth, one named *Paoletto* [Paulet] propounded a means of raising two millions of crowns yearly by permitting all Counsellours and Officers, as well as of Justice as of the Finances, to convey over their Offices after their death to their Heirs, or to sell them to others, reserving a certain annual sum to be duely paid. This was embraced and agreed unto, that upon payment of a certain annual sum, according to the worth of the Place, the Office or Place was to descend to the Heir; or the Possessor, if he pleased, might sell it whilst he lived, to any one that was capable of it. And that if any one should die without having paid this Annual Right, his Heirs should not enjoy the benefit of the Place, but that it should be left to the King's disposal. This Contract was to last for nine years onely; which time being expired, the Priviledge was to be continued, or abolished, as the King should please. Thus from this time forward, taking the name from the inventor of it, this Annual Right was called *la Paoletta* [Paulette].

Emery's Intention was, that the nine years of the *Paoletta* being expired, the King should totally abolish it; and that if any of the Officers should desire to dispose of their Offices after these nine years, he should make a new Agreement, advancing some considerable sum: By which means he thought to raise good store of Money, whereby the expence of War might be supplied without grieving the people.

This might have taken effect, had it not met with some opposition in the Parliament of *Paris*, by some troublesome Spirits, who had other particular ends. It was therefore thought fit to exempt it from the said abolition; which condescention, through weakness, was the cause from whence arose licentious Resolutions, which confounded all good Government.

But the Counsellours having adherences, friends and alliances with many other Lords and Officers of the Kingdom, suspected lest this being introduced into the parts farther off, might by little and little creep into their Employments; wherefore they began those Novelties, which shall be the subject of the ensuing Narrative.

Yet neither were the alteration of the *Paoletta,* nor the Grievances, nor the Gabels [*gabelles,* or compulsory salt purchases], the sole occasions which caused Disobedience: for such burthens were quietly suffer'd, and received without any innovation, under the management of *Richelieu,* who making use therein of the King's Power, maintained them by severity and force, as thinking Rigour to be a better way than Gentleness, whereby to govern a Nation naturally as apt to forget Injuries as good turns. But the proposal in the Edict of augmenting the number of the Masters of Requests, every of which Places were sold for more than 60,000 Crowns, was the true occasion of those troubles which interrupted the Prosperity of that Kingdom, and hastened the Revolutions, though under other reasons and motives, which seemed to aim more at the publick good, than at the private end of some particular men. These Masters of the Requests are conspicuous persons, who after having sat as Counsellours in Parliament, are admitted into that Order: They are admitted into the King's Privy Council, they practise much in Court, and are imployed in Embassies in Provinces, and in Armies for Justice, and for the Finances; so as they usually prove men of Courage.

All men were troubled and scandalized at the increasing of this number, the price being lessened thereby to those who were in the Places, being considerable persons: For nothing sways more with men, than their particular Interest and Advantage. They used therefore all means to keep the Cardinal from attempting this Novelty; thinking, that as he was the first Minister of State, he was the first motioner or promoter thereof. The Cardinal knew, that to touch upon what concerned those of Parliament, was but a slippery business, and therefore he did not in his heart approve entirely of the Proposal: but the business of Moneys being urgent, and the rest of his Majesty's Council not thinking to meet with any repugnancy in those who had such dependency upon the favour of the Court, and who desired to deserve those Employments which were wont to be confer'd by the King in Armies and in Provinces; the Edict stood good in substance, but was somewhat moderated by the Cardinal, who was forced to yield to the common desires. . . . Moreover, some, that they might render him odious to the Parliament and to the People, gave out that he (as being the prime Minister of State) was the first Author of the abolition of the *Paoletto,* and of creating new Masters of the Requests, though he had always withstood them; and that *Emery* was the onely occasioner of them, being backt by the rest of the Council: And they did this, intending that the Parliament resenting this, might make the Cardinal's conduct be ill thought of, and that by his fall, *Emery* thought to succeed him. These suspitions were increased by some conversation which he held with *Peter Brussel* [Broussel] a Counsellour of the Great Chamber, poorly spirited, but popular; and who instead of judging Processes [trials], was always busie in publick Affairs. He willingly took upon him the Petitions of the Poor, either out of real or feign'd Charity; and he was hereunto incited by *Peter Longuile* a Counsellour of the same Chamber, who spent all his talent in Intrigues and Cabals. *Brussel* applying himself to *Longuile's* Genius, though he were ignorant enough, and not very capable of what he went about, which made him be believed by those who knew not his true ends, to be a well-minded [having good intentions] man: But being displeased with the Court and Cardinal, for that his Son who was Ensigne to the Guard, was denied a Lieutenants place that was vacant, he set himself to beget an ill opinion of the Cardinal. This mean while the Masters of the Requests fearing lest if any of them should die, their Heirs might not succeed unto them in their Office, by reason of the distaste which they had already given unto the Queen, they publish'd a licentious Writing, whereby they did reciprocally oblige themselves to pay for the Place of any that should die, for the Heir of the deceased; which was thought a very bold thing. Nor did their designes cease here, but finding themselves not able of themselves alone to make good their party, they presented a Request in the name of the Publick, for the union and joyning of the whole Parliament; representing, that it was necessary for repairing the Ruines of the Kingdom, occasioned by the ill Administration of the Finances, which were more imploy'd in the profit of a few particular men, than for the use of the Crown, from whence the peoples grievances did proceed; by which appearances they made the people believe, that their end was onely to exempt them from all Impositions. . . . not long after, notwithstanding the King's inhibition, the joyning of all the Bodies of Tribunals was decreed, and met, where *Broussel, Blaumenil, Charton,* and others, spoke without any regard, against the Court-government: An Act of great Disobedience, and contrary to all Laws and Practice; all the Bodies not being accustomed to be called together nor to meet, but by extraordinary order from the King. But those who sought a propitious conjuncture of time to inhanse or exalt their pretended Authority by lessening that of the Kings, being desirous to winde themselves into the Affairs of State, laid hold of the pretence of wasting of the King's Finances, and gave way to this fatal Union, wherein they were applauded by many, not onely for the novelty of the Act, but out of hopes which other Male-contents and their idle followers conceived, that they should be eased of their Grievances by the punishment of those who imploy'd the King's Moneys ill, and that they should thereby have Peace, which they said was retarded out of the Officers particular ends. . . .

And in sequele of these giddy attempts, which are the usual food of the petulant Vulgar, it happened that Monsieur *di* [de] *Bachaumont* Son to President *Coigneux*, hearing his Father speak in the Parliament in behalf of the Court, being one night at Supper in *Monsieur di* [de] *Paris* his house, Marshal of the Field, and discoursing there with divers Friends touching the present Commotions, said jeastingly to his Companions, with whom he began to sport, throwing Oranges at one another, That he had a designe to sling to some purpose at his Father's Opinion. This Jeast was taken notice of, and thereupon when one declaimed boldly in pleading against any person of Quality, men would say, that *he slung soundly that morning:* so passing from one Jeast to another, he that railed most against the Government, was called a good Slinger. And this went through every ones mouth some months before there was any talk of the Faction called *la Fronde,* or the Sling; but the rise thereof was taken from the Boys, who sometimes slung Stones under the new Bridge when the water was low; whence the fore-named *Bachaumont* took occasion to say, that he would sling at his Father's Opinion, comparing the Whizze of a Sling to the force of Discourse in Rhetorick. . . .

As all these things were a mighty prejudice to the King's Soveraignty, and of very bad Example, and a great scandal in Subjects who were bound to obey; and the Cardinal being therewith sorely netled, took a firm resolution to defend by all possible means the Authority of the Minor-King, which was recommended to his trust: and very well knowing what sad fruit might proceed from this seed, employed first his most refined Judgment to keep it from increasing, making use of milde ways, spinning on the time, till the conjuncture of Affairs might afford him opportunity to make use of more powerful means: But this fair was doing no good, the Malady grew more contagious; which made him at last aware, that without making use of Fire and Sword, it would dayly take deeper root; for the Courts Lenity was interpreted Weakness, and the pride of some of these Gown-men (who were blinded by Passion, and by hope of bettering their condition by the ruine of others) grew to such a height, that being cloy'd with living quietly, they began to plot all the ways they could how to arrive at their desired end. That they might therefore irritate the hatred and fury of the people, they thought it necessary to appear Vindicators of their

Grievances, and to lay the fault upon those that govern'd. Wherefore they began to allure them by hopes of a present good, and by fear of an approaching mischief; attributing the continuing of War to the State-Ministers, that they might thereby provide themselves of Moneys squeezed out of the poor Subjects. So as an universal Impression being made by these colourable pretences, whereby Affairs were carried on to open Sedition, the King's Council thought it fit to lay aside all Lenity, and to put on more vigorous and rigid Resolutions. Wherefore they thought fit to make some of them an Example, thereby to make others more respectful and obedient: and because the famous Victory of *Lens* in *Germany* [actually in the Spanish Netherlands] happened at the same time, for which *Te Deum* was sung in the Cathedral Church, the King and his Guards being present, it was thought now a fit time to imprison *Brousel, Charton,* and President *Blaumeneile,* who were thought worse minded than the rest; since they could not do it otherwise without a great Army, especially upon old *Brousel,* who was protected by the people, with whom he had won such credit as if he had been a New *Cato.*

B. FRENCH COURIER

Cardinal Mazarin, seeing that the Court of Parlement of Paris was directly opposed to the plans he had made for the destruction and ruin of the French Royal Monarchy and for the establishment of a Tyrannical Monarchy, caused the members of his Council now at Saint-Germain-en-Laye to forge a document in the King's name which suspended this August Parlement. All the more does he show himself thereby to be the enemy of the State: for this amounts to destroying the strongest pillar of the State, the true basis of Royal Justice, or more precisely, the living Image of the Kings; for it is this Parlement of Parlements—the Court of Peers, erected, established and confirmed by a long sequence of kings for three hundred and forty years and more, to whose judgments numberless Princes, Kings, Emperors and even Popes have so often submitted their interests and their disputes—which transmits to the King the Grandeur and Majesty of their Justice. By the same declaration Mazarin attributes to several bailiwicks and presidencies in the jurisdiction of the said Parlement the power and Sovereign Jurisdiction which is a beam of the Royal authority distributed and divided arbitrarily according to the caprice of the said Cardinal; he thereby makes it clearly known that his intention is more to infringe and usurp this Authority than to preserve it.

As this declaration went directly against the authority of the King, when the people of the town of Orléans learned that several of their magistrates, being ill-disposed to His Majesty's service and favoring

Cardinal Mazarin's interests, had been so bold as to register the act, they took up arms to protect their town against the tyrannous yoke with which it was threatened and sent word of this attack to the Court of the Parlement. Whereupon the Court deliberated this present day, Monday, February 8, and gave orders that the judgments previously entered against Cardinal Mazarin and in favor of the safety of the towns should be published at the seat of the Presidial of Orléans and registered by the Lieutenant General and his officers, who are to execute them, under penalty of answering in their own individual names with the loss of their offices. . . .

Though in the past there may have been nations which raised statues, proclaimed triumphant celebrations, commanded sacrifices and established festivals in honor of those who had shown their noteworthiness by a victory or some other generous action, how much greater is our indebtedness to these venerable senators whom neither fear of disgrace nor the threats of mistreatment nor the violence used against several of them could turn away from the projects which they had so generously adopted for the relief of the people! How can we ever pay adequate recognition to them? Furthermore, if, having saved France from its bloodsuckers, remedied the disorders and abuses which were being committed in the government of the State,—if, having saved it and protected it from the imminent ruin to which it was exposed by the tyranny of this man who, abusing the authority of the King, uses it only to mistreat loyal and good Frenchmen,—if (I say), when we have seen the extinction of the present turmoil and the fires of disunity which this evil Minister has lit in this kingdom, we may soon be most happy to see the end and termination, thanks to the admirable conduct of this company, of that war which began so many years ago and has continued since, supported by the blood and substance of the poor people,—what sufficient recognition, then, can we give to such a multitude of obligations, what honors should we not prepare for them, since we owe them our peace for which they toiled so long? . . .

As there is nothing which can contribute more greatly to the strengthening and enlargement of a kingdom than union and perfect agreement between the Sovereign and his subjects, therefore, among the most considerable accidents which can happen to it, none is more dangerous than disunity and discord, which, once brought by misfortune into even the most flourishing of states, cause first a myriad of mishaps to individuals and then universal ruin and desolation.

By such incipient disunity France appeared to be preparing a theater of woe where Europe could see enacted the bloodiest tragedies. The havoc and disorder which occurred in the vicinity of the city of Paris would have been no more than a foretaste of the misfortunes which customarily form the accompaniment of civil wars, from which every good Frenchman wishes to be spared: so that the return of the Deputies of the Parlement having assured us of a firm peace, at the same time it gives us hope that we shall enjoy the delights which this sweet name of peace promises to each and all with the tranquility which is inseparable from it.

11 / JOSEPH SCHUMPETER: LOUIS XIV—A MODERN JUDGMENT

Louis XIV was not only the master of his own realm; he was also accused of seeking the "universal monarchy" of Europe—that is, seeking to impose his domination upon all other European states. The term "imperialism" had not yet been invented for territorial expansion and colonial aggrandizement, but the policy and practice were already known. Many different explanations of imperialism have been offered, but few which illuminate the interrelationship between the structure of society and the practice of politics as clearly as that of the economist and sociologist Joseph A. Schumpeter in his Imperialism and Social Classes *(1951). Schumpeter was born in Moravia, then part of the Austro-Hungarian monarchy, in 1883, taught economics at various European universities, and served as a government minister and adviser in Austria and Germany before coming to the United States in 1933. He died in 1950, the year before the publication of this work.*[22]

At the threshold of modern Europe there stands a form of imperialism that is of special interest to us. It is rooted in the nature of the absolutist state of the seventeenth and eighteenth centuries which was, everywhere on the Continent, the result of the victory of the monarchy over the estates and classes. Everywhere on the Continent, in the sixteenth and seventeenth centuries, these struggles broke the political

[22] Joseph A. Schumpeter, "Imperialism in the Modern Absolute Monarchy," in *Social Classes, Imperialism: Two Essays,* translated from the German by Heinz Norden (New York: Meridian Books, 1955), pp. 54–64. Reprinted by permission of the publishers from Joseph A. Schumpeter, *Imperialism and Social Classes.* Cambridge, Mass.: Harvard University Press. Copyright, 1951, by The Trustees of Elizabeth B. Schumpeter.

back of the people, leaving only the prince and his soldiers and officials on the devastated soil of earlier political factions. Of the whole family of constitutions in western and central Europe, only the English constitution maintained itself. Whenever there was enough power and activity in the autocratic state, imperialist tendencies began to stir, notably in Spain, France, and the larger territories of Germany. Let us take France as an example. . . .

Louis XIV . . . was master of the machinery of state. His ancestors had gradually created this position by military force; or rather, in a military sense, it had been created in the course of the development of the national state, for that course manifested itself in military struggle, and the centralized state could arise only when one of the military powers originally present triumphed over the others, absorbing what was left of them in the way of military strength and initiative. In France, as elsewhere, the absolutist national state meant the military organization of the martial elements of the nation, in effect a war machine. True, this was not its entire meaning and cultural significance. Now that national unity was achieved, now that, since the victory over Spain, no external enemy offered a serious threat any longer, there might have been disarmament—the military element might have been permitted to recede. The state would not have ceased to exist or failed to fulfill its function on that account. But the foundations of royal power rested on this military character of the state and on the social factors and psychological tendencies it expressed. Hence it *was* maintained, even though the causes that had brought it to the fore had disappeared. Hence the war machine continued to impress its mark on the state. Hence the king felt himself to be primarily a warlord, adorned himself preeminently with military emblems. Hence his chief concern was to maintain a large, well-equipped army, one that remained active and was directly tied to his person. All other functions he might delegate to his subordinates. But this one—supreme command of the army and with it the direction of foreign affairs—he claimed as his own prerogative. When he was unable to exercise it, he at least made a pretense of personal military efficiency. Any other inadequacy he and the dominant groups might have pardoned. Military shortcomings, however, were dangerous, and when they were present—which doubtless was the case with Louis XIV—they had to be carefully concealed. The king might not actually be a hero in battle, but he had to have the reputation of being one.

The necessity for this attitude flows from the social structure of the period. In a political sense neither the peasantry nor the working masses carried weight—and this was true in the social sense as well. In its fight against the nobility, the crown had occasionally championed both, but essentially they were and remained helots, to be disposed of at will—not only economically exploited but even, against their will, trained to be blindly obeying soldiers. The urban middle class was also virtually beholden to the crown, though not quite so unconditionally. Once a valuable ally in the struggle against the nobility, it had become a mere servant. It had to obey, was molded by the crown along the lines of greatest financial return. The Church likewise paid for its national opposition to Rome with strict submission to the royal power. To this extent the king was actually, not merely legally, the master. It was of little concern to him—within eventually quite wide limits—what all these people who were forced to submit to him thought. But that was not true of the aristocracy. It too had had to submit to the crown, surrendering its independence and political rights—or at least the opportunity to exercise them. The stiff-necked rural nobility that once had both feet firmly planted in the soil amid its people had turned into a court aristocracy of extreme outward servility. Yet its social position remained intact. It still had its estates, and its members had retained their prestige in their own immediate neighborhoods. The peasants were more or less at its mercy. Each of the great houses still had its dependent circle among the lower nobility. Thus the aristocracy as a whole was still a power factor that had to be taken into account. Its submission to the crown was more in the nature of a settlement than a surrender. It resembled an election—a compulsory one, to be sure—of the king as the leader and executive organ of the nobility. Politically the nobility ruled far more completely *through* the king than it once did while it challenged his power. At that time, after all, the still independent cities did form a modest counterpoise to the nobility. Had the king, for example, conceived the notion of translating into action his pose as the protector of the lowest population strata, the nobility would have been able to squelch any such attempt by mere passive resistance—as happened in Austria in the case of Joseph II. The nobles would have merely had to retire to their châteaux in order to bring into play, even outwardly, the actual foundations of their power, in order to become again a reasonably independent rural nobility which would have been capable of putting up a good fight.

The reason they did no such thing was, in essence, because the king did what they wanted and placed the domestic resources of the state at their disposal. But the king was aware of the danger. He was carefully intent on remaining the leader of the aristocracy. Hence he drew its members to his court, rewarded those that came, sought to injure and discredit those that did not. He endeavored successfully to have only those play a part who had entered into relations with him and to foster the view, within the aristocracy, that only the *gens de la cour*—court society—could be considered to have full and authoritative standing. Viewed in this light, those aspects that historians customarily

dispose of as court extravagance and arbitrary and avoidable mismanagement take on an altogether different meaning. It was a class rather
than an individual that was actually master of the state. That class
needed a brilliant center, and the court had to be such a center—otherwise it might all too readily have become a parliament. But whoever
remained away from his estates for long periods of time was likely to
suffer economic loss. The court had to indemnify him if it wished to
hold him—with missions, commands, offices, pensions—all of which had
to be lucrative and entail no work. The aristocracy remained loyal only
because the king did precisely this. The large surplus beyond the requirements of debt service and administration which had existed at
the outset of the era of Louis XIV, together with all the borrowings
the crown was able to contrive—all this fell only nominally to the crown.
Actually it had to be shared with the nobility which, in this fashion,
received a pension from the pockets of the taxpayers.

A system of this kind was essentially untenable. It placed shackles
of gold on real ability that sought outlet in action, bought up every
natural opportunity for such talent to apply itself. There they were at
Versailles, all these aristocrats—socially interned, consigned to amuse
themselves under the monarch's gracious smile. There was absolutely
nothing to do but to engage in flirtation, sports, and court festivities.
These are fine pastimes, but they are life-filling only for relatively rare
connoisseurs. Unless the nobles were to be allowed to revolt, they had
to be kept busy. Now all the noble families whose members were amusing themselves at Versailles could look back on a warlike past, martial
ideas and phrases, bellicose instincts. To ninety-nine out of a hundred
of them, "action" meant military action. If civil war was to be avoided,
then external wars were required. Foreign campaigns preoccupied and
satisfied the nobility. From the viewpoint of the crown they were harmless and even advantageous. As it was, the crown was in control of the
military machine, which must not be allowed to rust or languish. Tradition—as always surviving its usefulness—favored war as the natural
pursuit of kings. And finally, the monarchy needed outward successes
to maintain its position at home—how much it needed them was later
shown when the pendulum swung to the other extreme, under Louis
XV and Louis XVI. Small wonder that France took the field on every
possible occasion, with an excess of enthusiasm that becomes wholly
understandable from its position and that left it quite indifferent to the
actual nature of the occasion. Any war would do. If only there was war,
the details of foreign policy were gladly left to the king.

Thus the belligerence and war policy of the autocratic state are explained from the necessities of its social structure, from the inherited
dispositions of its ruling class, rather than from the immediate advantages to be derived by conquest. . . .

We do not seek to underestimate the immediate advantages, at the time, of an expansion of the national domain. This is an element that then had a significance much greater than it has today. At a time when communications were uncertain, making military protection of commerce necessary, every nation undoubtedly had an interest in national bases overseas as well as in Europe, and in colonies too, though not so much in the conquest of other European countries. Finally, for the absolute monarch conquest meant an increment in power, soldiers, and income. And had all the plans of Louis XIV succeeded, he would undoubtedly have "made a go of it." The inner necessity to engage in a policy of conquest was not distasteful to him. Yet that this element could play a part is explained only from the traditional habit of war and from the fact that the war machine stood ready at hand. Otherwise these instincts would have been inhibited, just as are predatory instincts in private life. Murder with intent to rob cannot be explained by the mere desire for the victim's money, any more than analogous suggestions explain the expansive policy of the absolutist state.

At the same time, it remains a peculiarity of this type of imperialism that the monarch's personal motives and interests are far more important to an understanding of its individual aspects than is true in the case of other types. The prince-become-state made foreign policy his own personal business and saw to it that it was the concern of no one else. His personal interests became the interests of the state. Hereditary claims, personal rancor and idiosyncrasy, family politics, individual generosity and similar traits cannot be denied a role as real factors shaping the surface situation. These things may have been no more than individual manifestations of a social situation, social data processed through an individual temperament; but superficially, at least, they did make history to the extent that they, in turn, had consequences that become elements of the social situation. It was this period that gave rise to the notion, so deeply rooted in the popular mind down to recent times, that foreign policy can be explained by the whims of sovereigns and their relations to one another. It gave rise to the whole approach that judges events from the viewpoint of monarchial interest, honor, and morality—an approach stemming directly from the social views of the time (as seen, for example, in the letters of Mme. de Sévigné) and one that adapts itself only slowly to changing times.

12 / BENEDICT DE SPINOZA: THE RIGHT OF FREE THOUGHT

The right of government to control the beliefs of subjects and to punish "wrong" and "dangerous" thoughts was seldom questioned before the eighteenth century. The affirmation, therefore, of the morality and utility of freedom of thought by Benedict de Spinoza (1632–1677) was an act of notable courage. This was all the more true because Spinoza, born a Sephardic Jew in the Dutch Republic, was expelled from the Jewish community for his rejection of rigid Judaic orthodoxy and faced repeated criticism from the Calvinist clergy for his treatment of the Bible as a historical document subject to the criteria of historical analysis. The translation of his Tractatus theologico-politicus *("Treatise on Theology and Politics," 1670), from which the following passages are taken, is by a modern British scholar.*[23]

Could thought be controlled as easily as speech, all governments would rule in safety, and none would be oppressive; for everyone would live as his rulers wanted, and his judgements of true and false, good and bad, fair and unfair, would be determined entirely by their will. However, . . . it is impossible for thought to be completely subject to another's control, because no one can give up to another his natural right to reason freely and form his own judgement about everything, nor can he be compelled to do so. This is why a government is regarded as oppressive if it tries to control men's minds, and why a sovereign is thought to wrong its subjects, and to usurp their right, if it seeks to tell them what they should embrace as true and reject as false, and to prescribe the beliefs which should inspire their minds with devotion to God; for in such matters an individual cannot alienate his right even if he wishes. Admittedly a man's judgement can be influenced in many ways, some of them hardly credible; so much so, in fact, that though not directly under another's command it may depend

[23] Benedict de Spinoza, *Tractatus theologico-politicus*, in *The Political Works*, edited and translated from the Latin by A. G. Wernham (Oxford: The Clarendon Press, 1958), pp. 227–9, 235–9. Reprinted by permission of The Clarendon Press.

entirely on his words, and thus in that respect can properly be called subject to his right. Yet in spite of all that political skill has been able to achieve in this field, it has never been completely successful; men have always found that individuals were full of their own ideas, and that opinions varied as much as tastes. Even Moses, who by extraordinary ability, and not by deception, had so captivated the mind of his people that it regarded him as a superman, divinely inspired in everything he said and did, was not immune from its criticisms and misrepresentations; and this is still more true of the other kings. Yet were such immunity conceivable at all it would be in a monarchy; not in a democracy where all or most men are colleagues in the government. The reason for this, I think, is plain to everyone.

Thus no matter how completely a ruler has convinced his subjects that he has the right to do everything, and is the interpreter of law and piety, he will never be able to prevent them from passing their own individual judgements on everything, and from feeling different emotions accordingly. It is true that he has the right to treat as enemies all who are not in complete agreement with him on every point; but what I am discussing now is not his right, but the good of the state. Admittedly he has the right to rule with the utmost violence, and to hale citizens off to execution on the most trivial pretexts; but everyone will deny that he can do so with the approval of sound reason. Indeed, just because he cannot do such things without great danger to the whole state, we may even deny that he has full power to do them, and hence deny that he has full right to do them either; since, as I have shown, a sovereign's right is determined by its power.

If no man, then, can surrender his freedom to judge and think as he pleases, and everyone is master of his own thoughts by perfect natural right, the attempt to make men speak only as the sovereign prescribes, no manner how different and opposed their ideas may be, must always meet with very little success in a state; for even men of great experience cannot hold their tongues, far less the mass of the people. It is a common human failing to confide one's plans to others even when secrecy is needed: hence government will be most oppressive where the individual is denied the freedom to express and communicate his opinions, and moderate where this freedom is allowed him. Yet it must also be admitted that words can be treasonable as well as deeds; and so, though it is impossible to deprive subjects of such freedom entirely, it will be quite disastrous to grant it to them in full. . . .

He who seeks to determine everything by law will aggravate vices rather than correct them. We must necessarily permit what we cannot prevent, even though it often leads to harm. Things like extravagance, envy, greed, and drunkenness are a source of much evil; yet we put up with them because they cannot be prevented by legal enactment, vices though in fact they are. Much more then must we allow independence of judgement; for it is certainly a virtue, and it cannot be suppressed. Besides, it leads to no trouble which cannot be forestalled by the influence of the magistrates (as I shall presently show); to say nothing of the fact that it is quite indispensable for the advancement of the arts and sciences, for these are cultivated with success only by men whose judgement is free and unbiased.

But let us assume that such freedom can be suppressed, and that men can be so thoroughly coerced that they dare not whisper a word which is not prescribed by the sovereign. Will it ever come to pass that they also think nothing but what it wills? Assuredly not. Then the inevitable result will be this. Every day men will be saying one thing and thinking another; belief in another's word, a prime necessity in a state, will thus be undermined, nauseating sycophancy and deceitfulness encouraged; and hence will come frauds and the destruction of all honest dealing. In fact, however, the assumption that everyone can be made to speak to order is quite impossible. The more the sovereign tries to deprive men of freedom of speech, the more stubbornly is it opposed; not indeed by money-grubbers, sycophants, and the rest of the shallow crew, whose supreme happiness is to gloat over the coins in their coffers and to have their bellies well stuffed, but by those who, because of their culture, integrity, and ability, have some independence of mind. Ordinary human nature is such that men find nothing more irritating than to have the views which they hold to be true branded as criminal, and the beliefs which inspire them to piety towards God and man held up against them as wickedness; this encourages them to denounce the laws, and to go to all lengths against the magistrate, in the belief that it is not disgraceful but highly laudable to stir up sedition and attempt the most outrageous crimes in such a cause. Given, then, that human nature is such, it follows that laws which proscribe beliefs do not affect the wicked but the liberalminded, that they are passed to annoy the good rather than to restrain the malicious, and that they cannot be upheld without great danger to the state. In any case, such laws are utterly useless; for those who regard the proscribed beliefs as sound will be unable to obey the laws which proscribe them, while those who reject such beliefs as false welcome these laws as privileges, and are so proud of them that the magistrate can never repeal them even if he wishes. . . . Finally, the readiness of magistrates to settle the disputes of scholars by legislation has been the main source of innumerable divisions in the church; for were men not captivated by the hope of getting the laws and the magistrate on their side, of triumphing over their opponents amid the general applause of the mob, and of attaining high office, they would never quarrel with such spite or be driven by such frenzy. And these are the findings of experience as well as of reason; for each new day brings instances to show that laws which prescribe what everyone must believe, and forbid men to say or write anything against this or that opinion, are often passed to gratify, or rather, to appease the anger of those who cannot abide independent minds, but by their savage influence can easily change the fervour of an unruly people into frenzy, and direct it against anyone they please. Yet how much better would it be to curb the furious anger of the mob, instead of passing useless laws which can only be broken by those who love the virtues and the arts, and reducing the state to such straits that it cannot support men of liberal views? What greater calamity to a state can be imagined than that good men should be sent into exile as malefactors because they hold unorthodox beliefs and cannot pretend otherwise? What, I say, is more disastrous than that men should be branded as public enemies and haled off to execution for no crime or misdeed, but simply because they have independent minds; and that the scaffold, the terror of the wicked, should become a glorious stage for presenting—to the signal disgrace of the sovereign—supreme examples of courage and endurance? For men whose consciences are clear do not fear death or beg for mercy like criminals, since their minds are not tormented by remorse for deeds of shame; they think it a merit, not a punishment, to die for a good cause, and an honour to die for freedom. And since they give their lives for a cause that is beyond the ken of fainéants and fools, hateful to the unruly, and dear to the good, what are men taught by their death? Only to emulate them, or at least to hold them in reverence.

If honesty, then, is to be valued above servility, and sovereigns are to retain full control, without being forced to yield to agitators, it is necessary to allow freedom of judgement, and so to govern men that they can express different and conflicting opinions without ceasing to live in harmony. This method of government is undoubtedly best, and least subject to inconveniences; for it is best suited to human nature. I have shown that in a democracy (which comes nearest to the natural condition) all make a covenant to act, but not to judge and think, in accordance with the common decision; that is, because all men cannot think alike, they agree that the proposal which gets the most votes shall have the force of a decree, but meanwhile retain the authority to revoke such decrees when they discover better. Thus the less freedom of judgement men are allowed, the greater is the departure from the most natural condition, and, in consequence, the more oppressive is the government.

13 / JOHN LOCKE: SOCIAL CONTRACT AND RESPONSIBLE GOVERNMENT

One of the key figures in the transition from the medieval to the modern pattern of debate over the right form and character of the state is the English philosopher John Locke (1632–1704). Educated as a physician, Locke was active chiefly as a philosophical, religious, and political thinker; but he was not strange to practical politics. He not only provided the Whig party with its weapons of doctrine, but also took part in the work of governmental administration when the Whigs were influential. His most important work of political theory, the Two Treatises of Government *(or* Civil Government, *as they are more usually called), was written almost a decade before its first publication in 1690, when it was adapted by addition of a few phrases to serve as a defense of the overthrow of James II and the enthronement of his son-in-law (and nephew) and daughter, William III and Mary II. The following passages from the* Two Treatises *are taken from a modern critical edition by an English scholar, which is based upon Locke's own emendations of the original printed text.[24]*

The great Question which in all Ages has disturbed Mankind, and brought on them the greatest part of those Mischiefs which have ruin'd Cities, depopulated Countries, and disordered the Peace of the World, has been, Not whether there be Power in the World, nor whence it came, but who should have it. The settling of this point being of no smaller moment than the security of Princes, and the peace and welfare of their Estates and Kingdoms, a Reformer of Politicks, one would think, should lay this sure, and be very clear in it. For if this remain disputable, all the rest will be to very little purpose; and the skill used in dressing up Power with all the Splendor and Temptation Absolute-

[24] John Locke, *Two Treatises of Government,* ed. Peter Laslett (Cambridge, Eng.: University Press, 1960), pp. 236–7, 286–9, 341–4, 346, 348–51, 368–71, 444–6. Reprinted by permission of Cambridge University Press.

ness can add to it, without shewing who has a Right to have it, will serve only to give a greater edge to Man's Natural Ambition, which of it self is but too keen. What can this do but set Men on the more eagerly to scramble, and so lay a sure and lasting Foundation of endless Contention and Disorder, instead of that Peace and Tranquility, which is the business of Government, and the end of Humane Society?

. . . I think it may not be amiss, to set down what I take to be Political Power. That the Power of a *Magistrate* over a Subject, may be distinguished from that of a *Father* over his Children, a *Master* over his Servant, a *Husband* over his Wife, and a *Lord* over his Slave. All which distinct Powers happening sometimes together in the same Man, if he be considered under these different Relations, it may help us to distinguish these Powers one from another, and shew the difference betwixt a Ruler of a Common-wealth, a Father of a Family, and a Captain of a Galley.

Political Power then I take to be a *Right* of making Laws with Penalties of Death, and consequently all less Penalties, for the Regulating and Preserving of Property, and of employing the force of the Community, in the Execution of such Laws, and in the defence of the Common-wealth from Foreign Injury, and all this only for the Publick Good.

To understand Political Power right, and derive it from its Original, we must consider what State all Men are naturally in, and that is, a *State of perfect Freedom* to order their Actions, and dispose of their Possessions, and Persons as they think fit, within the bounds of the Law of Nature, without asking leave, or depending upon the Will of any other Man.

A *State* also of *Equality,* wherein all the Power and Jurisdiction is reciprocal, no one having more than another: there being nothing more evident, than that Creatures of the same species and rank promiscuously born to all the same advantages of Nature, and the use of the same faculties, should also be equal one amongst another without Subordination or Subjection, unless the Lord and Master of them all, should by any manifest Declaration of his Will set one above another, and confer on him by an evident and clear appointment an undoubted Right to Dominion and Sovereignty. . . .

But though this be a *State of Liberty,* yet it is *not a State of Licence,* though Man in that State have an uncontroleable Liberty, to dispose of his Person or Possessions, yet he has not Liberty to destroy himself, or so much as any Creature in his Possession, but where some nobler use, than its bare Preservation calls for it. The *State of Nature* has a Law of Nature to govern it, which obliges every one: And Reason, which is that Law, teaches all Mankind, who will but consult it, that being all equal and independent, no one ought to harm another in his Life, Health, Liberty, or Possessions. For Men being all the Workmanship of one Omnipotent, and infinitely wise Maker; All the Servants of one Sovereign Master, sent into the World by his order and about his business, they are his Property, whose Workmanship they are, made to last during his, not one anothers Pleasure. And being furnished with like Faculties, sharing all in one Community of Nature, there cannot be supposed any such *Subordination* among us, that may Authorize us to destroy one another, as if we were made for one anothers uses, as the inferior ranks of Creatures are for ours. Every one as he is *bound to preserve himself,* and not to quit his Station wilfully; so by the like reason when his own Preservation comes not in competition, ought he, as much as he can, *to preserve the rest of Mankind,* and may not unless it be to do Justice on an Offender, take away, or impair the life, or what tends to the Preservation of the Life, the Liberty, Health, Limb or Goods of another. . . .

Man being born, as has been proved, with a Title to perfect Freedom, and an uncontrouled enjoyment of all the Rights and Priviledges of the Law of Nature, equally with any other Man, or Number of Men in the World, hath by Nature a Power, not only to preserve his Property, that is, his Life, Liberty and Estate, against the Injuries and Attempts of other Men; but to judge of, and punish the breaches of that Law in others, as he is perswaded the Offence deserves, even with Death it self, in Crimes where the heinousness of the Fact, in his Opinion, requires it. But because no *Political Society* can be, nor subsist without having in it self the Power to preserve the Property, and in order thereunto punish the Offences of all those of that Society; there, and there only is *Political Society,* where every one of the Members hath quitted this natural Power, resign'd it up into the hands of the Community in all cases that exclude him not from appealing for Protection to the Law established by it. And thus all private judgement of every particular Member being excluded, the Community comes to be Umpire, by settled standing Rules, indifferent, and the same to all Parties; and by Men having Authority from the Community, for the execution of those Rules, decides all the differences that may happen between any Members of that Society, concerning any matter of right; and punishes those Offences, which any Member hath committed against the Society, with such Penalties as the Law has established: Whereby it is easie to discern who are, and who are not, in *Political Society* together. Those who are united into one Body, and have a common establish'd Law and Judicature to appeal to, with Authority to decide Controversies between them, and punish Offenders, *are in Civil Society* one with another: but those who have no such common

Appeal, I mean on Earth, are still in the state of Nature, each being, where there is no other, Judge for himself, and Executioner; which is, as I have before shew'd it, the perfect *state of Nature.*

And thus the Commonwealth comes by a Power to set down, what punishment shall belong to the several transgressions which they think worthy of it, committed amongst the Members of that Society, (which is the *power of making Laws*) as well as it has the power to punish any Injury done unto any of its Members, by any one that is not of it, (which is the *power of War and Peace;*) and all this for the preservation of the property of all the Members of that Society, as far as is possible. But though every Man who has enter'd into civil Society, and is become a member of any Commonwealth, has thereby quitted his power to punish Offences against the Law of Nature, in prosecution of his own private Judgment; yet with the Judgment of Offences which he has given up to the Legislative in all Cases, where he can Appeal to the Magistrate, he has given a right to the Commonwealth to imploy his force, for the Execution of the Judgments of the Commonwealth, whenever he shall be called to it; which indeed are his own Judgments, they being made by himself, or his Representative. And herein we have the original of the *Legislative* and *Executive Power* of Civil Society, which is to judge by standing Laws how far Offences are to be punished, when committed within the Commonwealth; and also to determin, by occasional Judgments founded on the present Circumstances of the Fact, how far Injuries from without are to be vindicated, and in both these to imploy all the force of all the Members when there shall be need.

Where-ever therefore any number of Men are so united into one Society, as to quit every one his Executive Power of the Law of Nature, and to resign it to the publick, there and there only is a *Political, or Civil Society.* And this is done where-ever any number of Men, in the state of Nature, enter into Society to make one People, one Body Politick under one Supreme Government, or else when any one joyns himself to, and incorporates with any Government already made. For hereby he authorizes the Society, or which is all one, the Legislative thereof to make Laws for him as the publick good of the Society shall require; to the Execution whereof, his own assistance (as to his own Decrees) is due. And this *puts Men* out of a State of Nature *into* that of a *Commonwealth,* by setting up a Judge on Earth, with Authority to determine all the Controversies, and redress the Injuries, that may happen to any Member of the Commonwealth; which Judge is the Legislative, or Magistrates appointed by it. And where-ever there are any number of Men, however associated, that have no such decisive power to appeal to, there they are *still in the state of Nature.*

Here it is evident, that *Absolute Monarchy,* which by some Men is counted the only Government in the World, is indeed *inconsistent with Civil Society,* and so can be no Form of Civil Government at all. For the *end of Civil Society,* being to avoid, and remedy those inconveniences of the State of Nature, which necessarily follow from every Man's being Judge in his own Case, by setting up a known Authority, to which every one of that Society may Appeal upon any Injury received, or Controversie that may arise, and which every one of the Society ought to obey; where-ever any persons are, who have not such an Authority to Appeal to, for the decision of any difference between them, there those persons are still *in the state of Nature.* And so is every *Absolute Prince* in respect of those who are under his *Dominion. . . .*

In Absolute Monarchies indeed, as well as other Governments of the World, the Subjects have an Appeal to the Law, and Judges to decide any Controversies, and restrain any Violence that may happen betwixt the Subjects themselves, one amongst another. This every one thinks necessary, and believes he deserves to be thought a declared Enemy to Society and Mankind, who should go about to take it away. But whether this be from a true Love of Mankind and Society, and such a Charity as we owe all one to another, there is reason to doubt. For this is no more, than what every Man who loves his own Power, Profit, or Greatness, may, and naturally must do, keep those Animals from hurting or destroying one another who labour and drudge only for his Pleasure and Advantage, and so are taken care of, not out of any Love the Master has for them, but Love of himself, and the Profit they bring him. For if it be asked, what Security, *what Fence* is there in such a State, *against the Violence and Oppression of this Absolute Ruler?* The very Question can scarce be born. They are ready to tell you, that it deserves Death only to ask after Safety. Betwixt Subject and Subject, they will grant, there must be Measures, Laws, and Judges, for their mutual Peace and Security: But as for the *Ruler,* he ought to be *Absolute,* and is above all such Circumstances: because he has Power to do more hurt and wrong, 'tis right when he does it. To ask how you may be guarded from harm, or injury on that side where the strongest hand is to do it, is presently the Voice of Faction and Rebellion. As if when Men quitting the State of Nature entered into Society, they agreed that all of them but one, should be under the restraint of Laws, but that he should still retain all the Liberty of the State of Nature, increased with Power, and made licentious by Impunity. This is to think that Men are so foolish that they take care to avoid what Mischiefs may be done them by *Pole-Cats,* or *Foxes,* but are content, nay think it Safety, to be devoured by *Lions. . . .*

Men being, as has been said, by Nature, all free, equal and independent, no one can be put out of this Estate, and subjected to the

Political Power of another, without his own *Consent*. The only way whereby any one devests himself of his Natural Liberty, and *puts on the bonds of Civil Society* is by agreeing with other Men to joyn and unite into a Community, for their comfortable, safe, and peaceable living one amongst another, in a secure Enjoyment of their Properties, and a greater Security against any that are not of it. This any number of Men may do, because it injures not the Freedom of the rest; they are left as they were in the Liberty of the State of Nature. When any number of Men have so *consented to make one Community* or Government, they are thereby presently incorporated, and make *one Body Politick,* wherein the *Majority* have a Right to act and conclude the rest.

For when any number of Men have, by the consent of every individual, made a *Community,* they have thereby made that *Community* one Body, with a Power to Act as one Body, which is only by the will and determination of the *majority.* For that which acts any Community, being only the consent of the individuals of it, and it being necessary to that which is one body to move one way; it is necessary the Body should move that way whither the greater force carries it, which is the *consent of the majority:* or else it is impossible it should act or continue one Body, *one Community,* which the consent of every individual that united into it, agreed that it should; and so every one is bound by that consent to be concluded by the *majority.* And therefore we see that in Assemblies impowered to act by positive Laws where no number is set by that positive Law which impowers them, the *act of the Majority* passes for the act of the whole, and of course determines, as having by the Law of Nature and Reason, the power of the whole.

And thus every Man, by consenting with others to make one Body Politick under one Government, puts himself under an Obligation to every one of that Society, to submit to the determination of the *majority,* and to be concluded by it; or else this *original Compact,* whereby he with others incorporates into *one Society,* would signifie nothing, and be no Compact, if he be left free, and under no other ties, than he was in before in the State of Nature. For what appearance would there be of any Compact? What new Engagement if he were not farther tied by any Decrees of the Society, than he himself thought fit, and did actually consent to? This would be still as great a liberty, as he himself had before his Compact, or any one else in the State of Nature hath, who may submit himself and consent to any acts of it if he thinks fit. . . .

Whosoever therefore out of a state of Nature unite into a *Community,* must be understood to give up all the power, necessary to the ends for which they unite into Society, to the *majority* of the Community, unless they expressly agreed in any number greater than the majority. And this is done by barely agreeing to *unite into one Political*

Society, which is *all the Compact* that is, or needs be, between the Individuals, that enter into, or make up a *Common-wealth.* And thus that, which begins and actually *constitutes any Political Society,* is nothing but the consent of any number of Freemen capable of a majority to unite and incorporate into such a Society. And this is that, and that only, which did, or could give *beginning* to any *lawful Government* in the World. . . .

If Man in the State of Nature be so free, as has been said; If he be absolute Lord of his own Person and Possessions, equal to the greatest, and subject to no Body, why will he part with his Freedom? Why will he give up this Empire, and subject himself to the Dominion and Controul of any other Power? To which 'tis obvious to Answer, that though in the state of Nature he hath such a right, yet the Enjoyment of it is very uncertain, and constantly exposed to the Invasion of others. For all being Kings as much as he, every Man his Equal, and the greatest part no strict Observers of Equity and Justice, the enjoyment of the property he has in this state is very unsafe, very unsecure. This makes him willing to quit a Condition, which however free, is full of fears and continual dangers: And 'tis not without reason, that he seeks out, and is willing to joyn in Society with others who are already united, or have a mind to unite for the mutual *Preservation* of their Lives, Liberties and Estates, which I call by the general Name, *Property.*

The great and *chief end* therefore, of Mens uniting into Commonwealths, and putting themselves under Government, *is the Preservation of their Property.* To which in the state of Nature there are many things wanting.

First, There wants an *establish'd,* settled, known *Law,* received and allowed by common consent to be the Standard of Right and Wrong, and the common measure to decide all Controversies between them. For though the Law of Nature be plain and intelligible to all rational Creatures; yet Men being biassed by their Interest, as well as ignorant for want of study of it, are not apt to allow of it as a Law binding to them in the application of it to their particular Cases.

Secondly, In the State of Nature there wants *a known and indifferent Judge,* with Authority to determine all differences according to the established Law. For every one in that state being both Judge and Executioner of the Law of Nature, Men being partial to themselves, Passion and Revenge is very apt to carry them too far, and with too much heat, in their own Cases; as well as negligence, and unconcernedness, to make them too remiss, in other Mens.

Thirdly, In the state of Nature there often wants *Power* to back and support the Sentence when right, and to *give* it due *Execution.* They who by any Injustice offended, will seldom fail, where they are able, by force to make good their Injustice: such resistance many times makes the punishment dangerous, and frequently destructive, to those who attempt it.

Thus Mankind, notwithstanding all the Priviledges of the state of Nature, being but in an ill condition, while they remain in it, are quickly driven into Society. Hence it comes to pass, that we seldom find any number of Men living any time together in this State. The inconveniences, that they are therein exposed to, by the irregular and uncertain exercise of the Power every Man has of punishing the transgressions of others, make them take Sanctuary under the establish'd Laws of Government, and therein seek *the preservation of their Property*. 'Tis this makes them so willingly give up every one his single power of punishing to be exercised by such alone as shall be appointed to it amongst them; and by such Rules as the Community, or those authorised by them to that purpose, shall agree on. And in this we have the original *right and rise* of both *the Legislative and Executive Power,* as well as of the Governments and Societies themselves. . . .

But though Men when they enter into Society, give up the Equality, Liberty, and Executive Power they had in the State of Nature, into the hands of the Society, to be so far disposed of by the Legislature, as the good of the Society shall require; yet it being only with an intention in every one the better to preserve himself his Liberty and Property; (For no rational Creature can be supposed to change his condition with an intention to be worse) the power of the Society, or *Legislative* constituted by them, *can never be suppos'd to extend farther than the common good;* but is obliged to secure every ones Property by providing against those three defects above-mentioned, that made the State of Nature so unsafe and uneasie. And so whoever has the Legislative or Supream Power of any Common-wealth, is bound to govern by establish'd *standing Laws,* promulgated and known to the People, and not by Extemporary Decrees; by *indifferent* and upright *Judges,* who are to decide Controversies by those Laws; And to imploy the force of the Community at home, *only in the Execution of such Laws,* or abroad to prevent or redress Foreign Injuries, and secure the Community from Inroads and Invasion. And all this to be directed to no other *end,* but the *Peace, Safety,* and *publick good* of the People. . . .

Here, 'tis like, the common Question will be made, *Who shall be Judge* whether the Prince or Legislative act contrary to their Trust? This, perhaps, ill affected and factious Men may spread amongst the People, when the Prince only makes use of his due Prerogative. To this I reply, *The People shall be Judge;* for who shall be *Judge* whether his Trustee or Deputy acts well, and according to the Trust reposed in him, but he who deputes him, and must, by having deputed him have still a Power to discard him, when he fails in his Trust? If this be reasonable in particular Cases of private Men, why should it be otherwise in that of the greatest moment; where the Welfare of Millions is concerned, and also where the evil, if not prevented, is greater, and the Redress very difficult, dear, and dangerous?

But farther, this Question, (*Who shall be Judge?*) cannot mean, that there is no Judge at all. For where there is no Judicature on Earth, to decide Controversies amongst Men, *God* in Heaven is *Judge:* He alone, 'tis true, is Judge of the Right. But *every Man* is *Judge* for himself, as in all other Cases, so in this, whether another hath put himself into a State of War with him, and whether he should appeal to the Supreme Judge, as *Jephtha* did.

If a Controversie arise betwixt a Prince and some of the People, in a matter where the Law is silent, or doubtful, and the thing be of great Consequence, I should think the proper *Umpire*, in such a Case, should be the Body of the *People.* For in Cases where the Prince hath a Trust reposed in him, and is dispensed from the common ordinary Rules of the Law; there, if any Men find themselves aggrieved, and think the Prince acts contrary to, or beyond that Trust, who so proper to *Judge* as the Body of the *People,* (who, at first, lodg'd that Trust in him) how far they meant it should extend? But if the Prince, or whoever they be in the Administration, decline that way of Determination, the Appeal then lies no where but to Heaven. Force between either Persons, who have no known Superiour on Earth, or which permits no Appeal to a Judge on Earth, being properly a state of War, wherein the Appeal lies only to Heaven, and in that State the *injured Party must judge* for himself, when he will think fit to make use of that Appeal, and put himself upon it.

To conclude, the *Power that every individual gave the Society,* when he entered into it, can never revert to the Individuals again, as long as the Society lasts, but will always remain in the Community; because without this, there can be no Community, no Common-wealth, which is contrary to the original Agreement: So also when the Society hath placed the Legislative in any Assembly of Men, to continue in them and their Successors, with Direction and Authority for providing such Successors, *the Legislative can never revert to the People* whilst that Government lasts: Because having provided a Legislative with Power to continue for ever, they have given up their Political Power to the Legislative, and cannot resume it. But if they have set Limits to the Duration of their Legislative, and made this Supreme Power in any Person, or Assembly, only temporary: Or else when by the Miscarriages of those in Authority, it is forfeited; upon the Forfeiture of their Rulers, or at the Determination of the Time set, *it reverts to the Society,* and the People have a Right to act as Supreme, and continue the Legislative in themselves, or erect a new Form, or under the old form place it in new hands, as they think good.

14 / THE RIGHTS OF SUBJECTS

What Locke defended in doctrine in his Treatises on Civil Government *was established in practice by the Act of Succession of 1689, confirming the passage of the crown to William and Mary. This statute is also known as the Bill of Rights, because it incorporated into law the principles of constitutional monarchy, representative government, and the rights of subjects, which the Stuarts from James I to James II had sought to limit and—according to their opponents—to abolish. The following is the full text of "An Act declaring the Rights and Liberties of the Subject, and settling the Succession of the Crown."* [25]

Whereas the Lords Spiritual and Temporal and Commons assembled at Westminster, lawfully, fully and freely representing all the estates of the people of this realm, did upon the thiiteenth day of February in the year of our Lord one thousand six hundred eighty-eight [26] present unto their Majesties, then called and known by the names and style of William and Mary, prince and princess of Orange, being present in their proper persons, a certain declaration in writing made by the said Lords and Commons in the words following, viz.:

Whereas the late King James the Second, by the assistance of divers evil counsellors, judges and ministers employed by him, did endeavour to subvert and extirpate the Protestant religion and the laws and liberties of this kingdom;

By assuming and exercising a power of dispensing with and suspending of laws and the execution of laws without consent of Parliament;

By committing and prosecuting divers worthy prelates for humbly petitioning to be excused from concurring to the said assumed power;

By issuing and causing to be executed a commission under the great

[25] *The Statutes at Large, of England and of Great-Britain: from Magna Carta to the Union of the Kingdoms of Great Britain and Ireland* (London: George Eyre and Andrew Strahan, 1811), Vol. V, pp. 538–43.

[26] Old Style; 1689 New Style

seal for erecting a court called the Court of Commissioners for Ecclesiastical Causes;

By levying money for and to the use of the Crown by pretence of prerogative for other time and in other manner than the same was granted by Parliament;

By raising and keeping a standing army within this kingdom in time of peace without consent of Parliament, and quartering soldiers contrary to law;

By causing several good subjects being Protestants to be disarmed at the same time when papists were both armed and employed contrary to law;

By violating the freedom of election of members to serve in Parliament;

By prosecutions in the Court of King's Bench for matters and causes cognizable only in Parliament, and by divers other arbitrary and illegal courses;

And whereas of late years partial, corrupt and unqualified persons have been returned and served on juries in trials, and particularly divers jurors in trials for high treason which were not freeholders;

And excessive bail hath been required of persons committed in criminal cases to elude the benefit of the laws made for the liberty of the subjects;

And excessive fines have been imposed;

And illegal and cruel punishments inflicted;

And several grants and promises made of fines and forfeitures before any conviction or judgment against the persons upon whom the same were to be levied;

All which are utterly and directly contrary to the known laws and statutes and freedom of this realm;

And whereas the said late King James the Second having abdicated the government and the throne being thereby vacant, his Highness the prince of Orange (whom it hath pleased Almighty God to make the glorious instrument of delivering this kingdom from popery and arbitrary power) did (by the advice of the Lords Spiritual and Temporal and divers principal persons of the Commons) cause letters to be written to the Lords Spiritual and Temporal being Protestants, and other letters to the several counties, cities, universities, boroughs and cinque ports, for the choosing of such persons to represent them as were of right to be sent to Parliament, to meet and sit at Westminster upon the two and twentieth day of January in this year one thousand six hundred eighty and eight,[27] in order to such an establishment as that their religion, laws and liberties might not again be in danger of

[27] Old Style

being subverted, upon which letters elections having been accordingly made;

And thereupon the said Lords Spiritual and Temporal and Commons, pursuant to their respective letters and elections, being now assembled in a full and free representative of this nation, taking into their most serious consideration the best means for attaining the ends aforesaid, do in the first place (as their ancestors in like case have usually done) for the vindicating and asserting their ancient rights and liberties declare

That the pretended power of suspending of laws or the execution of laws by regal authority without consent of Parliament is illegal;

That the pretended power of dispensing with laws or the execution of laws by regal authority, as it hath been assumed and exercised of late, is illegal;

That the commission for erecting the late Court of Commissioners for Ecclesiastical Causes, and all other commissions and courts of like nature, are illegal and pernicious;

That levying money for or to the use of the Crown by pretence of prerogative, without grant of Parliament, for longer time, or in other manner than the same is or shall be granted, is illegal;

That it is the right of the subjects to petition the king, and all commitments and prosecutions for such petitioning are illegal;

That the raising or keeping a standing army within the kingdom in time of peace, unless it be with consent of Parliament, is against law;

That the subjects which are Protestants may have arms for their defence suitable to their conditions and as allowed by law;

That election of members of Parliament ought to be free;

That the freedom of speech and debates or proceedings in Parliament ought not to be impeached or questioned in any court or place out of Parliament;

That excessive bail ought not to be required, nor excessive fines imposed, nor cruel and unusual punishments inflicted;

That jurors ought to be duly impanelled and returned, and jurors which pass upon men in trials for high treason ought to be freeholders;

That all grants and promises of fines and forfeitures of particular persons before conviction are illegal and void;

And that for redress of all grievances, and for the amending, strengthening and preserving of the laws, Parliaments ought to be held frequently.

And they do claim, demand and insist upon all and singular the premises as their undoubted rights and liberties, and that no declarations, judgments, doings or proceedings to the prejudice of the people in any of the said premises ought in any wise to be drawn hereafter into consequence or example; to which demand of their rights they are particularly encouraged by the declaration of his Highness the prince of Orange as being the only means for obtaining a full redress and remedy therein. Having therefore an entire confidence that his said Highness the prince of Orange will perfect the deliverance so far advanced by him, and will still preserve them from the violation of their rights which they have here asserted, and from all other attempts upon their religion, rights and liberties, the said Lords Spiritual and Temporal and Commons assembled at Westminster do resolve that William and Mary, prince and princess of Orange, be and be declared king and queen of England, France and Ireland and the dominions thereunto belonging, to hold the crown and royal dignity of the said kingdoms and dominions to them, the said prince and princess, during their lives and the life of the survivor of them, and that the sole and full exercise of the regal power be only in and executed by the said prince of Orange in the names of the said prince and princess during their joint lives, and after their deceases the said crown and royal dignity of the said kingdoms and dominions to be to the heirs of the body of the said princess, and for default of such issue to the Princess Anne of Denmark and the heirs of her body, and for default of such issue to the heirs of the body of the said prince of Orange. And the Lords Spiritual and Temporal and Commons do pray the said prince and princess to accept the same accordingly.

And that the oaths hereafter mentioned be taken by all persons of whom the oaths of allegiance and supremacy might be required by law, instead of them, and that the said oaths of allegiance and supremacy be abrogated.

I, A.B., do sincerely promise and swear that I will be faithful and bear true allegiance to their Majesties King William and Queen Mary. So help me God.

I, A.B., do swear that I do from my heart abhor, detest and abjure as impious and heretical this damnable doctrine and position, that princes excommunicated or deprived by the Pope or any authority of the see of Rome may be deposed or murdered by their subjects or any other whatsoever. And I do declare that no foreign prince, person, prelate, state or potentate hath or ought to have any jurisdiction, power, superiority, pre-eminence or authority, ecclesiastical or spiritual, within this realm. So help me God.

Upon which their said Majesties did accept the crown and royal dignity of the kingdoms of England, France and Ireland, and the dominions thereunto belonging, according to the resolution and desire of the said Lords and Commons contained in the said declaration. And thereupon their Majesties were pleased that the said Lords Spiritual and Temporal and Commons, being the two Houses of Parliament, should continue to sit, and with their Majesties' royal concurrence make effectual provision for the settlement of the religion, laws and liberties of this kingdom, so that the same for the future might not be in danger again of being subverted, to which the said Lords Spiritual and Temporal and Commons did agree, and proceed to act accordingly. Now in pursuance of the premises the said Lords Spiritual and Temporal and Commons in Parliament assembled, for the ratifying, confirming and establishing the said declaration and the articles, clauses, matters and things therein contained by the force of a law made in due form by authority of Parliament, do pray that it may be declared and enacted that all and singular the rights and liberties asserted and claimed in the said declaration are the true, ancient and indubitable rights and liberties of the people of this kingdom, and so shall be esteemed, allowed, adjudged, deemed and taken to be; and that all and every the particulars aforesaid shall be firmly and strictly holden and observed as they are expressed in the said declaration, and all officers and ministers whatsoever shall serve their Majesties and their successors according to the same in all times to come. And the said Lords Spiritual and Temporal and Commons, seriously considering how it hath pleased Almighty God in his marvellous providence and merciful goodness to this nation to provide and preserve their said Majesties' royal persons most happily to reign over us upon the throne of their ancestors, for which they render unto him from the bottom of their hearts their humblest thanks and praises, do truly, firmly, assuredly and in the sincerity of their hearts think, and do hereby recognize, acknowledge and declare, that King James the Second having abdicated the government, and their Majesties having accepted the crown and royal dignity as aforesaid, their said Majesties did become, were, are and of right ought to be by the laws of this realm our sovereign liege lord and lady, king and queen of England, France and Ireland and the dominions thereunto belonging, in and to whose princely persons the royal state, crown and dignity of the said realms with all honours, styles, titles, regalities, prerogatives, powers, jurisdictions and authorities to the same belonging and appertaining are most fully, rightfully and entirely invested and incorporated, united and annexed. And for preventing all questions and divisions in this realm by reason of any pretended titles to the crown, and for preserving a certainty in the succession thereof, in and upon which the unity, peace, tranquillity and safety of this nation doth under God wholly consist and depend, the said Lords Spiritual and Temporal and Commons do beseech their Majesties that it may be enacted, established and declared, that the crown and regal government of the said kingdoms and dominions, with all and singular the premises thereunto belonging and appertaining, shall be and continue to their said Majesties and the survivor of them during their lives and the life of the survivor of them, and that the entire, perfect and full exercise of the regal power and government be only in and executed by his Majesty in the names of both their Majesties during their joint lives; and after their deceases the said crown and premises shall be and remain to the heirs of the body of her Majesty, and for default of such issue to her Royal Highness the Princess Anne of Denmark and the heirs of her body, and for default of such issue to the heirs of the body of his said Majesty; and thereunto the said Lords Spiritual and Temporal and Commons do in the name of all the people aforesaid most humbly and faithfully submit themselves, their heirs and posterities for ever, and do faithfully promise that they will stand to, maintain and defend their said Majesties, and also the limitation and succession of the crown herein specified and contained, to the utmost of their powers with their lives and estates against all persons whatsoever that shall attempt anything to the contrary. And whereas it hath been found by experience that it is inconsistent with the safety and welfare of this Protestant Kingdom to be governed by a popish prince, or by any king or queen marrying a papist, the said Lords Spiritual and Temporal and Commons do further pray that it may be enacted, that all and every person and persons that is, are or shall be reconciled to or shall hold communion with the see or Church of Rome, or shall profess the popish religion, or shall marry a papist, shall be excluded and be for ever incapable to inherit, possess or enjoy the crown and government of this realm and Ireland and the dominions thereunto belonging or any part of the same, or to have, use or exercise any regal power, authority or jurisdiction within the same; and in all and every such case or cases the people of these realms shall be and are hereby absolved of their allegiance; and the said crown and government shall from time to time descend to and be enjoyed by such person or persons being Protestants as should have inherited and enjoyed the same in case the said person or persons so reconciled, holding communion or professing or marrying as aforesaid were naturally dead; and that every king and queen of this realm who at any time hereafter shall come to and succeed in the imperial crown of this kingdom shall on the first day of the meeting of the first Parliament next after his or her coming to the crown, sitting in his or her throne in the House of Peers in the presence of the Lords and Commons therein assembled, or at his or her coronation before such person or persons who shall administer the coronation oath to him or her at the time of his or her taking the said oath (which shall first happen), make, subscribe and audibly repeat the declaration mentioned in the statute made in the thirtieth year of the reign of King Charles the Second entituled, *An Act for the more effectual preserving the king's person and government by disabling papists from sitting in either House of Parliament*. But if it shall happen that such king or queen upon his or her succession to the crown of this realm shall be under the age of twelve years, then every such king or queen shall make, subscribe and audibly repeat the said declaration at his or her coronation or the first day of the meeting of the first Parliament as aforesaid which shall first happen after such king or queen shall have attained the said age of twelve years. All which their Majesties are contented and pleased shall be declared, enacted and established by authority of this present Parliament, and shall stand, remain and be the law of this realm for ever; and the same are by their said Majesties, by and with the advice and consent of the Lords Spiritual and Temporal and Commons in Parliament assembled and by the authority of the same, declared, enacted and established accordingly.

II. And be it further declared and enacted by the authority aforesaid, that from and after this present session of Parliament no dispensation by *non obstante* of or to any statute or any part thereof shall be allowed, but that the same shall be held void and of no effect, except a dispensation be allowed of in such statute, and except in such cases as shall be specially provided for by one or more bill or bills to be passed during this present session of Parliament.

III. Provided that no charter or grant or pardon granted before the three and twentieth day of October in the year of our Lord one thousand six hundred eighty-nine shall be any ways impeached or invalidated by this Act, but that the same shall be and remain of the same force and effect in law and no other than as if this Act had never been made.

15 / FÉNELON: THE DUTIES OF A KING

Where Locke attacked absolute monarchy from the standpoint that monarchy should be limited and controlled by representative institutions, absolutism also faced critics who accepted its own tenets of divine and hereditary right. Most notable of these was the French churchman, François de Salignac de la Mothe-Fénelon (1651–1715). Fénelon came from the ranks of the great nobility, became tutor to the duke of Burgundy, grandson of Louis XIV, and was named bishop of Cambrai. He was best known for his utopian novel Télémaque *("Telemachus," 1699), with its picture of a perfect society and government. The following passages are taken from a "Self-Examination upon the Duties of Kingship, Composed for the Instruction of Louis of France, Duke of Bur-*

gundy," which is clearly intended to warn the young prince against the misuse and abuse of royal power that was characteristic of his grandfather.[28]

Have you taken anything from a single one of your subjects by virtue of your sole authority and in violation of the law? When you took a person's house or cancelled the annuity owed him by the state, did you reimburse him as a private individual would have done? Before you laid taxes upon your people, did you make a thorough examination of what the state really needed, considering whether the need for taxes was greater than the hardships they caused? Did you ask the opinion on this most important question of the best informed men, those most zealous for the public welfare, those readiest to tell you the truth without flattery or weakness? Have you never given the name of "necessities of state" to what really only furthered your ambition, such as wars waged in order to make conquests and to gain glory? If you hold personal claims upon the succession in one or another nearby state, you should pay the expenses of war in this cause out of the revenues of your own domain, out of your savings, out of loans made to you personally; at the least, you should take from the nation only such help as your people give you out of their love, and you should not burden them with taxes to support pretensions which have nothing to do with their interests; for your subjects will be no happier when you own another province. . . .

Have you never tolerated injustice even when you refrained from committing it? Have you chosen with sufficient care all those whom you placed in authority, the intendants, governors, ministers, etc.? Have you never chosen anyone out of a weakness for his sponsors, or in the secret hope that he would extend your authority and increase your income beyond their proper limits? Have you investigated the way they governed? Have you made it known that you were ready to hear complaints against them and mete out justice to them? Did you do so when you discovered their misdeeds?

Have you never excessively enriched your ministers of state, or permitted them to do so on their own, beyond what their services merited? There should always be a limit to the compensation which the prince gives to those who serve the state under him. It is not permissible to give them fortunes greater than those possessed by persons of the highest rank or beyond the actual resources of the state. Whatever services he may have given, a minister should never be allowed

---

[28] *Œuvres de Fénelon, archevêque de Cambrai* (Paris: J. Leroux et Jouby, 1850–1851), Vol. VII, pp. 89–90, 92–93. Translated from the French by the editor.

to gain immense fortunes in a short time while the people suffer and princes and lords of the first rank are in need. It is even less permissible to give such fortunes to favorites, who ordinarily have given even less service to the state than ministers. . . .

Have you sought ways to lighten the burden upon the people, so that you collected in taxes only what the real needs of the state compelled you to take for their own benefit? The people's property should be used only for the real advantage of the people themselves. You have your own domain, which you should clear of debt and bring back into your own hands: for its purpose is to provide for the support of your household. You should limit these expenses, especially when your revenues from the domain are pledged and your people are exhausted. The taxes paid by the people should be used to meet the real needs of the state. In times of public shortage you should seek ways to eliminate all offices which are not absolutely necessary. Have you consulted men of skill and good will who can inform you of the condition of the provinces, the tillage of the soil, the crop of recent years, or of the situation of trade, etc., so that you may know what the state is able to pay without hardship? Have you determined the annual taxes upon this basis? Have you given favorable attention to the remonstrances of upright men? Have you sought out such criticism and even anticipated it, as a good prince should, instead of suppressing it? You know that the king formerly took nothing from the people by his sole authority: it was the Parliament, that is, the assembly of the nation, which granted him the funds needed for the extraordinary needs of the state. Except for this, he lived upon the revenue of his domain. What has changed this state of affairs if not the absolute authority which the kings have assumed? In our own day, we still see that the *Parlements* [judicial courts], which are assemblies vastly inferior to the old Parliaments or Estates of the nation, remonstrate against the registration of fiscal edicts. In no case should you issue such edicts without having first consulted those who are incapable of flattering you and are truly zealous for the public welfare. Have you never introduced new taxes on the people in order to pay for your superfluous expenditures, the abundance of your table, the splendor of your retinue and your furniture, the embellishment of your gardens and your mansions, and the exorbitant gifts you have lavished upon your favorites? . . .

Have you never done injustice to a foreign nation? We hang the poor starving wretch who steals a few francs in a highway robbery, and we treat a conqueror, that is, one who unjustly subjugates the lands of a neighboring state, as a hero! The usurpation of a field or a vineyard is regarded as unpardonable sin in the judgment of God unless it be restored; but the usurpation of cities and provinces is counted as if it were nothing at all! To take a private person's field from him is a great sin; to take a great land from a nation is an innocent and glorious deed! Where are our ideas of justice? Will this be how God judges? *Existimasti iniquè quod ero tui similis.* ["Should I let thee think that I am just as thou?" Ps. 50: 21] May we be less just when we are great than when we are small? Is justice no longer justice when the greatest interests are at stake? Are the millions who make up a nation less our brothers than a single man? Shall we have no scruple to do unto millions in a whole country that injustice which we would not do to a single man for the sake of his field? Everything gained by conquest alone is therefore most unjustly gained and should be restored; and the same is true of everything gained in a war undertaken for unjust causes. Treaties of peace are no protection when you are the stronger and compel your neighbors to sign in order to avoid greater harm; for they sign in the same way that a man gives his purse to a thief who holds a pistol to his breast. . . . Your enemy is your brother; you cannot forget it without forgetting humanity. You may never do him harm when you can avoid it without harm to yourself. . . . The question in treaties is no longer one of arms and war but only of peace, justice, humanity and good faith. It is even more infamous and criminal to deceive in a treaty of peace with a neighboring people than in a contract with an individual. To introduce ambiguous and specious terms into a treaty is to sow the seeds of future war; it is placing kegs of powder in the cellars of the houses where one dwells.

When it was a question of war, did you personally examine your rights and have them examined by men of high intelligence, men unwilling to flatter you? Did you distrust the advice of those ministers who have an interest in involving you in war, who at the very least try to flatter your passions so that you will satisfy their own desires? Have you sought out all the reasons which argued against you? Did you take the time to learn the sentiments of all your wisest councilors, without forestalling them?

Have you never regarded your personal glory as a reason for one enterprise or another, lest you pass your life without distinguishing yourself above other princes? As if princes can find solid glory in ruining the happiness of the peoples to whom they are supposed to be fathers! As if the father of a family could win esteem by making his children wretched! As if a king could hope for glory elsewhere than in his virtue, that is, in his justice and his good government over his people! Have you never believed that war was necessary in order to acquire fortified places which fitted your convenience and protected your frontier? A strange rule! By such handy means one can advance little by little all the way to China. The safety of a frontier can be protected without taking anyone else's property—fortify your own places and do not usurp your neighbor's. Would you want a neighbor to take from you whatever he believed convenient to his own safety? Your safety does not constitute a title of ownership over the property of others. Your true safety lies in being just, in keeping your loyal allies by your upright and moderate conduct, by possessing a numerous, well-fed, well-disciplined and well-disposed people. But what is more contrary to your safety than to make your neighbors feel that they themselves can never be safe with you, that you are always ready to take from them whatever you find convenient? . . .

When a king is just, sincere and inviolably faithful to all his allies, when he is powerful within his country as the result of wise measures of government, then he possesses the means to keep down restless and unjust neighbors who may want to attack him: he possesses the love of his people and the confidence of his neighbors; everyone has an interest in supporting him. If his cause is just, he need act only with the greatest mildness before beginning war. Being already powerfully armed, he can offer to accept the decision of neutral and impartial neighbors; he can make concessions for peace, avoid anything which makes for bitterness, and attempt conciliation in every way. If all this is to no avail, he will wage war with greater confidence in God's protection, with greater zeal on the part of his subjects, with greater assistance from his allies. But it will seldom happen that he will have to wage war under such circumstances. Three-fourths of all wars are the result only of arrogance, subtlety, greed and excessive haste.

16 / THE HOLY ROMAN EMPIRE OF THE GERMAN NATION

The debate over absolutism took on a different form in Germany. In the Holy Roman Empire, particularly after the Peace of Westphalia of 1648, effective sovereignty passed into the hands of the multitude of "imperial princes," as the immediate vassals of the emperor were called. The difficulty in defining the political character of Germany within the traditional categories of monarchy, aristocracy, and republic is reflected in the works from which the next two selections are taken. The first (A), Teutscher Fürsten-Staat ("The German Princely State," first published in 1656), was written by Veit Ludwig von Seckendorff (1626–1692). He was an official in the service of a number of lesser German princes at various times, but it was his work as a political writer and historian that brought him modest fame.[29] *The problem of Germany's weakness as a state in the face of the power of the increasingly centralized monarchies on her borders, notably France and Sweden, was emphasized in the second of these two selections* (B), *Samuel Freiherr von Pufendorf's* Einleitung zu der Historie der vornehmsten Reiche und Staaten in Europa (*"Introduction to the History of the Principal Kingdoms and States of Europe,"* 1682–86). *Pufendorf* (1632–1694) *was a German jurist, historian, and political theorist who taught at the universities of Heidelberg, Germany, and Lund, Sweden, and was historiographer successively to the king of Sweden and the elector of Brandenburg.*[30]

A. SECKENDORFF

Thank God, we here in Germany know nothing of that kind of power which is held and exercised over the whole land by a single person who holds himself to be supreme over it, and who possesses, rightly or not, the largest share of authority over everyone else, *for his own use and advantage and subject only to his own will and pleasure,* in much the same way that a lord is accustomed to command his bondsmen and bondswomen to do this or that for the service of his house, or for such other thing as his inclination moves him to want.[31]

But princely government in the German principalities and provinces, as in virtually any legitimate and well-ordered state, *is nothing else than the supreme dominion of the rightful prince or lord of the land over his Estates and subjects, as well as over the land itself and the*

[29] Veit Ludwig von Seckendorff, *Teutscher Fürsten-Staat,* ed. Andres Simson Biechlingen, Die neueste Auflage (Jena: Johann Meyers Wittwe, 1720), pp. 32–35. Translated from the German by Herbert H. Rowen.

[30] Samuel Puffendorf, *An Introduction to the History of the Principal Kingdoms and States of Europe, made English from the Original, the High-Dutch: The Fourth Edition, with Additions* (London: Thomas Newborough and Martha Gilliflower, 1700), pp. 303–7.

[31] Although there are numerous examples of fawning servants who have tried to persuade their lords to make themselves *princes* of this kind under the pretext that it would be to their *interest,* experience still teaches that such things turn out badly. Since the beginning of the world all government has had as its only aim to achieve this, that among a group of family heads who have suffered together, the wisest and ablest should be their common head and by his leadership protect them against the crimes of evil men and enable them to live in prosperity. We shall have more to say in its place as to whether government of this kind, or that described in subsequent paragraphs, best serves this true interest. (Note in original)

affairs thereunto appertaining, to the end that the common interest and welfare among both churchmen and laymen be preserved and maintained, and that those rights fallen into disuse or abuse be affirmed.

But when we ascribe this supreme dominion to the person only of the lord of the land, which rule we therefore call "princely" or "lordly," we thereby exclude *all other persons* in the country. . . , whether or not they have received a lordship and dominion as a fief or gift from the prince or his forbears, or from other, foreign authorities; and they are, furthermore, according to the custom of the land, not merely vassals or proprietors, but also residents and subjects: and the supreme rule and government of the country does not belong to them individually or together, no matter how mighty and wealthy they may be, but they are all to be considered as individually and jointly the subjects of the prince of the land.

B. PUFENDORF

As for the Form of Government in *Germany*, it is to be considered, that it is not like some Kingdoms, where the Kings have the whole Power in their hands, and according to whose commands the Subjects are obliged to comport themselves; neither is the Sovereign Power here circumscribed within certain bounds, as it is in some Kingdoms of Europe, where the Kings cannot exercise an absolute Soveraignty without the consent of the Estates: But *Germany* has its particular Form of Government, the like is not to be met withal in any Kingdom of *Europe*, except that the ancient Form of Government in *France* came pretty near it. *Germany* acknowledges but one Supreme Head under the Title of the *Roman Emperor;* which Title did at first imply no more than the Sovereignty over the City of Rome, and the Protection of the Church of Rome and her Patrimony. This Dignity was first annexed to the *German* Empire by *Otto* I. but it is long ago since the Popes have robb'd the Kings of *Germany* of this Power, and only have left them the bare Name. But besides this, the Estates of *Germany* some of which have great and potent Countries in their possession, have a considerable share of the Sovereignty over their Subjects; and tho' they are Vassals of the Emperour and Empire, nevertheless they ought not to be consider'd as Subjects, or only as potent or rich Citizens in a Government; for they are actually possess'd of the supreme Jurisdiction in the Criminal Affairs; they have power to make Laws and to regulate Church Affairs, (which however is only to be understood of the Protestants) to dispose of the revenues rising out of their Own Territories; to make Alliances, as well among themselves as with Foreign States, provided the same are not intended against the Emperour and Empire; they may build and maintain Fortresses and Armies of their own, Coin Money, and the like. This grandeur of the Estates, 'tis true, is a main obstacle that the Emperour cannot make himself absolute in the Empire, except it be in his Hereditary Countries; yet this has been always observ'd the more potent the Emperour is, the more he has exercised his Authority, and the Estates have been forced to comply with his commands: and it is certain, that the grandure of the Estates, except what is contained in the *Golden Bull* concerning the Electoral Dignity was more founded upon ancient Customs and Precedents, than any real Constitutions; till in the *Westphalian* Peace their Rights and Authority have been expresly and particularly confirm'd and establish'd.

Tho' it is certain that *Germany* within its self is so Potent, that it might be formidable to all its Neighbours, if its strength was well united and rightly employ'd; nevertheless this strong Body has also its infirmities, which weaken its strength, and slacken its vigour: its irregular Constitution of Government is one of the chief causes of its Distemper; it being neither one entire Kingdom, neither properly a Confederacy, but participating of both kinds: For the Emperour has not the entire Sovereignty over the whole Empire, nor each state in particular over his Territories; and the former is more than a bare Administrator, yet the latter have a greater share in the Sovereignty than can be attributed to any Subjects or Citizens whatever, tho' never so great. . . . Yet do I not find any instances in History, that any of the ancient Emperours did endeavour to subdue the Princes, and to make himself absolute Master of *Germany*. But this ambitious Design *Charles* V. as it seems, was first put upon by the *Spaniards*, or, as some will have it, by *Nicholas Perenot Granvel*. And truly the Electors had the same reasons not to have admitted him to the Imperial Dignity, as they had not to admit *Francis* I. King of *France:* And common Reason tells us, that no Nation that has the Power of Electing a Prince, ought to choose such a one as is possess'd before of a considerable Hereditary Estate, that he may think it his Interest to take more care of that than the Elective Kingdom: For he either will certainly be very careless of the Interest of the Elective Kingdom, or else he will make the Interest of the Elective Kingdom subservient to that of his Hereditary Countries, and make use of the Strength of the first to maintain the latter, and render it more Powerful; or else he will endeavour, by making himself Sovereign over the Elective Kingdom, to make it dependent on his Hereditary Estate.

. . . The Estates of *Germany*, to preserve their Liberty, were oblig'd to seek for Foreign Aid, by which means they maintained their Liberty; but it had been questionless more advantageous to *Germany*, not to have wanted the assistance of Foreigners, who were not forgetful to make their own advantage by it. Now it may be supposed, that there are some remnants of the *Spanish* Leaven, it may easily be conjectur'd, what jealousie and distrusts must be betwixt the Members of the Empire, and how contrary and different their Counsels and Actions must needs be: and tho' perhaps by settling a good understanding betwist the Supreme Head and Estates, a medium might be found out to obviate this and some other inconveniences, yet there reign various and great Distempers amongst the Estates themselves, which seem to render the best Remedies and Counsels either ineffectual, or at least very difficult: Among these must be counted the Religious Differences betwixt the Catholicks and the Protestants in general; which Differences do not only depend on the several Opinions in Matters of Faith, but also on a Worldly Interest; the Catholicks endeavouring upon all occasions to recover such Possessions as were taken from them since the Reformation; and the Protestants being resolved to maintain themselves in the Possession of them. Wherefore it has been observ'd, that sometimes the *Roman* Catholicks have been more guided by their particular Interest, and by their Clergy, than by that of the publick. Nay, it is to be fear'd, that if *Germany* should be vigorously attack'd by a potent Foreign Enemy, that some of the Popish Bigots would not be so backward in submitting themselves under the yoke, and be willing to lose one Eye, provided the Protestants might lose both.

Besides, the Protestants are again sub-divided into two Parties; there being among them some differences concerning several Articles of Faith; which, by the heat of the Clergy, were widen'd to that degree, that both Parties were brought to the very brink of Ruine. The great number of Estates augments the Distemper, it being next to an impossibility, that among so many, there should not be some, who either prompted by their passions, obstinacy, or for want of Understanding, may not deviate from the true Interest, or be misled by ill Councellours to act against the same; so that it would be a miracle to see so many Heads not well united. The Estates are also very unequal in Power; from whence it often happens, that some of the most Potent are for being like Sovereigns; and therefore being inclin'd rather to act according to their particular Interest and Grandeur than for the Publick, they make little account how they Ruin the less powerful. These therefore, when they see that the Laws cannot protect them, are at last oblig'd to take more care of their own preservation, than of the Publick Liberty, as thinking it indifferent by whom they are oppress'd. Not to mention here, the Jealousie which is betwixt the three Colleges of the Empire, and the several pretentions and differences which are among some of the Estates: I could wish that I could find out as easie a remedy against these and some other the like Diseases, as I have enumerated them, and demonstrated their pernicious Consequences.

17 / RUSSIA AND THE WEST

The same period that saw the loss of united statehood as an effective force in Germany saw the first emergence of Russia as a major political force within Europe. The Russian state, originating in the grand duchy of Muscovy, had been largely isolated from the main currents of Western and Central European political life over the preceding centuries; yet its increasing power was such that it could no longer be safely neglected, as in the past, by those who were not its immediate neighbors. The problems of negotiation with Russian officials, who knew little of events and institutions in Western Europe and did not share its diplomatic customs, are here described by an Austrian diplomat, Augustin, Freiherr von Meyerberg (A). Meyerberg, a councilor of the Imperial Chamber, was sent by Leopold I to the court of Tsar Alexei Mikhailovitch in 1661–1663.[32]

The principal architect of the transformation of Russia into a great power was Peter I, called "The Great," younger son of Tsar Alexei. The difficulties faced by Peter, particularly in the economic and social conditions of Russia, are depicted here (B) by G. Weber, a German diplomat who resided in Russia from 1714 to 1720.[33]

One of the central questions of modern Russian history has been the relationship of Russia to Western Europe—whether to imitate or reject it. A classic discussion of Peter the Great's role in the Westernization of Russia was given by V. O. Klyuchevsky, an outstanding historian. Klyuchevsky (1842–1911) was a professor at the University of Moscow from 1885 until his death. The chapters on Peter I in his Kurs Russkoi Istorii *("Course of Russian History," 1904–10) have been translated and published separately as* Peter

[32] [Augustin, Freiherr von Meyerberg], *Voyage en Moscovie d'un Ambassadeur, Conseiller de la Chambre Impériale, Envoyé par l'Empereur Léopold au Czar Alexis Mihalowicz, Grand Duc de Moscovie* (Leiden: Friderik Harring, 1688), pp. 56–7, 124–6. Translated from the French version by the editor.

[33] [G. Weber], *The Present State of Russia*, Translated from the High Dutch [German] (London: W. Taylor *et al.*, 1723), Vol. I, pp. 47–9, 70–2.

the Great. *The following excerpts (C) are taken from the conclud-ing chapter.*[34]

A. FREIHERR VON MEYERBERG:
AN EMBASSY TO RUSSIA

To be sure, we had been informed that the Muscovites, none of whom is permitted by the Tsar to leave his state or to study within his own country, and who consequently lack all knowledge of other realms, hold their own nation in higher esteem than any other; and that, thanks to a prejudice which they never abandon, they place them-selves above the rest of the world and think more of the power and majesty of their Tsar than of the strength and greatness of all kings and emperors; and that, thus fancying their own excellence, they hold foreigners in such contempt as being far beneath them, that if they have to receive ambassadors of other monarchs on behalf of their own master, they even dare to demand, as something always due to them, the right to be the first to descend from a carriage or horse, and to put on their hats; and that, in escorting ambassadors, they do not refrain from taking the places of greatest honor with such stubborn-ness that they sometimes remain motionless for hours on end in dis-putes of this kind, seeking to instill the belief that civility compels them to abandon their rights once they consent to step down or to put on their hats at the same time as ambassadors. For this reason we deemed it wise to prevent such annoyances by ordering the interpreter to warn the commissioner when he met him that I was not new to diplomacy and knew full well what propriety required of us and of him, so that, when he received us, he should abstain from the conduct to which the members of his nation were accustomed in such meetings, for we had no intention whatever of accepting it.

When we crossed the river, we saw him coming down on horseback from the citadel and alighting by the bank to wait for us on his feet at a distance of about eight steps from the water, while we landed from the bark. As soon as the first of us set foot on the sand, he began to walk toward us so that he received us as both sides stepped forward at an equal pace. Nonetheless he was the first to take off his hat and we at once did likewise. . . .

The Muscovites are so addicted to duplicity from the cradle that they never speak with sincerity, as results show; so that, growing up in this fashion, they always back their lies by new lies with such impu-

[34] Vasili Klyuchevsky, *Peter the Great,* translated from the Russian by Liliana Archibald (London: Macmillan & Company Ltd.; New York: St. Martin's Press, Inc., 1958), pp. 262–72. Reprinted by permission of St. Martin's Press.

dence that however certain you may be of what they say, you remain in doubt as to what conclusion you should draw. If perchance you should prove them guilty of lying by incontestable reasons, they do not blush but rather smile, as if they had been caught doing something brave. The ambassadors of foreign princes should expect no greater sincerity from the Tsar's ministers, who deceive them by piling up all their subtleties either by putting forward falsehoods as truth or by suppressing necessary knowledge; and if it pleases them, they so weaken the force of agreements already made in conference by dint of a thousand deliberately involved interpretations, that their promises become spoiled and useless. They are so under the influence of prosperity and adversity that when they have good fortune on their side, they permit their swelling arrogance to carry them high above the clouds, but when luck is bad they lose all courage and fall into an abyss of despondency. This is why they are extremely fickle in their dealings, particularly since their deliberations are based for the most part solely upon the knowledge which they extract from the gazettes of Prussia and Holland which foreign merchants occasionally bring to Moscow, and which they trust as if they were the Oracles of the Delphic Apollo; or they rely upon the truths which they believe they draw from the mouths of the knaves or common soldiers whom they capture in war, who when they are put to torture say anything that comes to their mind which they think may make their tormentors relent, telling them what they want to hear, although these wretches have no knowledge of the secrets of their princes or their officers. All these things make the negotiation of ambassadors of foreign princes in Moscow so difficult and its success so unlikely that often they repent having accepted the post.

B. G. WEBER: PETER THE GREAT

This Month disclosed at length the Reason of the Czar's having for several Weeks appeared extremely pensive. He had searched to the Bottom of the Disorders crept into Administration since the Year 1706, and found out whence it proceeded that the Army had been so ill paid, and suffered so much for Want; that the German Officers had quitted the Service; that so many thousands of Workmen had most miserably perished; that such a Dearth had overspread all the Country, that the Inland-trade had decayed; in short, that the Finances were in such Confusion; and had taken a firm Resolution to remedy all those Evils, if not thoroughly, yet at least as far as possible, to which end he established towards the End of the Year a Grand Inquisition.

The Experience of twenty Years and upwards has shewn, that notwithstanding the great Expences which the Czar has been at in maintaining his Armies and Fleet, and carrying on so many vast Buildings, yet he was not obliged to contract Debts, but always found new Supplies in his Dominions to support his Undertakings. *Russia* abounds in Merchandize, but not in ready Money, and considering the vast Extent of its Empire, it is justly matter of Surprize, that there is such a Disproportion between its Extent and Revenues, there being many Provinces, which yield to none in the World in Fruitfulness and the plentiful Produce of all that is necessary for human Life. The Czar has indeed discovered great part of the Causes of this Defect, and in some measure redressed several of them; but it impossible for him as yet to remove the Difficulties still remaining; and as for the rest, he has had neither Time nor Opportunity to get a true Information about them. It cannot be denied that there are but few Towns, and many Forests and Desarts in *Russia,* and that the greater Part of the Land is barren, or rather lies untilled; but one of the chief Reasons of this is, that the War has deprived the Countrey of abundance of Inhabitants, and those who are left, labour under the Oppression of the Czar's Officers, and of the Nobility, to such a Degree, that they are quite disheartened from Industry, and content themselves with making a poor Shift of living from Hand to Mouth. For in the same manner as the Czars have exercized, time out of Mind, the Power of seizing the Estates of their Boyars, on any pretences they think sufficient; so the latter are of Opinion, that, by Parity of reason, they may exercise the same Power over their Peasants, from whence it proceeds, that all manner of Industry and Desire of Gain is extinguished among the Boors, and if by chance one happens privately to get a small Sum, he hides it out of Fear of his Lord under a Dunghil, where it lies dead to him. The Nobility, on the other Hand, having thus by Violence and Cunning drained the Peasants of their very Blood, and being afraid of making themselves obnoxious to the Court, by the Shew of their ill-gotten Wealth, commonly lock it, either up in their Coffers to moulder there, or others, who are grown wiser, convey it into the Banks of *London, Venice,* and *Amsterdam.* Consequently all the Money being thus concealed, both by the Nobility and Peasants, it has no Circulation, and the Country reaps no Benefit from it. The Czar was once advised to abolish *Slavery,* and to introduce a moderate Liberty, which would both encourage his Subjects, and promote his own interest at the same time; but the wild Temper of the Russians, who are not to be governed without Constraint, was a sufficient Reason for rejecting that Proposition at that Time. . . .

Excepting the abovementioned Taxes, neither the Townsmen nor Peasants are charged with any Contributions on account of their Possessions or Trade, so that if they knew how to make the best Advantage of those Blessings which Nature has bestowed upon them, those Imposts would appear easy enough: But the Peasants, on one side, not understanding either how to improve their Land, or to make the best of its Produce; and, on the other side, the Nobility exhausting their very Substance, the Country groans under the insupportable Burthen, and their Minds seem so darkned, and their Senses so stupified by Slavery, that though they are taught the most obvious improvements in Husbandry, yet they do not care to depart from the old way, thinking that no body can understand it better than their Ancestors did. And it is easy to judge what Account their fruitful Soil might turn to, if one looks out of *Russia* into the Country of the Cosacks, where the Ground is not near so good; for those People being far more industrious and active than the Russians who live among them, and managing their Husbandry much upon the same Foot as in *Poland,* thrive by it, notwithstanding the quartering of Soldiers, and other Oppressions, much better than the Russians, who have the Protection of the Government. The same Unthriftiness is the Reason that many Country Families run away from their Habitations, when they find themselves insolvent, being apprehensive of the Execution, which in these Parts falls little short of Torture. Some of those Fugitives run into the Forrests, and join the Party of *Raskolnikes,* who are a sort of Zealots that stickle for the ancient Liturgy, and will not own the present Russian Church to be orthodox, for having made some Alterations in point of Ceremony; others take their Refuge in some Nobleman's House in another *Province;* however at present hardly any body will harbour them, it being enacted by the Provincial Law, that if one finds his Peasant in another Man's Estate, the latter is bound not only to deliver up the Fugitive, but also to pay to his right Master twenty five Rubels for every Year, during which he shall have entertained him, so that no Body would be a great Gainer by such a Bargain, seeing a Peasant seldom pays half that Sum to his Lord. But they who suffer most by such a Run-away, are his Neighbours, for as they are under an Incapacity of manuring his Land, which, as it is easy to imagine, is commonly quite out of Heart, and yet are forced to make up the full Sum of the Czar's Taxes, as though there was no deficiency in the Number of Inhabitants; it follows of Course, that being at length quite ruined themselves, they follow the Example of their Brethren, and fly from their Habitations to the Forrests. Yet even these Disorders are not so prejudicial to the Country as the Mismanagement of the Provincial Commissioners, Chancellors, and Clerks, who are intrusted with the Collection of the Taxes. These Cormorants no sooner enter upon their Offices, but they make it their sole Study how to build their Fortunes upon the Ruin of the Contry People, and he that came among them having hardly Clothes to his Back, is often known in four or five Years time, to have scraped so much together, as to be able to build large Stone-Houses, when at the same Time the poor Subjects are forced to run way from their Cottages.

C. V. O. KLYUCHEVSKY: PETER THE GREAT—A MODERN VIEW

What was Peter's attitude to Western Europe? He had inherited the precept "Do everything after the example of foreign countries," that is to say Western European countries. This precept combines large doses of despondency, a lack of confidence in Russia's strength, and self-denial. How did Peter interpret this precept? What did he think of Russian relations with Western Europe? Did he see in Western Europe a model to imitate or a master who could be dismissed at the end of the lesson? Peter thought that the biggest loss suffered by Muscovy in the seventeenth century had been the Baltic littoral, by which Russia was deprived of contact with the civilised nations of the West. Yet why did he want this contact? Peter has often been accused of being a blind and inveterate Westerner who admired everything foreign, not because it was better than the Russian, but because it was unlike anything Russian; and it was believed that he wanted rather to assimilate Russia to Western Europe than to make Russia resemble Western Europe. It is difficult to believe that as sensible a man as Peter was troubled by such fantasies.

We have already seen how, in 1697, he had travelled incognito with the Great Embassy, with the intention of acquiring general technical knowledge and recruiting West European naval technicians. Indeed it was for technical reasons that the West was necessary to Peter. He was not a blind admirer of the West; on the contrary, he mistrusted it, and was not deluded into thinking that he could establish cordial relations with the West, for he knew that the West mistrusted his country, and was hostile to it. On the anniversary in 1724 of the Peace of Nystadt, Peter wrote that all countries had tried hard to exclude the Russians from knowledge in many subjects, and particularly military affairs, but somehow the countries had let information on military affairs escape them, as if their sight had been obscured, "as if everything was veiled in front of their eyes." Peter found this a miracle from God, and ordered the miracle to be forcefully expressed in the forthcoming celebrations "and boldly set out, for there is a lot of meaning here," by which he meant that the subject was very suggestive of ideas. Indeed we would gladly believe the legend which has come down to us, that Peter once said, as Osterman records it: "We need Europe for a few decades; later on we must turn our back on it." Thus for Peter association with Europe was only a means to an end, and not an end in itself.

What did Peter hope to gain from a rapprochement? . . . Peter
called on Western Europe to work and train Russians in financial and
administrative affairs, and in the technical sciences. He did not want
to borrow the results of Western technique, but wanted to appropriate
the skill and knowledge, and build industries on the Western European
model. The intelligent Russian of the seventeenth century realised that
it was essential to increase Russia's productive capacity, by exploiting
the country's natural and virgin riches, in order that the increased requirements of the state might be more easily met. Peter shared this
point of view, and gave effect to it as did nobody before or after him,
and he is therefore unique in the history of Russia. In foreign policy he
concentrated on solving the Baltic problem.

It would be difficult to assess the value of the many industries he
introduced. The evidence of the increased wealth was not a higher
standard of living, but increased revenue. All increased earnings were,
in fact, used to pay for the war. Peter's intention had been general
economic reform, but the only evidence of success was the improved
financial position. . . . In Peter's time men worked not for themselves
but for the state, and after working better and harder than their fathers,
probably died a great deal poorer. Peter did not leave the state in debt
for one kopeck, nor did he waste a working day at the expense of future
generations. . . . Were we to draw up a balance sheet of Peter's activities, excluding those affecting Russia's security and international position, but including those affecting the people's welfare, we would find
that his great economic ambitions (which were the basis for his reforms) failed in their purpose, and, in fact, their only success was
financial.

Thus Peter took from the old Russia the absolute power, the law,
and the class structure; from the West he borrowed the technical knowledge required to organise the army, the navy, the economy, and the
government. Where then was the revolution which renewed or transformed the Russian way of life, which introduced not only new institutions, but new principles (whether they were good or bad, is for the
moment immaterial). Peter's contemporaries, however, thought that
the reforms were revolutionary, and they communicated their opinion
to their descendants. But the reforms did not stop the Russians from
doing things in their own way, and it was not the innovations that agi-
tated them so much as the methods Peter used. Some of the results of
the reforms were only left in the future, and their significance was certainly not understood by everyone, and contemporaries anyhow only
knew the effect the reforms had on them. Some reactions, however,
were immediate, and these Peter had to account for.

The reforms were influenced not only by Peter's personality, but by
wars and internecine struggles. Although the war had caused Peter to

introduce reforms, it had an adverse influence on their development and success, because they were effected in an atmosphere of confusion usually consequent on war. The difficulties and demands of war forced Peter to do everything hastily. The requirements of war imposed a nervous and feverish tempo on the reforms, and an unhealthily fast pace. Peter's military preoccupations did not leave him time for critical analysis of a situation or careful consideration of his orders and the conditions in which they would be carried out. He could not wait patiently for natural improvement; he required rapid action and immediate results; at every delay or difficulty he would goad the officials with the threats which he used so often that they lost their power. . . .

Moreover the reforms were evolved in the middle of bitter internal struggles, which often burst into violence; four terrible uprisings and three or four conspiracies were directed against Peter's innovations, and all appealed to people's feeling for antiquity, to the old prejudices and ideas. These troubles reinforced Peter's hostility to the old customs and habits which to him symbolised the prejudices and ideas of the past. The political education he had received was primarily responsible for this hostility. From his childhood he had witnessed the struggle which had divided Russian society from the beginning of the seventeenth century. On one side were the advocates of change who turned to the West for help, and on the other were the political and religious Old Believers. The beards and clothes of the Old Believers were symbols adopted expressly to distinguish them from the Western Europeans. In themselves these trivialities of dress were no obstacle to reform, but the sentiments and convictions of their wearers were certainly an obstacle. Peter took the side of the innovators, and hotly opposed these trifling practices, as well as the ancient traditions that the Russian insisted on observing. The memories of childhood were responsible for the Tsar's excessive attention to these details. He associated these symbols with the risings of the Streltsy and the Old Believers. To him, the beard worn by an Old Believer was not a detail of masculine appearance, but, like the long-skirted coat, the mark of a political attitude, the spirit of opposition. He wanted to have clean-shaven subjects wearing foreign clothes, in the belief that this would help them to behave like Western Europeans. . . .

All this might be amusing if it were not so contemptible! It was the first time that Russian legislation abandoned its serious tone and concerned itself with trifles better left to hairdressers and tailors. These caprices aroused much hostility among the people. These petty annoyances explain the disproportion, which is so striking, between the sacrifices involved in Peter's internal reforms, and their actual achievements. Indeed it is astonishing to find the number of difficulties that had to be overcome to achieve even modest results. . . . Peter went against the wind, and by his rapid motion increased the resistance he encouraged. There were contradictions in his actions which he was unable to resolve, discordances which could not be harmonised.

As he grew older, and left his unruly youth behind him, he became more anxious than any other Tsar had been for the welfare of his people, and he directed the whole of his forceful energy to its improvement. . . .

Unfortunately Peter's methods alienated those indifferent to his reforms, and turned them into stubborn opponents. Peter used force, not example, and relied on mens' instincts, and not on their moral impulses. Governing his country from the post-chaise and stagehouse, he thought always of business, never of people, and, sure of his own power, he neglected to pay sufficient attention to the passive resistance of the masses. A reforming zeal and a faith in autocracy were Peter's two hands; unfortunately one hand paralysed the energy of the other. Peter thought that he could supplement the lack of proper resources by using power to urge people on, and aimed at the impossible. As a result the officials became so intimidated and inefficient that they lost their ability to do what they were normally quite capable of doing. As Peter, for all his zeal, was unable to use people's strength, so the people, in their state of inert and passive resistance, were unable to appreciate Peter's efforts.

Let us end by giving our opinion of Peter's reforms. The contradiction in his work, his errors, his hesitations, his obstinacy, his lack of judgment in civil affairs, his uncontrollable cruelty, and, on the other hand, his wholehearted love of his country, his stubborn devotion to his work, the broad, enlightened outlook he brought to bear on it, his daring plans conceived with creative genius and concluded with incomparable energy, and finally the success he achieved by the incredible sacrifices of his people and himself, all these different characteristics make it difficult to paint one painting. Moreover they explain the diverse impression he made on people; he sometimes provoked unqualified admiration, sometimes unqualified hostility. Generally the criticism prevailed because even his good actions were accompanied by disgusting methods.

Peter's reforms were the occasion for a struggle between the despot and the people's inertia. The Tsar hoped to arouse the energies and initiative of a society subdued by serfdom with the menace of his power, and strove, with the help of the noblemen, the oppressors of serfs, to introduce into Russia the European sciences and education which were essential to social progress. He also wanted the serf, while remaining a serf, to act responsibly and freely. The conjunction of despotism and liberty, of civilisation and serfdom, was a paradox which was not resolved in the two centuries after Peter. It is true that Russians of the eighteenth century tried to reconcile the Petrine reforms with humanitarian instincts, and Prince Shcherbatov, who was opposed to autocracy, devoted a treatise to explaining and even justifying Peter's vices and arbitrary conduct. Shcherbatov recognised that the enlightment introduced into Russia by Peter benefited the country, and attacked Peter's critics on the grounds that they themselves had been the recipients of a culture, bestowed on them by the autocracy, which permitted them to distinguish the evils inherent in the autocratic system. Peter's faith in the miraculous power of education, and his respect for scientific knowledge, inspired the servile with little understanding of the meaning of civilisation; this understanding grew slowly, and was eventually transformed into a desire for truth and liberty.

Autocracy as a political principle is in itself odious. Yet we can reconcile ourselves to the individual who exercises this unnatural power when he adds self-sacrifice to it, and, although an autocrat, devotes himself unsparingly to the public good, risking destruction even on difficulties caused by his own work. We reconcile ourselves in the same way to the impetuous showers of spring, which strip branches from the trees, but none the less refresh the air, and by their downpour bring on the growth of the new seed.

18 / ARNAULD DE POMPONNE: HOLLAND—THE TRIUMPH OF TRADE

Commerce continued to play the key role in the economic life of Europe through the seventeenth century and well into the eighteenth. Just as Venice had earlier provided the success story of strength through trade, the Dutch Republic—or Holland, as it was coming to be called after its principal province—displayed to envious Europeans the lineaments of triumphant commercial capitalism. A concise and penetrating account of Dutch commercial practice and policy was made by a French diplomat, Simon Nicolas Arnauld de Pomponne (1618–1699), in the form of a "relation" written for his friends. This narrative of his mission, notable for its first-hand account of the character of Dutch life, was in large part written by Pomponne while he was Louis XIV's am-

bassador at The Hague from 1669 to 1671, although it was not given final form till after Pomponne's period as French foreign minister from 1672 until 1679. It remained in manuscript form until 1955, when it was published in the Works of the Historical Society of Utrecht *in the Netherlands, from which the following section was translated.*[35]

It must be granted that this little republic can now be numbered among the mightiest powers of Europe. In this we have reason to admire the fruits of industry, shipping and trade, for these are the sources from which all their wealth flows with an abundance which is all the more remarkable because until now the skill and ability of Holland have kept this flow almost completely away from the other nations of Europe. . . .

Having struck down the Portuguese, the Dutch were for many years the sole masters of the Indies trade. The English had indeed established some trading posts after the Dutch example, but were content to confine their establishments to the lands of the princes with whom they traded, and their profits were moderate; hence the Dutch felt little rivalry with them. Since then the Royal [East India] Company which has been formed in London has grown larger; its ships now return in great numbers and with rich cargoes; and the trading establishments which it has already made in various places in the Indies, and to which it seeks to add, cause the Dutch much anxiety. This trade, to which both nations aspire equally, was the real cause of the war which broke out in 1653–1654 between Cromwell and the States General; it also caused the war between the Dutch and the king of England in 1665, which ended with the treaty of Breda; and in the future it will be a constant source of friction and disputes between them.

Following their examples, the other nations of Europe have also wished to take their shares of the treasures and envisioned the profits to be made from sending their ships to such far-off places. The Danes made their efforts quite a while back and still maintain a fort and a colony on the Coromandel coast. The Swedes have also sent their ships to the Indies, but with repeated failure. Various French vessels have made the voyage at different times, but as these were only the endeavors of individuals or a small company too weak for great undertakings, even when they made a profit, it was not such as to arouse a

[35] Simon Nicolas Arnauld de Pomponne, *Relation de mon ambassade en Hollande, 1669–1671,* ed. Herbert H. Rowen, in *Werken uitgegeven door het Historisch Genootschap te Utrecht,* 4th series, No. 2 (Utrecht: Kemink & Zoon, 1955), pp. 36, 39–42. Translated from the French by the editor.

desire in others to follow them upon such distant journeys. At the present time the East India Company [of France] which has been established under the authority of the King and enjoys his special protection, and in which His Majesty and individual persons have invested a considerable capital, gives hopes both great and legitimate, and perhaps not the least reason to anticipate its substantial success is that the Dutch have become concerned about its competition.

In addition to the earnings which they make upon the goods which they bring to us in Europe, the Dutch also make very large profits from the goods which they sell within the Indies, where they are the merchants and the carriers for all nations just as they are on our own coasts. They sell in one land what they buy in another, and the freight of their vessels contributes a large part of their profits, as it does in our own waters. . . .

The wares which they bring back are distributed upon their arrival among the cities of Holland, Zeeland and Friesland where the Company has its chambers. One part is sold publicly on days which are carefully publicized by notices distributed to the merchants of all Europe. The rest is kept in storehouses, and the Dutch shrewdly draw out only as much as other nations need, but not so much as would reduce prices.

The same cleverness which prompts this policy of restriction sometimes results in their selling wares in profusion. When another country, such as Spain or England, receives the same wares which they sell, the Dutch release their stores at a very low price, although they suffer considerable loss in doing so. They are satisfied if the loss is shared by those whose expansion in trade they fear, whom they compel to sell at the same price as themselves. They soon make good the loss which they suffer, and by discouraging competitors who do not have the same great wealth or the same head start as themselves, they remain the masters over a trade which others abandon to them.

This same desire to avoid a fall in the prices of their wares from the Indies as a result of oversupply has repeatedly caused them to throw overboard whole cargoes of pepper and to burn great piles of cinnamon, cloves and nutmeg which would have met the needs of all Europe for several years.

The profits from the sale of these goods provides the funds for refitting the ships which they send to the Indies. Apart from some cloth and brandy, they bring few wares from Europe. Trading there is conducted almost solely by means of gold, and as great quantities of gold are shipped there and little of it returns, we may say that with the passage of time the larger part of the gold which comes from America and Peru will pass on to the East Indies.

Once the Company has met its expenses, the remainder of its profits are distributed among those who share in its ownership. These dividends are greater or lesser depending on the value of the returning fleets and on whether or not wars, such as the last one with England [1665–1667], have prevented them from undertaking the voyage. During the time of my stay in Holland, I saw dividends issued amounting to 12 and 40 per cent upon the shares in the Company.

"Shares in the Company" is the name given to the sums which were originally invested in the initial capital of 6,400,000 *livres* on which the Company was established. These shares vary in size according to the individual contribution, but none is of less than 1,000 crowns. Dividends are issued upon the basis of this original investment, but since the Company has become much wealthier, shareholders have received large profits from their first investments. Depending on whether the returning fleets seem to promise a greater or lesser dividend, the shares rise or fall in price, and the trade in them constitutes one of the largest activities on the Amsterdam Exchange. In 1669, the year I arrived in Holland, the shares which had declined greatly during the war with England returned, peace having been made, to 450 crowns; this means that a man who owned, let us say, 100 crowns in the first capital of 6,400,000 *livres* could now sell this share for 450 crowns. The fleet which came in with a rich cargo not long after my arrival soon produced a dividend of 40 per cent, and during the next year, 1670, the return of 19 vessels increased the price of shares to 510.

This increased wealth is assuredly large for those who were original investors in the Company. But today almost all the shares have come into the market and no longer remain in the hands of their first owners, so that wealth of this kind, acquired at a higher price, does not produce such great profits, and is today a kind of gamble in which those who buy and sell are betting upon whether the returning fleets will be rich or poor.

Thus I have heard Pensionary De Witt [John de Witt, councilor-pensionary of Holland, the leading political figure of the Dutch Republic] say that when he struck an average of the price of shares between 1643 and 1668, and of the dividends which had been made, he found that the price of the ordinary share came to 338 *livres* and the dividend to 15 *livres* 19 *sous*, so that those who had bought and received earnings over all this time had not made 4 per cent interest upon their money.

But although it is therefore true to say that those who now invest their money in the Company receive a moderate profit, the advantage for the state as a whole is very great, and there is not a year in which it does not bring in 10 or 12 million *livres* which are then distributed to all the provinces.

19 / ENGLAND'S ANSWER: MERCANTILISM

Most successful of the European nations in meeting the challenge of Dutch commercial predominance was Great Britain, beginning with the government of Oliver Cromwell and continuing uninterrupted after the Stuart Restoration. British policy followed the lines of what later came to be called "mercantilism," which was also practiced by France and other European countries as well. The first principle of mercantilism was to confine the market, at home and in overseas possessions, as nearly as possible to merchants of one's own nation. The technique for preventing the Dutch from taking advantage of their greater efficiency and lower costs as shippers and traders was defined in the Navigation Act of October 9, 1651, which was re-enacted under the Stuarts. The Navigation Act was one of the immediate sources of the Anglo-Dutch War of 1652–54.[36]

An Act for increase of Shipping, and Encouragement of the Navigation of this Nation.

[9 October, 1651.]

For the Increase of the Shipping and the Encouragement of the Navigation of this Nation, which under the good Providence and Protection of God, is so great a means of the Welfare and Safety of this Commonwealth; Be it Enacted by this present Parliament, and the Authority thereof, That from and after the First day of December, One thousand six hundred fifty and one, and from thence forwards, no Goods or Commodities whatsoever, of the Growth, Production or Manufacture of Asia, Africa or America or of any part thereof; or of any Islands belonging to them, or any of them, or which are described or laid down in the usual Maps or Cards of those places, as well of the English Plantations as others, shall be Imported or brought into this Commonwealth of England, or into Ireland, or any other Lands, Islands, Plantations or Territories to this Commonwealth, belonging, or in their Possession, in any other Ship or Ships, Vessel or Vessels whatsoever,

[36] C. H. Firth and R. S. Rait, eds., *Acts and Ordinances of the Interregnum, 1642–1660* (London: His Majesty's Stationery Office, 1911), Vol. II, pp. 559–62. Reprinted by permission of the Controller of Her Britannic Majesty's Stationery Office.

but onely in such as do truly and without fraud belong onely to the People of this Commonwealth, or the Plantations thereof, as the Proprietors or right Owners thereof; and whereof the Master and Mariners are also for the most part of them, of the People of this Commonwealth, under the penalty of the forfeiture and loss of all the Goods that shall be Imported contrary to this Act; as also of the Ship (with all her Tackle, Guns and Apparel) in which the said Goods or Commodities shall be so brought in and Imported; the one moyety to the use of the Commonwealth, and the other moyety to the use and behoof of any person or persons who shall seize the said Goods or Commodities, and shall prosecute the same in any Court of Record within this Commonwealth.

And it is further Enacted by the Authority aforesaid, That no Goods or Commodities of the Growth, Production or Manufacture of Europe, or of any part thereof, shall after the First day of December, One thousand six hundred fifty and one, be imported or brought into this Commonwealth of England, or into Ireland, or any other Lands, Islands, Plantations or Territories to this Commonwealth belonging, or in their possession, in any Ship or Ships, Vessel or Vessels whatsoever, but in such as do truly and without fraud belong onely to the people of this Commonwealth, as the true Owners and Proprietors thereof, and in no other, except onely such Forein Ships and Vessels as do truly and properly belong to the people of that Countrey or Place, of which the said Goods are the Growth, Production or Manufacture; or to such Ports where the said Goods can onely be, or most usually are first shipped for Transportation; And that under the same penalty of forfeiture and loss expressed in the former Branch of this Act, the said Forfeitures to be recovered and imployed as is therein expressed.

And it is further Enacted by the Authority aforesaid, That no Goods or Commodities that are of Forein Growth, Production or Manufacture, and which are to be brought into this Commonwealth, in Shipping belonging to the People thereof, shall be by them Shipped or brought from any other place or places, Countrey or Countreys, but onely from those of their said Growth, Production or Manufacture; or from those Ports where the said Goods and Commodities can onely, or are, or usually have been first shipped for Transportation; and from none other Places or Countreys, under the same penalty of forfeiture and loss expressed in the first Branch of this Act, the said Forfeitures to be recovered and imployed as is therein expressed.

And it is further Enacted by the Authority aforesaid, That no sort of Cod-fish, Ling, Herring, Pilchard, or any other kinde of salted Fish, usually fished for and caught by the people of this Nation; nor any Oyle made, or that shall be made of any kinde of Fish whatsoever; nor any Whale-fins, or Whale-bones, shall from henceforth be Imported into this Commonwealth, or into Ireland, or any other Lands, Islands, Plantations, or Territories thereto belonging, or in their possession, but onely such as shall be caught in Vessels that do or shall truly and properly belong to the people of this Nation, as Proprietors and Right Owners thereof: And the said Fish to be cured, and the Oyl aforesaid made by the people of this Commonwealth, under the penalty and loss expressed in the said first Branch of this present Act; the said Forfeit to be recovered and imployed as is there expressed.

And it is further Enacted by the Authority aforesaid, That no sort of Cod, Ling, Herring, Pilchard, or any other kinde of Salted Fish whatsoever, which shall be caught and cured by the people of this Commonwealth, shall be from and after the First day of February, One thousand six hundred fifty three, exported from any place or places belonging to this Commonwealth, in any other Ship or Ships, Vessel or Vessels, save onely in such as do truly and properly appertain to the people of this Commonwealth, as Right Owners; and whereof the Master and Mariners are for the most part of them English, under the penalty and loss expressed in the said first Branch of this present Act; the said Forfeit to be recovered and imployed as is there expressed.

Provided always, That this Act, nor any thing therein contained, extend not, or be meant to restrain the Importation of any of the Commodities of the Straights or Levant Seas, loaden in the Shipping of this Nation as aforesaid, at the usual Ports or places for lading of them heretofore, within the said Straights or Levant Seas, though the said Commodities be not of the very Growth of the said places.

Provided also, That this Act nor any thing therein contained, extend not, nor be meant to restrain the Importing of any East-India Commodities loaden in the Shipping of this Nation, at the usual Port or places for Lading of them heretofore in any part of those Seas, to the Southward and Eastward of Cabo Bona Esperanza, although the said Ports be not the very places of their Growth.

Provided also, That it shall and may be lawful to and for any of the People of this Commonwealth, in Vessels or Ships to them belonging, and whereof the Master and Mariners are of this Nation as aforesaid, to load and bring in from any of the Ports of Spain and Portugal, all sorts of Goods or Commodities that have come from, or any way belonging unto the Plantations or Dominions of either of them respectively.

Be it also further Enacted by the authority aforesaid, That from henceforth it shall not be lawful to any person or persons whatsoever, to load or cause to be loaden and carried in any Bottom or Bottoms, Ship or Ships, Vessel or Vessels whatsoever, whereof any Stranger or Strangers born (unless such as be Denizens or Naturalized) be Owners, part Owners, or Master, any Fish, Victual, Wares, or things of what kinde or nature soever the same shall be, from one Port or Creek of this Commonwealth, to another Port or Creek of the same, under penalty to every one that shall offend contrary to the true meaning of this Branch of this present Act, to forfeit all the Goods that shall be so laden or carried, as also the Ship upon which they shall be so laden or carried, the same Forfeit to be recovered and imployed as directed in the first Branch of this present Act.

Lastly, That this Act nor any thing therein contained, extend not to Bullion, nor yet to any Goods taken, or that shall be taken by way of Reprizal by any Ship or Ships, having Commission from this Commonwealth.

Provided, That this Act, or any thing therein contained, shall not extend, nor be construed to extend to any Silk or Silk-wares which shall be brought by Land from any parts of Italy, and there bought with the proceed of English Commodities, sold either for Money or in Barter; but that it shall and may be lawful for any of the People of this Commonwealth to ship the same in English Vessels from Ostend, Newport, Roterdam, Middleburgh, Amsterdam, or any Ports thereabouts; the Owners and Proprietors first making Oath by themselves, or other credible Witness, before the Commissioners of the Customs for the time being, or their Deputies, or one of the Barons of the Exchequer, that the Goods aforesaid were so bought for his or their own proper accompt in Italy.

II / 1715-1789: THE AGE OF ENLIGHTEN-MENT

The eighteenth century—roughly defined as the period between the death of Louis XIV and the start of the French Revolution—was an age dominated less by a political than a philosophical attitude. It was an age of embattled "reason." "Reason" meant partly the application of logic to the world of experience, culminating in the method and the achievements of natural science; partly the attitude and the standards of "reasonable" men; and partly the rejection of beliefs and practices based on tradition, habit, and a supernatural view of the world in favor of judgments by men using their own knowledge for their own purposes. "Reason" in politics meant many things: the "reason of state" symbolized by Frederick II, which put logic and morals at the service of power; the "reason" of increased efficiency of government; the "reason," no less, of power dedicated to the general welfare of mankind rather than the self-service of rulers. "Reason," in a word, was as much a fashion as a fact; it was the characteristic eighteenth-century style in argument and action as much as particular ideas and deeds.

20 / FRANCESCO ALGAROTTI: POPULARIZATION OF THE NEW SCIENCE

During the eighteenth century Newtonian science ceased to be the possession of only those skilled in mathematics and scien-

*tific experimentation; it became part of the intellectual equipment
of thoughtful laymen. Popularized science cut away the "hard"—
and sometimes central—concepts of science in order to make it simple and understandable to the untrained mind. Characteristic of
such popularized science was* Il Neutonianesimo per le donne
*("Newtonianism for the Ladies," 1732), by the Italian man of
letters, Count Francesco Algarotti. The following excerpt is taken
from the edition of Algarotti's works published in 1791, in which
this work was retitled* Dialogues on Newtonian Optics. *Algarotti
(1712–1764) was a man of many parts, being a literary and art
critic as well as an occasional writer on politics and science; he
spent some years at the court of Frederick the Great as the Prussian
king's intellectual companion.*[1]

The next morning it was somewhat later when I was told that the
Marchesa's chambers were open and that I should enter. After the
usual courtesies, I began.—

"Madam, are you fully prepared to enter the sanctum of philosophy?
You know, of course, that those who lack reverence are excluded, as are
those who let themselves be tricked by globes, vortices, and other such-
like profane fantasies. Before crossing the threshold, one should totally
wipe from the mind that futile curiosity which gives rise to the proud
folly of those who invent general systems. For this sin, remember, they
seem to be condemned, like Sisyphus in the myth, to roll and lift up
huge boulders which soon after come tumbling down."

"Then our desire to know the cause of things must be without hope,"
said the Marchesa.

"There is hope," I replied, "if such a desire leads us to know things
as they really are."

"And shall we profit much thereby?" said the Marchesa. "For such
knowledge, should the philosopher be exalted above other men?"

"Madam," I replied, "don't you believe that it is much more worth-
while to know the real history of the effects which are observed in
nature than to lose oneself in the romance of their causes? Is not the
march of a Montecucculi[2] far more instructive than all the comings
and goings of Ariosto's[3] and Boiardo's[4] knights errant? Yet such is the

[1] *Opere del Conte Algarotti*, Edizione novissima (Venice: Carlo Palese, 1791),
Vol. II, pp. 101–8. Translated from the Italian by Donald Weinstein.

[2] Count Raimondo Montecucculi, duke of Melfi (1608–1680), a famed Italian-
born general in the service of the Hapsburg emperor (ed.)

[3] Lodovico Ariosto (1474–1533), Italian poet, author of the epic *Orlando Furi-
oso* (ed.)

[4] Matteo Boiardo (1440–1494), Italian poet, author of the chivalric romance
Orlando Innamorato (ed.)

condition of man that the ability to ascertain how things really are, to distinguish appearance from reality—the ability to see—is not given to everyone. Things are concealed from us as though by a heavy fog, especially those things that are most often before our eyes. Nature has hidden from us the primary and elementary effects almost as thoroughly, I should say, as she has hidden the causes themselves. Thus, if we cannot find the order and mutual dependence of all parts of the universe, nor discover first causes, perhaps, Madam, you will think it no small achievement to show the relationship among effects that appear to be very different, reducing them to a common principle, and to extract by observation from particular phenomena the general law which nature follows and by which she governs the world."

"So far," said the Marchesa, "the only value I have seen in observation is a destructive one. If a system is beautiful, elegant and simple, the observers immediately declare war upon it and do not rest until they have pulled it down. I must say they do seem to have some of the perverse humor of the man who tried to become famous and much talked about by ridiculing things of beauty."

"Among the systems that have appeared in the world," I replied, "the one that was dreamed up about the qualities of the moon's rays was perhaps not least important. Indeed, you may yourself have noted that it was once among those most in vogue. On the principle that the moon presides over the night as the sun over the day, that the color of the sun is related to gold while the color of the moon is related to silver, and other differences of the same kind, some theorists used to hold that the rays of the moon were endowed with qualities entirely antithetical to those of the sun. Therefore, if the rays of the sun are hot and dry, as we feel them to be every day, those of the moon were supposed to be cold and moist. From which it followed that they were also unhealthy. Indeed, as soon as the moon begins to rise above the horizon and its rays grow stronger, most people go indoors or if they stay out strolling in the open air and inhale some of the harmful potency of its light, they believe that it gives them a headache. But then the observers of natural phenomena chose to intervene and put this system into the crucible of experiment. They concentrated the power of the moon's rays by focusing them through lenses, and applied a thermometer to them. This is an instrument which displays heat and cold visually, thanks to its sensitivity and what we may call its irritability. It is made of a ball or vessel of glass into which some spirit of wine is placed. When it feels the slightest degree of heat, the spirit of wine expands and rises in the neck of the vessel. With the slightest degree of cold, the spirit of wine contracts and descends. Whereupon they observed that it did not contract at all, even though the moon's rays, moist and cold as they were supposed to be, were more concentrated and denser in the focus of these lenses than they ever are when they strike us directly. It followed that the rays of that planet have no special qualities other than to illuminate the night and to inspire a certain sweet-sad passion and languor in lovers' hearts."

"Now observations like that should please everyone," exclaimed the Marchesa. "They do not disrupt beautiful things and they cure us of idle and ill-founded fears."

"The philosophers who build systems," I resumed, "should be compared to the race of statesmen who promised us oceans and worlds by means of systems of another sort, and boast that they will enrich nations. Since everyone would like to become rich as well as wise in quick time, there are people enough to listen to them; the only difference is that while the latter discover that their treasure consists of worthless scraps of paper, the former find that theirs is made of compressive or rotatory motions and other, equally false scraps and counterfeit coin of philosophy. Thus we will owe no small debt to the method of observation if it cures us of such vain and ill-founded hopes. Who can be satisfied by

grand promises with small expectations;

by the desire to embrace the whole world which ends by clasping nothing? Surely it is better to build upon the small foundations one actually has. The true philosopher should be like those wise princes who are perfectly content to possess a single state which is more secure than it is large. On the other hand, has not the method of observation greatly extended the limits of our knowledge? You yourself, Madam, conceded only yesterday that thanks to observations with the microscope our vision has penetrated into the deepest recesses of bodies, and that by observations with the telescope it has scanned the breadth of the heavens to enrich natural history and astronomy with a thousand wonderful discoveries. Only through the study of observations has chemistry been perfected, so that it is now succeeding in analyzing bodies into their component elements and is on the verge of being able to put them together again. Only in this way has nautical science made such progress that now we can speed from one hemisphere to the other in great safety. It is undeniable, Madam, that in medicine, where hypothetical systems are very dangerous, only sober reason and, so to speak, passionate observation can bring improvement and development. What then remains for us? Nothing but the responsibility to observe ourselves attentively, to follow step by step the development of the child and the gradual progress of the mental faculties in the man, until we reach the point of discerning, in the profound darkness of metaphysics, the formation of our ideas. Newton has opened the hidden treasure of physics by making the finest use of observations and, as one of his countrymen has sung of him, by unfolding the transparent garment of day, he has brought forth and at last uncovered for men the hitherto concealed properties of the light which animates all things and brings happiness to the world. You will now see the most beautiful and wonderful texture of this light, Madam, and Newton's words will lead your mind toward truth."

21 / BECCARIA: REASONABLE JUSTICE

Another aspect of the Enlightenment's attempt to reduce the inhumanity of man to man was its criticism of the traditional forms and means of legal justice. Its targets were torture of the accused and the condemned, arbitrary and disproportionate punishments, and inequality of the laws for different sections of the population. Yet the philosophes *did not oppose strict enforcement of the laws as such, for, as subsequent selections will show, they relied upon the state to accomplish the reforms they proposed. The outstanding spokesman for the reform of justice was the Italian nobleman, Cesare Bonesane, marchese di Beccaria (1735–1794). He was a university professor at Milan, his native city, and wrote on such fields as economics, law, politics, and ethics. The* Tratto dei delitti e delle pene *("Essay on Crimes and Punishments," 1764), from which the following passages are selected, was the work which embodied his principal ideas.*[5]

In every human society there is an effort continually tending to confer on one part the height of power and happiness, and to reduce the other to the extreme of weakness and misery. The intent of good laws is to oppose this effort, and to diffuse their influence universally and equally. But men generally abandon the care of their most important concerns to the uncertain prudence and discretion of those whose interest it is to reject the best and wisest institutions; and it is not till they have been led into a thousand mistakes in matters the most essential to their lives and liberties, and are weary of suffering, that

[5] [Cesare Bonesano, Marchese di Beccaria], *An Essay on Crimes and Punishments,* Translated from the Italian, new ed. (Edinburgh: W. Gordon and W. Creech, 1778), pp. 11–13, 26–9, 41.

they can be induced to apply a remedy to the evils with which they are oppressed. It is then they begin to conceive and acknowledge the most palpable truths, which, from their very simplicity, commonly escape vulgar minds, incapable of analysing objects, accustomed to receive impressions without distinction, and to be determined rather by the opinions of others than by the result of their own examination.

If we look into history we shall find that laws, which are, or ought to be, conventions between men in the state of freedom, have been, for the most part, the work of the passions of a few, or the consequence of a fortuitous or temporary necessity; not dictated by a cool examiner of human nature, who knew how to collect in one point the actions of a multitude, and had this only end in view, *the greatest happiness of the greatest number*. Happy are those few nations who have not waited till the slow succession of human vicissitudes should, from the extremity of evil, produce a transition to good; but, by prudent laws, have facilitated the progress from one to the other! And how great are the obligations due from mankind to that philosopher who, from the obscurity of his closet, had the courage to scatter among the multitude the seeds of useful truths, so long unfruitful!

The art of printing has diffused the knowledge of those philosophical truths, by which the relations between sovereigns and their subjects, and between nations, are discovered. By this knowledge commerce is animated, and there has sprung up a spirit of emulation and industry, worthy of rational beings. These are the produce of this enlightened age; but the cruelty of punishments, and the irregularity of proceeding in criminal cases, so principal a part of the legislation, and so much neglected throughout Europe, has hardly ever been called in question. Errors, accumulated through many centuries, have never yet been exposed by ascending to general principles; nor has the force of acknowledged truths been ever opposed to the unbounded licentiousness of ill-directed power, which has continually produced so many authorized examples of the most unfeeling barbarity. Surely, the groans of the weak, sacrificed to the cruel ignorance and indolence of the powerful, the barbarous torments lavished, and multiplied with useless severity, for crimes either not proved, or in their nature impossible, the filth and horrors of a prison, increased by the most cruel tormentor of the miserable, uncertainty, ought to have roused the attention of those whose business is to direct the opinions of mankind. . . .

It is not only the common interest of mankind that crimes should not be committed, but that crimes of every kind should be less frequent, in proportion to the evil they produce to society. Therefore the means made use of by the legislature to prevent crimes should be more powerful, in proportion as they are destructive of the public safety and happiness, and as the inducements to commit them are stronger. Therefore there ought to be a fixed proportion between crimes and punishments.

It is impossible to prevent entirely all the disorders which the passions of mankind cause in society. These disorders increase in proportion to the number of people and the opposition of private interests. If we consult history, we shall find them increasing, in every state, with the extent of dominion. In political arithmetic, it is necessary to substitute a calculation of probabilities to mathematical exactness. That force which continually impels us to our own private interest, like gravity, acts incessantly, unless it meets with an obstacle to oppose it. The effects of this force are the confused series of human actions. Punishments, which I would call political obstacles, prevent the fatal effects of private interest, without destroying the impelling cause, which is that sensibility inseparable from man. The legislator acts, in this case, like a skilful architect, who endeavours to counteract the force of gravity by combining the circumstances which may contribute to the strength of his edifice.

The necessity of uniting in society being granted, together with the conventions which the opposite interests of individuals must necessarily require, a scale of crimes must be formed, of which the first degree should consist of those which immediately tend to the dissolution of society, and the last of the smallest possible injustice done to a private member of that society. Between these extremes will be comprehended all actions contrary to the public good which are called criminal, and which descend by insensible degrees, decreasing from the highest to the lowest. If mathematical calculation could be applied to the obscure and infinite combinations of human actions, there might be a corresponding scale of punishments, descending from the greatest to the least: but it will be sufficient that the wise legislator mark the principal divisions, without disturbing the order, lest to crimes of the *first* degree be assigned punishments of the *last*. If there were an exact and universal scale of crimes and punishments, we should there have a common measure of the degree of liberty and slavery, humanity and cruelty of different nations.

Any action which is not comprehended in the above-mentioned scale will not be called a crime, or punished as such, except by those who have an interest in the denomination. The uncertainty of the extreme points of this scale hath produced a system of morality which contradicts the laws, a multitude of laws that contradict each other, and many which expose the best men to the severest punishments, rendering the ideas of *vice* and *virtue* vague and fluctuating, and even their existence doubtful. Hence that fatal lethargy of political bodies, which terminates in their destruction. . . .

Pleasure and pain are the only springs of action in beings endowed with sensibility. Even amongst the motives which incite men to acts of religion, the invisible legislator has ordained rewards and punishments. From a partial distribution of these will arise that contradiction, so little observed because so common, I mean that of punishing by the laws the crimes which the laws have occasioned. If an equal punishment be ordained for two crimes that injure society in different degrees, there is nothing to deter men from committing the greater as often as it is attended with greater advantage. . . .

From the foregoing considerations it is evident, that the intent of punishments is not to torment a sensible being, nor to undo a crime already committed. Is it possible that torments and useless cruelty, the instrument of furious fanaticism or the impotency of tyrants, can be authorised by a political body, which, so far from being influenced by passion, should be the cool moderator of the passions of individuals? Can the groans of a tortured wretch recall the time past, or reverse the crime he has committed?

The end of punishment, therefore, is no other than to prevent the criminal from doing further injury to society, and to prevent others from committing the like offence. Such punishments, therefore, and such a mode of inflicting them, ought to be chosen, as will make the strongest and most lasting impressions on the minds of others, with the least torment to the body of the criminal.

22 / VOLTAIRE: "SCIENTIFIC" RELIGION — DEISM

The rise of the new science, with its mechanical interpretation of the physical world, encouraged the parallel religious system generally called deism. Deism attempted to remove all or most of the supernatural elements from traditional Christianity and presented the resulting creed as "natural religion," the religious counterpart of natural science. It placed particular stress upon the notion of God as the creator of the world according to fixed physical and moral laws. Most influential of the deists was the French writer François Marie Arouet, who took the name of Voltaire (1694–1778). He was the outstanding figure of the Enlightenment, beginning as a poet and dramatist and becoming over the years a philosopher, a political propagandist, a social satirist, and a his-

torian. He made a classic statement of deist doctrine in his Dictionnaire Philosophique ("Philosophical Dictionary," 1764) in the
articles "Theism" and "Theist." Although the term "theism" is nowadays customarily used to designate revealed religion, as distinct
from natural religion, Voltaire used it to distinguish natural religion
from atheism.[6]

THEISM

Theism is a religion diffused through all religions; it is a metal which
mixes itself with all the others, the veins of which extend under ground
to the four corners of the world. This mine is more openly worked in
China; everywhere else it is hidden, and the secret is only in the hands
of the adepts.

There is no country where there are more of these adepts than in
England. In the last century there were many atheists in that country
as well as in France and Italy. What the chancellor Bacon had said
proved true to the letter, that a little philosophy makes a man an
atheist, and that much philosophy leads to the knowledge of a God.
When it was believed with Epicurus, that chance made everything,
or with Aristotle, and even with several ancient theologians, that
nothing was created but through corruption, and that by matter and
motion alone the world goes on, then it was impossible to believe in
a providence. But since nature has been looked into, which the ancients
did not perceive at all; since it is observed that all is organized, that
everything has its germ; since it is well known that a mushroom is the
work of infinite wisdom, as well as all the worlds; then those who
thought, adored in the countries where their ancestors had blasphemed.
The physicians are become the heralds of providence; a catechist an-
nounces God to children, and a Newton demonstrates Him to the
learned.

Many persons ask whether theism, considered abstractedly, and
without any religious ceremony, is in fact a religion? The answer is
easy: he who recognizes only a creating God, he who views in God
only a Being infinitely powerful, and who sees in His creatures only
wonderful machines, is not religious towards Him any more than a
European, admiring the King of China, would thereby profess allegiance to that prince. But he who thinks that God has deigned to
place a relation between Himself and mankind; that He has made him
free, capable of good and evil; that He has given all of them that good

[6] François Marie Arouet de Voltaire, Philosophical Dictionary, in Works, translated by Tobias Smollett and William F. Fleming (Paris: E. R. DuMont, n.d.),
Vol. XIV, pp. 79–83.

sense which is the instinct of man, and on which the law of nature is founded; such a one undoubtedly has a religion, and a much better religion than all those sects who are beyond the pale of our Church; for all these sects are false, and the law of nature is true. Thus, theism is good sense not yet instructed by revelation; and other religions are good sense perverted by superstition.

All sects differ, because they come from men; morality is everywhere the same, because it comes from God. It is asked why, out of five or six hundred sects, there have scarcely been any who have not spilled blood; and why the theists, who are everywhere so numerous, have never caused the least disturbance? It is because they are philosophers. Now philosophers may reason badly, but they never intrigue. Those who persecute a philosopher, under the pretext that his opinions may be dangerous to the public, are as absurd as those who are afraid that the study of algebra will raise the price of bread in the market; one must pity a thinking being who errs; the persecutor is frantic and horrible. We are all brethren; if one of my brothers, full of respect and filial love, inspired by the most fraternal charity, does not salute our common Father with the same ceremonies as I do, ought I to cut his throat and tear out his heart?

What is a true theist? It is he who says to God: "I adore and serve You"; it is he who says to the Turk, to the Chinese, the Indian, and the Russian: "I love you." He doubts, perhaps, that Mahomet made a journey to the moon and put half of it in his pocket; he does not wish that after his death his wife should burn herself from devotion; he is sometimes tempted not to believe the story of the eleven thousand virgins, and that of St. Amable, whose hat and gloves were carried by a ray of the sun from Auvergne as far as Rome. But for all that he is a just man. Noah would have placed him in his ark, Numa Pompilius in his councils; he would have ascended the car of Zoroaster; he would have talked philosophy with the Platos, the Aristippuses, the Ciceros, the Atticuses—but would he not have drunk hemlock with Socrates?

THEIST

The theist is a man firmly persuaded of the existence of a Supreme Being equally good and powerful, who has formed all extended, vegetating, sentient, and reflecting existences; who perpetuates their species, who punishes crimes without cruelty, and rewards virtuous actions with kindness.

The theist does not know how God punishes, how He rewards, how He pardons; for he is not presumptuous enough to flatter himself that he understands how God acts; but he knows that God does act, and that He is just. The difficulties opposed to a providence do not stagger him in his faith, because they are only great difficulties, not proofs; he submits himself to that providence, although he only perceives some of its effects and some appearances; and judging of the things he does not see from those he does see, he thinks that this providence pervades all places and all ages.

United in this principle with the rest of the universe, he does not join any of the sects, who all contradict themselves; his religion is the most ancient and the most extended; for the simple adoration of a God has preceded all the systems in the world. He speaks a language which all nations understand, while they are unable to understand each other's. He has brethren from Pekin to Cayenne, and he reckons all the wise his brothers. He believes that religion consists neither in the opinions of incomprehensible metaphysics, nor in vain decorations, but in adoration and justice. To do good—that is his worship; to submit oneself to God—that is his doctrine. The Mahometan cries out to him: "Take care of yourself, if you do not make the pilgrimage to Mecca." "Woe be to thee," says a Franciscan, "if thou dost not make a journey to our Lady of Loretto." He laughs at Loretto and Mecca; but he succors the indigent and defends the oppressed.

23 / HOLBACH: "SCIENTIFIC" IRRELIGION—ATHEISM

A minority of Enlightenment thinkers went beyond the limits of deist doctrine to attack all religion. They drew arguments in favor of atheism both from the tension between the new science and the old creeds, and from the asserted harmful effects of religion in personal and social life. The most systematic of these eighteenth-century atheists was a German nobleman resident in France, Paul Thiry, Baron d'Holbach (1723–1789). His Système de la Nature ("System of Nature," 1770) was widely read and widely assailed for its total materialism. All of Holbach's works were published anonymously or pseudonymously, but the true authorship of The System of Nature *was an open secret. The translation from which the following passages are taken was made by an English radical who suffered imprisonment on charges of sedition during the period of the war against the French Revolution after 1792.*[7]

If a misanthrope, in hatred of the human race, had formed the project of throwing man into the greatest perplexity, could he have been able to have imagined a more efficacious means, than to occupy them without relaxation, with a being not only unknown, but also totally impossible to be known, which should, however, have been announced to them as the centre of all their thoughts, as the model and the only end of all their actions, as the object of all their researches, as a thing more important than life, since their present felicity, and their future happiness must necessarily depend upon it? What would it be, if to these ideas, already so suitable to disturb their brain, he also joined that of an absolute monarch, who followed no rule in his conduct, who was not bound by any duty, who could punish, to all eternity, the offences which they committed against him in the course of time; whose fury it is extremely easy to provoke, who is irritated by the ideas and thoughts of men, and of whom without even their knowledge they can incur the displeasure? The name of such a being, would assuredly be sufficient to carry trouble, affliction, and consternation in the souls of those, who should hear it pronounced; his idea would follow them every where, it would unceasingly afflict them, it would plunge them into despair. To what torture would not their mind put itself to discover this formidable being, to ascertain the secret of pleasing him, to imagine what would be able to disarm his anger! What fears would they not entertain of not having justly hit upon him! What disputes would they not have upon the nature, upon the qualities of a being equally unknown to all men, and seen variously by each of them! What variety in the means to which imagination would give birth, in order to find favour in his eyes or to remove his wrath!

Such is, word for word, the history of those effects which the name of God produces upon the earth. Men were always frightened at it, because they never had any fixed ideas of the being which this name represented. The qualities which some speculators, by dint of racking the brain, have believed they discovered in him, have done no more than disturb the repose of nations and of each of the citizens who compose it, alarm them without reason, fill them with spleen and animosity, render their existence unhappy, make them lose sight of the realities necessary to their happiness. By the magical charm of

[7] [Paul Thiry, Baron d'Holbach], *The System of Nature; or, The Laws of the Moral and Physical World,* translated from the French by William Hodgson (London: The Translator, 1795), Vol. III, pp. 146–51.

this formidable word, the human species have remained as if they were benumbed and stupefied, or else a blind fanaticism rendered them furious: sometimes desponding with fear, man cringed like a slave who bends under the scourge of an inexorable master, always ready to strike him; he believed he was only born to serve this master whom he never knew, and of whom they gave him the most terrible ideas; to tremble under his yoke; to labour to appease him; to dread his vengeance; to live in tears and misery. If he raised his eyes bathed in tears towards his god, it was in the excess of his grief; he nevertheless always mistrusted him, because he believed him unjust, severe, capricious, and implacable. He could neither labour for his happiness, cheer his heart, nor consult his reason, because he was always sighing, and he was never permitted to lose sight of his fears. He became the enemy of himself and of his fellow creatures, because they persuaded him that his well-being here below was interdicted. Every time there was a question of his cœlestial tyrant, he no longer had any judgment, he no longer reasoned, he fell into a state of infancy or of delirium, which submitted him to authority. Man was destined to this servitude as soon as he quitted the womb of his mother, and tyrannical opinion obliged him to wear his fetters during the rest of his days. A prey to the panic terrors with which they never ceased to inspire him, he appeared to have come upon the earth only to dream, to groan, to sigh, to injure himself, to deprive himself of all pleasures, to embitter his life, or disturb the felicity of others. Perpetually infected by the terrific chimeras which the delirium of the imagination presented to him without ceasing, he was abject, stupid, irrational, and he frequently became wicked, to honour the god whom they proposed to him for a model, or whom they told him to avenge.

It was thus that mortals prostrated themselves, from race to race, before the vain phantoms to which fear originally gave birth in the bosom of ignorance and the calamities of the earth. It was thus that they tremblingly adored those vain idols which they erected in the recesses of their own brain, where they have given them a sanctuary; nothing can make them feel that it is themselves whom they adore, that they fall on their knees before their own work, that they frighten themselves with the extravagant picture which they have themselves delineated; they obstinately persist in prostrating themselves, in perplexing themselves, in trembling; they make a crime even of the pleasure of dissipating their fears; they mistake the ridiculous production of their own folly; their conduct resembles that of children, who are afraid of themselves, when they see in a mirror their own peculiar traits which they have disfigured. Their extravagancies, so grievous to themselves, have their epoch in this world from the fatal notion of a god; they will continue them and renew them until such time as this unintelligible notion shall no longer be looked upon as important and necessary to the happiness of society. In the mean time, it is evident that the man who should arrive at the destruction of this fatal notion, or at least should diminish its terrible influence, would certainly be the friend of the human species.

24 / VOLTAIRE: RELIGIOUS TOLERANCE

Complex and varied as the Enlightenment was, no single idea permeated its conceptions and its moods more than that of tolerance. Such thinkers as Voltaire were especially repelled by the claim of the various creeds of traditional Christianity that they had the right and the duty to destroy those who differed with them. Toward religious persecutors the philosophes, *as the Enlightenment thinkers called themselves, felt no tolerance of their own, but denounced them in fiery words. One typical work of this kind is a pamphlet by Voltaire,* Le Philosophe ignorant *("The Ignorant Philosopher," 1766), from which the following passages are taken.*[8]

What a dreadful passion is that pride, which would force men to think like ourselves! But is it not the summit of folly to think of bringing them to our dogmas, through making them continually revolt by the most atrocious calumnies, by persecutions, dragging them to the galleys, to the gibbet, to the wheel, and to the flaming pile?

An Irish priest has lately advanced in a Pamphlet, that is, indeed, unknown, but which he has nevertheless written, and he has heard others assert, that we are come a hundred years too late to raise our voices against the want of toleration; that barbarity has taken place of gentleness; and this is not the time to complain. I shall reply to those who speak in this manner: Observe what passes under your own eyes, and if you have a human heart, you will join your compassion to ours. Eight unhappy preachers have been hanged in France since the year 1745. The bills of confession have excited infinite troubles;

---

[8] François Marie Arouet de Voltaire, *The Ignorant Philosopher. With an Address to the Public upon the Parricides imputed to the Families of Calas and Sirven,* translated from the French [with corrections by the editor] (London: S. Bladon, 1767), pp. 167–74.

and, at length, an unhappy fanatic from the dregs of the people, having attempted to assassinate the king in 1757, he answered, before the parlement upon his first interrogation, he had undertaken this parricide for a principle of religion; and he added these fatal words, "He that does no good but to himself, is good for nothing." By whom was he taught them? Who could teach a college-sweeper, a wretched varlet, to talk thus? He maintained when put to the torture, not only that this assassination was a meritorious deed, but that he had heard all the priests in the great hall of the palace where justice is administered, say the same.

The contagion of fanaticism then still subsists. The virus is so little eradicated, that a priest in the country of the Calas's and Sirvens, printed a few years since, an Apology for the Massacre of St. Bartholomew's. Another has published the Justification of the Murderers of the curate Grandier; and when that useful humane Treatise upon Toleration appeared in France, it could not be allowed a public sale. This Treatise has indeed done some good, it has dissipated some prejudices, it has inspired a horror for persecutions and fanaticism; but in this picture of religious barbarities, the author has omitted certain features that would have rendered the picture more terrible, and the instruction more striking.

The author has been reproached with going a little too far, when, in order to display how detestable and frantic is persecution, he introduces a report of Ravaillac proposing to the Jesuit le Tellier the confinement of all Jansenists. This fiction might, indeed, appear somewhat *outrée* to those who are unacquainted with the silly rage of fanaticism. It will appear very surprising, when it is known, that what is a fiction in the Treatise upon Toleration is an historical fact.

The fact is, we find in the History of the Reformation of Switzerland, that in order to prevent the great change that was ready to burst, some priests of Geneva, in 1536, corrupted a servant maid to poison three of the principal actors in the reformation; and that the poison not having been administered strong enough, they put some that was more violent in the bread and wine of the public communion, in order to exterminate all those of the reformed religion in a single morning, and to make the church of God triumph.

The author of the Treatise upon Toleration has not mentioned the shocking executions wherein so many unhappy victims perished in the valleys of Piedmont. He has passed over in silence the massacre of six hundred inhabitants of Valtelina, men, women, and children, who were murdered by the Catholics in the month of September, 1620. I will not say it was with the consent and assistance of the archbishop of Milan, Charles Borome, who was made a saint. Some passionate writers have averred this fact, which I am very far from believing; but I say, there is scarce any city or borough in Europe, where blood has not been spilt for religious quarrels; I say, that the human species has been perceptibly diminished, because women and girls were massacred as well as men; I say, that Europe would have had a third larger population, if there had been no theological disputes. In fine, I say, that so far from forgetting these abominable times, we should frequently take a view of them, to inspire an eternal horror for them; and that it is for our age to make reparation by toleration, for this long collection of crimes, which has taken place through the want of toleration, during sixteen barbarous centuries.

Let it not then be said, that there are no traces left of that shocking fanaticism, of the want of toleration; they are still everywhere to be met with, even in those countries that are esteemed the most humane. The Lutheran and Calvinist preachers, were they masters, would, perhaps, be as little inclined to pity, as obdurate, as insolent as they upbraid their antagonists with being. The barbarous law, whereby any Roman Catholic is forbidden to reside more than three days in certain countries, is not yet revoked. An Italian, a Frenchman, or an Austrian, cannot occupy a house, or possess an acre of land in their territories; whilst an unknown citizen of Genneva, or Shaffhousen, is, at least, allowed to purchase manors in France. If a Frenchman, on the contrary, wanted to purchase an estate in the Protestant republics of which I am speaking, and if the government wisely winked at it, there would be still some souls formed of such clods, as to rise up against this tolerating humanity.

25 / JOHN WESLEY: "METHODICAL" CHRISTIANITY

New ways of defending Christianity were devised and used in the very midst of the Enlightenment. None was more dramatic or effective than the "methodical" Christianity expounded by the Englishman John Wesley (1703–1791) during preaching tours estimated to have covered more than a quarter of a million miles. Wesley, ordained an Anglican clergyman, rejected the cool rationalism dominant in eighteenth-century Anglicanism and made his appeal to the emotions of his hearers in some forty thousand sermons. Eventually he formed his own denomination, called

*Methodism, independent of the Anglican church. The following
sections from his journal display his conception of active Christianity and his method of spreading it before the people of both high
class and low.*[9]

Mon. 11 [June, 1739].—I received a pressing letter from London (as
I had several others before) to come thither as soon as possible, our
brethren in Fetter Lane being in great confusion for want of my presence and advice. I therefore preached in the afternoon on these words:
"I take you to record this day, that I am pure from the blood of all
men; for I have not shunned to declare unto you all the counsel of
God." After sermon I commended them to the grace of God, in whom
they had believed. Surely God hath yet a work to do in this place. I
have not found such love, no, not in England; nor so child-like, artless,
teachable a temper, as He hath given to this people.

Yet during this whole time I had many thoughts concerning the unusual manner of my ministering among them. But after frequently
laying it before the Lord, and calmly weighing whatever objections
I heard against it, I could not but adhere to what I had some time since
wrote to a friend, who had freely spoken his sentiments concerning it.
An extract of that letter I here subjoin, that the matter may be placed
in a clear light.

DEAR SIR,
The best return I can make for the kind freedom you use is to use the
same to you. Oh may the God whom we serve sanctify it to us both, and
teach us the whole truth as it is in Jesus!

You say you cannot reconcile some parts of my behaviour with the character I have long supported. No, nor ever will. Therefore I have disclaimed
that character on every possible occasion. I told all in our ship, all at Savannah, all at Frederica, and that over and over, in express terms, "I am not a
Christian; I only follow after, if haply I may attain it." When they urged my
works and self-denial, I answered short, "Though I give all my goods to feed
the poor, and my body to be burned, I am nothing: for I have not charity;
I do not love God with all my heart." If they added, "Nay, but you could
not preach as you do, if you was not a Christian," I again confronted them
with St. Paul: "Though I speak with the tongue of men and angels, and have
not charity, I am nothing." Most earnestly, therefore, both in public and private, did I inculcate this: "Be not ye shaken, however I may fall, for the
foundation standeth sure."

If you ask on what principle, then, I acted, it was this: A desire to be a

---

[9] *The Journal of the Rev. John Wesley, A.M.*, ed. Nehemiah Curnock (London:
Epworth Press, 1938), Vol. II, pp. 216–18; Vol. IV, pp. 337–40. Reprinted by permission of Epworth Press.

Christian; and a conviction that, whatever I judge conducive thereto, that I am bound to do; wherever I judge I can best answer this end, thither it is my duty to go. On this principle I set out for America, on this I visited the Moravian Church, and on the same am I ready now (God being my helper) to go to Abyssinia or China, or whithersoever it shall please God, by this conviction, to call me.

As to your advice that I should settle in college, I have no business there, haivng now no office and no pupils. And whether the other branch of your proposal be expedient for me, viz. "To accept of a cure of souls," [10] it will be time enough to consider when one is offered to me.

But, in the meantime, you think I ought to sit still; because otherwise I should invade another's office if I interfered with other people's business, and intermeddled with souls that did not belong to me. You accordingly ask, "How is it that I assemble Christians, who are none of my charge, to sing psalms, and pray, and hear the Scriptures expounded?" and think it hard to justify doing this in other men's parishes, upon catholic principles.

Permit me to speak plainly. If by catholic principles you mean any other than scriptural, they weigh nothing with me. I allow no other rule, whether of faith or practice, than the Holy Scriptures; but, on scriptural principles, I do not think it hard to justify whatever I do. God in Scripture commands me, according to my power, to instruct the ignorant, reform the wicked, confirm the virtuous. Man forbids me to do this in another's parish: that is, in effect, to do it at all; seeing I have now no parish of my own, nor probably ever shall. Whom, then, shall I hear, God or man? "If it be just to obey man rather than God, judge you. A dispensation of the gospel is committed to me; and woe is me if I preach not the gospel." But where shall I preach it, upon the principles you mention? Why, not in Europe, Asia, Africa, or America; not in any of the Christian parts, at least, of the habitable earth. For all these are, after a sort, divided into parishes. If it be said, "Go back, then, to the heathens from whence you came": nay, but neither could I now (on your principles) preach to them; for all the heathens in Georgia belong to the parish either of Savannah or of Frederica.

Suffer me now to tell you my principles in this matter. I look upon all the world as my parish; thus far I mean, that, in whatever part of it I am, I judge it meet, right and my bounden duty to declare unto all that are willing to hear the glad tidings of salvation. This is the work which I know God has called me to; and sure I am that His blessing attends it. Great encouragement have I, therefore, to be faithful in fulfilling the work He hath given me to do. His servant I am, and, as such, am employed according to the plain direction of His word: "As I have opportunity, doing good unto all men." And His providence clearly concurs with His word, which has disengaged me from all things else that I might singly attend on this very thing, "and go about doing good."

If you ask me, "How can this be? How can one do good, of whom *men say all manner of evil?*" I will put you in mind (though you once knew this, yea, and much established me in that great truth) the more evil men say of

---

[10] appointment to a parish church (ed.)

me, for my Lord's sake, the more good will He do by me. That it is for His sake, I know, and He knoweth, and the event agreeth thereto; for He mightily confirms the words I speak, by the Holy Ghost given unto those that hear them. Oh my friend, my heart is moved toward you. I fear you have herein "made shipwreck of the faith." I fear "Satan, transformed into an angel of light," hath assaulted you, and prevailed also. I fear that offspring of hell, worldly or mystic prudence, has drawn you away from the simplicity of the gospel. How else could you ever conceive that the being reviled and "hated of all men" should make us less fit for our Master's service? How else could you ever think of "saving yourself and them that hear you" without being "the filth and offscouring of the world"? To this hour is this scripture true; and I therein rejoice; yea, and will rejoice. Blessed be God, I enjoy the reproach of Christ! Oh may you also be vile, exceeding vile, for His sake! God forbid that you should ever be other than generally scandalous; I had almost said universally. If any man tell you there is a new way of following Christ, "he is a liar, and the truth is not in him."

I am, &c.

. . .

Wed. 18 [July, 1759].—We called at the house where Mr. B[erridge] had been preaching in the morning, and found several there rejoicing in God and several mourning after Him. While I prayed with them many crowded into the house, some of whom burst into a strange, involuntary laughter, so that my voice could scarce be heard, and when I strove to speak louder a sudden hoarseness seized me. Then the laughter increased. I perceived it was Satan, and resolved to pray on. Immediately the Lord rebuked him that laughter was at an end, and so was my hoarseness. A vehement wrestling with God ran through the whole company, whether sorrowful or rejoicing, till, beside the three young women of the house, one young man and a girl about eleven years old, who had been counted one of the wickedest in Harlston, were exceedingly blest with the consolations of God.

Among those under conviction was an elderly woman, who had been a scoffer at the gospel, and a keen ridiculer of all that cried out; but she now cried louder than any present. . . .

We met Mr. B at Stapleford, five miles from Cambridge. His heart was particularly set on this people, because he was curate here five or six years; but never preached a gospel sermon among them till this evening. About one thousand five hundred persons met in a close to hear him, great part of whom were laughers and mockers. The work of God, however, quickly began among them that were serious, while not a few endeavoured to make sport by mimicking the gestures of them that were wounded. Both these and those who rejoiced in God gave great offence to some stern-looking men, who vehemently demanded to have those wretches horsewhipped out of the close. Need we wonder at this, when several of His own people are unwilling to let God work in His own way? And well may Satan be enraged at the cries of the people, and the prayers they make in the bitterness of their souls, seeing we know these are the chief times at which Satan is cast out.

However, in a while, many of the scoffers were weary, and went away; the rest continued as insensible as before. I had long been walking round the multitude, feeling a jealousy for my God, and praying Him to make the place of His feet glorious. My patience at last began to fail, and I prayed, "O king of glory, break some of them in pieces; but let it be to the saving of their souls!" I had but just spoke and I heard a dreadful noise on the farther side of the congregation, and, turning thither, saw one Thomas Skinner coming forward, the most horrible human figure I ever saw. His large wig and hair were coal black; his face distorted beyond all description. He roared incessantly, throwing and clapping his hands together with his whole force. Several were terrified, and hasted out of his way. I was glad to hear him, after a while, pray aloud. Not a few of the triflers grew serious, while his kindred and acquaintance were very unwilling to believe even their own eyes and ears. They would fain have got him away, but he fell to the earth, crying, "My burden My burden! I cannot bear it!" Some of his brother scoffers were calling for horse-whips, till they saw him extended on his back at full length. They then said he was dead. And, indeed, the only sign of life was the working of his breast and the distortions of his face, while the veins of his neck were swelled as if ready to burst. He was just before the chief captain of Satan's forces. None was by nature more fitted for mockery; none could swear more heroically to whip out of the close all who were affected by the preaching. His agonies lasted some hours; then his body and soul were eased.

When Mr. B had refreshed himself a little he returned to the close and bid the multitude take warning by Skinner, who still lay roaring and tormented on the ground. All the people were now deeply serious, and several hundreds, instead of going when Mr. B dismissed them, stayed in Mr. Jennings's yard. Many of these, especially men, were truly broken in heart. Mr. B talked with as many as could come into the house, and, seeing what numbers stood hungering without, sent me word to pray with them. This was a grievous cross! I knew it was the Lord's will, but felt such weakness of body and sinking of spirit, and was withal so hoarse, that I supposed few could hear out of some hundreds who stood before me. However, I attempted, and in a moment the Lord poured upon such a spirit of supplication, and gave me so clear and strong an utterance, that it seemed I was another man —a further instance that the servants of God are not sent a warfare on their own charge. . . .

It was late when I went to lodge about half a mile off, where I found a young woman reading hymns, and the power of the Lord falling on the hearers, especially one young man, who cried aloud in such bitter anguish that I soon desired we might join in prayer. This was the seventh time of my praying in public that day, and had I been faithful I should probably have prayed seven more.

26 / MONTESQUIEU: LIBERTY AND THE DIVISION OF POWERS

The central direction of the Enlightenment, for all its philosophical and moral concerns, was political. The philosophes *tended to emphasize the power of legislation in shaping society and hence saw the state as the principal agency for the achievement of reform. The first of the major political writers who can be clearly set within the pattern of Enlightenment was Charles de Secondat, Baron de la Brède et de Montesquieu (1689–1755). Montesquieu, by profession a jurist, resigned that career to become a man of letters. Although he was a nobleman and shared many of the convictions of his fellow aristocrats, his conception of political life went far beyond the immediate interests of his class, to reach judgments of extraordinary breadth. A keen historical thinker and one of the founders of sociological study, he crystallized his political thought in L'Esprit des lois ("The Spirit of the Laws," 1748), from which the following sections are taken.*[11]

In the widest meaning of the term, laws are those necessary relationships which flow from the nature of things. In this sense everything which exists has its laws: the Deity has his laws, the material world its laws, the spiritual beings of a higher order than man their laws, the beasts their laws, and man his own laws. . . .

Individual intelligent beings may have laws of their own making, but they also have laws which they did not make. Before they existed,

[11] Charles de Secondat, baron de la Brède et de Montesquieu, *De l'esprit des loix,* in *Œuvres de Montesquieu* (London: [no publisher named], 1787), Vol. I, pp. 1–4, 6–7, 13–14, 16–18, 24–6, 30–3, 35–6, 39, 41–2, 46–9, 52–3, 55, 319–26, 342–3, 347–8. Translated from the French by the editor.

intelligent beings were possible; therefore relationships among them were possible, and thus laws were possible too. Even before laws were made, relationships of justice were possible. To say that justice or injustice are no more than what positive laws command or forbid is no different from saying that the radii of a circle are not equal until one actually draws the circle. . . .

As a physical being, man is governed by invariable laws in the same way as other bodies. But as an intelligent being, he repeatedly violates the laws set down by God and he changes those which he himself has established. He is compelled to be his own guide and yet he has a finite intelligence, is subject to ignorance and error, and easily forgets the little that he knows. As a creature of the senses, he is subject to a thousand passions. At any moment such a creature as this may forget his Maker; God calls him back to himself by the laws of religion. At any moment such a creature as this may forget what he is; philosophers put him on his guard by the laws of morality. Man, who is made to live in society, may forget his fellow men; legislators remind him of his duty by political and civil laws. . . .

In general, law is human reason as it governs all the peoples upon earth; and the political and civil laws of each nation should be only this general human reason applied to particular cases.

They ought to be so adapted to the particular people for whom they are made that only by the merest accident will the laws of one nation be suitable for another.

They should be related to the particular nature and principle of the government, whether already established or proposed to be established; this is true both of political laws, which create the form of government, and civil laws, which uphold it.

They should be related to the *physical* character of the country; to its climate, whether frigid, torrid or temperate; to the character of the land, its situation and its size; to the way of life of the people, whether farmers, hunters or herdsmen. They should be related to the extent of liberty compatible with the constitution; to the religion of the inhabitants, to their propensities, wealth, number, trade, to their morals and manners. Lastly, there is an interrelationship of the laws, depending on their origin, the purpose of the legislator and the affairs to which they are directed. All these factors should be taken into consideration. . . .

There are three kinds of government: Republican, monarchical, and despotic. Their nature can be determined by anyone with even the very least education. I assume three definitions, or more exactly three facts: first, that "in a republican government the sovereign power belongs to the people as a whole, or to just a part of the people; in a monarchical government, one man governs, but only by means of settled and established laws; while in despotic government, one man subject to neither law nor rule controls everything according to his desire and caprice." . . .

Democracy consists in the possession of the sovereign power in a republic by the people as a whole. When the sovereign power is in the hands of a part of the people, it is called an *Aristocracy*.

In a democracy, the people is the monarch in some respects and the subject in others.

It is the monarch only by means of its votes, which are the expression of its will. The will of the sovereign is equal to the sovereign himself. Therefore the laws which establish the right to vote are fundamental in this form of government. Indeed, in a democracy it is as important to determine who shall give the vote, to whom and about what, as it is in a monarchy to know who the monarch is and how he ought to rule. . . .

It is beyond doubt that the people should cast their votes in public. This should be considered as a fundamental law of democracy. The common folk should be guided and restrained by men of eminence. Thus, in the Roman republic all was lost when voting was made secret, for no guidance could be given to the populace when it went astray. But when the body of the nobles vote in an aristocracy, or the senate in a democracy, no secrecy can be too great, for what matters then is only the prevention of intrigue. . . .

In aristocracy the sovereign power is in the hands of a limited number of persons, who make the laws and execute them. The rest of the people play the same part with respect to them that subjects do toward the monarch in a monarchy. . . .

The best aristocracy is that in which the section of the people who have no share whatever of power is so small and impoverished that the ruling section has no interest in oppressing them. . . . Aristocratic families should therefore be as much like the people as possible. The closer aristocracy comes to democracy, the more perfect it will be; and the closer to monarchy, the less perfect.

The most imperfect of all is that in which the section of the people which obeys are the civil slaves of those who command, like the aristocracy of Poland, in which the peasants are the slaves of the nobility.

The character of monarchical government, in which one man governs by means of fundamental laws, is determined by the intermediate, subordinate and dependent powers. I say the intermediate, subordinate and dependent powers because in monarchy the prince is the source of all political and civil power. The fundamental laws require the existence of intermediate channels through which power flows; for if the momentary and capricious will of a single man decides everything in the state, there can be nothing settled and firm, and hence no fundamental law.

The most natural form of intermediate and subordinate power is that of the nobility. In a way it belongs to the essence of monarchy, whose fundamental maxim is "No monarch, no nobility; no nobility, no monarch." . . .

It is not enough to have intermediate ranks in a monarchy; a depository of the laws is also necessary, which can be found only in the political bodies which inform the public of the laws upon their enactment and remind them of the laws which are forgotten. Because the nobility is by its nature ill-informed, inattentive and scornful of the government, a body is necessary which will always rescue the laws which lie forgotten in the dust. The prince's council is not an adequate body of this kind. By its nature, it is the depository of the momentary will of the prince who executes the laws and not the depository of the fundamental laws. Furthermore, the prince's council is in constant change; it is not permanent and cannot have many members, nor does it possess to a sufficient extent the confidence of the people; it therefore lacks the capacity to inform the people in times of difficulty or to end their disobedience when they break the law.

In despotic states which have no fundamental laws, there is likewise no depository of the laws. This is why religion is generally so strong a factor in such countries, for it constitutes a kind of depository, an element of permanence; if not religion, then the customs are venerated in place of the laws. . . .

Having examined the laws which are related to the nature of each government, we must see what laws are related to its principle.

This is the difference between the nature of a government and its principle: its nature is what makes it a government of the kind it is, and its principle is what makes it act. The first is its particular structure and the second the human passions that set it in motion.

Now, the laws should be related no less closely to the principle of each government than to its nature. . . .

Not much honesty is required for the maintenance or the preservation of a monarchical or despotic government. In the former the force of the law, in the other the always raised arm of the prince, do the whole work of directing affairs or maintaining order. But an additional motive force is required in a popular state, namely, *virtue*.[12]

___

[12] In the preface Montesquieu explains his specific meaning of virtue:
"In order to comprehend the first four books of this work, it must be noted that . . . what I call *virtue* in a republic is the love of the fatherland, that is, love of equality. This is neither moral nor Christian virtue, but political *virtue*." (ed.)

What I say here is confirmed by all history and conforms most exactly to the nature of things. For it is clear that in a monarchy, where the man who executes the law deems himself to be above the laws, less virtue is needed than in a popular government, where the man who enforces the laws feels that he himself is subject to them and will bear their weight.

It is clear, too, that a monarch who through ill counsel or neglect ceases to enforce the laws can easily repair the harm done—he need only change his council or correct the neglect himself. But when in a popular government the laws cease to be enforced, as results only from the corruption of the republic, the state is already lost. . . .

Virtue is needed in aristocratic government as well as in popular government, although it is true that this is not an absolute necessity. . . . *Moderation* is therefore the soul of this government, but such moderation, I add, as is based on virtue and not such as results from cowardice and lassitude of the soul.

In monarchies policy achieves great things with as little virtue as it can; just as in well-made machinery good design makes use of the fewest possible movements, motors and wheels. . . . But I must lose no time now in explaining that I am not satirizing monarchical government. No, indeed; although it lacks one motive force, it has another—HONOR, which is the prejudice of each person and each order of society in its own favor, takes the place of the political virtue of which I have spoken and acts in its stead. It can inspire the finest deeds, and when joined to the force of law it can bring about the goal of government like virtue itself. . . .

As we have said, monarchical government presupposes the existence of distinctions of eminence, of ranks, even of a hereditary nobility. It is in the nature of *honor* that some should be honored and distinguished above others; it belongs therefore in this kind of government.

Ambition is ruinous to a republic, but it produces useful results in a monarchy, to which it gives life; and there is this advantage that ambition is not dangerous in a monarchy because it can always be put down.

We may compare monarchy to the system of the universe, in which one force drives all things away from the center and the force of gravity brings them back. Honor sets all parts of the body politic into motion, binding them by its own action; and so it is that each man, believing that he is seeking his own interests, contributes to the common welfare.

It is true, philosophically speaking, that it is false honor which guides all parts of the state; but this false honor is no less useful to the public than true honor may be to individuals possessed of it.

Furthermore, is it not a great achievement to oblige men to perform all kinds of difficult and laborious deeds with no other recompense than the fame they earn thereby? . . .

Just as virtue is necessary in a republic and honor in a monarchy, so despotic government has need of FEAR; for virtue is wholly unnecessary and honor would be dangerous in it. . . .

No word has been defined in as many different ways, or made such varied impressions upon men's minds, as "liberty." Some have taken it to mean the ability to depose one to whom they had given tyrannical power; others, the power to elect those whom they must obey; others still, the right to bear arms and employ violence; and lastly, those for whom freedom means the privilege to be governed only by a man of their own nation or by their own laws. There is a nation which considered its freedom to be the right to wear long beards. Some have given this name to one form of government and denied it to others. Those who favored republican government gave it to this form, and those who benefited by monarchical government gave it to monarchy. In a word, men have called freedom that government which conformed to their customs or their tastes; and, as in republics the instruments of evil of which men complain are not always immediately before their eyes, as it seems to be more the laws than the law enforcers which are heard, it is customary to see freedom in republics and bar it from being present in monarchies. In a word, since the people appears to do almost anything it wants in a democracy, liberty has been felt to belong to this kind of government and the power of the people has been confused with the freedom of the people.

It is true that in democracies the people appears to do what it wants to, but political freedom does not at all consist in doing what one wants to. In a state, that is, in a society under law, freedom cannot consist in anything but doing what one should want to, and in not being compelled to do what one should not want to.

We must keep in mind the difference between independence and liberty. Liberty is the right to do whatever the laws permit; if a citizen could do what the laws forbade, he would have no freedom, for everyone else would have the same power.

Democracy and aristocracy are not free states by their own nature. Political liberty is found only in moderate governments, but not always even in them. It is present only when power is not abused. But experience constantly teaches us that any man with power is tempted to abuse it, and uses it until he discovers its limits. Strange to say, even virtue needs to be limited.

If power is not to be abused, things must be so arranged that power halts power. A constitution may compel no one to do such things as the law does not require of him, and not to do what the law permits him. . . .

There is furthermore one nation in the world where the immediate object of its constitution is political freedom. We shall examine the principle upon which it founds that freedom. If these principles are good, freedom will shine forth as in a mirror.

It takes little effort to discover political freedom in a constitution. If we can observe it where it already exists, where we have already found it, why seek further?

In every state there are three kinds of power—the legislative power; the executive power with regard to matters under the law of nations; and the executive power with regard to matters under the civil law.

By the first the prince or the magistrate makes temporary or permanent laws, and amends or abrogates existing laws. By the second he makes peace or wages war, sends or receives embassies, maintains public order and prevents invasion. By the third he punishes crimes and decides disputes between individuals. We shall call this last the right of judgment and the other simply the executive power of the state.

For a citizen political liberty is that tranquility of mind which arises out of each man's sense of his own safety. To provide this freedom, government must be such that each citizen need have no fear of any other citizen.

There is no freedom when the legislative power is combined with the executive power in the same person, or the same body of magistrates; for it may be feared that the same monarch or senate will enact tyrannical laws and enforce them tyrannically.

There is no freedom if the power of judgment is not separate from the legislative and executive powers. If it is combined with the legislative power, the power over the lives and the liberty of citizens becomes arbitrary, for the judge would be the legislator. If it is combined with the executive power, the judge would have the strength of an oppressor.

All would be lost if the same man, or the same body of leading men or of the nobility or of the people, exercised all three powers, to make the laws, to carry out public decisions and to judge crimes or disputes among individuals. . . .

This, then, is the fundamental constitution of the government of which we speak. The legislature is composed of two parts, each able to restrain the other by their mutual right to reject legislation. Both are bound by the executive power, which in turn is bound by the legislature.

These three powers might well result in quiescence or inaction. But since they are compelled to act by the necessary pressure of business, they are compelled to act in agreement. . . .

As all things human come to an end, so the state of which we speak will one day lose its freedom and perish. Rome, Lacedaemon [Sparta] and Carthage all perished. This state too will perish because the legislative power will become more corrupt than the executive power.

It is not my concern to examine whether the English enjoy this freedom or not at the present time. I need only say that it is established by their laws, and this is all I wish to know.

Nor do I desire in any way whatever to denigrate other governments, nor to say that this extreme political liberty should cause humiliation to those who enjoy only moderate freedom. I should be the last to say this, I who believe that it is not always desirable to push even reason beyond its limits, and that men almost always adapt themselves better to the middle than the extreme course.

27 / J. J. ROUSSEAU: POPULAR SOVEREIGNTY AND THE SOCIAL CONTRACT

The political thought of the Enlightenment culminated in the work of the Genevan-born French writer, Jean Jacques Rousseau. He attacked the question of sovereignty with all the relentless logic of a Jean Bodin two centuries before; if anything, he was harsher in his reasoning, for he made the central question of tyranny not how political power was used but who used it. No less important than the logic of his arguments was his passionate rhetoric, which broke through the cool style of the classical school to strike directly at men's souls. His intense and open emotionality made him one of the eighteenth-century sources of the Romantic movement of the next period. Rousseau (1712–1778) was a man of many sides and many talents. His first successes were as a musician and composer, but he later became a novelist whose novels were philosophical and educational tracts, a political writer, and an extraordinarily frank and probing autobiographer. His most influential work on politics was the Contrat social *("The So-*

cial Contract," 1762), from which the following selections are taken.[13]

My design in this treatise is to enquire whether, taking men such as they are, and laws such as they may be made, it is not possible to establish some just and certain rule for the administration of the civil order. In the course of my research I shall endeavour to unite what right permits with what interest prescribes, that justice and utility may not be separated.

I shall enter on my enquiry without saying anything about the importance of my subject. If I am asked whether I am a prince or a lawgiver, that I write on politics, I shall answer that I am neither, and for reason I am a political writer. If I were a prince or a lawgiver, I should not waste in theory the time which I ought to employ in practice; I would act or I would remain silent.

Born a citizen of a free State, and, as such, a member of its Sovereign, however weak the influence of my voice may prove in the determination of public affairs, the right of voting on such occasions imposes on me the duty of informing myself on the subject: and I am happy, whenever I meditate on governments, to find that my researches always afford me new reason to admire that of my own country.

Man is born free, and yet we see him everywhere in chains. Those who believe themselves the masters of others cease not to be even greater slaves than the people they govern. How this happens I am ignorant; but, if I am asked what renders it justifiable, I believe it may be in my power to resolve the question.

If I were only to consider force, and the effects of it, I should say, "When a people is constrained to obey, and does obey, it does well; but as soon as it can throw off its yoke, and does throw it off, it does better: for a people may certainly use, for the recovery of their liberty, the same right that was employed to deprive them of it: it was either justifiably recovered, or unjustifiably torn from them." But the social order is a sacred right which serves for the basis of all others. Yet this right comes not from nature; it is therefore founded on conventions. . . .

The strongest are still never sufficiently strong to ensure them continual mastership, unless they find means of transforming force into right, and obedience into duty. Hence the right of the strongest—a right which seems ironical in appearance, but is really established as

[13] Jean Jacques Rousseau, *The Social Contract*, an eighteenth-century translation from the French, revised by Charles Frankel (New York: Hafner Publishing Co., 1954), pp. 5–6, 8–9, 14–19, 24, 27–30.. Reprinted by permission of Hafner Publishing Co.

a principle. But shall we never have an explanation of this term? Force is a physical power; I do not see what morality can result from its effects. To yield to force is an act of necessity, not of inclination; or it is at best only an act of prudence. In what sense then can it be a duty? . . .

We must grant, therefore, that force does not constitute right, and that obedience is only due to legitimate powers. Thus everything goes back to my first question. . . .

I will suppose that men in the state of nature are arrived at that crisis when the strength of each individual is insufficient to overcome the resistance of the obstacles to his preservation. This primitive state can therefore subsist no longer; and the human race would perish unless it changed its manner of life.

As men cannot create for themselves new forces, but merely unite and direct those which already exist, the only means they can employ for their preservation is to form by aggregation an assemblage of forces that may be able to overcome the resistance, to be put in motion as one body, and to act in concert.

This assemblage of forces must be produced by the concurrence of many; but as the force and the liberty of each man are the chief instruments of his perservation, how can he engage elsewhere without danger to himself, and without neglecting the care which is due himself? This difficulty, which leads directly to my subject, may be expressed in these words:

"Where shall we find a form of association which will defend and protect with the whole common force the person and the property of each associate, and by which every person, while uniting himself with all, shall obey only himself and shall remain as free as before?" Such is the fundamental problem of which the Social Contract gives the solution.

The articles of this contract are so unalterably fixed by the nature of the act that the least modification renders them vain and of no effect; so that they are the same everywhere, and are everywhere tacitly understood and admitted, even though they may never have been formally announced; until, the social compact being violated, each individual is restored to his original rights, and resumes his native liberty, while losing the conventional liberty for which he renounced it.

The articles of the social contract will, when clearly understood, be found reducible to this single point: the total alienation of each associate, and all his rights, to the whole community; for, in the first place, as every individual gives himself up entirely, the condition of every person is alike; and being so, it would not be to the interest of any one to render that condition offensive to others.

Nay, more than this, the alienation being made without any reserve, the union is as complete as it can be, and no associate has any further claim to anything: for if any individual retained rights not enjoyed in general by all, as there would be no common superior to decide between him and the public, each person being in some points his own judge, would soon pretend to be so in everything; and thus would the state of nature be continued and the association necessarily become tyrannical or be annihilated.

Finally, each person gives himself to all, and so not to any one individual; and as there is no one associate over whom the same right is not acquired which is ceded to him by others, each gains an equivalent for what he loses, and finds his force increased for preserving that which he possesses.

If, therefore, we exclude from the social compact all that is not essential, we shall find it reduced to the following terms:

Each of us places in common his person and all his power under the supreme direction of the general will; and as one body we all receive each member as an indivisible part of the whole.

From that moment, instead of as many separate persons as there are contracting parties, this act of association produces a moral and collective body, composed of as many members as there are votes in the assembly, which from this act receives its unity, its common self, its life, and its will. This public person, which is thus formed by the union of all other persons, took formerly the name of "city," and now that of "republic" or "body politic." It is called by its members "State" when it is passive, "Sovereign" when in activity, and whenever it is compared with other bodies of a similar kind, it is denominated "power." The associates take collectively the name of "people," and separately, that of "citizens," as participating in the supreme authority, and of "subjects," because they are subjected to the laws of the State. But these terms are frequently confounded and used one for the other; and it is enough that a man understands how to distinguish them when they are employed in all their precision.

It appears from this formula that the act of association contains a reciprocal engagement between the public and individuals, and that each individual, contracting, as it were, with himself, is engaged under a double character; that is, as a member of the Sovereign engaging with individuals, and as a member of the State engaged with the Sovereign. But we cannot apply here the maxim of civil right, that no person is bound by any engagement which he makes with himself; for there is a material difference between an obligation to oneself individually, and an obligation to a collective body of which oneself constitutes a part.

It is necessary to observe here that public deliberation, which cannot bind all the subjects to the Sovereign, in consequence of the double character under which the members of that body appear, cannot, for the opposite reason, bind the Sovereign to itself; and consequently it is against the nature of the body politic for the sovereign power to impose on itself any law which it cannot break. . . .

Further, the Sovereign, being formed only of the individuals who compose it, neither has, nor can have, any interest contrary to theirs; consequently, the sovereign power need give no guarantee to its subjects, because it is impossible that the body should seek to injure all its members; and we shall see presently that it can do no injury to any individual in particular. The Sovereign, by its nature, is always everything it ought to be.

But this is not so with the relation of subjects towards the Sovereign, which, notwithstanding the common interest, has nothing to make them responsible for the performance of their engagements if some means is not found of ensuring their fidelity.

In fact, each individual may, as a man, have a private will, dissimilar or contrary to the general will which he has as a citizen. His own private interest may dictate to him very differently from the common interest; his absolute and naturally independent existence may make him regard what he owes to the common cause as a gratuitous contribution, the omission of which would be less injurious to others than the payment would be burdensome to himself; and considering the moral person which constitutes the State as a creature of the imagination, because it is not a man, he may wish to enjoy the rights of a citizen without being disposed to fulfil the duties of a subject. Such an injustice would in its progress cause the ruin of the body politic.

In order, therefore, to prevent the social compact from becoming an empty formula, it tacitly comprehends the engagement, which alone can give effect to the others—that whoever refuses to obey the general will shall be compelled to it by the whole body: this in fact only forces him to be free; for this is the condition which, by giving each citizen to his country, guarantees his absolute personal independence, a condition which gives motion and effect to the political machine. This alone renders all civil engagements justifiable, and without it they would be absurd, tyrannical, and subject to the most enormous abuses.

The passing from the state of nature to the civil state produces in man a very remarkable change, by substituting justice for instinct in his conduct, and giving to his actions a moral character which they lacked before. It is then only that the voice of duty succeeds to physical impulse, and a sense of what is right, to the incitements of appetite. Man, who had till then regarded none but himself, perceives that he must act on other principles, and learns to consult his reason before he listens to his inclinations. Although he is deprived in this new state of many advantages which he enjoyed from nature, he gains in return others so great, his faculties unfold themselves by being exercised, his ideas are so extended, his sentiments so exalted, and his whole mind so enlarged and refined, that if, by abusing his new condition, he did not sometimes degrade it even below that from which he emerged, he ought to bless continually the happy moment that snatched him forever from it, and transformed him from a circumscribed and stupid animal to an intelligent being and a man. . . .

The first and most important consequence of the principles already established is that the general will alone can direct the forces of the State agreeably to the end of its institution, which is the common good; for if the clashing of private interests has rendered the establishing of societies necessary, the agreement of the same interests has made such establishments possible. It is what is common in these different interests that forms the social bond; and if there was not some point in which they all unanimously centered, no society would exist. It is on the basis of this common interest alone that society must be governed.

I say, therefore, that sovereignty, being only the exercise of the general will, can never alienate itself, and that the Sovereign, which is only a collective being, cannot be represented but by itself: the *power* may well be transmitted but not the *will*. . . .

It follows from what has been said that the general will is always right and tends always to the public advantage; but it does not follow that the deliberations of the people have always the same rectitude. Our will always seeks our own good, but we do not always perceive what it is. The people are never corrupted, but they are often deceived, and only then do they seem to will what is bad.

There is frequently much difference between the *will of all* and the *general will*. The latter regards only the common interest; the former regards private interest, and is indeed but a sum of private wills: but remove from these same wills the pluses and minuses that cancel each other, and then the general will remains as the sum of the differences.

If, when the people, sufficiently informed, deliberated, there was to be no communication among them, from the grand total of trifling differences the general will would always result, and their resolutions be always good. But when cabals and partial associations are formed at the expense of the great association, the will of each such association, though *general* with regard to its members, is *private* with regard to the State: it can then be said no longer that there are as many voters as men, but only as many as there are associations. By this means the differences being less numerous, they produce a result less general. Finally, when one of these associations becomes so large that it prevails over all the rest, you have no longer the sum of many opinions dissenting in a small degree from each other, but one great dictating dissentient; from that moment there is no longer a general will, and the predominating opinion is only an individual one.

It is therefore of the utmost importance for obtaining the expression of the general will, that no partial society should be formed in the State, and that every citizen should speak his opinion entirely from himself. . . .

All the services which a citizen can render to the State ought to be rendered as soon as the Sovereign demands them; but the Sovereign cannot, on its side, impose any burden on the subject useless to the community; it cannot even have the inclination to do so; for, under the law of reason, nothing is done without a cause, any more than under the law of nature. . . .

By whatever path we return to our principle, we always arrive at the same conclusion—that is, that the social compact establishes among citizens such an equality that they are all engaged under the same conditions, and should all enjoy the same rights. Thus, by the nature of the compact all acts of sovereignty, that is to say, all authentic acts of the general will, oblige or favour all citizens alike in such a manner as evinces that the Sovereign knows no person but the body of the nation, and does not make any distinction among the individuals who compose it. What, therefore, is properly an act of sovereignty? It is not a convention between a superior and an inferior, but a convention of the body with each of its members—a justifiable convention because it has the social contract for its basis; equitable, because it is common to all; beneficial, because it can have no other object but the general good; and solid, because it is guaranteed by the public force and the supreme power. While subjects are under the governance of such conventions only, they obey no one but only their own will: and to enquire how far the respective rights of the Sovereign and citizens extend is to ask how far the citizens can engage with themselves, each towards all, and all towards each.

We see by this that the sovereign power, all absolute, all sacred, all inviolable as it is, neither will, nor can, exceed the bounds of general conventions, and that every man may fully dispose of what is left to him of his property and his liberty by these conventions; so that the Sovereign never has any right to lay a greater charge on one subject than on another, because then the affair would become personal, and in such cases the power of the Sovereign is no longer competent.

28 / CARON DE BEAUMARCHAIS: THE CONFLICT OF TALENT AND RANK

The Enlightenment spirit of dissatisfaction with the existing social order found expression not only in formal works of political and ethical theory but also in works of popular literature. Of these none is more characteristic, and none was more the rage at the time, than Beaumarchais' farcical comedy, Le Mariage de Figaro *("The Marriage of Figaro"), which was completed in 1778 but forbidden by the royal censorship until 1784, when it had its first performance. Pierre Augustin Caron de Beaumarchais (1732–1799) began his career as a clockmaker, his father's trade, but subsequently became a playwright and a financier. It was in this last capacity that he helped supply the American rebels against Great Britain with munitions in the period before France became their open ally. In the following scene from* The Marriage of Figaro, *the title character, a former barber who has become the valet of the Count of Almaviva, bewails the latter's apparent seduction of his bride, Susanna. The translation is from an adaptation for the contemporary English stage.*[14]

Manent Figaro *and* Doctor.

FIGARO. Oh Woman, Woman, Woman! Inconstant, weak, deceitful Woman!—But each Animal is obliged to follow the instinct of its Nature; and it is thine to betray!—What, after swearing this very Morning to remain for ever Faithful; and on the identical Day! The bridal Day!—

DOCTOR. Patience.

FIGARO. I even saw her laugh with Delight, while he read her Billet! —They think themselves secure, but perhaps they yet may be deceived. —No, my very worthy Lord and Master, you have not got her yet.— What! Because you are a great Man, you fancy yourself a Great Genius.

[14] Pierre Augustin Caron de Beaumarchais, *The Follies of a Day; or, The Marriage of Figaro,* translated from the French by Thomas Holcroft, new ed. (London: G. G. J. and J. Robinson, 1785), pp. 91–6.

—Which way?—How came you to be the rich and mighty Count Almaviva? Why truly, you gave yourself the Trouble to be born! While the
obscurity in which I have been cast demanded more Abilities to gain
a mere Subsistence that are requisite to govern Empires. And what,
most noble Count, are your Claims to Distinction, to pompous Titles,
and immense Wealth, of which you are so proud, and which, by Accident, you possess? For which of your Virtues? Your wisdom? Your
Generosity? Your Justice?—The Wisdom you have acquired consists
in vile Arts, to gratify vile Passions; your Generosity is lavished on your
hireling Instruments, but whose Necessities make them far less Contemptible than yourself; and your Justice is the inveterate Persecution
of those who have the Will and the Wit to resist your Depredations.
But this has ever been the Practice of the *little* Great; those they cannot degrade, they endeavour to crush.

DOCTOR. Be advised, Figaro—be calm—there has ever been a Respect
paid—

FIGARO. To Vice—where it is not due.—Shame light on them that pay
it.

DOCTOR. —Consider, he is—

FIGARO. A Lord—and I am—a Man!—Yes, I am a Man, but the noc-
turnal Spells of that enchantress Woman, soon shall make me a Monster. Why, what an Ass am I!—Acting here the idiot part of a (*Strikes
his forehead*)—a—*Husband*—Altho' I am but half finished. (*Agnes peeps
out of the Pavilion, and approaches a little way to listen.*)

AGNES. Is that Hannibal?

DOCTOR. I hear somebody! (*Agnes hears the voice of the Doctor, and
runs in again.*) I will retire, but if you are wise, you will wait the
Event patiently; your suspicions may be unjust,—should they prove
real, then shake her from you, as her Ingratitude deserves. (*Exit.*)

FIGARO. Oh, how easy it is for the prayer mumbling Priest to bid the
Wretch on the Rack suffer patiently. (*Figaro listens.*) I hear nothing—
all is silent—and dark as their designs. (*Figaro pulls off his Roquelaure,
and throws it on a Garden-bench.*) Why, what a Destiny is mine—Am
I for ever doom'd to be the foot-ball of Fortune?—Son of I knew not
who, stol'n I knew not how, and brought up to I knew not what, lying
and thieving excepted, I had the sense, tho' young, to despise a life so
base, and fled such infernal Tutors. My Genius, tho' cramp'd, could
not be totally subdued, and I spent what little time and money I could
spare in Books and Study. Alas! it was but time and money thrown
away. Desolate in the world, unfriended, unprotected, my poor stock
of knowledge not being whip'd into me by the masculine hic haec hoc
hand of a School-master, I could not get Bread, much less Preferment.
—Disheartened by the failure of all my projects, I yet had the audacity
to attempt a Comedy, but as I had the still greater audacity to attack

the favorite Vice of the favorite Mistress, of the favorite Footman of
the Favorite Minister, I could not get it licensed.—It happened about
that time, that the fashionable Question of the day was an enquiry
into the real and imaginary Wealth of Nations; and, as it is not necessary to possess the thing you write about, I, with lank Cheeks, penny-
less Purse, and all the simplicity of a Boy, or a Philosopher, freely
described the true causes of national Poverty: when suddenly I was
awaken'd in my bed at Mid-night, and entrusted to the tender care
of his Catholic Majesty's Mirmidons, whose Magic-power caused the
heavy gates of an old Castle to fly open at my approach, where I was
graciously received, lodged, and ornamented, according to the fashion
of the place, and provided with Straw, and Bread, and Water gratis.
My ardor for Liberty, sufficiently cool'd. I was once more turned adrift
in the wide World, with leave to provide Straw and Bread and Water
for myself.—On this my second birth, I found all Madrid in Raptures,
concerning a most generous Royal Edict, lately published, in favor of
the Liberty of the Press: and I soon learnt, that, provided I neither
spoke of the Wealth of Nations in my writings, nor of the Government, nor of Religion, nor of any Corporate-Companies, nor offended
the favorite Mistress of the Minister's Favorite Footman, nor said any
one thing which could be twisted into a reference, or hint, derogatory
to any one Individual, who had more powerful friends than I had, I
was at liberty to write, freely, all, and whatever I pleased, under the
inspection of some two or three Censors!—Soon after this, a Place happened to be vacant, which required a person well acquainted with
Calculation; I offered my Services; my Abilities were not questioned;
I waited, in anxious expectation of the Event, and, in three days, learnt
it had been bestowed, two days before, upon a Dancing-master.—Per-
secuted by Creditors, tired of starving, and unable, through the feeble-
ness of Youth to sustain so unequal a Struggle, I had the weakness,
at last, to sink before Temptation, and set up a Pharaoh Bank. And
now, for once, behold the Scene changed! See me equally familiar with
Lords as with their Lacquies! Every door was open to me! Every hand
held out! But, notwithstanding my desire to be Something in this world,
my detestation of the brazen Effrontery, profound Ignorance, and insupportable Insolence of these fashionable Friends of Nobility was
so innate that I found I could better endure all the Miseries of Poverty
than the Disgrace and Disgust of such Society.—Quitting, therefore,
with contempt this new Trade, and leaving false Shame behind me, as
a burthen too heavy for a Foot-passenger, I once more took up my
strap and hone, and travelled for employment from Town to Town.—
At Seville I found a Lord mad to marry his Mistress; my Wit procured
him what his could not, a Wife; and, in return, he gratefully endeavours
to Seduce mine—Strange concatenation of circumstance! My Parents

all at once claim me!—'Tis he, 'tis she, 'tis me, 'tis—I don't know who!—
I came into the world without my Knowledge, and I shall go out
without my Will; and thus do I continue to torment myself about this
Being of mine, without understanding what this Being is, what it was,
what it shall be, whence it came, where it is, or whither it shall go.—I
only know it to be a compound of Contradictions! A little, wise, foolish Animal, ardent in the pursuit of Pleasure, capricious through Vanity, laborious from Necessity, but indolent by Choice. After having
exhausted every Art for enjoyment, and every Profession for a livelihood, I found myself intoxicated by a heavenly Illusion, that has van-
ish'd at my approach!—Vanished!—And is it vanished?—Oh Susan!
Susan! (*Figaro sinks melancholy upon the garden-seat; but being suddenly roused by a noise, wraps himself up in his Rocquelaure.*)

29 / PETER GAY:
THE ENLIGHTENMENT—
A MODERN VIEW

*The essential character and significance of the Enlighten-
ment continue to be a subject of debate among historians. Some of
the most original and perceptive contributions to this debate have
come from an American historian, Peter Gay of Columbia University. Like so many of the thinkers about whom he writes, Gay
combines serious and subtle analysis with literary verve. The article from which the following selection is taken was based upon a
paper read before the American Historical Association in 1959.*[15]

The crisis of secularization . . . was slower and subtler than we have
been led to believe. It was also more pervasive. It was not confined
to educated Christians, tormented by the startling conclusions of physi-
cists. It was a problem for the *philosophes* themselves. It is not surprising that their anguish has received little attention—they covered it
well with urbanity and noisy anticlericalism.

But anguish there was. The *philosophes* had two enemies: the institutions of Christianity and the idea of hierarchy. And they had two

[15] Peter Gay, "The Unity of the French Enlightenment," *History* 3 (New York:
Meridian Books, The World Publishing Company, 1960), pp. 18–28. Reprinted
by permission of Peter Gay.

problems: God and the masses. Both the enemies and the problems were related and woven into the single task of rethinking their world. The old questions that Christianity had answered so fully for so many men and so many centuries, had to be asked anew: What, as Kant put it, What can I know? What ought I to do? What may I hope?

Science itself did not answer these questions. It only suggested—ever more insistently as the century went on—that the old answers were wrong. Now, the *philosophes* were products of Christian homes and Christian schools. If they became enemies of Christianity, they did so not from indifference or ignorance: they knew their Bible, their catechism, their Church Fathers, their apologetics. And they knew, because it had been drummed into them early, the fate that awaits heretics or atheists in the world to come. Their anticlerical humor therefore has the bitter intimacy of the family joke; to embrace materialism was an act of rejection.

The *philosophes'* crisis was a crisis of freedom. They did not fully understand it, but to the extent that they did understand it, they knew their situation to be filled with terror and delight. They felt the anxiety and exhilaration of the explorer who stands before the unknown.

To use such existentialist language may seem like rather a portentous way to describe men noted for their sociability and frivolity. It is of course true that the *philosophes* did not suffer alone: they had the comforting company of elegant salons and of respectable philosophical forebears.

Yet even the supple Voltaire, who had been initiated into unbelief by fashionable teachers, was not free from the symptoms of this crisis. Much of his mockery was a weapon in a grim fight, and a device to keep up his own morale. Much of his philosophical rumination on free will reveals the persistence of a troublesome inner struggle.

It may not be fair to call to witness Rousseau, whose malaise was perpetual. But the shape of his agony mirrors the agony of his century. Nothing is more pathetic than Rousseau's attempt to rescue at least some comforting aspects of his universe from the icy blasts of Voltaire's cosmic pessimism. "All the subtleties of metaphysics," he wrote Voltaire, seeking to answer the poem on the Lisbon earthquake, "will not make me doubt for a moment the immortality of the soul or a beneficent Providence. I feel it, I believe it, I want it, I hope for it, and I shall defend it to my last breath." But the edifice of Rousseau's faith was flimsily built on illogical hope: the immortality of the soul and a beneficent Providence are articles of faith to which a Christian happily subscribes, but to which the deist, nourished on scientific skepticism, has no right.

Diderot, the most ebullient of *philosophes,* the freest and most inventive of spirits, was driven from position to position and haunted by doubts. Born into a family richly endowed with priests, of pious parents and with a fanatical brother, long toying with entering the priesthood, Diderot moved from Catholicism to theism, from theism to deism, from deism to skepticism, and from skepticism to atheism. But atheism, with its cold determinism, repelled him even though he accepted it as true; while Catholicism, with its colorful ceremony, moved him even though he rejected it as false. Writing to his mistress, Sophie Volland, he cursed the philosophy—his own—that reduced their love to a blind encounter of atoms. "I am furious at being entangled in a confounded philosophy which my mind cannot refrain from approving and my heart from denying."

The materialists of course claimed to be defiantly happy at being cosmic orphans. But the question, If God is dead, what is permitted? was not a question calculated to make men sleep easy.

I am not simply arguing that the *philosophes* were less cheerful than they appeared in their social roles—most of us are. Nor that they suffered personal crises—philosophers, especially young philosophers, often do. I am arguing that the *philosophes'* anguish was related to the crisis in Christian civilization; that (to use different language) whatever childhood experience made them psychologically vulnerable in adult life, their obsessions, their self-questionings, their anxieties, were poured into their religious, moral, and political speculation.

But the *philosophes'* crisis was not only a crisis felt, it was also a crisis conquered. And this brings me back to the idea of work, and to the philosophy of energy.

There are several ways of dealing with a sense of helplessness. The *philosophes* might have given way to panic, despair, or paralyzing skepticism; they might have escaped from the terrifying spectacle of an empty universe by a doctrine of art for art's sake. Instead they overcame their anxiety by work. They escaped not from, but into reality.

The philosophy of energy was not a technical philosophical position, but a style of life. Whatever its form, it was confidence in the rational will, a humanist pride in man's possibilities tempered by an empiricist's humility before man's limitations. Men, Voltaire said, must dare to do more than they have done. "We do not want enough," he warned, and late in life he wrote to a friend, "We must battle nature and fortune until the last moment, and never despair of anything until we are good and dead."

Sometimes work was an escape. The drudgery of reading proofs on an *Encyclopédie* or of correcting a king's verses were bulwarks against uncertainty, loneliness, and *Weltschmerz*. "If I were by your side, I'd complain and you would comfort me; but you are absent, and work is the only means I have of diverting my thoughts from my sufferings."

Thus Diderot, depressed and alone in Paris, to his best friend Grimm. "To work and think of you, that's my life." Thus Voltaire, after his disastrous stay at the Prussian court, to his niece and mistress Madame Denis. Love and work: an energetic program to make an unpalatable world less unpalatable.

But work as consolation is only the most primitive level of the philosophy of energy. Its most familiar expression, which pervaded the *philosophes'* writings through the century, was the drive to assert man's power over the environment. Even the materialists, for all their determinism, taught the virtue of rational activity and the possibility of modifying nature.

Power over nature was more than a cliché: the *philosophes* knew precisely what they meant by it. They had learned it, partly from Bacon, partly (although rather less) from Descartes, and above all from the needs and possibilities of their time. Medieval man had not abjectly resigned himself to misery or pathetic dependence on divine intervention in his behalf. Yet even sympathetic historians have conceded that the Middle Ages were an age of precarious and violent existence. Men aged young and died young; those fortunate enough to survive infancy, epidemics, or famines, were likely victims of bandits, pirates, sudden war, or brutal migrations. "Beneath all social life," Marc Bloch writes, "there was a soil of primitivism, of submission to ungovernable powers."

To remedy this—to prolong life, clear the roads of assassins, keep men from starving, and give them hope of enjoying the fruits of their labors—required more than a stable political organization. It required a spiritual revolution, and the culmination of that revolution was the philosophy of the *philosophes*.

But words alone did not eliminate illness, starvation, or insecurity, scourges that continued to haunt the world of Bacon and even the world of Voltaire. French civilization of the eighteenth century still wore a half-finished look. Polish was bright, because it was new; the decline of religious fervor did not prevent occasional terrifying outbursts of hysteria, the advances of education did not eliminate brutal games, sadistic sports, or cruel riots.

The survival of coarseness was related to the continuing ravages of diseases and the pressures of hunger: the uncertainty of life did not allow the generous grace of conduct that comes with true ease. The fate of the royal family—the death in rapid succession of the only son and two of the grandsons of Louis XIV—dramatically underlined the general precariousness. At the age of forty-six, Diderot, on a visit to his native town, found most of his schoolmates gone, and mused darkly on the brevity of life.

Yet the *philosophes'* attitude to the blows of fate was one of defiance, not resignation. While deists continued to protest that the Lord gave, they saw no reason why they might not enjoy what he had given, and why they might not try to keep it as long as possible. In the Middle Ages, the accidents of nature had dominated man; in the eighteenth century, to use Diderot's phrase, men were seizing nature and tormenting her. Scientists were beginning to force from her reluctant lips the secrets of her operations.

Evidence for this sense of mastery is everywhere. It is in medicine, which had a place of honor among the *philosophes*. Some of them were physicians, others took an abiding interest in what La Mettrie, himself a doctor, praised as the supreme art of healing. It is, too, in Diderot's *Encyclopédie*. Its alphabetical arrangement vividly emphasizes its single-minded purpose. The anticlerical articles are not just playful bait to make the reader tolerate dull pieces on crafts; the articles on crafts are not just padding for daring heresies. Both fulfill one task: to reinterpret the world and by reinterpreting it, to change it. In a phrase which has become too familiar to have retained its original impact, Diderot said that he wanted his *Encyclopédie* to "change the general way of thinking."

The *philosophes*, men with a single career which took a variety of forms, also had a single task which took a variety of expressions. The philosophy of energy is the glass that collects all their activities in a single focus. Diderot spoke for them all: "Everything belongs together in the human understanding; the obscurity of one idea spreads over those that surround it. An error throws shadows over neighboring truths, and if it happens that there should be in society men interested in forming, as it were, centers of shadow, soon the people will find itself plunged into a profound darkness." The spreading of light operates by the same Keynesian multiplier: the *philosophes'* propaganda campaign, from the bulky *Encyclopédie* to the sprightly *Dictionnaire philosophique,* is a series of lamps from which others will find illumination and spread the light in their turn.

The *philosophes'* task cannot therefore be contained in the word "humanitarianism." It was greater than that: the campaign to abolish torture cannot be divorced from the campaign to abolish Jesuits or to spread technological knowledge—all are part of imposing man's rational will on the environment. Nor was it simply the acquisition of knowledge. As good Baconians, the *philosophes* preached that knowledge is power, but few of them were naïve enough to believe that knowledge automatically creates virtue: their writings are filled with warnings against the misuse of intelligence or the brutalizing of learning. They did argue that since knowledge is power, ignorance is impotence. It followed that the men who wanted to keep others in ignorance were enemies of humanity. What does one do with monsters who want to castrate mankind? All—or almost all—methods are fair against them.

The philosophers of energy face to face with their enemies: this confrontation leads us back to the beginning, for it helps to solve the puzzling contradictions that beset the interpreter of the Enlightenment. The French Enlightenment had its own history, and that history mirrors, and helped to shape, the history of the century. Something happened in Europe in the 1760's. It was the beginning of industrial society; the beginning of modern politics and the great democratic revolt against aristocratic regimes. It was a time of turmoil within the Christian world itself: witness the suppression of the Jesuits, and the outbursts of hysterical prosecutions of Huguenots and blasphemers.

In this time of trouble, the *philosophes* added to their sense of power over the environment a sense of mission. The moderate anticlericalism of a Montesquieu gave way to the belligerent cry, *Écrasez l'infâme;* democratic political ideas found a favorable hearing even from the skeptic Voltaire. The *philosophes* grew more radical, more combative, more convinced than ever that they were the prophets of a new age that would rise on the ruins of the old.

As they became more violently partisan, the contradictions in their views became more obvious. As a historian, Voltaire delighted in the past for its own sake; as an aesthetician, Diderot delighted in the play of light and shade on canvas. But as prophets, both found it necessary to import moral lessons into all their writings. If the old civilization must give way to the new, if men must learn to dare and to rely on themselves, if even the uneducated are to find their place in this revolution, then *philosophes* must teach, and teach again, and teach everywhere. Cultivated men possessed by a sense of mission temper their cultivation for the sake of their mission. This will lead to inconsistencies. But these inconsistencies do not destroy, indeed they express, the richness and the unity of the French Enlightenment.

30 / L. B. NAMIER:
KING AND PARTY
IN ENGLAND

The model country politically in the view of most philosophes was England, but often such thinkers as Montesquieu and Voltaire were describing Locke's theories rather than contemporary practice. Historical study of the British political system in the eighteenth century has been transformed by the work of a recent English historian, Sir Lewis Namier. His method consisted fundamentally in examining what the English politicians did and wrote rather than what others wrote about them. Namier (1888–1960) was professor of history at Manchester and London Universities. His ideas on the British monarchy and party system during the reign of George III are summarized in the Romanes Lecture which he delivered at Oxford in 1952. The following selections are taken from this lecture.[16]

According to contemporaries the complex system of the "mixed form of government" combined "by a skillful division of power" the best of monarchy, aristocracy, and democracy; and it was viewed by them with pride and satisfaction. Mechanically minded and with a bent towards the ingenious, they relished its "checks and controls," and the "mutual watchfulness and jealousy" which its delicate balance demanded from all concerned; and they cherished a constitution which safeguarded their rights and freedoms when "in almost every other nation of Europe" public liberty was "extremely upon the decline." George III, that much maligned monarch, was truly representative when, abhorring both "despotism" and "anarchy," he extolled "the beauty, excellence, and perfection of the British constitution as by law established." What was bound to escape contemporaries was the insoluble contradiction of a political system which, incongruously, associated a royal executive with parliamentary struggles for office. Yet the two had to coexist in an organic transition from royal to parliamentary government.

A parliamentary régime is based on the unhindered alternating of party-governments. But while contending party leaders can in turn fill the office of prime minister, how could the king freely pass from the one side to the other, and in turn captain opposite teams? It was far more consonant with his position to try to heal "the unhappy divisions that subsist between men" and form an administration from "the best of all parties" than to quit "one set of men for another." Could he give up with unconcern the ministers whom he had chosen and upheld, and in whose actions and policy he had participated? In 1779 it was but natural for him to stipulate that on a change of government past measures should "be treated with proper respect" and that "no blame

[16] Lewis B. Namier, *Monarchy and the Party System* (Oxford: The Clarendon Press, 1952), pp. 9–13, 24–30. Reprinted by permission of The Clarendon Press.

be laid" on them. And here is a naive but sincere statement of his position: "I have no wish but for the prosperity of my Dominions therefore must look on all who will not heartily assist me as bad men as well as ungrateful subjects." And on another occasion: ". . . whilst I have no wish but for the good and prosperity of my country, it is impossible that the nation shall not stand by me; if they will not, they shall have another King." He did not think in terms of parties: but their existence prevented the king, while he remained the actual head of the executive, from leading an undivided nation.

Yet it was impossible to eliminate party from parliament: an assembly whose leaders contend for office and power was bound to split into factions divided by personal animosities and trying to preserve their identity and coherence in and out of office. Consequently when in office they laid themselves open to the accusation of monopolizing power and of "keeping the King in fetters"; in opposition, of distressing the government with intention to "storm the Closet" and force themselves, unconstitutionally, on the king. No consistent defence of parties was possible under the "mixed form of government," and this undoubtedly retarded their development and consolidation. . . . Parliamentary struggles for office necessarily produce a dichotomy of "ins" and "outs"; and two party-names were current since the last quarter of the seventeenth century: hence in retrospect the appearances of a two-party system. In reality three broad divisions, based on type and not on party, can be distinguished in the eighteenth-century House of Commons: on the one side were the followers of Court and Administration, the "placemen," *par excellence* a group of permanent "ins"; on the opposite side, the independent country gentlemen, of their own choice permanent "outs"; and in between, occupying as it were the centre of the arena, and focusing upon themselves the attention of the public and of history, stood the political factions contending for power, the forerunners of parliamentary government based on a party-system. Though distinct, these groups were not sharply separated: wide borderlands intervened between them, in which heterogeneous types moved to and fro.

The Court and Administration party was a composite, differentiated body; but common to them all was a basic readiness to support any minister of the king's choice: even in their parliamentary capacity they professed direct political allegiance to the Crown, either on a traditional semi-feudal, or on a timeless civil-service basis, or merely as recipients, in one form on another, of the king's bounty; and adherence to the king's government, so long as compatible with conscience, was far more consonant with the avowed decencies of eighteenth-century politics than "formed opposition." A second, concomitant, characteristic of the group was that whether they were great noblemen, or minor ministers of an administrative type, or hard-working officials, or political parasites, they tried through a direct nexus with the Crown to secure permanency of employment: wherein they were, by and large, successful. A third common feature, induced by natural selection and inherent in the character of the group, was that its members did not play for the highest political prizes: peers of the first rank and great wealth and desirous of making a figure in the country, or great orators or statesmen in either House, would well-nigh automatically move into the centre of the arena and take their place among the leaders of political factions. . . .

Whig and Tory were "denominations"—names and creeds—which covered enduring types moulded by deeply ingrained differences in temperament and outlook. But when was a clear party division covered by them? Even before 1714 some scholars now discern merely a number of groups and connexions of a Tory or a Whig hue, or of uncertain colouring; for hardly ever was there anything like straight party voting. About the middle of the century the names were deprecated, described as outworn and meaningless, and yet they were used; for names there must be in a political dichotomy, even if their meaning is uncertain and their use misleading. In parliament even under the first two Georges disaffected Whigs supplied the most inveterate leaders of the Opposition and most of its voting strength. But in a good many constituencies the names of Whig and Tory still correspond to real divisions: partly perhaps because local factions could hardly have been denoted as "Government" and "Opposition," and partly because the most enduring distinction between Tory and Whig—High Church *versus* Low Church and Dissent—retained more vitality and significance in local struggles than at Westminster.

A ruling group will always try to place its opponents under a ban, and the natural consequence of the practice of Walpole and the Pelhams was that anyone who wished to play at politics and for office, adopted the name of Whig: the Finches, Seymours, Legges, Leveson-Gowers, Wyndhams, Foxes, &c. In fact by 1750 everyone at Court, in office, and in the centre arena was a Whig, while the name of Tories, by a process of natural selection, was left to the residuum who did not enter politics in pursuit of office, honours, or profits, that is, to the country gentlemen and to the forerunners of urban radicals. . . .

Who were now the "Tories"? The younger Pitt never used the name and after his death his successors went merely by that of "Mr. Pitt's friends" (apparently George Canning was the only one who occasionally called himself a "Tory"). . . . In short: here is once more the basic structure of eighteenth-century parliamentary politics, with increased regard for the country gentlemen but no trace of a two-party system, or at all of party in the modern sense; and the group which in 1760 went by the name of Tories, a generation later is referred to simply as "independent country gentlemen," the name of Tory being practically in abeyance. It is the history of those party-names, and how they were applied, which calls for careful study free of confusion between names and realities, or rather between the differing realities which the same names were made to cover; and next the history must be traced of party realities as shaped by interaction between the constituencies and the House of Commons. Nineteenth-century parliamentary historians now seem agreed in deferring the full emergence of the modern party till after the Second Reform Bill: what preceded it were intermediary forms which should not be treated anachronistically in terms of a later age.

With regard to the second half of the eighteenth century, the idea of party conducive to parliamentary government is usually linked up with the Whigs; which, for what it is worth, is a matter of nomenclature rather than of ideology: the politicians, and not the Court group or the independent country gentlemen, were the party-forming element, and the politicians called themselves Whigs. But among the politicians the attitude to sovereign and party did not depend on the degree of their Whiggery: those who enjoyed the favour of the Crown, and coalesced with the Court party, were naturally less of a party-forming element than those in disfavour, or uncertain of royal support, who had therefore to rely primarily on parliament and seek to form their following into a coherent party. . . .

Ideas and a political practice are things of slow growth; parliamentary government, wise as it is as a system, was not born like Pallas Athene.

To sum up: Parliamentary government based on the party-system, is not an ingenious device, the product of creative thought, for which credit is due to one set of men, while another is to be blamed for lack of foresight or virtue in not anticipating it. Its bases are deep down in the political structure of the nation, which was being gradually transformed during the period of so-called mixed government. An electorate thinking in terms of nation-wide parties is its indispensable basis; and it is therefore at least as much in the constituencies as in parliament that the growth of these parties will have to be traced. In the eighteenth century parliament was without that background of enfranchised masses thinking in terms of party; it was to a high degree a closed arena, with its own life and divisions, still dominated by Court and Country on the periphery, but containing the forerunners of political parties in the centre. To clear up these antecedents must be the contribution of us, eighteenth century historians, to the essential work on the least explored period of British constitutional history, the nineteenth century, now started by a group of keen, able, and what is important, mostly young historians.

31 / SIR WILLIAM KEITH: THE OLD COLONIAL SYSTEM

From the beginning of their colonial expansion, the European states had emphasized the economic and strategic advantages which they sought in overseas possessions. During the eighteenth century Great Britain began to face a new problem—rivalry not just with other European powers, but with the "colonials" themselves, that is, the European settlers in the "plantations" of North America. The difficulties faced by the British government and the fundamental policy which it followed for most of the period are set forth by Sir William Keith in his Short Discourse on the Present State of the Colonies in America, With Respect to the Interest of Great Britain, *which was presented to King George II in 1728. Keith (c.1669–1749), baronet of Ludquhairn, was governor of Pennsylvania from 1712 to 1726 and wrote an important* History of the British Plantations in America *(1738). The present excerpt from the* Short Discourse *is taken from a collection of Keith's writings published in 1740.*[17]

When either by Conquest or Increase of People, foreign Provinces are possessed, and Colonies planted abroad, it is convenient, and often necessary, to substitute little dependant provincial Governments, whose People being infranchized, and made Partakers of the Liberties and Privileges belonging to the original Mother State, are justly bound by its Laws, and become subservient to its Interests, as the true End of their Incorporation.

Every Act of a dependant Provincial Government therefore ought to terminate in the Advantage of the Mother State, unto whom it owes its Being, and by whom it is protected in all its valuable Privileges: Hence it follows, that all advantageous Projects, or commercial Gains in any Colony, which are truly prejudicial to, and inconsistent with

[17] Sir William Keith, *A Collection of Papers and other Tracts, Written occasionally on Various Subjects* (London: J. Mechell, 1740), pp. 169–75.

the Interest of the Mother State, must be understood to be illegal, and the Practice of them unwarrantable, because they contradict the End for which the Colony had a Being, and are incompatible with the Terms on which the People claim both Privilege and Protection.

Were these Things rightly understood among the Inhabitants of the *British* Colonies in *America,* there would be less Occasion for such Instructions and strict Prohibitions as are daily sent from *England* to regulate their Conduct in many Points; the very Nature of the Thing would be sufficient to direct their Choice in cultivating such Parts of Industry and Commerce only, as would bring some Advantage to the Interest and Trade of *Great Britain.* They would soon find by Experience, that this was the solid and true Foundation whereon to build a real Interest in their Mother Country, and the certain Means of acquiring Riches without Envy.

On the other hand, where the Government of a Provincial Colony is well regulated, and all its Business and Commerce truly adapted to the proper End and Design of the first Settlement, such a Province, like a choice Branch springing from the main Root, ought to be carefully nourished, and its just Interests well guarded. No little partial Project, or Party Gain, should be suffered to affect it; but rather it ought to be considered, and weighed in the general Ballance of the whole State, as an useful and profitable Member, for such is the End of all Colonies; and if this Use cannot be made of them, it would be much better for the State to be without them.

It has ever been the Maxim of all polite Nations, to regulate their Government to the best Advantage of their trading Interest: wherefore it may be helpful to take a short View of the principal Benefits arising to *Great Britain* from the Trade of the Colonies.

1. The Colonies take off and consume above one sixth Part of the Woollen Manufactures exported from *Britain,* which is the chief Staple of *England,* and main support of the landed Interest.

2. They take off and consume more than double that Value in Linen and Callicoes, which is either the Product of *Britain* and *Ireland,* or partly the profitable Returns made for that Product carried to foreign Countries.

3. The Luxury of the Colonies, which increases daily, consumes great Quantities of *English* manufactured Silk, Haberdashery, Houshold Furniture, and Trinkets of all Sorts; also a very considerable Value in *East-India* Goods.

4. A great Revenue is raised to the Crown of *Britain* by Returns made in the Produce of the Plantations, especially in Tobacco, which at the same time helps England to bring nearer to a Ballance their unprofitable Trade with *France.*

5. Those Colonies promote the Interest and Trade of *Britain,* by a

vast Increase of Shipping and Seamen, which enables them to carry great Quantities of Fish to *Spain, Portugal, Leghorn, &c.* Furs, Logwood, and Rice to *Holland*, whereby they help *Great Britain* considerably in the Ballance of Trade with those Countries.

6. If reasonably encouraged, the Colonies are now in a Condition to furnish *Britain* with as much of the following Commodities as it can demand, *viz.* Masting for the Navy, and all Sorts of Timber, Hemp, Flax, Pitch, Tar, Oil, Rosin, Copper Oar, with Pig and Bar Iron, by Means whereof the Ballance of Trade to *Russia* and the *Baltick* may be very much reduced in favour of *Great Britain.*

7. The Profits arising to all those Colonies by Trade is return'd in Bullion or other useful Effects to *Great Britain*, where the superfluous Cash, and other riches acquired in *America* must center, which is not one of the least Securities that *Britain* has to keep the Colonies always in due Subjection.

8. The Colonies upon the Main are the Granaries of *America*, and a necessary Support to the Sugar Plantations in the *West-Indies*, which could not subsist without them.

By this short View of Trade in general we may plainly understand, that those Colonies can be very beneficially employed both for *Great Britain* and themselves, without interfering with any of the staple Manufactures in *England;* and considering the Bulk and End of their whole Traffick, it were Pity that any material Branch of it should be depress'd, on Account of private and particular Interests, which, in Comparison with these, cannot justly be esteem'd a national Concern; for if the Trade of the Colonies be regulated to the Advantage of *Britain*, there is nothing more certain, than that the Discouragement of any material Branch for the sake of any Company, or private Interest, would be a Loss to the Nation. But in order to set this Point yet in a clearer Light, we will proceed to consider some of the most obvious Regulations on the *American* Trade, for rendering the Colonies truly serviceable to *Great Britain.*

1. That all the Product of the Colonies, for which the Manufacture and Trade of *Britain* has a constant Demand, be enumerated among the Goods which by Law must be first transported to *Britain*, before they can be carried to any other Market.

2. That every valuable Merchandize to be found in the *English Colonies*, and but rarely any where else, and for which there is a constant Demand in *Europe*, shall also be enumerated, in order to assist *Great Britain* in the Ballance of Trade with other Countries.

3. That all Kinds of Woollen Manufactures for which the Colonies have a Demand, shall continue to be brought from *Britain* only, and Linens from *Great Britain* and *Ireland.*

4. All other *European* Commodities to be carried to the Colonies,

(Salt excepted) Entry thereof to be first made in *Britain,* before they can be transported to any of the *English* Colonies.

5. The Colonies to be absolutely restrained in their several Governments from laying any Manner of Duties on Shipping or Trade from *Europe,* or upon *European* Good transported from one Colony to another.

6. That the Acts of Parliament relating to the Trade and Government of the Colonies, be revised and collected into one distinct Body of Laws, for the Use of the Plantations, and such as Trade with them.

Supposing these Things to be done, it will evidently follow, that the more extensive the Trade of the Colonies is, the greater will be the Advantages accruing to *Great Britain* therefrom; and consequently, that the Enlargement of the Colonies, and the Increase of their People, would still be an Addition to the national Strength. All smaller Improvements therefore pretended unto, and set up by lesser Societies for private Gain in *Great Britain,* or elsewhere, although they might have a just Pretence to bring some Sort of a publick Benefit along with them, yet if they shall appear to be more hurtful unto the much greater, and more national Concern of those useful trading Colonies, they ought in Justice to the Publick to be neglected in Favour of them; it being an unalterable Maxim, that a lesser publick Good must give place to a greater; and that it is of more Moment to maintain a greater, than a lesser Number of Subjects well employed to the Advantage of the State.

From what has been said of the Nature of Colonies, and the Restriction that ought to be laid on their Trade, it is plain that none of the *English* Plantations in *America* can with any Reason or good Sense pretend to claim an absolute legislative Power within themselves; so that let their several Constitutions be founded by antient Charters, Royal Patents, Customs by Prescription, or what other legal Authority you please; yet still they cannot be possessed of any rightful Capacity to contradict, or evade the true Intent and Force of any Act of Parliament, wherewith the Wisdom of *Great Britain* may think fit to affect them from Time to Time. In discoursing therefore on their legislative Powers, improperly so called, we are to consider them only as so many Incorporations at a Distance, invested with an Ability of making temporary By-Laws for themselves, agreeable to their respective Situations and Climates, but no ways interfering with the legal Prerogative of the Crown, or the true legislative Power of the Mother State.

32 / ABBÉ RAYNAL: SLAVERY DENOUNCED

One of the striking aspects of European colonial history was the criticism which arose in European society against the employment of Negro slave labor in the American colonies. Slavery itself was no novelty either in Africa, whence the slaves were imported, or in most other parts of the world, although it had become almost extinct in Europe. The assault upon this institution during the eighteenth century came more from the circles of the Enlightenment than from religious groups. Outstanding among the antislavery works was Guillaume Thomas François Raynal's Histoire philosophique et politique des établissements et du commerce des Européens dans les deux Indes *("Philosophical and Political History of the Settlements and Trade of the Europeans in the East and West Indies," 1770), from which the following selections are taken. Raynal (1713–1796) was usually called Abbé (Abbot) Raynal, in recognition of his early career as a Roman Catholic priest, but he was defrocked for his open hostility to the Church's doctrines and practices.*[18]

We will not here so far debase ourselves as to enlarge the ignominious list of those writers who devote their abilities to justify by policy what morality condemns. In an age where so many errors are boldly laid open, it would be unpardonable to conceal any truth that is of importance to humanity. If whatever we have hitherto advanced hath seemingly tended only to alleviate the burden of slavery, the reason is, that it was first necessary to give some comfort to those unhappy beings, whom we cannot set free, and convince their oppressors that they are cruel to the prejudice of their real interests. But, in the mean time, until some considerable revolution shall make the evidence of this great truth felt, it may not be improper to pursue this subject further. We shall then first prove, that there is no reason of state that can authorise slavery. We shall not be afraid to cite to the

[18] Abbé Guillaume Thomas François Raynal, *A Philosophical and Political History of the Settlements and Trade of the Europeans in the East and West Indies,* translated by J. Justamond (with corrections by the editor), 3rd edition (London: T. Cadell, 1777), Vol. III, pp. 424–30, 433–7.

tribunal of reason and justice those governments which tolerate this cruelty, or which even are not ashamed to make it the basis of their power. . . .

Will it be said, that he who wants to make me a slave does me no injury, but that he only makes use of his rights? Where are those rights? Who hath stamped upon them so sacred a character as to silence mine? From nature I hold the right of self-defence; nature, therefore, has not given another the right of attacking me. If thou thinkest thyself authorised to oppress me, because thou are stronger and more ingenious than I am; do not complain if my vigorous arm shall plunge a dagger into thy breast; do not complain, when in thy tortured entrails thou shalt feel the pangs of death conveyed by poison into thy food: I am stronger and more ingenious than thou: fall a victim, therefore, in thy turn; and expiate the crime of having been an oppressor.

He who supports the system of slavery is the enemy of the whole human race. He divides it into two societies of legal assassins: the oppressors and the oppressed. It is the same thing as proclaiming to the world, if you would preserve your life, instantly take away mine, for I want to have yours.

But the right of slavery, you say, extends only to the right of labour and the privation of liberty, not of life. What! does not the master, who disposes of my strength at his pleasure, likewise dispose of my life, which depends on the voluntary and proper use of my faculties? What is existence to him, who has not the disposal of it? I cannot kill my slave; but I can make him bleed upon the whip of an executioner; I can overwhelm him with sorrows, drudgery and want, I can injure him every way, and secretly undermine the principles and springs of his life; I can smother by slow punishments the wretched infant which a negro woman carries in her womb. Thus the laws protect the slave against a violent death, only to leave to my cruelty the right of making him die by degrees.

Let us proceed a step further: the right of slavery is that of perpetrating all sorts of crimes: those crimes which invade property, for slaves are not suffered to have any even in their own persons: those crimes which destroy personal safety; for the slave may be sacrificed to the caprice of his master: those crimes which make modesty shudder. —My blood rises at these horrid images. I detest, I abhor the human species, made up only of victims and executioners, and if it is never to become better, may it be annihilated! . . .

The subject of an absolute prince is the same as the slave in a state repugnant to nature. Everything that contributes to keep a man in such a state is an attempt against his person. Every power of obedience; his neighbour, who set him the example of it; his enemies: and all those who are about him are the authors or abettors of this violence.

His mother, who taught him the first lessons of obedience; his neighbour, who set him the example of it; his superiors who compelled him into this state; and his equals, who led him into it by their opinion: all these are the ministers and instruments of tyranny. The tyrant can do nothing of himself; he is only the first mover of those efforts which all his subjects exert to their own mutual oppression. He keeps them in a state of perpetual war, which renders robberies, treasons, assassinations lawful. Thus, like the blood which flows in his veins, all crimes originate from his heart, and return thither as to their primary source. Caligula used to say, that if the whole human race had but one head, he should have taken pleasure in cutting it off. Socrates would have said, that if all the crimes were heaped upon one head, that should be the one which ought to be struck off.

Let us, therefore, endeavour to make the light of reason and the sentiments of nature take place of the blind ferocity of our ancestors. Let us break the bonds of so many victims to our mercenary principles, should we even be obliged to discard a commerce which is founded only on injustice, and whose object is luxury.

But even this is not necessary. There is no occasion to give up those conveniences which custom hath so much endeared to us. We may draw them from our colonies, without peopling them with slaves. These crops may be cultivated by the hands of freemen, and then be reaped without remorse. . . .

At the time that we gradually confer liberty on these unhappy beings as a reward for their œconomy, their good behaviour, and their industry, we must be careful to subject them to our laws and manners, and to offer them our superfluities. We must give them a country, give them interests to study, crops to cultivate, and an object adequate to their particular tastes, and our colonies will never want hands, which being eased of their chains, will be more active and robust.

In order to overturn the whole system of slavery, which is supported by passions so universal, by laws so authentic, by the emulation of such powerful nations, by prejudices still more powerful, to what tribunal shall we refer the cause of humanity, which so many men are in confederacy to betray? Sovereigns of the earth, you alone can bring about this revolution. If you do not sport with the rest of mortals, if you do not regard the power of kings as the right of a successful plunder, and the obedience of subjects as artfully obtained from their ignorance, reflect on your own obligations. Refuse the sanction of your authority to the infamous and criminal traffic of men turned into so many herds of cattle, and this trade will cease. For once unite for the happiness of the world, those powers and designs which have been so often exerted for its ruin. If some one among you would venture to found the expectation of his opulence and grandeur on the generosity of all the rest, he instantly becomes an enemy of mankind, who ought to be destroyed. You may carry fire and sword into his territories. Your armies will soon be inspired with the sacred enthusiasm of humanity. You will then perceive what difference virtue makes between men who succour the oppressed, and mercenaries who serve tyrants.

But what am I saying? Let the ineffectual calls of humanity be no longer pleaded with the people and their masters: perhaps, they have never been attended to in any public transactions. If then, ye nations of Europe, interest alone can exert its influence over you, listen to me once more. Your slaves stand in no need either of your generosity or your counsels, in order to break the sacrilegious yoke of their oppression. Nature speaks a more powerful language than philosophy, or interest. Some white people already massacred, have expiated a part of our crimes; already have two colonies of fugitive negroes been established, to whom treaties and power give a perfect security from your attacks. Poison hath at different times been the instrument of their vengeance. Several have eluded your oppression by suicide. These enterprises are so many indications of the impending storm, and the negroes only lack a chief, sufficiently courageous, to lead them to vengeance and slaughter.

Where is the great man to be found, whom nature, perhaps, owes to the honour of the human species? Where is this new Spartacus, who will not find a Crassus? Then will the *black code* be no more; and the *white code* will be a dreadful one, if the conqueror only takes heed of the right of reprisal.

Till this revolution takes place, the negroes groan under the yoke of oppression, the description of which cannot but involve us more and more in their destiny.

33 / FRANÇOIS QUESNAY: ECONOMIC REFORM FOR A COUNTRY OF FARMERS

François Quesnay (1694–1774), founder of the school of Physiocrats, was trained as a physician and served as surgeon to Louis XV. His articles on economics contributed to the Encyclopédie *expounded a theory of economic analysis and proposed re-*

forms which were later expanded in the Tableau économique, *a mathematical model of the operation of a national economy. As an economic theory, physiocracy stressed the central importance of agriculture, considered to be the only true producer of new wealth. Politically, it combined support of the monarch as the sole sovereign with a program of reforms that undermined the traditional structure of royal government and French society. The reforms proposed by the Physiocrats are succinctly outlined in Quesnay's* General Maxims, *published as an appendix to the first edition of his* Tableau économique, *printed at Versailles in December, 1758.*[19]

MAXIM I

That sovereign authority is unique and placed above every individual in society and above all unfair undertakings by selfish persons; the purpose of ruling and obeying is to make everyone safe and provide for everyone's legitimate interests. The theory of government by means of countervailing forces is harmful; it displays only discord among the strong and despondency among the weak. The division of society into different orders of citizens, some exercising sovereign authority over others, destroys the general interest of the nation and introduces dissension of special interests among the different classes of citizens. This is a division which inverts the order of government in an agricultural kingdom, which should bring together all interests in a supreme purpose—the prosperity of agriculture—which is the source of the whole wealth of the State and of each of its citizens.

II

That the nation should be taught the general laws of the natural order, which constitute that form of government which is plainly most perfect. The study of man-made laws is not enough to train statesmen; those whose aim is a post in government must be required to study the natural order, which is of greatest profit to men combined in society. It is also necessary that the practical, informational knowledge which a nation acquires through experience and reflection be brought together with the general science of government, so that the sovereign authority, always guided by facts, may introduce the best of laws and

---

[19] François Quesnay, "Maximes générales du gouvernement économique d'un royaume agricole," in Auguste Oncken, ed., *Œuvres économiques et philosophiques de F. Quesnay, fondateur du système physiocratique* (Frankfurt: Joseph Baer; Paris: Jules Peelman, 1888), pp. 329–337. Translated by Herbert H. Rowen.

enforce them strictly, in order to make everyone safe and to achieve the greatest possible prosperity for society.

III

That the sovereign and the nation should never lose from sight the fact that the land is the only source of wealth, which is multiplied only by agriculture. For the increase of wealth makes the growth of population certain; men and wealth make agriculture prosper, extend trade, enliven industry and cause wealth to increase and become permanent. Wealth is the permanent foundation upon which the success of every part of the government of the kingdom depends.

IV

That the ownership of real estate and chattels should be assured to those who are their rightful possessors; for THE SAFETY OF PROPERTY IS THE ESSENTIAL FOUNDATION OF THE ECONOMIC ORDER OF SOCIETY. Unless the right of property is made secure, the country will remain a wasteland. There will be neither landowners nor tenants to make the necessary outlays for developing land and bringing it into cultivation, if those who make these expenditures are not safeguarded in their capital and their earnings. It is the safety of permanent possession which spurs labor and the use of wealth for the improvement and cultivation of land and commercial and industrial enterprises. It is only the sovereign power which can safeguard the property of subjects and which has a primary right in the distribution of the fruits of the soil, the only source of wealth.

V

That taxes should be neither destructive nor out of proportion to the total income of the nation; that an increase in taxes should come after an increase in incomes; that they should be collected directly from the net product of real estate, and not from men's wages, nor from commodities, which would multiply the cost of collection, damage trade, and annually destroy a portion of the nation's wealth. Nor should taxes be collected directly from the wealth of the tenants of landed property; for THE PROGRESS MADE BY AGRICULTURE IN A KINGDOM SHOULD BE CONSIDERED AS A KIND OF VALUABLE REAL ESTATE WHICH MUST BE PROTECTED IN ORDER TO PROVIDE TAXES, INCOME, AND SUBSISTENCE FOR ALL CLASSES OF CITIZENS: otherwise taxes would be degraded into a form of robbery and cause a decline from which the ruin of the State would soon result.

VI

That farmers' earnings should be sufficient to provide for annual investment in the cultivation of the land and hence to produce the largest product possible; for if the profits are not large enough, the expenses of cultivation are proportionally greater and result in a smaller net product.

VII

That the total national income should go back into circulation every year and be employed throughout the country; that no one should build up a monetary fortune, or at least that there should be a balance between such fortunes and the return of money to circulation; for otherwise the formation of such fortunes would halt the distribution of a portion of the annual national income and retard the savings of the kingdom, to the detriment of farmers' earnings, payment of workmen's wages, and the necessary consumption by the various classes of men engaged in gainful professions. This interception of savings would slow renewal of income and taxes.

VIII

That an economical government should devote itself only to encouraging productive investment and trade in foodstuffs grown within the country, and that it should refrain from unproductive expenditures.

IX

That a nation with a large quantity of farmland and the means for engaging in large-scale trade in foodstuffs grown within the country, should not employ too much money and too many persons in the manufacture and sale of luxury goods, to the detriment of labor and investment in agriculture; for THE KINGDOM SHOULD POSSSESS A NUMEROUS POPULATION OF WEALTHY FARMERS in preference to everything else.

X

That a portion of the total income should not go unless it returns as money or merchandise.

XI

That the emigration of residents who take their wealth out of the country should be avoided.

XII

That the children of rich farmers should settle in *the countryside, to support the tillers;* for if they are harassed into leaving the countryside and settling in the towns, they take away the wealth of their fathers which had been employed in farming. IT IS NO SO MUCH MEN AS WEALTH WHICH MUST BE ATTRACTED TO THE COUNTRYSIDE; for the more wealth is employed in farming, the fewer men are needed, the more prosperous it is and the greater income it produces. This is true, for example, of large grain farms run by rich farmers, as compared with small farms operated by poor sharecroppers who use oxen or even cows to till the soil.

XIII

That each person should be free to grow in his fields the crops which his interests, his skills, and the kind of terrain suggest to him, in order to get the biggest crop possible. No favor should be shown to the monopoly of a particular crop on the farms, for it is harmful to the general income of the nation. The prejudice which causes men to prefer abundance of articles of prime necessity rather than of other goods, to the detriment of the selling price of one or the other, is a short-sighted view which does not perceive the results of mutual foreign trade, which provides everything and fixes the price of the goods which each nation can cultivate most profitably. AFTER WEALTH IN EXPLOITATION OF FARM-LAND, IT IS INCOME AND TAXES WHICH ARE THE PRIME NECESSITIES of a State, in order that it be able to defend subjects against famine and enemies and support the glory and power of the monarch and the prosperity of the nation.

XIV

That the raising of livestock should be encouraged; for they furnish manure for the land and make big crops possible.

XV

That lands used for growing grain be combined as much as possible into large farms operated by big farmers; for there is less expense in the maintenance and upkeep of buildings, and proportionately much less expense and much more net produce in larger than in smaller agricultural enterprises. A large number of small farmers has a deleterious effect upon population. A population which is supported by net product is one which provides the surest and most available labor for different occupations and different tasks. Any savings to the benefit of profits, by work which can be performed by animals, machines, streams, etc., is to the advantage of the population and the State, because an increase in net product results in more profit for men to be used for other services or work.

XVI

That foreign trade in produce grown within the country should not be prevented; for THE STATE OF THE MARKET DETERMINES NEW PRODUCTION.

XVII

That the marketing and transport of goods produced by labor, should be facilitated by the improvement of highways and canals, rivers and the sea; for the more is saved in the expenses of trade, the more the income of the country is increased.

XVIII

That the price of foodstuffs and commodities within should not be kept low; for mutual trade within foreign countries will become disadvantageous to this nation. THE SELLING PRICE DETERMINES INCOME: Abundance and low prices do not mean wealth. Scarcity and high prices mean hardship. Abundance and high prices mean opulence.

XIX

That the opinion which holds that the little people benefit from a low price of food should be rejected; for a low price for food reduces the wages of the common people, diminishes their prosperity, means fewer good-paying jobs for them, and destroys the income of the nation.

XX

That the prosperity of the highest class of citizens should not be reduced; for they would not contribute enough to consumption of foods which can be consumed only within the country, which would bring about a diminution of the reproduction and revenue of the nation.

XXI

That landowners and those in gain professions should not indulge in unproductive saving, which withdraws a portion of their income or their profits from circulation and distribution.

XXII

That the luxury of embellishment should not be encouraged to the detriment of expenditures in developing and improving agriculture, and expenditures upon consumption.

XXIII

That the nation should not suffer losses in mutual trade with foreign countries, even though this trade may be profitable to merchants who earn profits by the sale to their fellow-citizens of the goods they import. For then the growth of the fortune of these merchants causes retrenchment in the circulation of income which is harmful to the distribution and reproduction of income.

XXIV

That we should not be deceived by apparent advantages in mutual trade with foreign countries, as we are when we judge only by the balance of monetary payments without examining how much more or less profit is earned upon the goods which are sold and bought. For often it is the nation which receives a monetary surplus which is the loser, and this loss is to the detriment of the distribution and reproduction of income.

XXV

That complete freedom of trade should be maintained; for THE SYSTEM OF DOMESTIC AND FOREIGN TRADE WHICH IS MOST SURE, MOST EXACT AND MOST PROFITABLE TO THE NATION AND THE STATE IS THAT WHICH RESTS UPON COMPLETE FREEDOM OF COMPETITION.

XXVI

That less attention should be paid to expanding population than to increasing income; for a greater prosperity which produces large incomes is preferable to the pressure of subsistence which is required by a population which is greater than the available income, and there are more resources for the needs of the State when the people are prosperous, and also more means to make agriculture prosper.

XXVII

That the government should be concerned less with accumulating savings than with the activities necessary for the prosperity of the king-dom; for the growth of wealth means that even very large expenditures cease to be excessive. But we should not confuse simple expenditures and abuses; for abuses can swallow up the entire wealth of the nation and the sovereign.

XXVIII

That fiscal administration, either in tax collection or government spending, should not be the source of personal monetary fortunes, which withdraw a portion of income from circulation, distribution, and repro-duction.

XXIX

That we should put our hopes for resources to meet the extraordinary needs of a State only in the prosperity of the nation and not in credits granted by financiers; for PRIVATE MONETARY FORTUNES ARE CLANDES-TINE WEALTH WHICH KNOWS NEITHER KING NOR FATHERLAND.

XXX

That the State should avoid borrowing by means of government bonds, which place upon it a burden of debilitating indebtedness and give rise to trading in financial obligations, through the intermediary of commercial paper which, when discounted, increases private mon-etary fortunes even more. Such fortunes separate finance from agri-culture and deprive the countryside of the necessary wealth for the improvement of the land and its cultivation.

34 / ADAM SMITH: FREEDOM OF ENTERPRISE

In 1776, the very year the American declaration of inde-pendence indicated the political failure of the "old colonial sys-tem," the policy of mercantilism came under fire from the side of economic theory. A systematic rebuttal of the assumptions and workings of mercantilism was put forward by Adam Smith (1723–1790), a Scottish philosopher and economist, in his Inquiry into the Nature and Causes of the Wealth of Nations *(1776). Smith was a professor of moral philosophy at Glasgow before resigning his chair to travel and then to work at his major study, the* Wealth of Nations, *which became the foundation stone of classical economics. The following sections from the* Wealth of Nations *show both its critical and constructive sides.*[20]

The general industry of the society never can exceed what the capital of the society can employ. As the number of workmen that can be kept in employment by any particular person must bear a certain proportion to his capital, so the number of those that can be continually employed by all the members of a great society, must bear a certain proportion to the whole capital of that society, and never can exceed that proportion. No regulation of commerce can increase the quantity of industry in any society beyond what its capital can maintain. It can only divert a part of it into a direction into which it might not otherwise have gone; and it is by no means certain that this artificial direction is likely to be more advantageous to the society than that into which it would have gone of its own accord.

Every individual is continually exerting himself to find out the most advantageous employment for whatever capital he can command. It is his own advantage, indeed, and not that of his society, which he has in view. But the study of his own advantage naturally, or rather necessarily leads him to prefer that employment which is most advantageous to the society.

First, every individual endeavours to employ his capital as near home as he can, and consequently as much as he can in the support of domestic industry; provided always that he can thereby obtain the ordinary, or not a great deal less than the ordinary profits of stock. . . .

Secondly, every individual who employs his capital in the support of domestic industry, necessarily endeavours so to direct that industry, that its produce may be of the greatest possible value.

The produce of industry is what it adds to the subject or materials upon which it is employed. In proportion as the value of this produce is great or small, so will likewise be the profits of the employer. But it is only for the sake of profit that any man employs a capital in the support of industry; and he will always, therefore, endeavour to employ

[20] Adam Smith, *An Inquiry into the Nature and Causes of the Wealth of Nations,* in *Works* (London: T. Cadell, *et al.,* 1811), Vol. III, pp. 177–8, 180–4.

it in the support of that industry of which the produce is likely to be of the greatest value, or to exchange for the greatest quantity either of money or of other goods.

But the annual revenue of every society is always precisely equal to the exchangeable value of the whole annual produce of its industry, or rather is precisely the same thing with that exchangeable value. As every individual, therefore, endeavours as much as he can both to employ his capital in the support of domestic industry, and so to direct that industry that its produce may be of the greatest value; every individual necessarily labours to render the annual revenue of the society as great as he can. He generally, indeed, neither intends to promote the public interest, nor knows how much he is promoting it. By preferring the support of domestic to that of foreign industry, he intends only his own security; and be directing that industry in such a manner as its produce may be of the greatest value, he intends only his own gain, and he is in this, as in many other cases, led by an invisible hand to promote an end which was no part of his intention. Nor is it always the worse for the society that it was no part of it. By pursuing his own interest he frequently promotes that of the society more effectually than when he really intends to promote it. I have never known much good done by those who affected to trade for the public good. It is an affectation, indeed, not very common among merchants, and very few words need be employed in dissuading them from it.

What is the species of domestic industry which his capital can employ, and of which the produce is likely to be of the greatest value, every individual, it is evident, can, in his local situation, judge much better than any statesman or lawgiver can do for him. The statesman, who should attempt to direct private people in what manner they ought to employ their capitals, would not only load himself with a most unnecessary attention, but assume an authority which could safely be trusted, not only to no single person, but to no council or senate whatever, and which would no-where be so dangerous as in the hands of a man who had folly and presumption enough to fancy himself fit to exercise it.

To give the monopoly of the home-market to the produce of domestic industry, in any particular art or manufacture, is in some measure to direct private people in what manner they ought to employ their capitals, and must, in almost all cases, be either a useless or a hurtful regulation. If the produce of domestic can be brought there as cheap as that of foreign industry, the regulation is evidently useless. If it cannot, it must generally be hurtful. It is the maxim of every prudent master of a family, never to attempt to make at home what it will cost him more to make than to buy. The taylor does not attempt to make his own shoes, but buys them of the shoemaker. The shoemaker does not attempt to make his own clothes, but employs a taylor. The farmer attempts to make neither the one nor the other, but employs those different artificers. All of them find it for their interest to employ their whole industry in a way in which they have some advantage over their neighbours, and to purchase with a part of its produce, or what is the same thing, with the price of a part of it, whatever else they have occasion for.

What is prudence in the conduct of every private family, can scarce be folly in that of a great kingdom. If a foreign country can supply us with a commodity cheaper than we ourselves can make it, better buy it of them with some part of the produce of our own industry, employed in a way in which we have some advantage. The general industry of the country, being always in proportion to the capital which employs it, will not thereby be diminished, no more than that of the above-mentioned artificers; but only left to find out the way in which it can be employed with the greatest advantage. It is certainly not employed to the greatest advantage, when it is thus directed towards an object which it can buy cheaper than it can make. The value of its annual produce is certainly more or less diminished, when it is thus turned away from producing commodities evidently of more value than the commodity which it is directed to produce. According to the supposition, that commodity could be purchased from foreign countries cheaper than it can be made at home. It could, therefore, have been purchased with a part only of the commodities, or, what is the same thing, with a part only of the price of the commodities, which the industry employed by an equal capital would have produced at home, had it been left to follow its natural course. The industry of the country, therefore, is thus turned away from a more, to a less advantageous employment, and the exchangeable value of its annual produce, instead of being increased, according to the intention of the lawgiver, must necessarily be diminished by every such regulation.

35 / JOHN AIKIN: INDUSTRIAL REVOLUTION

Although Adam Smith wrote during the age of the early Industrial Revolution in England, he considered industry primarily as it was before the appearance of large-scale machinery and the factory system. John Aikin (1747–1822), an English physician who busied himself as a writer on many nonmedical topics, discussed the process of industrialization, without Smith's powerful theoretical insight but with evident familiarity of firsthand observation, in his Description of the Country from thirty to forty Miles round Manchester *(1795). The Lancashire town of Manchester was one of the centers of the Industrial Revolution.*[21]

In 1773 a survey of Manchester was executed with accuracy, which gave the following results:

	MANCHESTER	SALFORD	TOTAL
Houses, inhabited	3,402	866	4,268
Families	5,317	1099	6,416
Male inhabitants	10,548	2248	12,796
Female ditto	11,933	2517	14,450
Both sexes	22,481	4765	27,246

Persons to a house, 6⅓.   To a family, 4¼.

At the same period, the township of Manchester (detached from the town) contained 311 houses, 361 families, 947 males, 958 females; total, 1905.

And the whole parish of Manchester, comprizing thirty-one townships in a compass of sixty square miles, contained 2371 houses, 2525 families, 6942 males, 6844 females; total, 13,786 inhabitants.

The whole number, then, of inhabitants in the town, township, and parish of Manchester, and in Salford, amounted to 42,927.

At Christmas 1788, the numbers by enumeration were, in the township of Manchester, 5916 houses, 8570 families, 42,821 persons; in the township of Salford, about 1260 houses. The whole number of people in both towns might then be reckoned at more than 50,000.

During the year 1791, the christenings in these towns amounted to 2960; the burials to 2286. These numbers, by the usual mode of calculating, will give from sixty-five to seventy-four thousand inhabitants —an increase almost unparalleled! . . .

The acquisition of these last branches, with the great increase of the export trade, have given such employment to large capitals here, that the interior business of the country is in great measure given up to the middle class of manufacturers and petty chapmen; but no exertions of the masters or workmen could have answered the demands of trade without the introduction of *spinning machines.*

These were first used by the country people on a confined scale,

[21] J. Aikin, *A Description of the Country from thirty to forty Miles round Manchester* (London: John Stockdale, 1795), pp. 156–7, 167–9, 176–7.

twelve spindles being thought a great matter; while the awkward posture required to spin on them was discouraging to grown up people, who saw with surprize children from nine to twelve years of age manage them with dexterity, whereby plenty was brought into families formerly overburthened with children, and the poor weavers were delivered from the bondage in which they had lain from the insolence of the spinners. The following state of the case will explain this matter. From the time that the original system in the fustian branch, of buying pieces in the grey from the weaver, was changed, by delivering them out work, the custom of giving them weft in the cops, which obtained for a while, grew into disuse, as there was no detecting the knavery of spinners till a piece came in woven; so that the practice was altered, and wool given with warps, the weaver answering for the spinning. And the weavers in a scarcity of spinning have sometimes been paid less for the weft than they gave the spinner, but durst not complain, much less abate the spinner, lest their looms should be unemployed. But when spinning-jennies were introduced, and children could work upon them, the case was reversed.

The plenty of weft produced by this means gave uneasiness to the country people, and the weavers were afraid lest the manufacturers should demand finer weft woven at the former prices, which occasioned some risings, and the demolition of jennies in some places by the uninformed populace. At length Doring Rasbotham, Esq. a worthy magistrate near Bolton, wrote and printed a sensible address to the weavers, in order to convince them of their own interest in encouraging these engines, which happily produced a general acquiescence in their use to a certain number of spindles. These were soon multiplied to three or four times the number; nor did the invention of mechanics rest here, for the demand for twist for warps was greater as weft grew more plentiful, whence engines were soon constructed for this purpose.

The improvements kept increasing, till the capital engines for twist were perfected, by which thousands of spindles are put in motion by a water wheel, and managed mostly by children, without confusion and with less waste of cotton than by the former methods. But the carding and slubbing preparatory to twisting required a greater range of invention. The first attempts were in carding engines, which are very curious, and now brought to a great degree of perfection; and an engine has been contrived for converting the carded wool to slubbing, by drawing it to about the thickness of candlewick preparatory to throwing it into twist. When these larger machines that moved by water were first set to work, they produced such excellent twist for warps, that they soon outrivalled the warps made on the larger jennies, which had yielded good profits to the owners. In consequence of this, according to the usual short-sighted policy of narrow-minded and interested men, the country was excited against the water-machines, and some of them were demolished before protection could be obtained. Yet a little reflection would have shown the country people, that if more warps were made, there would be a greater demand for weft from their jennies, and a better price for it. This has since been fully experienced in the introduction of muslins; for no contrivance in the other machines could make the thread hold when it is so slack thrown as to suit for weft; nor can it be supposed that the attempt would be made, as the demand for twist for warps will fully employ them. For when cotton bears a reasonable price, the warps made of this twist will be as cheap as those made with yarn, and keep the money at home which used to be sent abroad for that article; there being no comparison between yarn and cotton warps in goodness. In fact, cotton warps have lately been introduced to a great extent, where yarn had before been used. As these machines are now to be seen by the curious, and specifications of their construction may be had at the Patent office, no delicacy is necessary in laying descriptions of them fully before the public. . . .

The prodigious extension of the several branches of the Manchester manufactures has likewise greatly increased the business of several trades and manufactures connected with or dependent upon them. The making of paper at mills in the vicinity has been brought to great perfection, and now includes all kinds, from the strongest parcelling paper to the finest writing sorts, and that on which banker's bills are printed. To the ironmongers' shops, which are greatly increased of late, are generally annexed smithies, where many articles are made, even to nails. A considerable iron foundry is established in Salford, in which are cast most of the articles wanted in Manchester and its neighbourhood, consisting chiefly of large cast wheels for the cotton machines; cylinders, boilers, and pipes for steam engines; cast ovens, and grates of all sizes. This work belongs to Batemen and Sharrard, gen[tle]men every way qualified for so great an undertaking. Mr. Sharrard is a very ingenious and able engineer, who has improved upon and brought the steam engine to great perfection. Most of those that are used and set up in and about Manchester are of their make and fitting up. They are in general of a small size, very compact, stand in a small space, work smooth and easy, and are scarcely heard in the building where erected. They are now used in cotton mills, and for every purpose of the water wheel, where a stream is not to be got, and for winding up coals from a great depth in the coal pits, which is performed with a quickness and ease not to be conceived.

Some few are also erected in this neighbourhood by Messrs. Bolton and Watts of Birmingham, who have far excelled all others in their improvement of the steam engine, for which they have obtained a patent, that has been the source of great and deserved emolument. The boilers are generally of plate iron or copper; but some few for the smaller engines are of cast iron.

36 / MERCIER DE LA RIVIÈRE: ENLIGHTENED DESPOTISM DEFINED

The Enlightenment did not long remain at the level of pure doctrine, but received practical application—of a kind—in the rule of the "enlightened despots." For them enlightenment meant principally weakening the power of the traditional "estates" or quasi-representative "orders of society," furthering the centralization of governmental administration and moderating the intolerance of the established churches. Despotism meant only "absolute" monarchy, not tyranny. This distinction is explored in the work of the French political and economic thinker, Pierre François Joachim Henri Mercier de la Rivière, in his work, L'ordre naturel et essentiel des sociétés politiques *("The Natural and Essential Order of Political Societies," 1767), from which the following passages are taken.*[22]

Under *legal* despotism, the majesty of the Sovereign and his despotic authority are constantly represented everywhere in his kingdom, no matter how far the king himself may be, by immutable laws which are manifestly just and necessary. As the sovereign's will is only the expression of the public order, to be obeyed it needs only to be known; and the sovereign governs his state by means of laws whose wisdom is manifest, in the same way that God, whose image he is, governs the

[22] [Pierre François Joachim Henri Mercier de la Rivière], *L'ordre naturel et essentiel des sociétés politiques* (London: Jean Nourse; Paris: Desaint, 1767), pp. 180–2, 185–9. Translated from the French by the editor.

universe, in which, as we see, all secondary causes are subject *without variation* to laws from which they cannot depart. Hence such a Monarch devotes his attention solely to the good works which cannot be performed except by him and through him. The peace which reigns constantly within his person bestows its priceless benefits upon the world without; and the more these benefits multiply for others, the more they multiply for him. The armed guard around him is just a superficial ornamentation, not a necessary precaution; his person is everywhere safe among a people whose wealth, numbers and happiness could not be greater. The king's glance, we may say, makes the most barren lands fruitful; the happiness of a multitude of subjects who adore him in the firm belief that they owe their joys to him becomes his own happiness; and the abundance which arises everywhere is shared between them and him only so that it may become an ever-flowing source of benefactions.

Such a sovereign must have all foreign nations for his friends and admirers; in my mind I see them, filled with veneration and respect for a power which may cause them awe but never fear, coming to the foot of his throne to mingle their homages with those which his subjects daily hasten to render him in filial love; in everything that comes before his eyes he discovers another ground of glory, another object of delight; he is less a man on earth than a beneficent deity, whose temple is in every heart but who seemingly has put on human shape so as to add to the benefits procured by his wisdom and the pleasures that are felt in his presence. . . .

What an enormous difference there is between the situation of a Sovereign whom every one regards as a good which he fears to lose, and that of an arbitrary despot whom every one looks upon as an evil to be suffered only as long as it cannot be thrown off. The authority of an *arbitrary* despot cannot help but be precarious and unstable, because it is impossible to hold in steady balance the diverse opinions, interests and claims upon which it rests; that of the *legal* despot is unshakeable, because its principle, which is manifest justice and necessity, is invariable and always produces the same effects. . . .

Euclid is a true despot, and the geometric laws which he has handed down to us are truly despotic laws: their legal despotism and the personal despotism of this Lawmaker are one and the same thing, the irresistible force of manifest truth. This is the means by which Euclid the despot has ruled for centuries without contradiction over all enlightened peoples; and he will not cease to exercise the same despotism over them so long as there is no contradiction to meet from the side of ignorance. The stubborn resistance of this blind force is the only one over which personal and legal despotism needs to triumph; hence education and freedom of debate are the arms which it should employ to combat it, because it needs only to make its justice and necessity manifest to assure its sway. . . .

If the kings are truly great, truly kings, it is only through a government of this kind—all authority belongs to them and to no others; and because all their purposes are dictated by manifest justice and necessity, it can be said, in a way, that they are associated with *supreme reason* in the government of the earth; that in this quality his divine wisdom, which is communicated to them in the quality of manifest justice and necessity, and which always dwells within them, compels them to do good and makes them unable to do evil; so that, by their mediation, heaven and earth touch and the justice and goodness of God does not cease to be made manifest to men, being present to them in the Agents of his authority.

Thus the guilt of the crime of high treason and *lèse-majesté* falls upon those who seek to legitimize all the abuses of authority in the hope of their own profit, and secretly strive to insinuate to Sovereigns that their despotism is *arbitrary* and absolutely independent of all rules, that their purposes alone determine what is just and unjust. This perfidy can succeed only when favored by the Sovereign's lack of understanding, which does not enable him to see *manifestly* that the social order is *naturally and necessarily* based upon the physical order itself; not knowing this truth, they permit themselves to be persuaded that an *arbitrary* power can be highly useful to them in doing good; but an *arbitrary* power can serve only to do evil; for it is only evil which can be arbitrary, either in form or in substance—whatever is in order has *immutable* laws which are anything but *arbitrary,* and which *necessarily* produce the good for which they are instituted: thus it is only to the extent that a despot turns away from the laws of order to surrender to disorder that he can make *arbitrary* use of his power; now it has been demonstrated that order is wholly to the advantage of the Sovereign and sovereignty, that disorder can only create havoc with him personally and with his authority, which cannot be separated from the intuitive and determinative force of manifest justice and necessity without being at the mercy of all the arbitrary claims to which ignorance and opinions, the only enemies which his power has need to fear, can give rise.

How happy are the nations which enjoy the despotism of manifest justice and necessity: peace, justice, abundance, the purest felicity dwell endlessly among them; happier still are the Sovereigns to whom one can say without offending them: "Powerful masters of the earth, *your power* comes from God; it is from him that you hold your absolute authority because it is the authority of the manifest justice and necessity which God has instituted. Take care not to exchange this sacred authority for a power which can be arbitrary in you only insofar as it is so in its origins: your power, which is natural, absolute, independent, would be no more than an artificial, uncertain authority, dependent upon the very people whom it is supposed to govern. You are kings, but you are men—as men, you can make laws *arbitrarily;* as kings, you can only proclaim laws already established by the deity whose agents you are; as men, you are free to choose between good and evil, and human ignorance can lead you astray; as kings, evil and error cannot reside in you, because they cannot reside in God who, having established you as the Agents of his will, makes it visible to you in its manifest justice and necessity; the *personal* and *legal* despotism which they assure you for all time is the same as that which belongs to the King of Kings. Like him you are despots; like him, you will always be despots, because it is not in the nature of manifest justice and necessity that you should cease to be so; and your despotism will lavish glory and prosperity of every kind upon you; but it does not lie within order, in which you are instructed by manifest justice and necessity, that the best possible condition of the peoples should not be the best possible condition of Sovereigns."

37 / MACHIAVELLIANISM AND FREDERICK THE GREAT

One of the primary questions of political life has always been the proper use of the power of the state. The eighteenth century continued to feel the corrosive effect of Machiavelli's Prince, *with its propositions that the true measure of statesmanship was success in maintaining and extending power and that in this quest the end justified the use of any means, however immoral. One of the most unequivocal rebuttals of the* Prince *ever attempted came in 1740 from the pen of the Crown Prince of Prussia, Frederick of Hohenzollern, under the title of* Anti-Machiavel *("Anti-Machiavelli"). Although published anonymously, it was soon known who the author was, and interest in the little book rose rapidly when Frederick, becoming king of Prussia later in 1740, launched his attack upon the Austrian province of Silesia—an act which most people considered to be flagrant Machiavellianism. The following excerpts (A) from the* Anti-Machiavel *are taken from the first English translation, which appeared a year later.*[23]

Frederick II admitted to at least a degree of Machiavellianism after he had seized and held Silesia during the first war of the Austrian succession (1740–45). He discussed the problems of the means-end relationship in politics and the duties of a ruler in the selection used here (B) from his Histoire de mon temps, 1740–1745 *("History of My Own Times, 1740–1745," 1746).*[24]

A French observer, Honoré Gabriel Riqueti, comte de Mirabeau, probed to the core of weakness in the Prussian monarchy in his work, De la monarchie prussienne sous Frédéric le Grand *("The Prussian Monarchy under Frederick the Great"), published in London two years after the king's death in 1786. Mirabeau (1749–1791), after an early career as a rakehell whom his father caused to be repeatedly imprisoned for the sake of the family, became a learned and cogent writer on political matters. He was the first major leader during the French Revolution, which he strove to consolidate in the form of a constitutional monarchy. The excerpts (C) are taken from his study of Prussia under Frederick II.*[25]

An estimate of Frederick II's accomplishment as the paramount builder of Prussia was made by an outstanding German historian, Gerhard Ritter, a little less than two centuries after Frederick's accession. The portrait and judgment of Frederick given in Ritter's Friedrich der Grosse: Ein historisches Profil *("Frederick the Great: A Historical Profile," 1936) is complex, many-sided and subtle, where most works upon the Prussian king are works of either unabashed praise or simple-minded blame. The passages chosen (D) are too brief to reproduce the full variety of Ritter's view of Frederick, but they do indicate his method and his standards of judgment. Ritter (b. 1888), a historian of strongly nationalist convictions, became one of the leaders of the German resistance to Hitler during the last years of World War II.*[26]

[23] [Frederick II, king of Prussia], *Anti-Machiavel: or, an Examination of Machiavel's Prince, with Notes Historical and Political,* published by Mr. de Voltaire, translated from the French (London: T. Woodward, 1741), pp. 165–9, 192–8, 294–5.

[24] Frederick II, king of Prussia, *The History of My Own Times,* translated from the French by Thomas Holcroft, Part I (London: G. G. J. and J. Robinson, 1789), pp. xvi–xx.

[25] Honoré Gabriel Riqueti, comte de Mirabeau, *De la monarchie prussienne sous Frédéric le Grand* (London: n. p., 1788), Vol. I, pp. 133–5, 190–2, 333–4, 348–9. Translated from the French by the editor.

[26] Gerhard Ritter, *Friedrich der Grosse: Ein historisches Profil* (Leipzig: Verlag

A. FREDERICK II: ANTI-MACHIAVELLI

Painters and Historians have this in common, that they ought to copy Nature. The former draw the Features and Complexions of Men, the latter their Actions and Characters. There are some Painters of such a singular Cast, that they draw nothing but Monsters and Devils. *Machiavel* is of this Stamp; he makes a Hell of the Universe, and represents all Men as being in the State of the Damned. One would think this Politician had a mind to defame the whole human Race, from a particular Hatred he bore to it; and that he had undertaken to annihilate Virtue, perhaps with a View to make all the Inhabitants of this Continent as bad as the Prince he would form.

Machiavel maintains, that, in this wicked and degenerate World, it is certain Ruin to be strictly honest: For my part, I affirm, that in order to be safe, it is necessary to be virtuous. Men are commonly neither wholly good, nor wholly bad; but both good and bad; and such as are between the two will unanimously revere a powerful Prince, who is just and virtuous. I had much rather make War upon a Tyrant than upon a good King, upon a *Lewis* XI. than upon a *Lewis* XII., upon a *Domitian* rather than upon a *Trajan;* for the good King will be well served, whereas the Tyrant's Subjects will join my Troops. Let me go into *Italy* with Ten thousand Men against an *Alexander* VI., half *Italy* will side with me: But let me march with Forty thousand against an *Innocent* XI. and all *Italy* will rise in his Defence. No wise and good King in *England* was ever dethroned by great Armies; all their bad Kings have been ruined by Competitors, who, when they began the War, could not muster Four thousand regular troops. Every wise Prince therefore will look upon Virtue as his chief Security, and as the Means of gaining and preserving the Attachment and Fidelity of his Subjects, and striking Terror into his Enemies. . . .

Machiavel, the Preceptor of Tyrants, has the Boldness to affirm, that Princes may impose upon the World by Dissimulation. This is the first Position which I shall endeavour to refute. The extreme Curiosity of the Publick is well known; it is a Being that sees every thing, hears every thing, and divulges whatever it has heard or seen. If its Curiosity examines the Conduct of Particular Men, 'tis only to fill up idle Hours; but if it considers the Characters of Princes, 'tis with an Eye to its own Interest. And indeed Princes are more exposed than all other Men, to the Conjectures, Comments and Judgment of the World; they are a sort of Stars, at which a whole People of Astronomers are continually levelling their Telescopes and Cross-staves; Courtiers

Quelle & Meyer, 1936), pp. 92-4, 98-100. Translated from the German by the editor. Reprinted by permission of Verlag Quelle & Meyer.

who are near them are daily taking their Observations; a single Gesture, a single Glance of the Eye, discovers them; and the People who observe them at a greater Distance, magnify them by Conjectures; in short, as well may the Sun hide its Spots, as great Princes their Vices and their genuine Character, from the Eyes of so many curious Observers.

If the Mask of Dissimulation should cover, for a time, the natural Deformity of a Prince, yet he could never keep his Mask always on; he would sometimes be obliged, was it only for a Breathing, to throw it off; and one View of his naked Features would be sufficient to content the Curious. It will therefore be in vain for Dissimulation to dwell in the Mouths of Princes; Craftiness in their Discourses and Actions will have no Effect: To judge of Men by their Words and Professions, would be the way to be always mistaken; we therefore compare their Actions with one another, and then with their Words; and against this repeated Examination, Falsity and Deceit will find no Refuge: No Man can well act any Part but his own; he must really have the same Character which he would bear in the World: Without this, the Man who thinks to impose upon the Publick, imposes upon none but himself.

Sixtus Quintus, Philip II. passed for Hypocrites, and enterprising Men, but not for being virtuous. Let a Prince be as artful as he would, he will never be able, even by following all our Author's Maxims, to gain the Character of Virtue which he has not, and avoid the Scandal of Crimes which belong to him.

Machiavel argues no better, in the Reasons he assigns for employing Trick and Hypocrisy. The ingenious, but fallacious Application of the Fable of the Centaur proves nothing; for if that Animal was half Man, half Horse, does it follow from thence, that Princes ought to be crafty and false? A Man must have a strong Inclination to inculcate Crime, who employs Arguments so weak and so far-fetched as this of the Centaur.

But here follows a Reasoning as false as any we have yet met with. Our Politician affirms, that a Prince ought to have the Qualities both of the Lion and the Fox; of the Lion, to destroy the Wolves; and of the Fox, to avoid Snares: From whence he infers, that a wise Prince neither can nor should fulfil his Engagements: Here is a Conclusion without Premises. Would not any other Man blush to throw out such impious Sophistry?

If *Machiavel's* confused Notions could be strained into good Sense, and sound Morality, they might be represented thus: The World resembles a Match at Gaming, where Sharpers and fair Players are promiscuously engaged: A Prince therefore who is in the Game, and would not be cheated himself, should be well acquainted with all the Ways of cheating others; not in order to put any of these Lessons in

Practice, but only that he may hinder them from being practised upon him by Gamesters.

But to return to *Machiavel's* Sophistry. Because all Men, says he, are wicked, and at all times break their Faith and Promise to you, there is no Obligation upon you to keep yours with them. Now here is a manifest Contradiction; for he says a few Lines after, that Dissemblers will always find People simple enough to be imposed upon. How can this be reconciled with the other? All Men are wicked, and yet you find Men simple enough to be imposed upon! But it is not true, that all Men are wicked: One must have a strange misanthropic Turn, not to perceive, that in every Society there are a great many honest Men, and that the major Part are neither good nor bad. But without supposing all the World to be wicked, how could *Machiavel* have supported his detestable Maxims? Nay, granting that Men are as wicked as he represents them, would it follow that we ought to imitate their Example? If any Man robs, or commits Murder, I conclude that he deserves to be hanged, not that I must act accordingly. If Honour and Virtue were to be banished the World, said *Charles* the Wise, they ought to find an Asylum with Princes. . . .

It is with the Office of a Prince, as with all others; no Man, whatever his Employment may be, can gain the Confidence of others, without Justice and Integrity, as well as Prudence: The most vicious Men always chuse to deal with the most virtuous; in the same manner as those Princes who have the least Capacity for Governing, trust to him who passes with them for having the most. And why should Vice be more necessary to the Office of Sovereignty, than to that of the meanest Magistrate? Upon the whole, a Prince who would preserve his Dominions, as he must gain the Hearts of the People, so for that purpose he is obliged to be just, virtuous, and beneficent, and not, as *Machiavel* through the whole of this Work endeavours to form him, unjust, cruel, ambitious, and solely intent upon aggrandizing himself, by any means whatever.

Thus have I endeavoured to unmask this Politician, who passed in his own Age for an extraordinary Man, whom several Ministers of State have thought a dangerous Writer, and yet have followed his abominable Maxims, and recommended the Study of them to their Masters, an Author who yet was never expertly answered, and whom several Statesmen follow, without thinking it any Reproach to them. Happy would be the Man who were able to banish such Doctrines out of the World. I have here endeavoured to shew the Inconsistency of them; and it is incumbent on those who rule over others, to shew it by their Example, and to set the Publick right, with regard to the false Notion they entertain of Politicks, which should only be a System of Wisdom, but commonly passes for a Breviary of Fraud and Imposture:

It is incumbent on them to banish Subtleties and Insincerity, which are so common in Treaties; to revive Honesty and Candour, which, in Truth, are very rare among Sovereigns, and to shew themselves as indifferent about conquering the Provinces of their Neighbours, as jealous of preserving their own. The Prince who would possess every thing, is not less absurd than the Man who would devour every thing, and expects he could digest as much as he devours. Whereas he who is content to govern wisely what he justly possesses, is like the Man who loads his Stomach with nothing more than it is able to digest.

B. FREDERICK II: MEANS AND ENDS

Posterity, perhaps, will see with surprise, in these memoirs, a recital of treaties concluded and broken. Numerous as such examples are, example would not justify the author of this work, if he had not better reasons to excuse his conduct.

The interests of the state ought to serve as the rule to the monarch.

Cases in which alliances may be broken are, 1. When the ally fails in fulfilling his engagements; 2. When the ally meditates deceit, and there is no other resource than that of being the first to deceive; 3. When a superior force oppresses and renders the breaking of a treaty an act of necessity; 4, and lastly, The want of means to continue the war. That despicable thing called money, by I know not what fatality, influences all affairs. Princes are slaves to their means; the interest of the state prescribes law to them, and that law is inviolable. If the prince is under an obligation even to sacrifice his life for the safety of his subjects, how much more ought he to sacrifice those connections the continuation of which would to them become prejudicial! Examples of treaties in like manner broken are frequent. It is not our intention to justify them all, yet dare we affirm there are some treaties which either necessity, wisdom, prudence, or the good of the nation, oblige us to transgress; for kings only possess these means of avoiding ruin. Had Francis I. fulfilled the treaty of Madrid, he would by the loss of Burgundy, have established an enemy in the heart of his dominions. This would have reduced France to the unhappy condition in which she was in the reign of Louis XI. and Louis XII. If after the battle of Muhlberg, won by Charles V. the protestant league in Germany had not strengthened itself by the support of France, it could not but have worn those chains which the emperor had long been forging. Had not the English broken the alliance, so contrary to their interests, by which Charles II. was united with Louis XIV. a diminution of their power would have been risked, and the more so because France would have had greatly the advantage over England in the political balance of Europe. Sages, who predict effects from causes, ought early to resist all such causes as are thus diametrically opposite to their interests. Suffer me to explain myself exactly, on so delicate a subject, which has seldom been otherwise than dogmatically treated. To me it appears evident that a private person ought to be scrupulously tenacious of his promise, though he should have made it inconsiderately. If he is injured he can have recourse to the protection of the laws, and, be the issue what it may, an individual only suffers. But where is the tribunal that can redress a monarch's wrongs, should another monarch forfeit his engagement? The word of an individual can only involve an individual in misfortune, while that of a sovereign may draw down calamities on nations. The question then will be reduced to this, must the people perish or must the prince infringe a treaty? And where is the man weak enough to hesitate a moment concerning his answer? Hence, from the case we have supposed, is deduced the necessity of first carefully examining the circumstances under which the monarch acts, the conduct of his allies, the resources he may be able to obtain, or his incapacity to fulfil his engagements, before any decisive judgment ought to be passed upon his proceedings. For, as we have already said, the good or ill state of the finances is the pulse of the kingdom, which has a greater influence than is either known or believed on political and military operations. Ignorant of this, the public judges only from appearances, and consequently is deceived in its judgments. Prudence will not admit that they should be better informed, for it would be the excess of phrenzy to vaingloriously publish the weak side of a nation. Delighted by such a discovery, its enemies would not fail to profit by the intelligence. Wisdom therefore requires we should leave to the public the rash liberty of deciding, and, unable to justify ourselves, while we live, without danger to the state, we must rest satisfied with that justification which may be obtained from disinterested posterity.

C. MIRABEAU: FREDERICK THE GREAT

Frederick II was no less remarkable as an administrator than as a political king and a warrior; his successes and his mistakes both provide important lessons. He lacked understanding of a number of subjects, but the firm will to govern his provinces well never failed him. It may be said that he went to such trouble for the sake of his own interests, that it was for himself that he increased the population of his country, its income, its army and its power. Of course—but it is fortunately in the nature of things that the sovereign's true advantage and his people's welfare constitute one and the same interest. Happy is the prince who knows this truth and has the courage to make it the principle of his life! Such a prince truly deserves the surname of "Great."

The king of Prussia, as we know, rose at five o'clock in the morning and then worked for two or three hours, not with his ministers but with his secretaries. The difference is immense. Ministers have authority and opinions, and exert influence upon the purposes even of enlightened princes, while they direct those of ordinary sovereigns. The secretaries of the king of Prussia were only scribes. His own name for them was *die Schreiber,* the writers. Had any of them been so rash as to express his opinion regarding the matters on which he was reporting, the king would have thought that the man had lost his mind. These "writers" daily received all communications addressed to the sovereign. They arranged and labeled them and then came to the king with their portfolios; they read him the labels, which briefly stated the content of the papers. The king at once decided what should be said, written or done as a consequence, and the secretary noted the decision. In the evening the secretary returned with the written replies, which the king signed. This procedure was repeated daily, and in this way this man of unchanging habits disposed of as many as two hundred matters a day. It is easy to understand that he could read neither all the dispatches which were placed before him nor all the replies which he signed. But he never failed to read several of the papers received and several of those to be dispatched, so that no secretary should ever dare to deceive him. . . .

But it is sad that all these great benefits [bestowed on Prussia by Frederick II], several incalculable in their possible consequences, should have remained only resources! Otherwise his monarchy would rest upon a solid and unshakeable foundation, not as now upon one which is unstable; which, although the genius of the late king erected upon it the vast edifice of his power, can be turned topsy-turvy by a single storm—an edifice which may even be brought down by the very props unskilfully used in an attempt to hold it up. His provinces would nourish a larger, and above all a more confident, population, because they would be prosperous and their livelihood would not depend upon artificial and precarious means. Agriculture, trade and industry, and as a result income, would all continue to grow. The state, strengthened by its own solidity, would be able to sustain the torpor of a weak and indolent king, the lavishness of a vain or open-handed one, or the reversals of fortune which are sometimes inevitable in the nature of things. In a word, the king of Prussia would not be the only rich man in his kingdom, and three-quarters of the country would not be exposed to the danger of dying of destitution if the king lost his fortune, or just his mind. The mistakes of kings must be included when one reckons the strength of states. The Prussian monarchy is so constituted that it can support no calamity whatever, not even the one which is inevitable in the long run—a government without ability.

Even with all the late king's skill, this complicated machine could not continue the work. The erroneous measure of a system in which revenues were paramount undermined the state. Frederick II plied it with stimulants to no avail. The body politic is wasting away; it needs a radical cure, one which it is quite difficult to administer in the midst of its present crisis. . . .

As we see, the position of a king of Prussia is extremely critical. His entire power derives in the first instance from the delicate mainspring which drives his political machine. He needs an immense treasure and a superior army. The military system and the most inflexible economy must therefore always be the palladium of this monarchy; but in addition it needs help, and powerful help. One man, even the best of men, cannot do everything. . . .

But is it in the order of things human that no prince of the House of Brandenburg shall ever have a penchant for spending, ostentation and the luxuries of a court, that they will all resolve to live in their residences as in an army camp? And yet the existence of the Prussian army depends on it. If ever a prince without much intelligence ascends this throne, we shall see this formidable giant suddenly come crashing down without apparent cause, and astonished Europe will perceive only a sickly pigmy in its place. Then all the causes of destruction which arise from a harmful system of political economy and a harmful system of recruiting troops, with the enlistment of foreign soldiers who require an entire system of discipline in order to be kept under control—all these causes will act with redoubled force to dissolve the body politic; we shall see Prussia fall as once Sweden did, and we shall keep only the memory of the brilliant role which one man alone enabled it to play. Let us avert our eyes from this misfortune. Long may the guardian angel of Europe delay it!

D. GERHARD RITTER: A MODERN JUDGMENT ON FREDERICK II

From the very first day, the goal of his [Frederick II's] foreign policy was to make clear to the world that a new period of Prussian history had begun and that in his person a new disturbing factor had entered the company of European great states. Frederick was wholly convinced that what his Prussia most lacked was "reputation"—the aspect of a power to be feared in a showdown. It was not news to him that Vienna had considered his father to be nothing more than a "poltroon" whose threats and tantrums did not have to be taken seriously. He knew from his own painful experience in the affair of his marriage how the Imperial envoy Seckendorff had kept Berlin's policy "on the leash" by combined slyness and superciliousness. . . . There burned in him the youthfully ardent desire to be revenged for this succession of slights and humiliations (as Frederick considered them), and to make the other powers feel at last the full weight of Prussian military might. Nothing better expressed his attitude than the celebrated instructions which he gave to Colonel von Camas, his special envoy to Paris: Camas was to describe the young Prussian king as a hothead of incalculable vanity, calling attention to his armaments (which were being made with deliberate bustle and ado) and hinting that Frederick, in his unquenchable eagerness for action, was quite capable of "setting all Europe afire." With such cool calculation did he employ his own youthful fire as a technique of diplomatic pressure! . . .

It was a most fortunate accident for the satisfaction of this need "to make his reputation" as quickly as possible that Emperor Charles VI died in October, 1740, only five months after Frederick came to power. The death of the 55-year-old emperor threw the entire existing political system into turmoil. Charles VI was the last ruling Hapsburg in the male line. All Europe had awaited his death with tension for many years. He had obtained by great sacrifices the solemn recognition of all the major courts of Europe for his "Pragmatic Sanction," which promised the succession in all his hereditary lands to his daughter Maria Theresa. But what was the value of paper treaties as a guard against the ambitions of powerful neighbors with a thirst for territorial expansion? Frederick had been convinced for many years that they would all throw off their obligations, each on a different pretext, and lay covetous hands upon portions of the Hapsburg inheritance. It seemed to be of great consequence to Prussia, whose need for territorial expansion was the most urgent, to be in position before the other powers. It was important to create an accomplished fact before they even began to act; otherwise, as repeated experience had shown, the most recent arrival among the great powers would end up empty-handed.

These were, as we see, the very simple arguments which moved Frederick to seize Silesia by a sudden blow. It was at this time that he told the Italian writer Algarotti that he didn't have to cudgel his brains over the death of Charles VI—he had mentally prepared all plans for Prussia's policy in this eventuality and now it was only a question of carrying out his plans. To be sure, this was youthful exaggeration, for nothing had been prepared. The campaign in Silesia was not an enterprise carefully devised over the years; it was essentially an improvisation of genius. Had it been otherwise, it probably would never have been undertaken. But from the very first moment, the young king took it for granted that he could not lose this favorable moment to make a great gain for Prussia and to take revenge on the Imperial power for old affronts. A state like Prussia, wedged in between mighty neighbors and constantly endangered by hostile coalitions, could progress only by rapidly discovering the favorable moment and acting with deliberation and speed. Frederick felt with utmost sharpness that an opportunity for Prussia once missed would never return. The general European situation appeared to him as uncommonly favorable for carrying out a bold enterprise. . . .

This was the world situation which offered such good prospects to a young and ambitious great power like Brandenburg-Prussia. But from the beginning the upstart ran the danger of appearing as the disagreeable troublemaker who imperiled the hard-built balance of power, who once more loosed the floods of war upon Europe and called into question the treaty order established in recent decades. From the beginning it was the fate of Frederician Prussia to bear the reputation of a violent and arrogant upstart. The policy of the newest of the great powers could succeed only by means of a surprise attack, so that it soon took on the appearance of a morally callous, warlike and "militarist" state. As the policy of the weaker side, it was often compelled to change camps quickly and to take unhesitating advantage of the swiftly altering situation; and thus it soon acquired the reputation of being especially sly, perfidious and Machiavellian. . . . [The English] wished to maintain Austria for the sake of the European balance of power. Frederick's attack upon Silesia therefore seemed to England to be an attack upon the most sacred foundations of European politics. It is always easier for the insular power, which by its very nature has no interest in the frontier squabbles of the continental powers, to present its special interests as coinciding with the interest, real or apparent, of all Europe. There is something frightening for the true Englishman in the idea that the fate of nations and decisions of war and peace should depend upon the ambition, the vainglory or even the scrupulosity of a single man. Furthermore, something of the belief of the Christian Middle Ages in the inviolable validity of eternal principles of right and justice, superior to any nation's motives, has continued to live on there (to this very day). The English have experienced, since the days of the Renaissance, fewer of those catastrophes in foreign relations which might have shattered this belief and blunted their legalism, than have the powers of continental Europe. And hence they are readier than we to pass moral condemnation upon acts based on a policy of strength, considering them as deeds of violence in defiance of the ideal of humanity. The way in which Frederick began his Silesian campaign caused him to appear before the world as a malevolent aggressor and notorious lawbreaker.

What most mattered was that he attacked Silesia in the midst of

peace and put it under military occupation before he began any negotiations in Vienna. We know why he did so: because he considered
negotiations regarding his territorial claims in Silesia to be hopeless
until he had created an accomplished fact. In this he was certainly
right. But he who would correctly evaluate the historical phenomenon
whose name is Frederick the Second must first of all clearly realize
how unprecedented and essentially reckless his action was. No one
could have discarded with greater and more astonishing abruptness
the principles of strict morality by which his father and most of his
forebears had conducted their foreign policy. What remained of his
own impassioned assurances in the *Anti-Machiavel* that true and enlightened policy has no need to violate morality? Completely isolated
and wholly without allies or diplomatic preparation, he confronted
Europe, trusting solely in the logic of facts—and in his weapons. Though
in his own mind he might consider his conduct as politically urgent,
even necessary, as retaliation for a long-standing evasion of his rights,
and though he might defend it as such before the world, nonetheless
it was a challenge to all Europe. Frederick's own confidential advisers,
General von Schwerin and cabinet minister von Podewils, felt the
enterprise to be an adventure; they tried in vain to prevent it, to post-
pone it, to turn it in another direction. He listened to them but followed
his demon. They foresaw what came to pass. Frederick had to devote
all the rest of his life to overcoming the consequences of this adventure,
to meeting the dangers which rose out of it. But he stood the test. In
so doing he laid the basis for the greatness of Prussia; and this is the
justification before history of what he did, that it was an act *sui generis*
[unique of its kind], the daring but unavoidable breakthrough of a
state which sought by violent means to rise above the narrowness and
obscurity of its petty condition to a place on the stage of world history.

38 / JOSEPH II: ENLIGHTENED DESPOTISM ENTHRONED

*Like Frederick II of Prussia, Emperor Joseph II, the ruler
of Austria, is numbered among the foremost "enlightened despots"
of the age. Joseph's view of his "enlightened" goals are clearly set
forth in the following letters. Joseph II (1740–1790) of Hapsburg
became Holy Roman Emperor in 1765 and shared rule over the*

Hapsburg dominions with his mother, Maria Theresa, until her death in 1780, after which he ruled alone.[27]

To Cardinal Herzan, Imperial Royal Minister in Rome

Monsieur le Cardinal,—Since I have ascended the throne, and wear the first diadem in the world, I have made philosophy the legislator of my empire.

In consequence of its logic, Austria will assume another form, the authority of the Ulemas will be restricted, and the rights of majesty will be restored to their primitive extent. It is necessary I should remove certain things out of the domain of religion which never did belong to it.

As I myself detest superstition and the Sadducean doctrines, I will free my people of them; with this view, I will dismiss the monks, I will suppress their monasteries, and will subject them to the bishops of their diocese.

In Rome they will declare this an infringement of the rights of God: I know they will cry aloud, "the greatness of Israel is fallen"; they will complain, that I take away from the people their tribunes, and that I draw a line of separation between dogma and philosophy; but they will be still more enraged when I undertake all this without the approbation of the servant of the servants of God.

To these things we owe the degradation of the human mind. A servant of the altar will never admit that the state is putting him into his proper place, when it leaves him no other occupation than the gospel, and when by laws it prevents the children of Levi from carrying on a monopoly with the human understanding.

The principles of monachism, from Pachomius up to our time, have been directly opposed to the light of reason; respect for their founders ultimately became adoration itself, so that we behold again the Israelites going up to Bethel, in order to adore golden calves.

These false conceptions of religion were transmitted to the common people; they no longer knew God, and expected every thing from their saints.

The rights of the bishops, which I will re-establish, must assist in reforming the ideas of the people; instead of the monk, I will have the priest to preach, not the romances of the canonised, but the holy gospel and morality.

---

[27] "Letters of Joseph II. Written to Distinguished Princes and Statesmen, on Various Interesting Subjects. Now first translated from the German," *The Pamphleteer* (London), Vol. XIX, No. 38, 1822, pp. 274-5, 288-91.

I shall take care that the edifice, which I have erected for posterity, be durable. The general seminaries are nurseries for my priests; whence, on going out into the world, they will take with them a purified mind, and communicate it to the people by wise instruction.

Thus, after the lapse of centuries, we shall have Christians; thus, when I shall have executed my plan, the people of my empire will better know the duties they owe to God, to the country, and to their fellow-creatures; thus shall we yet be blessed by our posterity, for having delivered them from the overgrown power of Rome; for having brought back the priests within the limits of their duties; and for having subjected their future life to the Lord, and their present life to the country alone.

Vienna, October, 1781   JOSEPH.

To * * *

My friend,—Because there have been Neroes, and a Dionysius, who exceeded the limits of their authority; because there have been tyrants, who abused the power which destiny confided to them;—is it for that reason just, that, under the pretext of fear lest the rights of a nation might suffer, a people should throw all possible obstacles in the way of a prince, in his arrangements of government, which have no other aim than the welfare of his subjects?

Since my accession to the throne, I have ever been anxious to conquer the prejudices against my station, and have taken pains to gain the confidence of my people; I have several times since given proof, that the welfare of my subjects is my passion; that to satisfy it, I shun neither labor, nor trouble, nor even vexations, and reflect well on the means which are likely to promote my views; and yet in my reforms, I everywhere find opposition from people, of whom I least expected it.

As a monarch, I do not deserve the distrust of my subjects; as the Regent of a great empire, I must have the whole extent of my state before my eyes, and embrace the whole in one view; I cannot always listen to the voices of single provinces, which consider only their own narrow sphere.

Private advantage is a chimera, and while on the one hand I lose it in order to make a sacrifice to my country, I may on the other hand share in the common welfare.—But how few think of this!

If I were unacquainted with the duties of my station—if I were not morally convinced, that I am destined by Providence to wear my diadem, together with all the load of obligations which it imposes upon me—melancholy, discontent, and the wish not to exist, would fill my bosom. But I know my heart; I am internally convinced of the honesty of my intentions, and hope that when I am no more, posterity will examine, and judge more equitably, more justly, and more impartially, all that I have done for my people.

Vienna, October, 1787.   JOSEPH.

To van Swieten

Sir,—Till now the Protestant religion has been opposed in my states; its adherents have been treated like foreigners; civil rights, possession of estates, title, and appointments, all were refused them.

I determined from the very commencement of my reign to adorn my diadem with the love of my people, to act in the administration of affairs according to just, impartial, and liberal principles; consequently, I granted toleration, and removed the yoke which had oppressed the protestants for centuries.

Fanaticism shall in future be known in my states only by the contempt I have for it; nobody shall any longer be exposed to hardships on account of his creed; no man shall be compelled in future to profess the religion of the state, if it be contrary to his persuasion, and if he have other ideas of the right way of insuring blessedness.

In future my Empire shall not be the scene of abominable intolerance. Fortunately no sacrifices like those of Calas and Sirven have ever disgraced any reign in this country.

If, in former times, the will of the monarch furnished opportunities for injustice, if the limits of executive power were exceeded, and private hatred acted her part, I can only pity those monarchs who were nothing but kings.

Tolerance is an effect of that beneficent increase of knowledge which now enlightens Europe, and which is owing to philosophy and the efforts of great men; it is a convincing proof of the improvement of the human mind, which has boldly reopened a road through the dominions of superstition, which was trodden centuries ago by Zoroaster and Confucius, and which, fortunately for mankinds, has now become the highway of monarchs. Adieu!

Vienna, December, 1787.   JOSEPH.

39 / ALEXANDER RADISHCHEV: SERFDOM IN RUSSIA

Serfdom, the characteristically medieval form of peasant status in Western Europe, had either disappeared from there by the eighteenth century or had been reduced to a burdensome legalism. In Eastern Europe, however, it became strong and widespread, especially between the sixteenth and eighteenth centuries. One of the first criticisms of serfdom in Russia was made by a liberal nobleman, Alexander Nikolaevich Radishchev (1749–1802), during the reign of Empress Catherine II. His work, cast in the form of a travel account, Puteshestvie ot Peterburga do Moskvy *("A Journey from St. Petersburg to Moscow," 1790), earned him the frightened contempt of Empress Catherine, who had him sent into exile in Siberia. The following excerpts from his work include some of Catherine's comments upon it.*[28]

But who among us wears the fetters, who feels the burden of slavery? The agriculturist! The man who feeds us in our leanness and satisfies our hunger, who gives us health and prolongs our life, without having the right to dispose of what he cultivates nor of what he produces. But who has a greater right to a field than the man who cultivates it? Let us imagine that men have come into a wilderness to establish a community. Mindful of their need of sustenance, they divide up the uncultivated land. Who deserves a share in this division? Is it not he who knows how to plough the land, he who has the strength and the determination requisite for the task? The land will be useless to a child, an old man, a weak, sick, or lazy man. It will remain a wilderness, and the wind will not rustle any grain growing upon it. If it is useless to the owner, it is equally useless to society, for the owner cannot render the surplus to society when he does not even have what he needs for

[28] Aleksandr Nikolaevich Radishchev, *A Journey from St. Petersburg to Moscow*, translated by Leo Weiner; Roderick Page Thaler, ed. (Cambridge, Mass.: Harvard University Press, 1958), pp. 146–7, 151–4, 155–6, 239, 248. Reprinted by permission of the publishers from Aleksandr Nikolaevich Radishchev, *A Journey from St. Petersburg to Moscow*. Cambridge, Mass.: Harvard University Press, Copyright, 1958, by The President and Fellows of Harvard College.

himself. Hence, in primitive society, he who was able to cultivate his field had a proprietary right to it, and by virtue of cultivating it, had the exclusive enjoyment of it. But how very far we have departed from the primitive social relation to property! With us, he who has the natural right to it is not only completely excluded from it, but, while working another's field, sees his sustenance dependent on another's power! To your enlightened minds these truths cannot be incomprehensible, but your acts, in the application of these truths, are impeded, as we have already said, by prejudice and self-interest. Even so, can your hearts, which are full of love for humanity, prefer self-interest to the sentiments that soothe the heart? But wherein does your profit consist? Can a country in which two thirds of the citizens are deprived of their civil rights and to some extent are dead to the law be called happy? Can the civic condition of the peasant in Russia be called happy? Only an insatiable bloodsucker will say that the peasant is happy, for he has no conception of a better state of affairs. . . .

But, to return to our more immediate concern with the condition of the agriculturists, we find it most harmful to society. It is harmful because it prevents the increase of products and population, harmful by its example, and dangerous in the unrest it creates. Man, motivated by self-interest, undertakes that which may be to his immediate or later advantage, and avoids that from which he expects no present of future gain. Following this natural instinct, everything we do for our own sake, everything we do without compulsion, we do carefully, industriously, and well. On the other hand, all that we do not do for our own advantage, we do carelessly, lazily, and all awry. Thus we find the agriculturists in our country. The field is not their own, the fruit thereof does not belong to them. Hence they cultivate the land lazily and do not care whether it goes to waste because of their poor work. Compare this field with the one the haughty proprietor gives the worker for his own meager sustenance. The worker is unsparing in the labors which he spends on it. Nothing distracts him from his work. The savagery of the weather he overcomes bravely; the hours intended for rest he spends at work; he shuns pleasure even on the days set aside for it. For he looks after his own interest, works for himself, is his own master. Thus his field will give him an abundant harvest; while all the fruits of the work done on the proprietor's demesne will die or bear no future harvest; whereas they would grow and be ample for the sustenance of the citizens, if the cultivation of the fields were done with loving care, if it were free.

But if forced labor brings smaller harvests, crops which fail to reach the goal of adequate production also stop the increase of the population. Where there is nothing to eat, there will soon be no eaters, for all will die from exhaustion. Thus the enslaved field, by giving an insufficient return, starves to death the citizens for whom nature had intended her superabundance. But this is not the only thing in slavery that interferes with abundant life. To insufficiency of food and clothing they have added work to the point of exhaustion. Add to this the spurns of arrogance and the abuse of power, even over man's tenderest sentiments, and you see with horror the pernicious effects of slavery, which differs from victory and conquest only by not allowing what victory cuts down to be born anew. But it causes even greater harm. It is easy to see that the one devastates accidentally and momentarily, the other destroys continuously over a long period of time; the one, when its onrush is over, puts an end to its ravages, the other only begins where the first ends, and cannot change except by upheavals which are always dangerous to its whole internal structure.

But nothing is more harmful than to see forever before one the partners in slavery, master and slave. On the one side there is born conceit, on the other, servile fear. There can be no bond between them other than force. And this, concentrated in a small range, extends its oppressive autocratic power everywhere. But the champions of slavery, who, though they hold the sharp edge of power in their hands, are themselves cast into fetters, become its most fanatical preachers. It appears that the spirit of freedom is so dried up in the slaves that they not only have no desire to end their sufferings, but cannot bear to see others free. They love their fetters, if it is possible for man to love his own ruination. I think I can see in them the serpent that wrought the fall of the first man. The examples of arbitrary power are infectious. We must confess that we ourselves, armed with the mace of courage and the law of nature for the crushing of the hundred-headed monster that gulps down the food prepared for the people's general sustenance—we ourselves, perhaps, have been misled into autocratic acts, and, although our intentions have always been good and have aimed at the general happiness, yet our arbitrary behavior cannot be justified by its usefulness. Therefore we now implore your forgiveness for our unintentional presumption.

Do you not know, dear fellow citizens, what destruction threatens us and in what peril we stand? All the hardened feelings of the slaves, not given vent by a kindly gesture of freedom, strengthen and intensify their inner longings. A stream that is barred in its course becomes more powerful in proportion to the opposition it meets. Once it has burst the dam, nothing can stem its flood. Such are our brothers whom we keep enchained. They are waiting for a favorable chance and time. The alarum bell rings. And the destructive force of bestiality breaks loose with terrifying speed. Round about us we shall see sword and poison. Death and fiery desolation will be the meed for our harshness and inhumanity. And the more procrastinating and stubborn we have been about the loosening of their fetters, the more violent they will be in their vengefulness. Bring back to your memory the events of former times. Recall how deception roused the slaves to destroy their masters. Enticed by a crude pretender, they hastened to follow him, and wished only to free themselves from the yoke of their masters; and in their ignorance they could think of no other means to do this than to kill their masters. They spared neither sex nor age. They sought more the joy of vengeance than the benefit of broken shackles.

That is what awaits us, this is what we must expect. Danger is steadily mounting, peril is already hovering over our heads. Time has already raised its scythe and is only awaiting an opportunity. The first demagogue or humanitarian who rises up to awaken the unfortunates will hasten the scythe's fierce sweep. Beware!

But if the terror of destruction and the danger of the loss of property can move those among you who are weak, shall we not be brave enough to overcome our prejudices, to suppress our selfishness, to free our brothers from the bonds of slavery, and to reestablish the natural equality of all? Knowing the disposition of your hearts, I am sure that you will be convinced more readily by arguments drawn from the human heart than by the calculations of selfish reason, and still less by the fears of danger. Go, my dear ones, go to the dwellings of your brothers and proclaim to them the change in their lot. Proclaim with deep feeling: "Moved to pity by your fate, sympathizing with our fellow men, having come to recognize your equality, and convinced that our interests are mutual, we have come to embrace our brothers. We have abandoned the haughty discrimination which for so long a time has separated us from you, we have forgotten the inequality that has existed between us, we rejoice now in our mutual victory, and this day on which the shackles of our fellow citizens are broken shall become the most famous day in our annals. Forget our former injustice to you, and let us sincerely love one another."

Such will be your utterance; deep down in your hearts you already hear it. Do not delay, my dear ones. Time flies; our days go by and we do nothing. Let us not end our lives merely fostering good intentions which we have not been able to carry out. Let not our posterity take advantage of this, win our rightful crown of glory, and say contemptuously of us: "They had their day."

This is what I read in the mud-stained paper which I picked up in front of the posthut as I left my carriage. . . .

. . . A whole bundle of papers and drafts of laws referred to the abolition of serfdom in Russia. But my friend, realizing that the supreme power was not strong enough to cope with a sudden change of opinions, had outlined a program of temporary legislation leading to a gradual emancipation of the agriculturists in Russia. I will sketch here the main lines of his scheme. The first law provides for the distinction between rural and domestic serfdom. The latter is abolished first of all, and the landlords are forbidden to take into their houses any peasant or anybody registered in the last census as a village dweller. If a landlord takes a peasant into his house as a servant or artisan, he at once becomes free. Peasants are to be allowed to marry without asking their masters' permission. Marriage license fees are prohibited. The second law has to do with the property and protection of the peasants. They shall own individually the plot that they cultivate, for they shall pay the head tax themselves. Property acquired by a peasant shall belong to him, and no one shall arbitrarily deprive him of it. The peasant is to be reinstated as a citizen. He shall be judged by his peers, that is, in courts in which manorial peasants, among others, are to be chosen to serve. The peasant shall be permitted to acquire real estate, that is, to buy land. He may without hindrance obtain his freedom by paying his master a fixed sum to release him. Arbitrary punishment without due process of law is prohibited. "Avaunt, barbarous custom; perish, power of the tigers!" says our legislator.—Thereupon follows the complete abolition of serfdom.

THE EMPRESS CATHERINE II'S NOTES
ON THE JOURNEY

This book was printed in 1790 without mention of the printing press and without any visible permission at the beginning, although at the end it says: "With the permission of the Department of Public Morals." This is probably a lie, or else carelessness. The purpose of this book is clear on every page: its author, infected and full of the French madness, is trying in every possible way to break down respect for authority and for the authorities, to stir up in the people indignation against their superiors and against the government. . . .

On page 341 begins the pitiful story of a family sold at auction for their master's debts. . . . On 349 it ends with these words: "freedom is not to be expected from their counsels (the landed proprietors), but from the heavy burden of slavery itself." That is, he puts his hopes in a peasant rebellion.

Pages 340 to 369 contain, in the guise of a discussion of prosody, an ode most clearly, manifestly revolutionary, in which tsars are threatened with the block. Cromwell's example is cited and praised. These pages are of criminal intent, completely revolutionary. Ask the author what is the meaning of this ode and by whom it was composed.

III / 1789-1815:
THE AGE OF REVOLUTION

Revolution was the central fact of the quarter-century that began with the meeting of the Estates General in France and ended with the fall of Emperor Napoleon I. This was the age that gave the word "revolution" its modern meaning—the violent overthrow of a state and a society and the deliberate attempt to create in their stead a new state and a better society. This was the specific time of transition between the Old and the New Regimes, between a world fundamentally dedicated to privilege and a world making freedom and equality its stated goals. It was also the time when conservatism, political and intellectual, emerged in its modern shape—as the rejection of revolution and the deliberate transformation of state and society. It was, lastly, a time which thrust to the fore the always troubling problems of the relationship between power and morality, between the use of the state to do good and the evil that men do in the name of the good.

40 / ABBÉ SIEYÈS:
A NEW CLASS
DEMANDS POWER

During the revolutionary crisis of 1787–1789, the loose alliance of aristocrats and middle-class commoners against the crown gradually broke down as the nobility revealed that their hostility was more against reform than against the absolute monarchy. When the Estates General were convoked for 1789, the position of the Third Estate, the order of commoners, was given forceful expression in a pamphlet, Qu'est-ce que le Tiers-État? ("What is the Third Estate?"). Its author was a churchman, Emmanuel

Joseph Sieyès (1748–1836), known as the Abbé Sieyès although he held no higher office than vicar general to the bishop of Chartres. Sieyès, who was of middle-class origins, turned against his order and supported the reformers. Made famous by his provocative pamphlet, he played a secondary role during the next decade. Becoming a member of the Directory in 1799, he helped Napoleon Bonaparte come to power and was rewarded with the title of imperial count.[1]

The plan of this work is quite simple. We have three questions to put to ourselves:

1. What is the Third Estate?—Everything.
2. What has it been in the political order until now?—Nothing.
3. What does it want?—To become something.

We shall see if these are the right answers. Then we shall examine the measures which have been tried and those which ought to be adopted in order that the Third Estate may in fact become *something*. We shall therefore state:

4. What the ministers have *attempted* and what the privileged classes themselves propose on its behalf.

5. What *ought* to have been done.

6. Finally, what *remains* for the Third Estate to do in order to take its rightful place.

The Third Estate is a complete nation.

What is necessary for a nation to live and prosper? The work of *individuals* and the services of the *state*.

All the work of individuals can be included within four classes:

1. Since land and water provide the basic materials for man's needs, the first class in our list will comprise all families engaged in rural work.

2. From the time these materials are first sold until they are finally consumed or used, they receive additional value, of greater or lesser complexity, from the addition of further labor of varying quantity. Human industry thereby successfully improves the benefits bestowed by nature and adds two, ten, even a hundred times to the value of the raw material. This is the work of the second class.

3. Between production and consumption, as well as between the different stages of production, a host of intermediate agents, useful equally to producers and consumers, takes their place; these are businessmen (*négociants*) and merchants. The businessmen, who con-

---

[1] [Emmanuel Joseph Sieyès,] *Qu'est-ce que le Tiers-État?* (Paris: n. p., 1789), pp. 1–4, 6–7, 9. Translated from the French by the editor.

stantly bring into balance the needs of different places and times, speculate upon the profits to be earned by the storing and transporting of goods; the merchants, in the final analysis, have the task of selling goods, either at wholesale or retail. This kind of useful activity defines the third class.

4. In addition to these three classes of hard-working and useful citizens who produce *objects* for consumption and use, society also requires a very great number of special occupations and concerns which provide *direct* utility or pleasure to *persons*. The fourth class comprises groups as diverse as the most distinguished scientific and liberal professions on the one extreme, and the basest household services on the other.

These are the tasks upon which society rests. Who performs them? The Third Estate.

Similarly public duties may be arranged under four customary headings: the Sword, the Robe, the Church, and the Administration. We can see without detailed inquiry that the Third Estate constitutes nineteen-twentieths of all these groups, with the one difference that it has to perform all the really hard work, all the tasks that the privileged order refuses to perform. The places of profit and honor are the only ones occupied by the members of the privileged order. . . .

If this exclusion is a social crime against the Third Estate, can we at least say that it is useful to the state? But are we unaware of the results of this monopoly? Don't we know that while it discourages those it rejects, it also spoils the abilities of those it favors? Don't we know that anything done in the absence of free competition is more expensive and worse made? . . .

Who, then, would dare to say that the Third Estate does not possess within itself all that is needed to make a complete nation? It is a strong and sturdy man with one arm still in chains. Minus the privileged order, the nation would be greater, not less than it is. What, therefore, is the Third Estate? Everything—but in shackles and oppressed. What would it be without the privileged order? Everything—but free and prospering. Without the Third Estate, nothing can be done; without the privileged order, everything would be done infinitely better.

It is not enough to have shown that the privileged class, far from being useful to the nation, can only weaken and harm it; it must also be proved that the noble estate is actually not a part of the social organization, that it may well be a *burden* upon the nation but cannot be a part of it. . . .

The Third Estate, therefore, embraces everything which belongs to the nation; and whatever is not part of the Third Estate may not be treated as part of the nation. What is the Third Estate? Everything.

41 / THE DECLARATION OF RIGHTS

The mood to which Sieyès gave voice in a pamphlet received solemn expression within the first months of the Revolution in the Declaration of the Rights of Man and the Citizen. This statement of principles was adopted by the National Assembly—as the Estates General were now called—on August 27, 1789. It reflects many influences, from the doctrines of the Enlightenment to the English Bill of Rights enacted exactly a century before to the American Declaration of Independence of 1776. Though it was conceived as an all-inclusive program of principles, it reveals quite precisely which rights seemed most important to the bourgeoisie —the commoners of wealth and talents—in 1789, as political power passed into their hands. The full text of the Declaration is reproduced here (A) in a translation by an eminent American student of the French Revolution.[2]

The historical significance of the Declaration of the Rights of Man has been frequently debated, some seeing it as the basis of the virtues of the modern democratic order, others as the expression of its inadequacies and dangers. A modern German historian, Martin Göhring, sees the Declaration as the culmination of a long process of transformation of political ideas and practices in France. His Weg und Sieg der modernen Staatsidee in Frankreich *("The Development and Triumph of the Modern Idea of the State in France," 1946) was written during the final years of the Nazi regime, when the liberal and democratic principles which Göhring here praises (B) were treated as criminal heresies; it was published only after the end of World War II. Göhring (b. 1903) has been the outstanding German historian of the French Revolution since the early 1930's.[3]*

[2] John Hall Stewart, *A Documentary Survey of the French Revolution* (New York: The Macmillan Company, 1951), pp. 113–15. Translated from the French by John Hall Stewart. Copyright 1951 by The Macmillan Company and used with their permission.

[3] Martin Göhring, *Weg und Sieg der modernen Staatsidee in Frankreich* (Tübingen: J. C. B. Mohr [Paul Siebeck], 1946), pp. 278–81. Translated from the German by the editor. By permission of the publisher.

A. TEXT OF THE DECLARATION

The representatives of the French people, organized in National Assembly, considering that ignorance, forgetfulness, or contempt of the rights of man are the sole causes of public misfortunes and of the corruption of governments, have resolved to set forth in a solemn declaration the natural, inalienable, and sacred rights of man, in order that such declaration, continually before all members of the social body, may be a perpetual reminder of their rights and duties; in order that the acts of the legislative power and those of the executive power may constantly be compared with the aim of every political institution and may accordingly be more respected; in order that the demands of the citizens, founded henceforth upon simple and incontestable principles, may always be directed towards the maintenance of the Constitution and the welfare of all.

Accordingly, the National Assembly recognizes and proclaims, in the presence and under the auspices of the Supreme Being, the following rights of man and the citizen.

1. Men are born and remain free and equal in rights; social distinctions may be based only upon general usefulness.

2. The aim of every political association is the preservation of the natural and inalienable rights of man; these rights are liberty, property, security, and resistance to oppression.

3. The source of all sovereignty resides essentially in the nation; no group, no individual may exercise authority not emanating expressly therefrom.

4. Liberty consists of the power to do whatever is not injurious to others; thus the enjoyment of the natural rights of every man has for its limits only those that assure other members of society the enjoyment of those same rights; such limits may be determined only by law.

5. The law has the right to forbid only actions which are injurious to society. Whatever is not forbidden by law may not be prevented, and no one may be constrained to do what it does not prescribe.

6. Law is the expression of the general will; all citizens have the right to concur personally, or through their representatives, in its formation; it must be the same for all, whether it protects or punishes. All citizens, being equal before it, are equally admissible to all public offices, positions, and employments, according to their capacity, and without other distinction than that of virtues and talents.

7. No man may be accused, arrested, or detained except in the cases determined by law, and according to the forms prescribed thereby. Whoever solicits, expedites, or executes arbitrary orders, or has them executed, must be punished; but every citizen summoned or appre-

hended in pursuance of the law must obey immediately; he renders himself culpable by resistance.

8. The law is to establish only penalties that are absolutely and obviously necessary; and no one may be punished except by virtue of a law established and promulgated prior to the offence and legally applied.

9. Since every man is presumed innocent until declared guilty, if arrest be deemed indispensable, all unnecessary severity for securing the person of the accused must be severely repressed by law.

10. No one is to be disquieted because of his opinions, even religious, provided their manifestation does not disturb the public order established by law.

11. Free communication of ideas and opinions is one of the most precious of the rights of man. Consequently, every citizen may speak, write, and print freely, subject to responsibility for the abuse of such liberty in the cases determined by law.

12. The guarantee of the rights of man and the citizen necessitates a public force; such a force, therefore, is instituted for the advantage of all and not for the particular benefit of those to whom it is entrusted.

13. For the maintenance of the public force and for the expenses of administration a common tax is indispensable; it must be assessed equally on all citizens in proportion to their means.

14. Citizens have the right to ascertain, by themselves or through their representatives, the necessity of the public tax, to consent to it freely, to supervise its use, and to determine its quota, assessment, payment, and duration.

15. Society has the right to require of every public agent an accounting of his administration.

16. Every society in which the guarantee of rights is not assured or the separation of powers not determined has no constitution at all.

17. Since property is a sacred and inviolable right, no one may be deprived thereof unless a legally established public necessity obviously requires it, and upon condition of a just and previous indemnity.

B. MARTIN GÖHRING: HISTORICAL SIGNIFICANCE OF THE DECLARATION

Thus we have come to the threshold of the Great French Revolution. The small revolution was at an end. It was small not as measured by the ardor of the battle and the length of its duration, but only by its results. These were negative for those who waged it. They retained nothing from their triumph over absolutism. The privilege-based state which they had fought to control was doomed to destruction by the very way they had fought it. The higher orders fought with faces turned toward the past, and yet they had conjured up in the heavens the dawn of a new time. They had not taken notice of the universally prevailing discrepancy between the established institutions and the prevailing ideas and values, between the existing conditions and the laws; they did not realize that there was no longer any real possibility of putting their ideas into practice. A contemporary who emphasized the transformed character of the feudal system painted the true situation to a "T." The nobility, he wrote, had sought to reawaken the proud spirit of feudalism at a time when it had ceased to exist in reality. "They sought to transplant the chivalric ideal from the twelfth century to the eighteenth, the century of the Enlightenment. The corporations and estates were not aware that as they grew old, their maxims grew old too, and they did not understand that once everything else had changed, they too had either to change or go under." The feudal edifice could stand only as long as it had the respect of public opinion. The feudal order had to end when the people made their claims, when feudalism became hollow and fragile thanks to its own divisions, when it lost solidity, when the nobility ceased to enjoy general respect. "When the common citizen could become a noble by the payment of money, men no longer believed that the nobles constituted a special race. And when the wealth and economic progress of the commoners placed them on the same footing as the nobles, when the writers and scholars with whom the nobles shared their life became aware of their own superiority to them, when the feudal countryside became covered with academies rich in poets, important artists, wealthy merchants and educated citizens, all of whom considered themselves to be of at least equal value to the nobility, then the old belief lost its force, and old beliefs do not resume at the same place they started. A new spirit arose which could be attacked by saber and cannon only in vain." These are words of truth. The ideal which triumphed in 1789, like the chivalric ideal of the Middle Ages before it, conquered the world and maintained itself victoriously against all the coalitions of the old powers. This lay in the nature of things, for mankind became aware that a new time had indeed begun. Events capable of causing the Königsberg philosopher [Kant] to break his stride and violate his strict daily schedule had to be revolutionary in character. The storming of the Bastille had a revolutionary effect, but it was the symbolism of the act which created even more enthusiasm than the act as such. France rightly declared the day to be a national holiday.

Did the history of the events leading up to the Revolution decree that it had to turn out exactly as it did? No. Things would have taken a different shape had the crown followed a clear and creative policy, had it understood the signs of the times, had it made an alliance with the third estate and thereby joined forces with the new spirit. This was possible; it was what the bourgeoisie wanted. They did not want to

abandon the state but to work within it, admittedly in order to transform it. But just as the crown lacked the courage to sell its soul to the
privileged orders at the decisive moment, so too did it lack the strength
to do the opposite. It acted as if the great controversy was of immediate concern only to itself. This was to adhere to a principle which had
proved false in practice and which it too had inwardly ceased to believe. The result was to rush events and cause mistakes. But what did
that matter in comparison with what developed?

It was a unique event that a nation rose up in the face of a centuries-
old and still absolute power such as the monarchy continued to be,
declared itself to be sovereign, laid down the conditions of its future
existence upon the basis of its sovereignty, and thereby gave expression
to something that the best individuals in all civilized nations had already acknowledged, something worthy of serving the future generations of all peoples as a guiding star. This is the significance of the
Declaration of the Rights of Man. To be sure, it was not the first event
of its kind. There were similar declarations in English history, and the
American people had proclaimed a declaration of rights in 1783. But
the English declarations were concerned only with England, the American only with America. It remained therefore for France to give its
declaration the character of universality in space and time and to speak
to all the nations.

In the declaration of 1789 lay the quintessence of the political
thought of the philosophers of the continent as well as the political
ambitions and actions of the peoples, the French people first of all. It
was not wholly without significance that the soldier of freedom, La-
fayette, who had fought for the independence of America and had
been present when the American declaration was proclaimed, was the
first to propose a declaration of rights to the National Assembly; but
he had done no more than to take up and at most give form to impulses
which arose from the people themselves. The act was demanded by the
political situation and the need to reach European thinkers; by the
political situation insofar as it sought to protect forever the nation
which thereby declared its own sovereignty against any violent attempt
to undo what had been done. In view of the duality of forces at work
in the state, it presented to the menacing executive power a categorical
imperative in the provisions that sovereignty by its nature rests in the
people, that no society and no individual can exercise any authority
which does not derive from them, that the law must be the expression
of the general will, in which all citizens may participate personally or
by their representatives, and that the law may forbid only such actions
as are harmful to society, that no tax may be raised without the approval of the nation, that every public official is responsible to the
public, and that a constitutional condition exists only when the powers

of government are divided and the guarantee of natural rights is assured. These rights are freedom, property, security, and resistance to oppression. For in fact the only purpose of organizing a state is to protect the rights of men. But men are born and remain free and equal in rights; social differences can be justified only upon the basis of the general interest.

This was a beacon for all time. If nothing else had remained from the Revolution besides this proclamation, it would still be the most powerful political event of modern times. But more remained than that. On August 4, 1789, the deputies met in a memorable night session and proclaimed, amid undescribable enthusiasm and with both solemnity and generosity, the sacrifice upon the altar of the fatherland of all privileges, rights and immunities belonging to individuals, cities and provinces, which had been attained as the result of long struggle. This was the entombment of the old France. The feudal order was dead forever. Henceforth only Frenchmen with equal rights and provinces of equal status faced each other. France took one night to do what other nations were to require another hundred years to achieve. The prerequisites were laid down for the truly modern national state based upon unity and law. The Revolution created this state and preserved it through many trials. The creation was in such perfect conformity with the French character that one of its critics could say of it that it had proved "how far the human spirit can venture in desiring and in daring whatever it finds within itself that is founded upon the eternal duties of reason." But such a venture is good.

The great Revolution is not yet at an end. Its still creative power has not yet died out. It has proved itself victorious against all other forces of the spirit; for it was the Enlightenment put into practice and hence an avowal of the ideals of thinkers who stand in the ranks of those whom we honor as the greatest heroes of the spirit.

42 / CONDORCET:
THE VISION OF PROGRESS

The better world which was supposed to be built upon the principles of the Declaration of the Rights of Man was, in the revolutionaries' dream, the culmination of the long history of mankind. It was, in the phrase of the American historian Carl Becker, "the heavenly city of the eighteenth-century philosophers." Yet most of the thinkers of the Enlightenment had not been revolutionaries in intent, and few of those who remained active during the revolution fared well. This was the fate of Antoine Nicolas de Caritat, marquis de Condorcet, author of the Esquisse d'un tableau historique des progrès de l'esprit humain *("Sketch for a Historical Picture of the Progress of the Human Mind," 1795), from which the following excerpts are taken. Embodying in his activity and his ideas many of the characteristic elements of the Enlightenment, Condorcet (1743–1794) was born a nobleman but abandoned his title at the time of the revolution. He was hostile to the Jacobin Reign of Terror, during which he was outlawed. Arrested in 1794, he died in prison, probably a suicide, before he could be guillotined.[4]*

All errors in politics and morals are based on philosophical errors and these in turn are connected with scientific errors. There is not a religious system nor a supernatural extravagance that is not founded on ignorance of the laws of nature. The inventors, the defenders of these absurdities could not foresee the successive perfection of the human mind. Convinced that men in their day knew everything that they could ever know and would always believe what they then believed, they confidently supported their idle dreams on the current opinions of their country and their age.

Advances in the physical sciences are all the more fatal to these errors in that they often destroy them without appearing to attack them, and that they can shower on those who defend them so obstinately the humiliating taunt of ignorance.

At the same time the habit of correct reasoning about the objects of these sciences, the precise ideas gained by their methods, and the means of recognizing or proving the truth of a belief should naturally lead us to compare the sentiment that forces us to accept well-founded opinions credible for good reasons, with that which ties us to habitual prejudices or forces us to submit to authority. Such a comparison is enough to teach us to mistrust opinions of the latter kind, to convince us that we do not really believe them even when we boast of believing them, even when we profess them with the purest sincerity. This secret, once discovered, makes their destruction immediate and certain. Finally this progress of the physical sciences which neither the passions nor self-interest can disturb, in which neither birth, nor profession, nor

[4] Antoine Nicolas de Condorcet, *Sketch for a Historical Picture of the Progress of the Human Mind* (New York: The Noonday Press, 1955), pp. 163–4, 167–9, 189–91, 201–2. Translated from the French by June Barraclough. Reprinted by permission of The Noonday Press.

position are thought to confer on one the right to judge what one is not in a condition to understand, this inexorable progress cannot be contemplated by men of enlightenment without their wishing to make the other sciences follow the same path. It offers them at every step a model to emulate and one by which they may judge of their own efforts, recognize the false roads on which they may have set out and preserve themselves equally from pyrrhonism, from credulity, from extreme diffidence, and from a too great submission even to the authority of learning and fame. . . .

The progress of philosophy and the sciences has favoured and extended the progress of letters, and this in turn has served to make the study of the sciences easier, and that of philosophy more popular. The sciences and the arts have assisted one another despite the efforts of the ignorant and the foolish to separate them and make them enemies. Scholarship, which seemed doomed by its respect for the past and its deference towards authority always to lend its support to harmful superstitions, has nevertheless contributed to their eradication, for it was able to borrow the torch of a sounder criticism from philosophy and the sciences. It already knew how to weigh up authorities and compare them; it now learned how to bring every authority before the bar of Reason. It had already discounted prodigies, fantastic anecdotes, facts contrary to all probability; but after attacking the evidence on which such absurdities relied, it now learned that all extraordinary facts must always be rejected, however impressive the evidence in their favour, unless this can truly turn the scale against the weight of their physical or moral probability.

Thus all the intellectual activities of man, however different they may be in their aims, their methods, or the qualities of mind they exact, have combined to further the progress of human reason. Indeed, the whole system of human labour is like a well-made machine, whose several parts have been systematically distinguished but none the less, being intimately bound together, form a single whole, and work towards a single end.

Turning our attention to the human race in general, we shall show how the discovery of the correct method of procedure in the sciences, the growth of scientific theories, their application to every part of the natural world, to the subject of every human need, the lines of communication established between one science and another, the great number of men who cultivate the sciences, and most important of all, the spread of printing, how together all these advances ensure that no science will ever fall below the point it has reached. We shall point out that the principles of philosophy, the slogans of liberty, the recognition of the true rights of man and his real interests, have spread through far too great a number of nations, and now direct in each of them the opinions of far too great a number of enlightened men, for us to fear that they will ever be allowed to relapse into oblivion. And indeed what reason could we have for fear, when we consider that the languages most widely spoken are the languages of the two peoples who enjoy liberty to the fullest extent and who best understand its principles, and that no league of tyrants, no political intrigues, could prevent the resolute defence, in these two languages, of the rights of reason and of liberty?

But although everything tells us that the human race will never relapse into its former state of barbarism, although everything combines to reassure us against that corrupt and cowardly political theory which would condemn it to oscillate forever between truth and error, liberty and servitude, nevertheless we still see the forces of enlightenment in possession of no more than a very small portion of the globe, and the truly enlightened vastly outnumbered by the great mass of men who are still given over to ignorance and prejudice. We still see vast areas in which men groan in slavery, vast areas offering the spectacle of nations either degraded by the vices of a civilization whose progress is impeded by corruption, or still vegetating in the infant condition of early times. We observe that the labours of recent ages have done much for the progress of the human mind, but little for the perfection of the human race; that they have done much for the honour of man, something for his liberty, but so far almost nothing for his happiness. At a few points our eyes are dazzled with a brilliant light; but thick darkness still covers an immense stretch of the horizon. There are a few circumstances from which the philosopher can take consolation; but he is still afflicted by the spectacle of the stupidity, slavery, barbarism and extravagance of mankind; and the friend of humanity can find unmixed pleasure only in tasting the sweet delights of hope for the future. . . .

Since the discovery, or rather the exact analysis of the first principles of metaphysics, morals and politics is still recent and was preceded by the knowledge of a large number of detailed truths, the false notion that they have thereby attained their destination, has gained ready acceptance; men imagine that, because there are no more crude errors to refute, no more fundamental truths to establish, nothing remains to be done.

But it is easy to see how imperfect is the present analysis of man's moral and intellectual faculties; how much further the knowledge of his duties which presumes a knowledge of the influence of his actions upon the welfare of his fellow men and upon the society to which he belongs, can still be increased through a more profound, more accurate, more considered observation of that influence; how many questions have to be solved, how many social relations to be examined, before we can have precise knowledge of the individual rights of man and the rights that the state confers upon each in regard to all. Have we yet ascertained at all accurately the limits of the rights that exist between different societies in times of war, or that are enjoyed by society over its members in times of trouble and schism, or that belong to individuals, or spontaneous associations at the moment of their original, free formation or their necessary disintegration?

If we pass on to the theory which ought to direct the application of particular principles and serve as the foundation for the social art, do we not see the necessity of acquiring a precision that these elementary truths cannot possess so long as they are absolutely general? Have we yet reached the point when we can reckon as the only foundation of law either justice or a proved and acknowledged utility instead of the vague, uncertain, arbitrary views of alleged political expediency? Are we yet in possession of any precise rules for selecting out of the almost infinite variety of possible systems in which the general principles of equality and natural rights are respected, those which will best secure the preservation of these rights, which will afford the freest scope for their exercise and their enjoyment, and which will moreover insure the leisure and welfare of individuals and the strength, prosperity and peace of nations?

The application of the calculus of combinations and probabilities to these sciences promises even greater improvement, since it is the only way of achieving results of an almost mathematical exactitude and of assessing the degree of their probability or likelihood. Sometimes, it is true, the evidence upon which these results are based may lead us, without any calculation, at the first glance, to some general truth and teach us whether the effect produced by such-and-such a cause was or was not favourable, but if this evidence cannot be weighed and measured, and if these effects cannot be subjected to precise measurement, then we cannot know exactly how much good or evil they contain; or, again, if the good and evil nearly balance each other, if the difference between them is slight, we cannot pronounce with any certainty to which side the balance really inclines. Without the application of the calculus it would be almost impossible to choose with any certainty between two combinations that have the same purpose and between which there is no apparent difference in merit. Without the calculus these sciences would always remain crude and limited for want of instruments delicate enough to catch the fleeting truth, of machines precise enough to plumb the depths where so much that is of value to science lies hidden.

However, such an application, notwithstanding the happy efforts of

certain geometers, is still in the earliest stages: and it will be left to
the generations to come to use this source of knowledge which is as
inexhaustible as the calculus itself, or as the number of combinations, relations and facts that may be included in its sphere of operation. . . .

How consoling for the philosopher who laments the errors, the
crimes, the injustices which still pollute the earth and of which he is
often the victim is this view of the human race, emancipated from its
shackles, released from the empire of fate and from that of the enemies
of its progress, advancing with a firm and sure step along the path of
truth, virtue and happiness! It is the contemplation of this prospect
that rewards him for all his efforts to assist the progress of reason and
the defence of liberty. He dares to regard these strivings as part of the
eternal chain of human destiny; and in this persuasion he is filled with
the true delight of virtue and the pleasure of having done some lasting
good which fate can never destroy by a sinister stroke of revenge, by
calling back the reign of slavery and prejudice. Such contemplation is
for him an asylum, in which the memory of his persecutors cannot
pursue him; there he lives in thought with man restored to his natural
rights and dignity, forgets man tormented and corrupted by greed, fear
or envy; there he lives with his peers in an Elysium created by reason
and graced by the purest pleasures known to the love of mankind.

43 / JEAN PAUL MARAT: THE FALL OF LOUIS XVI

*The beheading of Louis XVI on January 21, 1793, like that
of Charles I a century and a half before, was the very symbol of
revolution for a world still largely monarchist in feeling and belief.
It played much the same role for the ardent revolutionaries, who
knew full well that they had struck down not only a man but an
institution hallowed by tradition and religion. The revolutionary
exultation over the king's execution was expressed two days later
by Jean Paul Marat, the outstanding journalist of the revolution,
in an article in the newspaper* Journal de la République Française
*("Journal of the French Republic"), from which the following ex-
cerpt is taken. Marat (1744–1793) was a Swiss-born physician and
scientist who had a notable medical career in France and England
before becoming a journalist and extreme Jacobin during the revolution. He was assassinated by a young woman supporter of the*

Girondins, the more moderate revolutionary party suppressed by the Jacobins.[5]

The tyrant's head has just fallen beneath the blade of the law. By the same act the foundations of monarchy among us have been overthrown: now at last I believe in the republic.

How vain were the fears which the dethroned despot's henchmen sought to arouse in us concerning the consequences of his death, in the hope of saving him from execution! To be sure, the precautions taken to keep order were impressive and were dictated by prudence, but they proved superfluous. All along the route from the Temple to the scaffold public wrath could be trusted to stand guard. Not a voice was heard during the execution to ask that the king be spared, not a voice was raised on behalf of the man who once decided the destinies of France; all about him profound silence reigned until his head was displayed to the people, when everywhere shouts rose up, "Long live the nation!" "Long live the republic!"

The rest of the day was perfectly calm. For the first time since the [massacre of the] Federation, the people seemed to be moved by serene joy; it was as if they had just witnessed a religious ceremony and were at last released from the burden of oppression which had weighed down upon them for so long, and they were imbued with the feeling of brotherhood. Every heart opened itself to the hope of a happier future.

This delicious satisfaction was disturbed only by anger over the monstrous attack upon a representative of the nation [Le Peletier de Saint-Fargeau] who was assassinated the day before by a former member of the royal bodyguard because he had voted in favor of the death of the tyrant.

The execution of Louis XVI is one of those memorable events which begin a new era in the history of nations. It will have a prodigious influence upon the fate of the despots of Europe and of the peoples who have not yet broken their shackles.

The National Convention no doubt showed its greatness when it sentenced to death the tyrant of France, but it obeyed the will of the nation. The way in which the people observed the punishment of their former master raised them even above their representatives, for you may be sure that the feelings of the citizens of Paris and the *fédérés* [provincial delegates] are shared by the citizens in every department.

[5] Jean Paul Marat, "Le tyran puni," *Journal de la République Française*, No. 105, Wednesday, January 23, 1793. Reprinted in Jean Paul Marat, *Textes choisis*, ed. Lucien Scheler (Paris: Éditions de Minuit, 1945), pp. 165–8. Translated from the French by the editor. Reprinted by permission of the publisher.

Far from disturbing the peace of the state, the execution of Louis XVI will serve only to strengthen it by restraining, through terror, the enemies inside and outside the country. It will also give the nation new energy and strength to repel the ferocious hordes of foreign satellites who dare to bear arms against her; for there is no better means of driving them back. Our present position is one in which we must triumph or perish. Cambon expressed this plain truth in a sublime image yesterday morning while on the speaker's platform: "We have just landed upon the Isle of Liberty, and we have burned the ship which brought us here."

If we are to defeat the countless legions of our foes, we must first of all be united among ourselves. If the national senate had been purged of the tyrant's accomplices, of these intriguers who have made so many attempts to strengthen the throne at the expense of public liberty, then it would have achieved unity without fail, instead of being troubled by dissension, as it still is. But he [Louis XVI] became a fanatic: in the conviction that he could not save himself by informing upon those who collaborated in his plots, he kept silent and tried to appear a martyr when he died.

In the letter he sent to his judges two days before his execution, he requested a delay of three days—a long enough time perhaps for the despot's henchmen to assure him impunity; for hordes of assassins were ready to slay every patriotic deputy who voted the death penalty. They all received threatening letters; one fell beneath an assassin's blows, and others were attacked. He also requested that provision be made for his family and the unfortunates whose only income was a royal pension; but he said not a word about his sentence and, strange to say, he forgot to protest his innocence.

44 / MAXIMILIEN ROBESPIERRE: THE DOCTRINE OF JACOBIN REVOLUTION

The revolution in France had become the work of the bourgeoisie from the first sessions of the Estates General, but from the time of Bastille Day (July 14, 1789) it was also evident that the hard and dangerous task of overcoming the opposition to the revolution fell especially upon the common people, particularly the

Paris "crowd." The Jacobins in particular relied upon popular insurrections to drive forward their revolutionary transformation of France; but they were also disturbed, like their less extreme revolutionary predecessors, by the desire of the poor to improve their condition by limiting the rights of private property. Maximilien Robespierre (1758–1794), the mind and voice of the Jacobins, sought to reconcile somehow the conflicting demands of the bourgeoisie and the populace. He appealed to the National Convention on April 24, 1793, to modify the rights of property in a new Declaration of Rights then under debate. His speech (A) on that occasion is translated here.[6]

How to reconcile the dream of government by the people with the fact of dictatorship was another disturbing problem confronting the French revolutionaries, particularly after the Jacobins took power. Robespierre's answer, which has come to be called the doctrine of "democratic dictatorship," was presented to the Convention in a speech on December 25, 1793. The impromptu character of his address is retained in the following translation (B) of the principal passages.[7]

A. RIGHTS OF PROPERTY

I shall first propose a number of articles required to fill out your theory of property. Let none among you take fright at this word. You souls in the mire who esteem only gold, I do not want to touch your treasures, however impure may be their source. You should know that the agrarian law [8] which you speak of so often is nothing but a bogeyman created by scoundrels to scare fools with.

We can be sure of this: a revolution was not needed to teach the world that extreme inequality of wealth is the source of many evils and crimes; but nonetheless we continue to be convinced that equality of wealth is a chimera. As for me, I believe it to be even less necessary for private happiness than for public felicity; it is much more important to make poverty honorable than to outlaw opulence; there is no reason for the hut of Fabricius to be jealous of Crassus's palace. As

[6] Marc Bouloiseau *et al.*, eds., *Œuvres de Maximilien Robespierre* (Paris: Presses Universitaires de France, 1958), Vol. IX, pp. 459–63. Translated from the French by Herbert H. Rowen. By permission of the publisher.

[7] *Discours et rapports de Robespierre*, edited by Charles Vellay (Paris: Charpentier et Fasquelle, 1908), pp. 311–6. Translated from the French by Herbert H. Rowen.

[8] a law providing for the redistribution of landed property upon an egalitarian basis (ed.)

far as I am concerned, I would much rather be one of Aristides' sons, raised in the Prytaneum at the expense of the Republic, than the heir presumptive to Xerxes, born in the filth of the Court and destined to occupy a throne ornamented with the degradation of the peoples and brilliant with the destitution of the public.

Let us therefore set down in good faith the principles of the right of property. This is all the more necessary because there is no right which prejudiced and vicious men have sought to wrap in thicker fog.

Ask that merchant in human flesh what property is; as he points out that long coffin which he calls a ship, in which he has confined and chained men who seem to be alive, he will tell you, "This is my property; I bought it at so much a head." Ask that gentleman who owns estates and serfs, or who believes that the world has been over-turned when he no longer does, and he will give you just about the same notion of property.

Ask the august members of the Capetian dynasty; they will tell you that the most sacred of all properties is without contradiction the hereditary right which from time immemorial they have enjoyed to oppress, degrade and squeeze down, legally and monarchically, the twenty-five million men who inhabit the territory of France, as their own good pleasure may dictate.

As such people see it, property bears no relation to any principle of morality. It excludes all notions of justice and injustice. Why does your declaration of rights apparently commit the same mistakes? When you defined liberty, the first of man's goods, the most sacred of the rights which he holds from nature, you rightly said that its limits lay in the rights of others. Why did you not apply this principle to property, which is a social institution? This was as if the eternal laws of nature were less inviolable than the covenants of men. You have multiplied clauses in order to assure the greatest freedom for the use of property, but you have not said a word to fix the limits of its legitimate charac-ter, so that your declaration seems to have been drawn up not for men but for rich men, monopolists, speculators and tyrants. My proposal to you is to reform these vices by enshrining the following truths:

Article 1.—Property is the right which each citizen has to enjoy and dispose of the portion of wealth which is guaranteed to him by law.

Article 2.—The right of property is limited like all other rights by the obligation to respect the rights of others.

Article 3.—It may not be used to the detriment of the safety, freedom, existence or property of our fellow men.

Article 4.—Any possession or business which violates this principle is illegal and immoral.

You all speak of taxation in order to establish the incontestable principle that it can emanate only from the will of the people or its representatives; but you forget a provision which is required by the interests of mankind—you forget to establish the basis of progressive taxation. Now, is there a principle in the matter of public taxation which follows more manifestly from the nature of things and from eternal justice than that which places upon the citizenry the obligation to contribute to public expenditures at a progressive rate, according to the extent of their fortune, that is, according to the size of the benefits which they draw from society?

I propose that you inscribe this principle in an article in the following terms:

"Citizens whose income does not exceed the amount needed for their subsistence shall be relieved from contributing to public expenditures; others shall make their contributions at a progressive rate, according to the size of their fortune."

The committee has completely forgotten to recall the duties of brotherhood which unite all men and all nations, and their rights to mutual assistance; it seems to have been unaware of the foundations of the eternal alliance of the peoples against the tyrants; we might say that your declaration was drawn up for a troop of human creatures penned up in some distant corner of the globe, and not for the immense family to which nature has given the earth for their residence and their domain. I propose that you fill this great gap by the following articles; they will only win you the respect of the peoples. It is true that they may have the drawback of involving you in a dispute with the kings from which there will be no turning back. I admit that this drawback does not scare me; it will not scare those who do not want to be reconciled with the kings.

Article 1.—The men of all countries are brothers, and the different peoples should assist each other to the extent of their power, like citizens of the same state.

Article 2.—He who oppresses one nation declares himself to be the enemy of all.

Article 3.—Those who wage war upon one people in order to halt the progress of freedom and to destroy the rights of man must be hunted down not as ordinary enemies but as assassins and rebellious brigands.

Article 4.—Kings, aristocrats and tyrants are all of them slaves in revolt against the sovereign of the earth, that is, the human race, and against the lawgiver of the universe, that is, nature.

B. "DEMOCRATIC DICTATORSHIP"

The theory of revolutionary government is as new as the revolution which created it. We need not look for this theory in the books of writers on politics, who utterly failed to foresee this revolution, nor should we look for it in the laws of tyrants, who are satisfied to misuse their power and seldom bother to prove that it is legitimate. For aristocrats, therefore, this word "revolution" is only the source of their terrors, or the pretext for their slanders; for tyrants, it is only a scandalous thing; and for many persons it is only an enigma. We must explain to all what it really means, so that at least those who are good citizens will support the principles of the public interest.

The function of government is to guide the moral and physical energies of the nation toward the goal for which it was established.

The goal of constitutional government is to preserve the Republic; the goal of revolutionary government, to establish it.

The revolution is the war waged by freedom against its foes; the constitution is the rule of freedom when it has triumphed and is at peace.

The very fact that revolutionary government is at war compels it to do an extraordinary number of things. Because it finds itself in stormy and changing circumstances and is constantly forced to meet new and pressing dangers—this is especially important—with new and immediately available resources, the rules to which it is subject are less uniform and rigorous.

The principal concern of constitutional government is civil liberty; of revolutionary government, public liberty. Under a constitutional regime little more is necessary than to protect individuals against abuses by the state; under a revolutionary regime it is the state which is compelled to defend itself against attacking factions on every side.

To good citizens revolutionary government owes the complete protection of the nation; to the enemies of the people it owes only death.

These ideas are sufficient to explain the origin and the nature of what we call revolutionary laws. Those who call them arbitrary or tyrannical are stupid, or they are perverse sophists who persist in confusing opposite things; they would establish the same rule for war and peace, for health and sickness. What they really want is the resurrection of tyranny and the death of the fatherland. If they call for literal enforcement of the provisions of the constitution, their purpose is only to be able themselves to violate these rules with impunity. They are cowardly murderers who want to strangle the Republic in its cradle without running danger to themselves, and therefore they try to choke it with vague maxims: but they themselves find no difficulty in throwing off the bonds of these maxims.

The ship of the constitution was not built to remain on the ways forever: but do we have to launch it just when the storm is at its worst and the winds are contrary? This is what is wanted by the tyrants and the slaves who were opposed to our even building this ship—but the French people have commanded you to wait until calm returns. With a unanimity which immediately drowns the clamors of the aristocrats and the federalists,[9] they order that your first act be to save them from all their enemies.

The temples of the gods are not built to serve as sanctuaries for the desecrators who come to profane them, nor was the Constitution designed to protect the plots of tyrants who seek to destroy it.

Is a revolutionary government less just and less legitimate because it must be freer in its movements and more active than an ordinary government? No! for it rests upon the sanest of all laws—the safety of the people—and the most indisputable of all rights—necessity.

It too has its rules, all based upon justice and public order. It has nothing in common with anarchy or disorder; on the contrary, its aims are to put down anarchy and disorder, to establish and to consolidate the reign of law. It has nothing in common with arbitrary power; it must be guided not by the passions of individuals but by the public interest.

It should follow the ordinary general principles in all cases where these can be strictly applied without endangering public liberty. But against conspirators it should employ all the force required to meet their boldness or treachery. The more terrible it is to evildoers, the more merciful it should be to good men. The more it is compelled by circumstances to act with necessary rigor, the more it should refrain from measures which needlessly interfere with freedom and disturb private interests without any public advantage. . . .

If we have to choose between an excess of patriotic zeal and the nothingness of bad citizenship, or even the morass of the principle of moderation, we will not hesitate. A vigorous body which suffers from an overabundance of vital juices is a greater source of strength than a corpse.

Let us be supremely careful that we do not kill patriotism in our endeavor to heal it.

By its nature patriotism is ardent. Who can love his homeland with a cool love? Patriotism belongs particularly to simple people, who have had little training in determining the political consequences of an act of state from its concealed motives. Where is the patriot, however well informed, who has never made a mistake? If we admit, then, that there are those who are moderate and cowardly with the best of intentions, why shouldn't there be patriots with the best of intentions who at times are carried too far by laudable feelings? Therefore, if we are to consider as criminal all those in the revolutionary movement who step over the precise line dictated by prudence, we will sweep into a common condemnation both bad citizens and all those who are the natural

---

[9] advocates of a decentralized, or federal, republic (ed.)

friends of freedom, your own friends, the supporters of the Republic. The adroit emissaries of tyranny will first trick them and then become their accusers and perhaps their judges.

Who then will untangle all these subtleties? Who will draw a line to mark off all the different excesses? It will be done by the love of fatherland, the love of truth. Kings and knaves will always try to stamp out this love, for they do not wish to face either reason or truth.

While we have shown the duties of revolutionary government, we have also pointed out the reefs which lie in front of it. The greater its power, the swifter and freer its actions, the more it must be guided by honest purposes. Let it fall into impure or traitorous hands, and on that very day its name will become a pretext and an excuse for nothing less than a counterrevolution. It will be strong then in the way a violent poison is strong.

The confidence of the French people is therefore given even more to the character of the National Convention than to the institution itself.

By placing all their power in your hands, they expect your government to bestow benefits upon patriots and to strike terror among the enemies of the fatherland. They have given you the task of doing several things at once—to act with all courage in support of the policy needed to crush the enemy; and even more to maintain unity among yourselves, as you must do in order to fulfill your great destiny.

The establishment of the French Republic is not a child's game. It cannot be done by a whim, without seriousness of purpose; it cannot be just the accidental result of the collision of the totality of all individual purposes and revolutionary forces. Wisdom and power presided together over the creation of the universe. When you gave to certain members selected from your midst the redoubtable task of constantly guarding the fate of the fatherland, you accepted the obligation to support them with your strength and your confidence. If the revolutionary government is not supported by the energy, knowledge, patriotism and good will of all the representatives of the people, how will it have enough strength to meet the attacks of Europe, the assaults of the foes of freedom, on every side?

Woe unto us if we open our souls to the treacherous insinuations of our enemies, who must divide us if they are to conquer. Woe unto us if we break our unity instead of strengthening it, if we listen to offended vanity instead of to the fatherland and to truth!

45 / GRACCHUS BABEUF: THE PLAINT OF THE PROPERTYLESS

Hostility among the lower classes to differences of wealth continued even after egalitarian movements were crushed by the Jacobins, who rejected Robespierre's plea for conciliation. Leadership of this opposition passed into the hands of François Noël Babeuf (1760–1797), who took the revolutionary pseudonym of Gracchus Babeuf. Although his specific program of action aimed principally at equalizing ownership of land, Babeuf went beyond egalitarianism in doctrine to attack the institution of private property as such. His criticism was expressed in his own newspaper, Le Tribun du Peuple *("The People's Tribune"), and in correspondence sent to other newspapers. The letter from which the following excerpts are translated was written but never sent to the newspaper* Les Hommes Libres *("The Free Men") and was seized in his rooms when he was arrested in 1796 for attempting to organize an insurrection against the Directory. Babeuf's views were considered so repulsive to the judgment of most men by the Directory, that it had the seized writings published after his execution; this letter was one of those reproduced.[10]*

Before making public a thesis such as this which I maintain here, I reflected upon it at length. As you know, I promised from the beginning to defend it before all and against all. After having raised such a question, I should be guilty of a crime against mankind if I permitted its most essential conclusion to be attacked without resistance when I believe I possess every means to enable it to triumph.

This is no little matter, for it involves determining whether I have presented to the world the easily reached *nec plus ultra* [ultimate boundary] of social welfare or have only presented a splendid illusion.

At least there is more pleasure in pleading this case before the tribunal of sages who listen, examine and debate than before the tribunal

[10] *Haute Cour de Justice, Suite de la Copie des Pièces Saisies dans le local que Baboeuf occupoit lors de son arrestation* (Paris: Imprimerie Nationale, 1798), pp. 10–14. Translated from the French by the editor.

211

of inquisitors and censors who begin by condemning, slandering and forbidding. This is why the judgment of a persuaded public opinion has much greater power than the judgment of force. The flood of philosophy sweeps along the nations and the ages; the influence of bayonets and the ruffians of the law barely reaches particular moments and places. . . .

I dispute the opinion that we would have been better off to have come sooner into the world in order to accomplish the mission of destroying the illusion of the alleged right of property. Who will persuade me that I am deceived in believing that it is precisely the present age which is the most favorable, infinitely more so than it was a thousand years ago? Men do not ordinarily think of destroying an abuse before they have felt the damage it does. However, mankind (always heedless of the future) had no foreboding of all the disadvantages of the right of property at the time it permitted it to be established. Their level of understanding at the time, their inexperience, hardly permitted them to make such a calculation. And even if someone had shouted a warning, "You will be lost if you forget that the fruits of the earth belong to everyone and the earth to no one," I doubt that any one would have listened, or would have believed if they had. The baneful results did not make themselves felt for a long time, so that even after hundreds of years there would have been no better chance of getting a reform adopted. Later, when the harm was felt more sharply, it occurred imperceptibly over a long period of time; men got into the habit of considering it to be quite natural; no one knew whence it came; in any case the result was that long usage made it habitual and it was consequently taken to be an unchangeable and necessary state of affairs. Ignorance, superstition and authority joined forces to prevent any one from detecting its true origin or becoming strong enough to attack it. But today, when the gangrene has extended its ravages so far that nothing remains for it to consume; when the whole people have first been reduced to receiving two ounces of bread a day and then paying for it at sixty *livres* a pound; when the mass, the majority, have been compelled to sell their last tatters in order to buy some bread and then must do without when it is sold out; when the people has been enlightened, is capable of understanding, and is disposed by all the circumstances of its position to grasp eagerly the precious truth that "The fruits of the earth belong to everyone and the earth to no one," . . . I do not see why it should not be possible to persuade the people, who of necessity desire what is good for them and consequently desire what is just and good, that they should proclaim their wish to live in the only state of *society which is peaceful and truly happy*. Far from our being able to say that this fatal institution has roots too deep for it to be extirpated, at this time when the abuse of the right of property has been carried to the final extremity, it seems to me on the contrary that it is losing most of its fibers, which no longer hold together the mainstays of the tree and hence expose it to being blown down by the smallest wind. Create a host of propertyless men, abandon them to the consuming selfishness of a handful of invaders, and *the roots of the fatal institution of property cease to be ineradicable*. Soon the dispossessed will consider the matter of their own accord, and will recognize, like those who considered it before them, that "the fruits of the earth belong to everyone and the earth to no one," that we are *lost* only because we forget it, that the majority of citizens permit themselves to be outrageously swindled when they remain the slaves and victims of the oppression of a minority; that it is worse than ridiculous not to throw off this yoke, not to embrace that state of society *which alone is just, good and in conformity with the pure sentiments of nature*—that state outside of which *there cannot exist peaceful and truly happy societies*. The French Revolution has provided us with repeated proof that abuses are not ineradicable because they are ancient, that on the contrary it was the excesses and the lassitude of their long existence which called most imperatively for their destruction. The Revolution has provided us with repeated proof that the French people are not incapable of adopting the greatest changes in their institutions and consenting to the greatest sacrifices for their improvement, simply because they are *a great and ancient people*. Has not everything changed since 1789 except this one institution of property? Why this single exception when we recognize so certainly that it affects the worst of the abuses, *the most deplorable creation of our fantasies?* Will the antiquity of the abuse fail to work here when it did not do so for all the other abuses which have been overturned? Will its importance and gravity provide reason to treat it more gently?

46 / MARC BLOCH: CHANGE AND CONTINUITY IN REVOLUTION

The changes in the pattern of land ownership in France during the revolution are shown by the historian Marc Bloch to have been highly varied in character, rather than a simple transfer

*in property, as has been so often held. The revolutionary transfor-
mations in the countryside are the culmination of Bloch's* Les
caractères originaux de l'histoire rurale française (*"The Novel
Characteristics of the Rural History of France," first published in
1933), from which the following passages are translated. Bloch
(1886–1944) rose to eminence as a medievalist during the period
between World Wars I and II, but his interests extended more
widely in time and theme. He emphasized not only the interrela-
tionships among the various fields of history, but also between the
different social sciences. He joined the resistance to the Nazis after
the defeat of France in 1940, was arrested, and was executed in
1944 as a hostage.*[11]

As a result, first, of the massive entry of the officeholding bourgeoisie
into the nobility and, second, of the formation of the judiciary into a
true caste by the operation of the system of inheritance and venality
of offices, the royal courts of law became populated with manorial
lords (*seigneurs*). Thereafter the most honest of judges was unable
to see things except through the spectacles of class spirit. In Germany
the electoral assemblies or "Estates," in which the squirearchy dominated, in England the Commons, which represented most of all the
gentry, the justices of the peace who were the political masters of the
countryside and were recruited from the same class—these formed the
firmest supports of the seignorial system. This role was played in
France principally by the bailiwick and seneschalship courts, the presidial courts and the Parlements. If they did not go so far as to permit
the eviction of tenants (this would have been a truly unthinkable
juridical revolution, and no one dared to demand it), they did allow
a host of lesser encroachments which in the long run amounted to a
great deal.

Fortunately for the peasants, the French seignorial class, although
it extended its ascendancy to the judicial hierarchy, lacked that full
control of the other mechanisms of control which the English gentry
(since the Revolutions) and the German *Junkertum* (until the re-
establishment of the monarchy) had firmly in hand—the political power,
the unimpeded direction of the great administrative services. Beginning with the seventeenth century, the intendants, who were the direct
representatives of the king in each province, became by the very necessities of their tasks the perpetual rivals of the officeholding magistracy,

[11] Marc Bloch, *Les caractères originaux de l'histoire rurale française,* new ed.
(Paris: Librairie Armand Colin, 1952), Vol. I, pp. 138–9, 153–4, 246–9. Translated from the French by the editor. By permission of the publisher.

although they personally belonged to the seignorial world by their origins. Furthermore, being primarily fiscal agents, it was their duty to protect the rural communities—a tax base if there ever was one— against the excesses of seignorial exploitation. In more general terms, it was their function to protect the subjects of the Prince. In England, the downfall of absolutism permitted the expansion of the famous movement of "enclosures" to the profit of the gentry; this involved a transformation of the technique of farming, but also, either directly or in consequence of its effects, the practical ruin or dispossession of numberless tenants. In France, by an analogous but inverse process, the victory of absolute monarchy limited the amplitude of the "feudal reaction." But it limited it, nothing more. The agents of the monarchy continued as before to consider the seignorial regime as one of the key elements of the state and the social order. They did not grasp the danger of that paradox which Fortescue had seen earlier, on the threshold of modern times, that the peasant was being more and more heavily burdened by the taxation of the state, while the old burden of obligations to the lord of the manor which he was still compelled to carry was neither abolished nor even adequately lightened, even though the lord, in the final analysis, had now become only a private person. . . .

The slow process of change by which the peasantry were apparently escaping the hold of the manorial lords came to a halt. The lords once more strongly fastened upon the peasants' backs their old bundle of obligations. Although the lord was often a newcomer, he still felt himself to have the soul of a master—even more so than his predecessor! Nothing is more characteristic than the importance attached to honorific rights in certain land registers when they were brought up to date. "When the lord or lady of Bretennières or their family enters or leaves church, all inhabitants and members of the parish of the said place are to keep silence and bow to them": these are the words of a register in Burgundy from the year 1734. The preceding register has nothing of the kind.

It is a matter of common knowledge that the seignorial edifice collapsed between 1789 and 1792 and that it brought down with it a monarchical order which had identified itself with it.

Although the new model lord of the manor claimed to be the master of the peasantry, he also became once more a large-scale farmer—perhaps this more than anything else (and more than one plain bourgeois underwent the same evolution). If the Revolution had broken out around 1480 (to venture an absurd hypothesis), in suppressing manorial dues it would have turned the land almost exclusively over to a host of small farmers. But from 1480 to 1789 three centuries passed which brought about the re-establishment of large-scale property. To be sure, it did not extend to almost every corner of the land, as in

England or eastern Germany. Vast areas remained in the hands of peasant proprietors, areas which in their total extent may well have been larger than those owned by large proprietors. Nonetheless, large-scale ownership of land spread to a sizeable area, although to an extent that was different in different regions. It was to survive the Revolution without too much damage. . . .

The great crisis which opened in 1789 did not destroy large-scale property as it had been reconstituted over the preceding centuries. Those nobles and estate-collecting bourgeois who did not emigrate (and they were much more numerous, even among the nobility, than is sometimes imagined) retained their possessions. Even some of the *émigrés* managed to keep their lands either by the device of having relatives or middlemen repurchase them on their behalf, or because they were restored to them by the Consulate and the Empire. The survival of noble fortunes in certain regions of France, notably in the West, is one of the least studied but most incontestable facts of our recent history. Nor did the sale of "national wealth"—the possessions of the clergy and the *émigrés*—strike a very hard blow at large-scale property; for the very mechanism of the transactions was not unfavorable to the purchase of large parcels or even of entire farms. Large-scale tenants became large-scale owners; bourgeois continued the patient and efficacious rural labors of previous generations; prosperous farmers increased their patrimony and passed once and for all into the ranks of rural capitalists.

Nonetheless, the Revolution did strengthen small-scale property by throwing numerous estates upon the market. Many peasants of modest means, especially in the regions of an intense collective life where the pressure of the communities was felt even in the conditions of sale, also acquired tracts of land and thus consolidated their economic position. Here and there even farm laborers got hold of some of the booty and raised themselves into the class of landowners. The division of common lands had a similar effect. This division was ordered, with the exception of the woodlands, by the Legislative Assembly after the abolition of feudalism on August 10, 1789; it was one of several measures designed, as deputy François de Neufchâteau admitted, to "tie the inhabitants of the countryside to the Revolution.". . . Finally, by taking the burden of manorial dues off the peasant's back, the revolutionary assemblies rescued him from one of the most powerful causes of that process of indebtedness which, since the sixteenth century, had so dangerously compromised the peasant's command over the soil. All in all, considering the matter broadly and disregarding the nuances (which, however, it is of primary importance to establish precisely), large-scale agricultural property under capitalist ownership and small-scale peasant property, as the Old Regime had created them, continued to coexist in France even as it was transformed by the Revolution.

Most of the revolutionaries, except for those who at the height of battle glimpsed the necessity of basing themselves upon the lower classes, had little more consideration for the day laborers than did the reformers of the eighteenth century. . . . In fact, the abolition of the rights of common usage was a blow to the rural proletariat from which they never recovered. To be sure, they found some advantage in the breakup of the common lands thanks to the royal edicts and the revolutionary laws, and here and there they acquired a few fragments of "national wealth." But these gains were often illusory; many disappointments awaited those who brought poor lands into cultivation, often in farms of inadequate size. All was not false in the forecast of the day laborers of Frenelle-la-Grande, who prophesied in 1789 that a temporary surplus of births would result from the partition of the land, followed by drastic impoverishment. The attraction of urban jobs, the decline of the rural industries by which the farm laborers had formerly added to their livelihood, the difficulties of adapting to the new economy, the very changes which took place in their collective mentality as they began to lose their old attachment to the traditional kinds of work, a new liking for comfort which sharpened their antipathy to the wretched conditions of a farm worker's life—these did the rest. . . . Day laborers and small farmers abandoned the fields in great numbers. The exodus from the countryside, which was already perceptible under the July Monarchy (1830–1848) and increased at an almost constantly accelerating rate after mid-nineteenth century, was the result primarily of this process.

47 / THE REVOLUTION REBUTTED

When the British parliamentarian and man of letters, Edmund Burke, was moved by the events in France to wrath at English supporters of the French Revolution, he made his central argument the peril of deliberate attempts to transform society and the state. This seemed to him to have been the aim of the philosophes *of the Enlightenment, and upon them, therefore, fell the burden of blame for the revolution. His rebuttal of their principles in his* Reflection on the Revolution in France *(1790), from which the following passages are taken (A), became the first clarion call of deliberately conservative thought. Burke (1729–1797) had earlier been an advocate of British reforms, notably in relations with Ireland, his country of birth, and with the American colonies. Both as orator and writer, Burke was one of the supreme figures of English literature of the eighteenth century, if not of all time.[12]*

Another direct assault against the concepts of popular sovereignty and rationalist philosophy was made by the Savoyard political writer, Joseph de Maistre. The following passages (B) translated from his Essai sur le principe générateur des Constitutions politiques et des autres institutions humaines, *which first appeared in 1810 in Russia and was reprinted in France in 1814, are characteristic of his thought. De Maistre (1754–1821) came from a family of French origins which had been long settled in Savoy. He served the king of Sardinia, his prince, as a diplomatic minister to St. Petersburg during the Napoleonic period, when his homeland was under French occupation.[13]*

A. EDMUND BURKE

You will observe, that from Magna Charta to the Declaration of Right, it has been the uniform policy of our constitution, to claim and assert our liberties, as an *entailed inheritance* derived to us from our forefathers, and to be transmitted to our posterity; as an estate specially belonging to the people of this kingdom, without any reference whatever to any other more general or prior right. By this means our constitution preserves an unity in so great a diversity of its parts. We have an inheritable crown; an inheritable peerage; and an house of commons and a people inheriting privileges, franchises, and liberties, from a long line of ancestors.

This policy appears to me to be the result of profound reflection; or rather the happy effect of following nature, which is wisdom without reflection, and above it. A spirit of innovation is generally the result of a selfish temper and confined views. People will not look forward to posterity, who never look backward to their ancestors. Besides, the people of England well know, that the idea of inheritance furnishes a sure principle of conservation, and a sure principle of transmission;

---

[12] Edmund Burke, *Reflections on the Revolution in France, and on the Proceedings in Certain Societies in London Relative to that Event, In a Letter Intended to Have Been Sent to a Gentleman in Paris* (London: J. Dodsley, 1790).

[13] Joseph Marie, comte de Maistre, *Essai sur le principe générateur des Constitutions politiques et des autres institutions humaines* (Paris: n. pub., 1821), pp. 310–16. Translated from the French by the editor.

without at all excluding a principle of improvement. It leaves acquisition free; but it secures what it acquires. Whatever advantages are obtained by a state proceeding on these maxims, are locked fast as in a sort of family settlement; grasped as in a kind of mortmain forever. By a constitutional policy, working after the pattern of nature, we receive, we hold, we transmit, our government and our privileges, in the same manner in which we enjoy and transmit our property and our lives. The institutions of policy, the goods of fortune, the gifts of Providence, are handed down, to us and from us, in the same course and order. Our political system is placed in a just correspondence and symmetry with the order of the world, and with the mode of existence decreed to a permanent body composed of transitory parts; wherein, by the disposition of a stupendous wisdom, moulding together the great mysterious incorporation of the human race, the whole, at one time, is never old, or middle-aged, or young, but in a condition of unchangeable constancy, moves on through the varied tenour of perpetual decay, fall, renovation, and progression. Thus, by preserving the method of nature in the conduct of the state, in what we improve we are never wholly new; in what we retain we are never wholly obsolete. By adhering in this manner and on those principles to our forefathers, we are guided not by the superstition of antiquarians, but by the spirit of philosophic analogy. In this choice of inheritance we have given to our frame of polity the image of a relation in blood; binding up the constitution of our country with our dearest domestic ties; adopting our fundamental laws into the bosom of our family affections; keeping inseparable, and cherishing with the warmth of all their combined and mutually reflected charities, our state, our hearths, our sepulchres, and our altars.

Through the same plan of a conformity to nature in our artificial institutions, and by calling in the aid of her unerring and powerful instincts, to fortify the fallible and feeble contrivances of our reason, we have derived several other, and those no small benefits, from considering our liberties in the light of an inheritance. Always acting as if in the presence of canonized forefathers, the spirit of freedom, leading in itself to misrule and excess, is tempered with an awful gravity. This idea of a liberal descent inspires us with a sense of habitual native dignity, which prevents that upstart insolence almost inevitably adhering to and disgracing those who are the first acquirers of any distinction. By this means our liberty becomes a noble freedom. It carries an imposing and majestic aspect. It had a pedigree, and illustrating ancestors. It has its bearings, and its ensigns armorial. It has its gallery of portraits; its monumental inscriptions; its records, evidences, and titles. We procure reverence to our civil institutions on the principle upon which nature teaches us to revere individual men; on account of their age; and on account of those from whom they are descended. All your sophisters cannot produce any thing better adapted to preserve a rational and manly freedom than the course that we have pursued, who have chosen our nature rather than our speculations, our breasts rather than our inventions, for the great conservatories and magazines of our rights and privileges.

You might, if you pleased, have profited of our example, and have given to your recovered freedom a correspondent dignity. Your privileges, though discontinued, were not lost to memory. Your constitution, it is true, whilst you were out of possession, suffered waste and dilapidation; but you possessed in some parts the walls, and in all the foundations of a noble and venerable castle. You might have repaired those walls; you might have built on those old foundations. Your constitution was suspended before it was perfected; but you had the elements of a constitution very nearly as good as could be wished. In your old states you possessed that variety of parts corresponding with the various descriptions of which your community was happily composed; you had all that combination, and all that opposition of interests, you had that action and counteraction which, in the natural and in the political world, from the reciprocal struggle of discordant powers, draws out the harmony of the universe. These opposed and conflicting interests, which you considered as so great a blemish in your old and in our present constitution, interpose a salutary check to all precipitate resolutions; they render deliberation a matter not of choice, but of necessity; they make all change a subject of *compromise;* which naturally begets moderation; they produce *temperaments,* preventing the sore evil of harsh, crude, unqualified reformations; and rendering all the headlong exertions of arbitrary power, in the few or in the many, for ever impracticable. Through that diversity of members and interests, general liberty had as many securities as there were separate views in the several orders; whilst by pressing down the whole by the weight of a real monarchy, the separate parts would have been prevented from warping and starting from their allotted places.

You had all these advantages in your ancient states; but you chose to act as if you had never been moulded into civil society, and had every thing to begin anew. You began ill, because you began by despising every thing that belonged to you. You set up your trade without a capital. If the last generations of your country appeared without much lustre in your eyes, you might have passed them by, and derived your claims from a more early race of ancestors. Under a pious predilection to those ancestors, your imaginations would have realized in them a standard of virtue and wisdom, beyond the vulgar practice of the hour: and you would have risen with the example to whose imitation

you aspired. Respecting your forefathers, you would have been taught
to respect yourselves. You would not have chosen to consider the
French as a people of yesterday, as a nation of low-born servile
wretches until the emancipating year of 1789. In order to furnish, at
the expense of your honour, an excuse to your apologists here for several enormities of yours, you would not have been content to be represented as a gang of Maroon slaves, suddenly broke loose from the
house of bondage, and therefore to be pardoned for your abuse of
the liberty to which you were not accustomed and ill fitted. Would it
not, my worthy friend, have been wiser to have you thought, what I,
for one, always thought you, a generous and gallant nation, long misled to your disadvantage by your high and romantic sentiments of
fidelity, honour, and loyalty; that events have been unfavourable to
you, but that you were not enslaved through any illiberal or servile
disposition; that in your most devoted submission, you were actuated
by a principle of public spirit, and that it was your country you wor-
shipped, in the person of your king? Had you made it to be understood, that in the delusion of this amiable error you had gone further
than your wise ancestors; that you were resolved to resume your ancient privileges, whilst you preserved the spirit of your ancient and
your recent loyalty and honour; or, if diffident of yourselves, and not
clearly discerning the almost obliterated constitution of your ancestors,
you had looked to your neighbours in this land, who had kept alive
the ancient principles and models of the old common law of Europe
meliorated and adapted to its present state—by following wise examples you would have given new examples of wisdom to the world. You
would have rendered the cause of liberty venerable in the eyes of
every worthy mind in every nation. You would have shamed despotism
from the earth, by shewing that freedom was not only reconcileable,
but as, when well disciplined it is, auxiliary to law. You would have
had an unoppressive but a productive revenue. You would have had
a flourishing commerce to feed it. You would have had a free constitution; a potent monarchy; a disciplined army; a reformed and venerated clergy; a mitigated but spirited nobility, to lead your virtue, not
to overlay it; you would have had a liberal order of commons, to emulate and to recruit that nobility; you would have had a protected, satisfied, laborious, and obedient people, taught to seek and to recognize
that happiness that is to be found by virtue in all conditions; in which
consists the true moral equality of mankind, and not in that monstrous
fiction, which, by inspiring false ideas and vain expectations into men
destined to travel in the obscure walk of laborious life, serves only to
aggravate and imbitter that real inequality, which it never can remove;
and which the order of civil life establishes as much for the benefit of

those whom it must leave in an humble state, as those whom it is able to exalt to a condition more splendid, but not more happy. You had a smooth and easy career of felicity and glory laid open to you, beyond any thing recorded in the history of the world; but you have shewn that difficulty is good for man.

Compute your gains: see what is got by those extravagant and presumptuous speculations which have taught your leaders to despise all their predecessors, and all their contemporaries, and even to despise themselves, until the moment in which they became truly despicable. By following those false lights, France has bought undisguised calamities at a higher price than any nation has purchased the most unequivocal blessings! France has bought poverty by crime! France has not sacrificed her virtue to her interest; but she has abandoned her interest, that she might prostitute her virtue. All other nations have begun the fabric of a new government, or the reformation of an old, by establishing originally, or by enforcing with greater exactness some rites or other of religion. All other people have laid the foundations of civil freedom in severer manners, and a system of a more austere and masculine morality. France, when she let loose the reins of regal authority, doubled the licence, of a ferocious dissoluteness in manners, and of an insolent irreligion in opinions and practices; and has extended through all ranks of life, as if she were communicating some privilege, or laying open some secluded benefit, all the unhappy corruptions that usually were the disease of wealth and power. This is one of the new principles of equality in France.

B. JOSEPH DE MAISTRE

I recall reading somewhere that *there are very few sovereignties able to defend the legitimacy of their origin.* Let us admit that the charge is just, yet it will bring not the faintest stain upon the successors of a leader against whose acts some accusation might be made: the clouds in which his authority would be more or less enshrouded would be only an unfortunate but necessary consequence of a law of morality. If it were otherwise, the result would be to prevent any sovereign from reigning legitimately unless he had been elected by the decision of the entire population, that is, by *popular right;* but this will never happen, for nothing is truer than what was said by the author of the *Considérations sur la France:* "The people will always accept their masters and will never choose them." The origin of sovereignty must always be kept outside the sphere of human power, so that even those men who seem to be directly involved nonetheless appear as part of the circumstances. As for legitimacy, however ambiguous its origins may seem,

God gives his explanation through his prime minister for the affairs of this world, *Time.* It is quite true nonetheless that certain contemporary omens cease to be deceptive when they are examined closely; but details in this respect belong to another work.

It all comes back to the general rule: *Men cannot make a constitution; and no legitimate constitution can be a written one.* No one has ever written and no one will ever write *a priori* the collection of fundamental laws by which a civil or religious society is established. It is only when the society has already been established, no one can say how, that it is possible for certain individual articles to be proclaimed or explained in writing; but such proclamations are almost always either the result or the cause of very great evils, and they always cost the peoples more than they are worth.

Only one exception is known to this general rule that *no constitution can be written or made a priori:* the law of Moses. We might say that it, and it alone, was *cast* like a statue, that a man of miracles, saying "FIAT!" ["Let it be done!"], wrote it down to the last detail and that his work has never since required correction, addition or modification either by himself or anyone else. It alone has defied time, because it owed nothing to time and expected nothing from time. . . .

But, every constitution being divine in origin, it follows that man can do nothing in relation to them unless he bases himself upon God, whose instrument he then becomes. Now this is a truth of which the entire human race has given striking proof throughout its existence. Open the book of history—which is experimental politics—and we shall always see in it that nations in their cradle are always surrounded by priests and that men in their weakness always call upon the help of the Deity. Mythology, which, for eyes ready to see, holds much more truth than ancient history, brings even stronger proof. It is always an oracle that founds cities; it is always an oracle that proclaims divine protection and the success of the founding hero. Kings in particular, the leaders of emerging empires, are repeatedly designated and almost *marked out* by Heaven in some extraordinary fashion. How many frivolous men have laughed at the Holy Ampulla, unaware that the Holy Ampulla is a hieroglyph which we need only know how to read!

The coronation of Kings arises from the same origin. Never has there been a more meaningful, a more venerable ceremony, or, to give it a more corect name, profession of faith. There is always the act of the Pontiff in touching the brow of emergent sovereignty with his finger. The numerous writers who have seen in these august rites nothing more than ambitious designs and even the deliberate agreement of superstition and tyranny, wrote contrary to the truth, and almost all contrary to their conscience also. . . . It is enough to insist here upon the common and perpetual opinion which calls upon divine power to establish empires.

48 / CATHERINE II: THE REVOLUTION COMBATTED

What Burke expressed in ideas—a hatred of the revolution in France as a vile thing deserving to be destroyed—was turned into a program for action by Catherine II, Empress of Russia. In 1792 Catherine drew up a memorandum on the prospects for armed intervention by Europeans to restore Louis XVI and his power. Excerpts from this document, published by a French historian during the nineteenth century, are translated below. Catherine (1729–1796), a German-born noblewoman, had married the heir to the Russian throne and had then become empress in her own name in 1762 after her husband, who had just become tsar as Peter III, was overthrown and assassinated by conspirators, among whom was her lover. Until the beginning of revolution in France, Catherine played the part of friend and patron to the Enlightenment, but never at the sacrifice of any portion of her political power or at the risk of any concrete political interest. Indeed, she did not actually join in the First Alliance against France, but used the opportunity to arrange the Second Partition of Poland.[14]

The cause of the king of France is every king's cause.

Europe's interest lies in having France regain the place which is proper for a great kingdom.

At the present moment a corps of ten thousand men would be strong enough to cross France from one end to the other.

A half million in money would suffice to establish this force, and such a modest sum could be obtained at Genoa. France would pay off this debt over a period of time.

The regions bordering on the Rhine which belong to the bishops of Speyer and Strasbourg, or to some other princes concerned, would be

[14] Ch. de Larivière, *Catherine II et la Révolution française* (Paris: H. Le Soudier, 1895), pp. 362–5, 372–5. Translated from the French by the editor.

best situated for assembling this force. As the proverb says, "If you have the money, you can have the Switzers too." All the expatriate nobles would join this corps without fail and perhaps the troops of the princes of Germany too. With this force France could be rescued from the bandits; the monarchy and the monarch would be re-established; the imposters would be driven out and a few scoundrels punished; the kingdom would be saved from oppression; and a general amnesty and indulgence would be quickly published for all who submit and return to the obedience of their legitimate master. In the beginning a fortified town would be needed, but even the smallest would provide a sufficient base. The clergy of France will have returned to them whatever portion of their property remains unsold; the nobles will regain the privileges on which their rank depends; and the provinces with representative assemblies [*pays d'États*] will obtain their demands.

It will be necessary to hold firm on the question of order and obedience, but force should be used only against resistance. If the National Assembly declares these actions to be a crime against the nation, we should reply by declaring its actions harmful to the kingdom, destructive of the monarchy, and contrary to its laws and principles, to be a crime against divine and human majesty. The Parlements would make no difficulty about confirming our declarations. . . .

It is obvious that at the very beginning foreign troops will prove better in service than native French forces. Nonetheless, many of the French nobility will assemble, sword in hand, to form a squadron under the name of the Royal Guard, and will act to rescue the king and the kingdom from the oppression, the pillage and the ruin of tyrants and bandits. General officers will take command of this force as it is formed. This Royal Guard composed of the nobility should not be abolished; if it had existed earlier, it is probable that the royal authority would not have been defeated. Never were there a cause more just nor incentives greater and more capable of arousing zeal and courage. There is no denying that the only result of success will be to restore to its legitimate possessor the authority which is properly his over an almost ruined kingdom. But by means of a wise system of government he will be able to reduce misfortune and make good its losses. Did not the reigns of Henry IV and Louis XIV re-establish the stability of the realm after the greatest of misfortunes? Did not the repute which France regained under the latter reign endure among the public until our own day? . . .

Since our purpose is to re-establish monarchical government in France, the ancient customs which inspire respect for rank in the public must be neither neglected nor treated with contempt. For example, no soldier should be permitted to come before princes or superior officers in the field unless in military uniform. Persons of superior rank should never appear in the theater or in public except when wearing their distinctive insignia, like cordons, etc., and full decorations. The princes should admit to their presence no one in a dress-coat, or dressed otherwise than with the decorations befitting the rank and quality of each in the kingdom, so as to repudiate the idea of perfect equality. They should re-establish the dignity which befits their rank on all occasions. This dignity will in no wise interfere with their being polite, winning and affable in manner with all, for what is involved is not vanity but the place which is proper to each in the monarchy.

It would be desirable for the liberator of France to take precautions that the money and troops will be employed for their proper purpose, that is, to re-establish the monarchy and to maintain the Roman Catholic religion, and for no other aim; in order to achieve this, it will not be useless to agree upon certain points and *even to make an agreement on these with the expatriate princes. . . .*

It is also obvious that there is a principle in this affair which should not be neglected, that is, to be particularly on guard against the frivolous and flighty spirit and the inborn recklessness of the French nation, which have become stronger than ever in this time of misfortune; but these traits may also be a means to bring them under control so long as we do not allow ourselves to be swept along; for of a certainty great affairs are not brought to success by frivolous epigrams, recklessness, and imprudence.

All reports are agreed on one point, that no two of the French who most favor the re-establishment of the monarchy have the same opinion on other matters; it has therefore been held that a proclamation of principles could provide the basis of unity. Those who sign this proclamation of unity will accept the following principles:

1. The maintenance of the Roman Catholic religion in its integrity.
2. Fidelity to the king.
3. His rescue.
4. The re-establishment of the government according to the unanimous wishes of the nation as set forth in the *cahiers* of the provinces, and hence the maintenance of the three Estates in their existence, their property and their security.
5. All contrary oaths shall be declared null and void.
6. A promise to obey the chief of the federation as the basis of the unity of those whose wills are now divided.
7. A promise to contribute to the re-establishment of public peace and tranquility.
8. A promise to maintain military order and discipline.

All points on which it will be difficult to reach agreement should be kept out of this formal proclamation of unity which they will sign, but no one should be accepted for service as an officer under the king and the princes without giving his signature upon his honor.

The most recent reports say that the Princes of the Blood are busy with counterrevolution, but they are said to be downcast, abandoned and pitiful. Such an attitude can only harm their purpose. In order to succeed, they must show a noble and confident air, a serene visage, a firm conviction in the justice of their cause and their enterprise, speaking little of what they really have in mind, but letting it be felt that great-hearted men of intelligence and courage always have at their disposal resources of which the ordinary man is not aware and hence that they always know far more about events than the ordinary person; let them add to this bearing that politeness and benevolence which win men's minds, and they will make great progress; let their bearing encourage, attract and console their fellows. All France is sick with discouragement.

In such a great affair as this of which we have just spoken, what matters is to be possessed utterly by one's purpose, to desire it passionately, and then to communicate one's own convictions to others; hence to act without hesitation as soon as a decision has been taken and thereafter to show the greatest calm in the midst of trouble and never to show agitation or anxiety over events.

This is what the truest, most sincere and purest intentions dictate. These ideas may be imperfect, but they are inspired by the purest desire to seek the triumph of the good and just cause.

49 / ROBERT R. PALMER: NAPOLEON AND JEFFERSON—TWO FACES OF THE NEW AGE

Napoleon I, Emperor of the French, and Thomas Jefferson, third President of the United States of America, both sons of the Enlightenment, epitomized its ambiguous heritage. One recreated the absolute monarchy at the same time as he consolidated the social and economic changes wrought by the French Revolution. The other guided for eight years the democratic republic whose Declaration of Independence he had written. The two men, and what they symbolized, are contrasted by the American historian

Robert R. Palmer in the concluding passages of his probing and illuminating work, The Age of the Democratic Revolution. *This section, "Two Men on Horseback," is reprinted here.*[15]

In the end we retreat into symbolism. Revolutions, agitations, social movements, and glacially slow readjustments in a democratic direction were to go on for a long time, but a historical period came to a close with the century itself, and the Age of the Democratic Revolution may be thought of as ending in a final scene of two men on horseback.

On the first day of the new century, January 1, 1801, the vice-president of the United States, Thomas Jefferson, soon to be president, left the boarding-house in which he resided with a few colleagues among vacant lots and half-finished buildings, on an unpaved and untidy thoroughfare known as C Street, in the new Federal City. The vice-president was hardly an inexperienced provincial, for he had known the court of Versailles well enough in former days, and been present in Paris at the time of the fall of the Bastille; but he accepted the peculiarities of life in America. Going down from C Street, he took the public ferry across the Potomac, and at Alexandria hired a horse, for which he paid three dollars. He rode for some ten miles to Mount Vernon for a social call on Mrs. George Washington. He had sometimes disagreed with her late husband, but her high-columned establishment overlooking the river already represented a common grounnd of American politics. He then returned as he had come, a solitary figure on a slow-moving, placid beast, of a kind that anyone was free to ride, or at least anyone who was white and had three dollars.

At about this same time the painter David, an old Jacobin of 1793, was at work on one of his memorable compositions, which may now be seen near the empty royal apartments at the palace of Versailles. He conceived of a horse and rider against a rocky Alpine background, moving steeply uphill, the horse a highstepping, tense, and furious charger, with startled eye and mane flowing in the wind, the rider a uniformed officer seated securely on his restless mount, transfixing the spectator with an imperious gaze, and while lightly holding the reins in one hand, pointing with the other over the mountains and into the future. It was a glorified picture of the master of the New Order in Europe—"Bonaparte crossing the St. Bernard Pass"—just before his descent for the second time into the Po valley, where in June 1800 he

[15] R. R. Palmer, *The Age of the Democratic Revolution: A Political History of Europe and America, 1760–1800,* Vol. II, *The Struggle* (Princeton, N.J.: Princeton University Press, 1964), pp. 569–575. Reprinted by permission of Princeton University Press.

defeated the Austrians at Marengo. This victory restored the Cisalpine Republic, and finally broke up the Second Coalition. Democracy in Europe had not exactly succeeded, but the great conservative and aristocratic counter-offensive had utterly failed.

That Bonaparte and Jefferson were very different human beings, as different as the horses they rode on, hardly needs to be pointed out. Jefferson, like American republicans generally, had once admired Bonaparte; even today there are at least six places in the United States named "Marengo." But Jefferson turned against the increasingly despotic ways and mad egotism of his one-time hero. "Do you call this a Republic?" asked the disgusted Thomas Paine in 1802. The author of the *Rights of Man* had had enough of Europe, and returned to America, and his abandonment of the old continent was also symbolic. As the great republican enthusiasms of the 1790's subsided, and as Europe went on with its chronic wars, there came to prevail for a long time in the United States a feeling of self-chosen and fortunate isolation, a belief that the vices of Europe were incorrigible, and that Americans should be as little involved as possible with an old world where true liberty could not exist. It was hard for the man on the three-dollar horse to understand the man on the charger, to comprehend why decent people could so long uphold Bonaparte, to think in terms of alternatives instead of ideals, to see that some things taken for granted in America, like "equality before the law," might in Europe have to be fought for.

Bonaparte and Jefferson had this much in common: both were detested as "Jacobins" in some quarters, yet under Bonaparte as First Consul and Emperor, and under Jefferson as President, the democratic and republican agitation quieted down. Revolutionary excitement was over. In America republicanism faded off into the general attitude of most people in the country. In Europe, where Bonaparte for a time treated republicans and royalists pretty much alike, giving them jobs if they could be useful, and imprisoning or even executing those who persisted in conspiracy or subversion, the forces making for change were content for a while to operate within an authoritarian framework which he provided. Men of practical bent and modern outlook, freed both from popular demands and from old-noble pretensions, relieved of the fear of both revolution and reaction, and protected by armed force, until 1813, against the inroads of ever-reviving Coalitions, worked together at a liquidation of the Old Regime in various countries, in an area much like that of the New Republican Order of 1798. This area was the Continental heartland of Western Civilization, comprising France and Italy, Switzerland and what are now called the Benelux countries, to which was soon added Germany as far as the Elbe—the sphere of Napoleon's empire, and of the "Europe" of 1960. The very

German philosopher Hegel, as he watched the Emperor of the French ride through the streets of Jena in 1806, just before annihilating the Prussian army, saw the movement of history, of humanity, and of true liberty embodied before his eyes—"the World-Soul sitting on a horse."

In the twentieth century both the World-Soul and the horse have become archaic, and the dialectic of Hegel has become unconvincing. It is not as easy to generalize about the grand sweep of human events as it once was. It is not easy to summarize what happened in the world of Western Civilization in the forty years from 1760 to 1800, or to be certain of the meaning of these years for the subsequent history of mankind. For the ideas set forth at the outset of the first volume of this book a thousand pages of evidence have now been offered. In history, for large ideas, there is no such thing as proof; no view, however much demonstrated, can pretend to be conclusive or final. It is hoped, however, that the reader can now see these events of the eighteenth century as a single movement, revolutionary in character, for which the word "democratic" is appropriate and enlightening; a movement which, however different in different countries, was everywhere aimed against closed élites, self-selecting power groups, hereditary castes, and forms of special advantage or discrimination that no longer served any useful purpose. These were summed up in such terms as feudalism, aristocracy, and privilege, against which the idea of common citizenship in a more centralized state, or of common membership in a free political nation, was offered as a more satisfactory basis for the human community.

What had happened by 1800, even in countries where it was temporarily suppressed, was the assertion of "equality" as a prime social desideratum. It was an equality that meant a wider diffusion of liberty. That the assurance of some liberties meant the curtailment of others was well understood, so that, more on the continent of Europe than elsewhere, the democratic movement brought a consolidation of public authority, or of the state. It was not an equality that could long accept the surrender of liberty; the solution provided by Bonaparte could not prove to be durable. Nor was it an equality that repudiated the power of government; the world of Thomas Jefferson would also pass.

In forty years, from 1760 to 1800, "equality" took on a wealth of meanings, to which few new ones have been added since that time. It could mean an equality between colonials and residents of a mother country, as in America; between nobles and commoners, as in France; patricians and burghers, as at Geneva; ruling townsmen and subject country people, as at Zurich and elsewhere; between Catholic and Protestant, Anglican and Dissenter, Christian and Jew, religionist and unbeliever, or between Greek and Turk in Rhigas Velestinlis' memo-

rable phrase. It might refer to the equal right of gildsmen and out-
siders to enter upon a particular kind of trade or manufacture. For
some few it included greater equality between men and women.
Equality for ex-slaves and between races was not overlooked. For
popular democrats, like the Paris sans-culottes, it meant the hope for a
more adequate livelihood, more schooling and education, the right to
stroll on the boulevards with the upper classes, and for more recognition and more respect; and it passed on to the extreme claim for an
exact equality of material circumstances, which was rarely in fact made
during the Revolutionary era, but was feared as an ultimate consequence of it by conservatives, and expressed in Babeuf's blunt formula,
"stomachs are equal."

Monarchy, religion, the church, the law, and the economic system—
along with the British Parliament, the Dutch Union of Utrecht, the old
folk-democracies of the upland Swiss, the gentry republic in Poland,
and the patrician communes of Italy—were brought into question so
far as they upheld inequalities that were thought to be unjust. "Everywhere inequality is a cause of revolution," said Aristotle long ago, and
his observation may remain as the last word on the subject. The problem of the historian in deciding upon the causes of revolution, as of
rulers in preventing or guiding it, is to identify the sore spots, the political, economic, sociological, or psychological matters which arouse,
in a significant number of relatively normal human beings, the em-
bittered sense of inequality which is the sense of injustice.

The present book began with a quotation from Alexis de Tocqueville, and may close with another. For Tocqueville the course of all
history revealed a continuing movement toward a greater "equality of
conditons." In the introduction to his *Democracy in America,* thinking
of both France and the United States, and indeed of all Europe since
the Middle Ages, he explained his view of world history, in which he
was less oracular than Hegel, and less dogmatic than Marx.

"The gradual trend toward equality of conditions," he said, "is a
fact of Providence, of which it bears the principal characteristics: it is
universal, it is enduring, it constantly eludes human powers of control;
all events and all men contribute to its development.

"Would it be wise to think that a social movement of such remote
origin can be suspended by the efforts of one generation? Can it be
supposed that democracy, after destroying feudalism and overwhelming kings, will yield before the powers of money and business—*devant
les bourgeois et les riches?* [16]

"What then does the future hold? No one can say."

Here was no prediction of revolution to come, no conservative theory,

---

[16] before the bourgeois and the wealthy.

as with Friedrich Gentz, that one revolution must lead endlessly to another, to show what a great evil the French Revolution had been; no neo-revolutionary message, as with Karl Marx, to show that since one revolution that he called "bourgeois" had occurred, another that he called "proletarian" must surely follow. It was only a prediction that the future would see an increasing equality of conditions, brought about in ways that could not be foreseen, and were not prescribed. It was a prediction that even inequalities of wealth and income, like others, would be reduced either by revolution or otherwise. Such has in fact proved to be the case.

For Tocqueville it was a troubled anticipation, in which difficulties and losses were to be expected as well as gains. In substance, however, it was the anticipation that had inspired the last days of Condorcet, who had rejoiced to see, in 1794, at the end of the "Progress of the Human Mind," the vision of a future world in which all invidious differences between human beings would be erased.

All revolutions since 1800, in Europe, Latin America, Asia, and Africa, have learned from the eighteenth-century Revolution of Western Civilization. They have been inspired by its successes, echoed its ideals, used its methods. It does not follow that one revolution need lead to another, or that revolution as such need be glorified as a social process. No revolution need be thought of as inevitable. In the eighteenth century there might have been no revolution, if only the old upper and ruling classes had made more sagacious concessions, if, indeed, the contrary tendencies toward a positive assertion of aristocratic values had not been so strong. What seems to be inevitable, in both human affairs and in social science, must be put in contingent form—if x, then y. If a sense of inequality or injustice persists too long untreated, it will produce social disorganization. In a general breakdown, if a constructive doctrine and program are at hand, such as were furnished in the eighteenth century by the European Enlightenment, if the capacities of leaders and followers are adequate to the purpose, and if they are strong enough to prevail over their adversaries, then a revolution may not only occur and survive, but open the way toward a better society. The conditions are hard to meet, but the stakes are high, for the alternative may be worse.

50 / CLEMENS VON METTERNICH: NAPOLEON, THE MAN AND HIS WORK

In 1799 the revolution and France itself passed into the control of General Napoleon Bonaparte, who became Emperor of the French and the creator of a French Empire extending over most of Europe between the Atlantic and Russia. His complex personality often baffled those who were not blinded by either admiration or hatred. One of the most penetrating analyses of the phenomenon of Napoleon I was penned by Prince Clemens von Metternich, the Austrian statesman who knew him as ambassador to France and then as the Austrian chancellor who helped organize the coalition that finally overthrew him. Metternich wrote in French, still the customary language of diplomacy, as had Frederick II and Catherine II before him. Metternich (1773–1859) came of a Rhenish noble family and entered Austrian service during the French Revolution. After the Peace of Vienna (1814–1815) he became the principal defender of intransigent political conservatism.[17]

My opinion of Napoleon has not varied during the different phases of [our] relations. I saw and studied him when he was at the height of his greatness; I saw and followed him when he was in decline, and although he may have attempted to deceive me about himself . . . he never succeeded. . . .

Judgment is often influenced by first impressions. I had never seen Napoleon before the audience he granted me to present my credentials. I found him standing in the middle of a salon with the minister of foreign affairs and six other personages of the Court. He wore the uniform of the infantry of the Guard and had a hat upon his head. This

[17] Prince Clemens von Metternich, *Mémoires, documents et écrits divers,* eds. Prince Richard de Metternich and M. A. de Klinkowstroem (Paris: E. Plon, 1879), Vol. I, pp. 295–301, 308, 310–11. Translated from the French by Herbert H. Rowen.

latter circumstance, improper in every respect since the audience was not at all public, struck me as a misplaced pretention which reeked of the upstart; it even made me hesitate for a moment with the thought of also putting on my hat. Nonetheless I made a brief speech, which in its conciseness and precision fundamentally differed from the kind of address which was customary at the Court of France.

His attitude semed to reveal discomfort and even embarrassment. His short squat figure, the careless way in which he held himself while he attempted to appear imposing—these destroyed my already dwindling awe such as one naturally feels for a man before whom the world trembles. I never wholly lost this impression, and it was present during the most important interview which I had with Napoleon. It is possible that it contributed to showing me the man as he was behind the mask which he was able to put on for self-concealment. In his flashes of sarcasm, his outbursts of anger, his sharp questions, I grew accustomed to seeing only prepared scenes, studied and calculated for the effect that he was prepared to produce upon the interlocutor. . . .

Just as everything was clear and precise in his conceptions, similarly he found neither difficulty nor uncertainty when confronted with the need for action. Accepted rules seldom got in his way. In practice as in discusion, he marched right to his goal without lingering for matters which he treated as secondary and which too often he scorned as unimportant. The straightest road to his objective was the one which he preferred to take and which he followed to the very end so long as there was no reason to leave it. But he was not the slave of his plans; he knew how to drop them or modify them whenever his point of view changed, or when new circumstances offered a means of achieving his purposes more effectively by different roads.

He knew little about science. His supporters have made a special effort to persuade people that he was a great mathematician. His knowledge of mathematics would not have raised him above any other officer trained like himself as an artilleryman; but his natural abilities made good what he lacked in science. The temper of his mind was such that he always sought the positive; he thrust aside vague ideas and felt equal abhorrence for the dreams of visionaries and the abstractions of ideologues. In science he really respected only what could be checked and verified by means of the sciences, what rested upon observation and experience. He always felt a profound contempt for the false philosophy and false philanthropy of the eighteenth century. Among the worthies of that movement Voltaire was the particular object of his antipathy, a feeling which he carried so far as to attack upon every possible occasion the general respect for Voltaire's literary merits.

Napoleon was not irreligious in the ordinary meaning of the word. He denied that there had ever existed a sincere atheist; he condemned deism as the product of rash speculation. As a Christian and a Catholic, he granted only positive religion the right to govern human society. He looked upon Christianity as the foundation of all true civilization, Catholicism as the creed most favorable to the preservation of the order and tranquility of the moral world, and Protestantism as a source of trouble and dissension. Personally indifferent to religious practices, he respected them too much ever to permit himself to mock those who engaged in them. It is possible that religion was for him less an affair of the emotions than the result of an enlightened policy; but whatever he may have felt in the secrecy of his heart, he took care not to betray it. His opinion of men was concentrated in a single idea, which acquired, to his misfortune, the force of an axiom in his mind. He was convinced that no one who appeared upon the public stage or even engaged in the active pursuits of life was moved or could be moved by any other motive than self-interest. He did not deny virtue and honor, but asserted that neither of these sentiments has ever served as the principal guide of conduct for anyone except those he labeled dreamers, to whom he therefore denied in his mind any of the necessary abilities for taking a successful part in the business of society. I spent many a moment discussing this thesis with him, which I sincerely rejected and which I tried to show him to be false, at least if applied as broadly as he did. I was never able to shake him on this article of faith.

He possessed a special flair for discovering those who could be useful to him. He quickly found out how to make the most effective use of them. Intent on guaranteeing their loyalty by their self-interest, he took care to bind them to his own fortune and therefore so compromised them that they could not return to other obligations. . . . His heroes were Alexander, Caesar and especially Charlemagne. The claim to be *de facto* and *de jure* the successor of Charlemagne was one of his special preoccupations. I have seen him lose himself in discussing with me this strange paradox which he supported with the feeblest arguments. Apparently it was my position as ambassador of Austria which earned me his obstinate attention in this regard.

One of his sharpest and most constant regrets was that he could not invoke the principle of legitimacy as the basis of his power. Few men have felt more strongly than he how precarious and brittle is authority which lacks this foundation, how open to attack from the flank. Nonetheless he never missed any opportunity to protest vigorously against those who thought that he occupied the throne as a usurper. "The throne of France," he said to me more than once, "was vacant. Louis XVI had not been able to maintain himself. If I had been in his place, the Revolution, despite the immense progress which it had made over the previous reigns, would never have taken place. Once the king fell, the Republic seized the territory of France, and it was the

Republic which I pushed aside. The ancient throne was buried beneath the rubble; I had to establish a new one. The Bourbons could not rule upon what I have created; my strength lies in my fortune; I am as new as the Empire; hence there is perfect homogeneity between the Empire and myself.". . .

The question has often been asked whether Napoleon was basically good or evil. It has always seemed to me that these adjectives cannot be applied in their ordinary sense to a character like his. . . . Napoleon had two faces. As a private man he was easy-going and manageable, although neither good nor evil. As a statesman, he permitted himself no emotions, he made his decisions upon the basis neither of affection nor hatred. He pushed his foes to the side or crushed them with no other thought than whether it was necessary or advantageous to get rid of them. Once this goal was achieved, he forgot them and did not persecute them. . . .

The opinion of mankind is still divided, and probably will always be, on the question whether Napoleon truly merited the title of a great man. It would be impossible to deny great qualities to one who rose from obscurity to become in a few years the strongest and most powerful of his contemporaries. But strength, power, superiority are more or less relative terms. In order correctly to estimate the degree of genius that a man needs to dominate his age, we must be able to take the measure of the age. This is the origin of the fundamental dispute in the judgment of Napoleon. If the era of the French Revolution was the most brilliant and glorious period of modern history, as its admirers believe, Napoleon, who was able to reach and keep the highest rank for fifteen years was assuredly one of the greatest men that has ever been seen. If, on the contrary, he had only to rise like a meteor above the fogs of general dissolution, if all about him he found only a society ruined by the excesses of a false civilization, if he had to combat nothing more than opponents already enfeebled by the universal weariness, nothing more than powerless rivals and ignoble passions, nothing more than adversaries paralyzed by their disunity both within and without the country, then it is certain that the luster of his success diminishes in proportion to the ease with which he achieved it. However, since in our opinion this was indeed the state of affairs, we are in no danger of exaggerating the idea of Napoleon's greatness even though we recognize what was extraordinary and impressive in his career.

The vast edifice which he constructed was exclusively the work of his own hands, and he himself was its keystone; but this gigantic building was essentially without a foundation; the materials it was built from were only the ruins of other buildings, and were already rotten or flimsy when they were first used. When the keystone was taken away, the building totally collapsed.

In a word, that was the history of the French Empire which Napoleon conceived and created. It existed in him alone and with him it had to pass away.

51 / J. G. FICHTE: THE UPSURGE OF NATIONALISM

The very nationalism which gave so much strength to the French revolutionary and Napoleonic regimes was aroused in other countries of Europe by the French conquests. In Germany, where the sense of ethnic and cultural nationhood had existed for centuries although German political unity had virtually vanished since the Middle Ages, the impulse to reunite the cultural and the political nations was particularly strong. The German philosopher, Johann Gottlieb Fichte, gave intellectual expression to this mood in his Reden an die deutsche Nation *("Addresses to the German Nation"), delivered in Berlin during the winter of 1807–1808. Fichte (1762–1814) began life in poverty, but rose to a professorship of philosophy at Jena and then at the new Prussian university of Berlin. He devoted considerable attention to ethical and political questions in addition to his specifically metaphysical studies.*[18]

People and fatherland in this sense, as a support and guarantee of eternity on earth and as that which can be eternal here below, far transcend the State in the ordinary sense of the word, viz., the social order as comprehended by mere intellectual conception and as established and maintained under the guidance of this conception. The aim of the State is positive law, internal peace, and a condition of affairs in which everyone may by diligence earn his daily bread and satisfy the needs of his material existence, so long as God permits him to live.

[18] Johann Gottlieb Fichte, *Addresses to the German Nation,* translated from the German by R. F. Jones and G. H. Turnbull (Chicago: Open Court Publishing Co., 1922), pp. 138–9, 226–30. Reprinted by permission of the publisher.

All this is only a means, a condition, and a framework for what love of fatherland really wants, viz., that the eternal and the divine may blossom in the world and never cease to become more and more pure, perfect, and excellent. That is why this love of fatherland must itself govern the State and be the supreme, final, and absolute authority. Its first exercise of this authority will be to limit the State's choice of means to secure its immediate object—internal peace. To attain this object, the natural freedom of the individual must, of course, be limited in many ways. If the only consideration and intention in regard to individuals were to secure internal peace, it would be well to limit that liberty as much as possible, to bring all their activities under a uniform rule, and to keep them under unceasing supervision. Even supposing such strictness were unnecessary, it could at any rate do no harm, if this were the sole object. It is only the higher view of the human race and of peoples which extends this narrow calculation. Freedom, including freedom in the activities of external life, is the soil in which higher culture germinates; a legislation which keeps the higher culture in view will allow to freedom as wide a field as possible, even at the risk of securing a smaller degree of uniform peace and quietness, and of making the work of government a little harder and more troublesome. . . .

This well-known system of a balance of power in Europe, therefore, assumes two things: first, a prey to which no one at all has any right, but for which all have a like desire; and second, the universal, ever-present, and unceasingly active lust for booty. Indeed, on these assumptions, this balance of power would be the only means of maintaining peace, if only one could find the second means, namely, that of creating the equilibrium and transforming it from an empty thought into a thing of reality.

But were these assumptions in fact to be made universally and without any exception? Had not the mighty German nation, in the middle of Europe, kept its hands off this prey, and was it not untainted by any craving for it, and almost incapable of making a claim to it? If only the German nation had remained united, with a common will and a common strength! Then, though the other Europeans might have wanted to murder each other on every sea and shore, and on every island too, in the middle of Europe the firm wall of the Germans would have prevented them from reaching each other. Here peace would have remained, and the Germans would have maintained themselves, and with themselves also a part of the other European peoples, in quiet and prosperity.

That things should remain thus did not suit the selfishness of foreign countries, whose calculations did not look more than one moment ahead. They found German bravery useful in waging their wars and German hands useful to snatch the booty from their rivals. A means had to be found to attain this end, and foreign cunning won an easy victory over German ingenuousness and lack of suspicion. It was foreign countries which first made use of the division of mind produced by religious disputes in Germany—Germany, which presented on a small scale the features of Christian Europe as a whole—foreign countries, I say, made use of these disputes to break up the close inner unity of Germany into separate and disconnected parts. Foreign countries had already destroyed their own unity naturally, by splitting into parts over a common prey; and now they artificially destroyed German unity. They knew how to present each of these separate States that had thus arisen in the lap of the one nation—which had no enemy except those foreign countries themselves, and no concern except the common one of setting itself with united strength against their seductive craft and cunning—foreign countries, I say, knew how to present each of these States to the others as a natural enemy, against which each State must be perpetually on its guard. On the other hand, they knew how to make themselves appear to the German States as natural allies against the danger threatening them from their own countrymen—as allies with whom alone they would themselves stand or fall, and whose enterprises they must in turn support with all their might. It was only because of this artificial bond that all the disputes which might arise about any matter whatever in the Old World or the New became disputes of the German races in their relation to each other. Every war, no matter what its cause, had to be fought out on German soil and with German blood; every disturbance of the balance had to be adjusted in that nation to which the whole fountainhead of such relationships was unknown; and the German States, whose separate existence was in itself contrary to all nature and reason, were compelled, in order that they might count for something, to act as make-weights to the chief forces in the scale of the European equilibrium, whose movement they followed blindly and without any will of their own. Just as in many States abroad the citizens are designated as belonging to this or that foreign party, or voting for this or that foreign alliance, but no name is found for those who belong to the party of their own country, so it was with the Germans; for long enough they belonged only to some foreign party or other, and one seldom came across a man who supported the party of the Germans and was of the opinion that this country ought to make an alliance with itself.

This, then, is the true origin and meaning, this the result for Germany and for the world, of that notorious doctrine of a balance of power to be artificially maintained between the European States. If Christian Europe had remained one, as it ought to be and as it originally was, there would never have been any occasion to think of such a thing. That which is one rests upon itself and supports itself, and does not split up into conflicting forces which must be brought to an equilibrium. Only when Europe became divided and without a law did the thought of a balance acquire a meaning from necessity. To this Europe, divided and without a law, Germany did not belong. If only Germany at any rate had remained one, it would have rested on itself in the centre of the civilized world like the sun in the centre of the universe; it would have kept itself at peace, and with itself the adjacent countries; and without any artificial measures it would have kept everything in equilibrium by the mere fact of its natural existence. It was only the deceit of foreign countries that dragged Germany into their own lawlessness and their own disputes; it was they who taught Germany the treacherous notion of the balance of power, for they knew it to be one of the most effective means of deluding Germany as to its own true advantage and of keeping it in that state of delusion. This aim is now sufficiently attained, and the result that was intended is now complete before our eyes. Even if we cannot do away with this result, why should we not at any rate extirpate the source of it in our own understanding, which is now almost the only thing over which we still have sovereign power? Why should the old dream still be placed before our eyes, now that disaster has awakened us from sleep? Why should we not now at any rate see the truth and perceive the only means that could have saved us? Perhaps our descendants may do what we see ought to be done, just as we now suffer because our fathers dreamed. Let us understand that the conception of an equilibrium to be artificially maintained might have been a consoling dream for foreign countries amid the guilt and evil that oppressed them, but that this conception, being an entirely foreign product, ought never to have taken root in the mind of a German, and that the Germans ought never to have been so situated that it could take root among them. Let us understand that now at any rate we must perceive the utter worthlessness of such a conception, and must see that the salvation of all is to be found, not in it, but solely in the unity of the Germans among themselves.

52 / KARL VON CLAUSEWITZ: NAPOLEON IN RUSSIA

The key event in the downfall of the Napoleonic empire was the Russian campaign of 1812. The causes of Napoleon's disaster in Russia—the frigid weather, the Russian strategy, the

French strategy, the burning of Moscow—have been much debated. An eyewitness to the campaign on the Russian side was the Prussian officer and military theoretician Karl von Clausewitz, who withdrew from the Prussian service in order to join the Russian forces. The following passages are taken from his Der Feldzug von 1812 in Russland *("The Campaign of 1812 in Russia," 1835). Clausewitz (1780–1831) served in the Prussian army from the age of twelve, with the exception of the period he spent in Russia (1812–1814). In 1818 he became head of the Prussian General Military School, acquiring fame as the outstanding military theoretician of his own, and perhaps of all time.*[19]

It may now be allowed the Author to give his opinion on Buonaparte's plan of operation in this much-discussed campaign.

Buonaparte determined to conduct and terminate the war in Russia as he had so many others. To begin with decisive battles, and to profit by their advantages; to gain others still more decisive, and thus to go on playing double or quits till he broke the bank—this was his manner; and we must admit, that to this manner he owed the enormous success of his career; and that the attainment of such success was scarcely conceivable in any other manner.

In Spain it had failed. The Austrian campaign of 1809 had saved Spain, by hindering him from driving the English out of Portugal. He had since subsided there into a defensive war, which cost him prodigious exertions, and, to a certain extent, lamed him of one arm. It is extraordinary, and perhaps the greatest error he ever committed, that he did not visit the Peninsula in person in 1810, in order to end the war in Portugal, by which that in Spain would by degrees have been extinguished; for the Spanish insurrection and the Anglo-Portuguese struggle incontestably fomented each other. Buonaparte would, however, have been always compelled to leave a considerable army in Spain.

It was naturally, and also very justly, a main object with him, in the case of this new war, to avoid being involved in a similarly tedious and costly defensive struggle, upon a theatre so much more distant. He was then under a pressing necessity of ending the war in, at the most, two campaigns.

To beat the enemy—to shatter him—to gain the capital—to drive the

[19] Karl von Clausewitz, *The Campaign of 1812 in Russia,* translated from the German (London: John Murray, 1843), pp. 252–5, 258–60. "Buonaparte," as Napoleon is called here, was the original Corsican spelling of the emperor's name and was usually retained by his opponents.

government into the last corner of the empire—and then, while the confusion was fresh, to dictate a peace—had been hitherto the plan of operation in his wars. In the case of Russia, he had against him the prodigious extent of the empire, and the circumstance of its having two capitals at a great distance from each other. He hoped to balance the moral disadvantages of these two circumstances by two others—by the weakness of the Russian government, and the dissension which he might hope to succeed in establishing between that government and the *noblesse*. He was deceived in both these grounds of reliance; and this it was which made the desertion and destruction of Moscow so vexatious to him. He had hoped, from that centre, to influence by opinion Petersburgh and the whole of Russia.

That under these circumstances Buonaparte should attempt to reach Moscow at a rush was only natural.

The effect of territorial extension, and of a possible national war—in short, the pressure of a vast state with its whole weight—could only make itself felt after a season, and might be overwhelming, if not itself overwhelmed, at the first onset.

If Buonaparte was really obliged to calculate on ending the war in two campaigns, it then made a great difference, whether he conquered Moscow or not in the first. This capital once taken, he might hope to undermine the preparations for further resistance, by imposing with the force which he had remaining—to mislead public opinion—to set feeling at variance with duty.

If Moscow remained in the hands of the Russians, perhaps a resistance for the next campaign might form itself on that basis to which the necessarily weakened force of Buonaparte would be unequal. In short, with the conquest of Moscow, he thought himself over the ridge.

This has always appeared to us the natural view for a man like Buonaparte. The question arises, whether this plan was altogether impracticable, and whether there was not another to be preferred to it?

We are not of such opinion. The Russian army might be beaten, scattered: Moscow might be conquered in one campaign; but we are of opinion that one essential condition was wanting in Buonaparte's execution of the plan—this was to remain formidable after the acquisition of Moscow.

We believe that this was neglected by Buonaparte only in consequence of his characteristic negligence in such matters.

He reached Moscow with 90,000 men, he should have reached it with 200,000.

This would have been possible if he had handled his army with more care and forbearance. But these were qualities unknown to him. He would, perhaps, have lost 30,000 men fewer in action if he had not chosen on every occasion to take the bull by the horns. With more precaution and better regulations as to subsistence, with more careful consideration of the direction of his marches, which would have prevented the unnecessary and enormous accumulation of masses on one and the same road, he would have obviated the starvation which attended his advance from its outset, and have preserved his army in a more effective condition.

Whether 200,000 men placed in the heart of the Russian empire would have produced the requisite moral effect, and commanded a peace, is certainly still a question; but it seems to us that it was allowable to reason *à priori* to that effect. It was not to be anticipated with certainty that the Russians would desert and destroy the city, and enter upon a war of extermination; perhaps it was not probable: if they were to do so, however, the whole object of the war was frustrated, carry it on as he would.

It is, moreover, to be considered as a great neglect on the part of Buonaparte to have made so little preparation as he did for retreat. . . .

The main difficulty was, however, that a country which has been pressed upon by enormous military and foreign masses is not in a condition to make great military exertions. Extraordinary efforts on the part of the citizens of a state have their limits; if they are called for in one direction they cannot be available in another. If the peasant be compelled to remain on the road the entire day with his cattle, for the transport of the supplies of an army, if he has his house full of soldiers, if the proprietor must give up his stores for the said army's subsistence, when the first necessities are hourly pressing and barely provided for, voluntary offerings of money, money's worth, and personal service, are hardly to be looked for.

Concede we, nevertheless, the possibility that such a campaign might have fulfilled its object, and prepared the way for a further advance in the following season. Let us, however, remember what we have to consider on the other side—that Buonaparte found the Russians but half prepared, that he could throw upon them an enormous superiority of force, with a fair prospect of forcing a victory, and giving to the execution of his undertaking the rapidity necessary for a surprise, with all but the certainty of gaining Moscow at one onset, with the possibility of having a peace in his pocket within a quarter of a year. Let us compare these views and reflections with the results of a so-called methodical campaign; it will be very doubtful, all things compared, whether Buonaparte's plan did not involve greater probability of final success than the other, and in this case it was, in fact, the methodical one, and the least audacious and hazardous of the two. However this may be, it is easy to understand that a man like Buonaparte did not hesitate between them.

The dangers of the moment are those by which men are chiefly influenced, and therefore that often appears a desperate course, which is in fact, in the last instance, the only road to safety, and the greatest evidence of foresight. It is seldom that mere acuteness of understanding suffices to fortify men to this degree, and the foresight which leads them in such paths can only be derived from an innate audacity of character. The famous conqueror in question was so far from deficient in this quality, that he would have chosen the most audacious course from inclination, even if his genius had not suggested it to him as the wisest.

We repeat it. He owed every thing to this boldness of determination, and his most brilliant campaigns would have been exposed to the same imputations as have attached to the one we have described, if they had not succeeded.

53 / FREDERICK WILLIAM III: MONARCHY AND NATIONALISM

The defeat of Napoleon in Russia led to the formation of a new coalition in 1813 which caused his downfall in the next year and made it permanent by the battle of Waterloo in 1815. Prussia, which had been totally beaten by Napoleon eight years earlier, was one of the powers which re-entered the war in 1813. Following is the appeal of Frederick William III, king of Prussia, to his people, dated at Breslau, Silesia, on March 10 and published in the Schlesische privilegirte Zeitung *("Silesian Authorized Newspaper") ten days later.*[20]

TO MY PEOPLE

There is as little need to explain to My loyal people as to the Ger-

[20] *Schlesische privilegirte Zeitung*, No. 34, Sunday, March 20, 1813, reproduced in Friedrich Meinecke, *Das Zeitalter der deutschen Erhebung, 1795–1815* (Bielefeld and Leipzig: Velhagen & Klasing, 1906). Translated from the German by the editor. By permission of Frau Antonie Meinecke.

mans the causes of the war which is now beginning. They are clear for undeluded Europe to see.

We succumbed to the superior power of France. The peace which wrested half of My subjects from Me did not bestow its blessings upon us, for it inflicted even deeper wounds upon us than did the war itself. The lifeblood of the country was sucked away, the principal fortresses remained occupied by the enemy, agriculture was crippled, as was the once-prosperous industries of our cities. Freedom of commerce was impeded, thus choking off the sources of profit and prosperity. The country became the prey of impoverishment.

By strictly fulfilling the obligations into which I had entered, I hoped to make things easier for My people and finally to convince the French emperor that it was to his own advantage to leave Prussia its independence. But my wholly innocent intentions were rendered useless by his arrogance and faithlessness, and we saw only too clearly that the emperor's treaties, even more than his wars, would be our slow but certain ruination. Now the moment has come when all illusions about our situation are at an end.

Brandenburgers, Prussians, Silesians, Pomeranians, Lithuanians! You know what you have endured for seven years, you know what tragic fate will be yours if we do not end with honor the fight which now begins. Remember the past, the Great Elector, the great Frederick. Keep in mind the benefits which our forefathers won under them in bloody battle: freedom of conscience, honor, independence, commerce, industry and science. Think of the great example of our mighty allies, the Russians; think of the Spaniards, the Portuguese. Even smaller nations have joined battle with mightier foes for such benefits and have triumphed. Remember the heroic Swiss and Dutch.

Great sacrifices will be demanded from all orders, for we are beginning on a large scale and our enemy's numbers and means are no less large. You will prefer to make sacrifices for the fatherland and for your hereditary king than for an alien ruler, who, as we have learned so often, will employ your sons and your last resources for goals which are not at all yours. Trust in God; endurance, courage, and the mighty assistance of our allies will be the victorious repayment for our honorable exertions.

But no matter what sacrifices may be demanded of individuals, they do not balance the holy boons for which we make them, for the sake of which we struggle and must triumph, if we do not wish to cease to be Prussians and Germans.

We are engaged in the final decisive battle for our existence, our independence, our prosperity; we have no choice except between an honorable peace and a glorious defeat. You will go forward boldly even to the latter for the sake of honor, because a Prussian and a German cannot live without honor. But we must have complete confidence: God and our firm will shall bring victory to our just cause, and with it a secure and glorious peace and the return of better times.

Frederick William

Breslau, March 17, 1813.

54 / RENÉ DE CHATEAUBRIAND: CHRISTIANITY REAFFIRMED

The rise of political conservatism was linked with a reaffirmation of traditional Christianity. One of the leaders in this movement was the French statesman and man of letters, François René, vicomte de Chateaubriand. Yet his Génie du Christianisme *("The Genius of Christianity," 1802) introduced a novel element into the argument in favor of orthodox religion: its appeal to the esthetic sense. The work was frequently reprinted in many languages during the nineteenth century; the following is an excerpt from an English translation published in the United States in 1864. Chateaubriand (1768–1848) was a royalist during the Revolution, but returned to France upon Napoleon's rise to power and served him briefly as a diplomat. He supported the restoration of the Bourbons in 1814, becoming an eminent parliamentarian and diplomat under Louis XVIII. He was one of the founders of the literary movement of Romanticism.*[21]

Every religion has its mysteries. All nature is a secret.

The Christian mysteries are the most sublime that can be; they are the archetypes of the system of man and of the world.

The sacraments are moral laws, and present pictures of a highly poetical character.

[21] René Viscount de Chateaubriand, *The Genius of Christianity; or the Spirit and Beauty of the Christian Religion,* translated from the French by Charles I. White (Baltimore: John Murphy & Co., 1864), pp. 664–8.

Faith is a force, charity a love, hope complete happiness, or, as religion expresses it, a complete virtue.

The laws of God constitute the most perfect code of natural justice.

The fall of our first parents is a universal tradition.

A new proof of it may be found in the constitution of the moral man, which is contrary to the general constitution of beings.

The prohibition to touch the fruit of knowledge was a sublime command, and the only one worthy of the Almighty.

All the arguments which pretend to demonstrate the antiquity of the earth may be contested.

The doctrine of the existence of a God is demonstrated by the wonders of the universe. A design of Providence is evident in the instincts of animals and in the beauty of nature.

Morality of itself proves the immortality of the soul. Man feels a desire of happiness, and is the only creature who cannot attain it; there is consequently a felicity beyond the present life; for we cannot wish for what does not exist.

The system of atheism is founded solely on exceptions. It is not the body that acts upon the soul, but the soul that acts upon the body. Man is not subject to the general laws of matter; he diminishes where the animal increases.

Atheism can benefit no class of people:—neither the unfortunate, whom it bereaves of hope, nor the prosperous, whose joys it renders insipid, nor the soldier, of whom it makes a coward, nor the woman, whose beauty and sensibility it mars, nor the mother who has a son to lose, nor the rulers of men, who have no surer pledge of the fidelity of their subjects than religion.

The punishments and rewards which Christianity holds out in another life are consistent with reason and the nature of the soul.

In literature, characters appear more interesting and the passions more energetic under the Christian dispensation than they were under polytheism. The latter exhibited no dramatic feature, no struggles between natural desire and virtue.

Mythology contracted nature, and for this reason the ancients had no descriptive poetry. Christianity restores to the wilderness both its pictures and its solitudes.

The Christian marvellous may sustain a comparison with the marvellous of fable. The ancients founded their poetry on Homer, while the Christians found theirs on the Bible: and the beauties of the Bible surpass the beauties of Homer.

To Christianity the fine arts owe their revival and their perfection.

In philosophy it is not hostile to any natural truth. If it has sometimes opposed the sciences, it followed the spirit of the age and the opinions of the greatest legislators of antiquity.

In history we should have been inferior to the ancients but for the new character of images, reflections, and thoughts, to which Christianity has given birth. Modern eloquence furnishes the same observation.

The relics of the fine arts, the solitude of monasteries, the charms of ruins, the pleasing superstitions of the common people, the harmonies of the heart, religion, and the desert, lead to the examination of the Christian worship.

This worship everywhere exhibits a union of pomp and majesty with a moral design and with a prayer either affecting or sublime. Religion gives life and animation to the sepulchre. From the laborer who reposes in a rural cemetery to the king who is interred at St. Dennis, the grave of the Christian is full of poetry. Job and David, reclining upon the Christian tomb, sing in their turn the sleep of death by which man awakes to eternity.

We have seen how much the world is indebted to the clergy and to the institutions and spirit of Christianity. If Schoonbeck, Bonnani, Giustiniani, and Helyot, had followed a better order in their laborious researches, we might have presented here a complete catalogue of the services rendered by religion to humanity. We would have commenced with a list of all the calamities incident to the soul or the body of man, and mentioned under each affliction the Christian order devoted to its relief. It is no exaggeration to assert that, whatever distress or suffering we may think of, religion has, in all probability, anticipated us and provided a remedy for it. From as accurate a calculation as we were able to make, we have obtained the following results:—

There are computed to be on the surface of Christian Europe about four thousand three hundred towns and villages. Of these four thousand three hundred towns and villages, three thousand two hundred and ninety-four are of the first, second, third, and fourth rank. Allowing one hospital to each of these three thousand two hundred and ninety-four places, (which is far below the truth,) you will have three thousand two hundred and ninety-four hospitals, almost all founded by the spirit of Christianity, endowed by the Church, and attended by religious orders. Supposing that, upon an average, each of these hospitals contains one hundred beds, or, if you please, fifty beds for two patients each, you will find that religion, exclusively of the immense number of poor which she supports, has afforded daily relief and subsistence for more than a thousand years to about three hundred and twenty-nine thousand four hundred persons.

On summing up the colleges and universities, we find nearly the same results; and we may safely assert that they afford instruction to at least three hundred thousand youths in the different states of Europe.

In this statement we have not included either the Christian hospitals and colleges in the other three quarters of the globe, or the female youth educated by nuns.

To these results must be added the catalogue of the celebrated men produced by the Church, who form nearly two-thirds of the distinguished characters of modern times. We must repeat, as we have shown, that to the Church we owe the revival of the arts and sciences and of letters; that to her are due most of the great modern discoveries, as gunpowder, clocks, the mariner's compass, and, in government, the representative system; that agriculture and commerce, the laws and political science, are under innumerable obligations to her; that her missions introduced the arts and sciences among civilized nations and laws among savage tribes; that her institution of chivalry powerfully contributed to save Europe from an invasion of new barbarians; that to her mankind is indebted for

The worship of one only God;

The more firm establishment of the belief in the existence of that Supreme Being;

A clearer idea of the immortality of the soul, and also of a future state of rewards and punishments;

A more enlarged and active humanity;

A perfect virtue, which alone is equivalent to all the others—Charity.

A political law and the law of nations, unknown to the ancients, and, above all, the abolition of slavery.

Who is there but must be convinced of the beauty and the grandeur of Christianity? Who but must be overwhelmed with this stupendous mass of benefits?

55 / THOMAS MALTHUS: THE PROBLEM OF POPULATION

The optimistic belief in inevitable progress, which the political conservatives opposed, was called into question on different grounds by an English economist, Thomas Robert Malthus (1766–1834). His Essay on the Principle of Population *is one of the central documents in the rise of the modern social science of demography (population study). The essay was first published anonymously in 1798 because of the boldness of its "uncharitable" argument; but Malthus put his name on the title page of the expanded edition, published in 1803 and reprinted frequently thereafter. The following passages are taken from the fifth edition.*[22]

In an inquiry concerning the improvement of society, the mode of conducting the subject which naturally presents itself, is,

1. To investigate the causes that have hitherto impeded the progress of mankind towards happiness; and,

2. To examine the probability of the total or partial removal of these causes in future.

To enter fully into this question, and to enumerate all the causes that have hitherto influenced human improvement, would be much beyond the power of an individual. The principal object of the present essay is to examine the effects of one great cause intimately united with the very nature of man; which, though it has been constantly and powerfully operating since the commencement of society, has been little noticed by the writers who have treated this subject. The facts which establish the existence of this cause have, indeed, been repeatedly stated and acknowledged; but its natural and necessary effects have been almost totally overlooked; though probably among these effects may be reckoned a very considerable portion of that vice and misery, and of that unequal distribution of the bounties of nature, which it has been the unceasing object of the enlightened philanthropist in all ages to correct.

The cause to which I allude, is the constant tendency of all animated life to increase beyond the nourishment prepared for it.

It is observed by Dr. Franklin, that there is no bound to the prolific nature of plants or animals, but what is made by their crowding and interfering with each other's means of subsistence. . . .

This is incontrovertibly true. Through the animal and vegetable kingdoms Nature has scattered the seeds of life abroad with the most profuse and liberal hand; but has been comparatively sparing in the room and the nourishment necessary to rear them. The germs of existence contained in this earth, if they could freely develope themselves, would fill millions of worlds in the course of a few thousand years. Necessity, that imperious, all-pervading law of nature, restrains them within the prescribed bounds. The race of plants and the race of animals shrink under this great restrictive law; and man cannot by any efforts of reason escape from it.

[22] T. R. Malthus, *An Essay on the Principle of Population; or, A View of Its Past and Present Effects on Human Happiness; with an Inquiry into Our Prospects Respecting the Future Removal or Mitigation of the Evils which It Occasions,* 5th ed. (London: John Murray, 1817), Vol. I, pp. 1–5, 9–10, 17–21, 23; Vol. III, pp. 63–4, 82, 87–8.

In plants and irrational animals, the view of the subject is simple. They are all impelled by a powerful instinct to the increase of their species; and this instinct is interrupted by no doubts about providing for their offspring. Wherever therefore there is liberty, the power of increase is exerted; and the superabundant effects are repressed afterwards by want of room and nourishment.

The effects of this check on man are more complicated. Impelled to the increase of his species by an equally powerful instinct, reason interrupts his career, and asks him whether he may not bring beings into the world, for whom he cannot provide the means of support. If he attend to this natural suggestion, the restriction too frequently produces vice. If he hear it not, the human race will be constantly endeavouring to increase beyond the means of subsistence. But as, by that law of our nature which makes food necessary to the life of man, population can never actually increase beyond the lowest nourishment capable of supporting it, a strong check on population, from the difficulty of acquiring food, must be constantly in operation. This difficulty must fall somewhere, and must necessarily be severely felt in some or other of the various forms of misery, or the fear of misery, by a large portion of mankind. . . .

It may safely be pronounced . . . that population, when unchecked, goes on doubling itself every twenty-five years, or increases in a geometrical ratio.

The rate according to which the productions of the earth may be supposed to increase, it will not be so easy to determine. Of this, however, we may be perfectly certain, that the ratio of their increase must be totally of a different nature from the ratio of the increase of population. A thousand millions are just as easily doubled every twenty-five years by the power of population as a thousand. But the food to support the increase from the greater number will by no means be obtained with the same facility. Man is necessarily confined in room. When acre has been added to acre till all the fertile land is occupied, the yearly increase of food must depend upon the melioration of the land already in possession. This is a fund, which, from the nature of all soils, instead of increasing, must be gradually diminishing. But population, could it be supplied with food, would go on with unexhausted vigour; and the increase of one period would furnish the power of a greater increase the next, and this without any limit. . . .

The ultimate check to population appears then to be a want of food, arising necessarily from the different ratios according to which population and food increase. But this ultimate check is never the immediate check, except in cases of actual famine.

The immediate check may be stated to consist in all those customs, and all those diseases, which seem to be generated by a scarcity of the means of subsistence; and all those causes, independent of this scarcity, whether of a moral or physical nature, which tend prematurely to weaken and destroy the human frame.

These checks to population, which are constantly operating with more or less force in every society, and keep down the number to the level of the means of subsistence, may be classed under two general heads—the preventive, and the positive checks.

The preventive check, as far as it is voluntary, is peculiar to man, and arises from that distinctive superiority in his reasoning faculties, which enables him to calculate distant consequences. The checks to the indefinite increase of plants and irrational animals are all either positive, or, if preventive, involuntary. But man cannot look around him, and see the distress which frequently presses upon those who have large families; he cannot contemplate his present possessions or earnings, which he now nearly consumes himself, and calculate the amount of each share, when with very little addition they must be divided, perhaps, among seven or eight, without feeling a doubt whether, if he follow the bent of his inclinations, he may be able to support the offspring which he will probably bring into the world. In a state of equality, if such can exist, this would be the simple question. In the present state of society other considerations occur. Will he not lower his rank in life, and be obliged to give up in great measure his former habits? Does any mode of employment present itself by which he may reasonably hope to maintain a family? Will he not at any rate subject himself to greater difficulties, and more severe labour, than in his single state? Will he not be unable to transmit to his children the same advantages of education and improvement that he had himself possessed? Does he even feel secure that, should he have a large family, his utmost exertions can save them from rags and squalid poverty, and their consequent degradation in the community? And may he not be reduced to the grating necessity of forfeiting his independence, and of being obliged to the sparing hand of Charity for support?

These considerations are calculated to prevent, and certainly do prevent, a great number of persons in all civilized nations from pursuing the dictate of nature in an early attachment to one woman.

If this restraint does not produce vice, it is undoubtedly the least evil that can arise from the principle of population. . . . When this restraint produces vice, the evils which follow are but too conspicuous. A promiscuous intercourse to such a degree as to prevent the birth of children seems to lower, in the most marked manner, the dignity of human nature. It cannot be without its effect on men, and nothing can be more obvious than its tendency to degrade the female character, and to destroy all its most amiable and distinguishing characteristics. Add to which, that among those unfortunate females, with which all great towns abound, more real distress and aggravated misery are, perhaps, to be found, than in any other department of human life. . . .

Promiscuous intercourse, unnatural passions, violations of the marriage bed, and improper arts to conceal the consequences of irregular connexions, are preventive checks that clearly come under the head of vice. . . .

As it appears that, in the actual state of every society which has come within our review, the natural progress of population has been constantly and powerfully checked; and as it seems evident that no improved form of government, no plans of emigration, no benevolent institutions, and no degree or direction of national industry, can prevent the continued action of a great check to population in some form or other; it follows that we must submit to it as an inevitable law of nature; and the only inquiry that remains is, how it may take place with the least possible prejudice to the virtue and happiness of human society. All the immediate checks to population, which have been observed to prevail in the same and different countries, seem to be resolvable into moral restraint, vice and misery; and if our choice be confined to these three, we cannot long hesitate in our decision respecting which it would be most eligible to encourage. . . .

It is of the very utmost importance to the happiness of mankind, that the population should not increase too fast; but it does not appear, that the object to be accomplished would admit of any considerable diminution in the desire of marriage. It is clearly the duty of each individual not to marry till he has a prospect of supporting his children; but it is at the same time to be wished that he should retain undiminished his desire of marriage, in order that he may exert himself to realize this prospect, and be stimulated to make provision for the support of greater numbers. . . .

The interval between the age of puberty and the period at which each individual might venture on marriage must, according to the supposition, be passed in strict chastity; because of the law of chastity cannot be violated without producing evil. The effect of anything like a promiscuous intercourse, which prevents the birth of children, is evidently to weaken the best affections of the heart, and in a very marked manner to degrade the female character. And any other intercourse would, without improper arts, bring as many children into the society as marriage, with a much greater probability of their becoming a burden to it.

These considerations shew that the virtue of chastity is not, as some have supposed, a forced produce of artificial society; but that it has the most real and solid foundation in nature and reason; being apparently the only virtuous mean of avoiding the vice and misery which result so often from the principle of population.

IV / 1815-1848: THE AGE OF RESTORATION

In 1814–1815 the defenders of the Old Regime won a total victory over Napoleon, in whom they fought not only the military conqueror but also the carrier of revolution from France to the rest of Europe. Military triumph was easier to achieve, however, than its political and social consolidation. For three decades the kings and the aristocracies endeavored to restore the Old Regime, but found that they could not halt the changes in economic, social, and political life which they so feared. The forces of innovation were not destroyed but merely defeated; after a while, they regrouped and took the initiative again. The Age of Restoration was marked by repeated revolutions and ended in the great revolutionary upsurge of 1848.

56 / FRIEDRICH VON GENTZ: ALLIANCE FOR THE STATUS QUO

In 1815 the ideal of the rulers of Europe was the re-establishment of the Old Regime. One great change, however, they had to accept. Under the old political system the powers had considered revolution to be a danger only to the state involved, and to be for others rather an opportunity for aggrandizement; now they felt "liberalism" (the name given to advocacy of the New Regime), no matter where it flourished, to be a peril to all conservative powers. The collaboration of the powers in the face of such dangers was the purpose of the half-dozen international conferences held in the decade after 1815. The significance of one of the most important of these "congresses" is analyzed by Friedrich von

Gentz, a German diplomat and political writer in the service of the Austrian chancellor, Metternich. This memorandum, "The Results of the Congress of Aix-la-Chapelle [Aachen], 1818," was submitted by Gentz to Metternich in November, 1818; the following passages from it are translated from the edition of Metternich's memoirs, in which it was first published. Gentz (1764–1832) was born in Silesia and served in the Prussian diplomatic corps before following Metternich into the Austrian service. He was one of the most thoughtful defenders of the old order.[1]

All the powers of Europe have been united since 1813 in what is, properly, not an alliance but a harmonious system based upon generally recognized principles and upon treaties which give to every state, large or small, the place befitting it. It may be denied that this state of affairs possesses the characteristics of a federative system or a balance of power according to older political ideas; but for all that, it is no less certain that in the present European situation, which will continue for some time, the existing system corresponds most closely to its needs and that the dissolution of this system would be a frightful calamity; for, as none of the states therein could maintain itself in isolation, the result for all of them would be new political combinations, new measures of security, and consequently new alliances, shifts, rapprochements, intrigues, and incalculable combinations, which in the course of a thousand different accidents, each as baleful as the next, would lead us to a new general war, that is (for the two terms are almost synonymous), to a final overthrow of the social order in Europe.

A fraction of these terrible dangers, it must be granted, did occupy, in the period from 1817 until the summer of 1818, not only the idle speculations of the public but also the considered thoughts of statesmen, in whom it aroused keen anxiety and sinister forebodings. During that time there was fear particularly of a change of policy in Russia; various events, misjudged perhaps at the time, gave rise to the suspicion that Emperor Alexander was seeking a system of close alliance with the Houses of Bourbon in France, Spain and Italy. Such a combination would have placed all states lying between them in the most critical position. It would inevitably have provoked a counter-combination of Austria, Prussia and England. The powers of the second and third rank would have joined one or the other standard; Germany, the

[1] *Mémoires, documents et écrits divers laissés par le Prince de Metternich, chancelier de Cour et d'État*, ed. Prince Richard de Metternich and M. A. de Klinkowstroem, 2nd ed. (Paris: E. Plon, 1881), Vol. III, pp. 172–6. Translated from the French by Herbert H. Rowen.

center of Europe, which is now united, would have run the risk of again being torn apart from several directions. Rivalries, fears, disputes and the provocations inseparable from such a situation would have soon placed these two opposed political bodies in a completely hostile stance, and the first serious dispute would have set off the explosion.

It is true that these suspicions and anxieties had already largely disappeared several months before the meeting at Aachen, yet the meeting did produce two priceless benefits: first, it wholly cleared the ground, removed all doubts, and fully re-established confidence in each Government in the conduct and the principles of the others, and in the stability of general unity; second, by means of private conferences, searching discussion, and the insights obtained by everyone of good intentions, it imbued the Sovereigns and their ministers with a sense of the necessity of maintaining intact a system which, whatever merits and faults may be found with it in theory, remains today the only one which works in practice, the only one which meets the rightly understood interests of all the powers, and is the anchor of salvation for Europe.

The confirmation of the quadruple alliance for the case of the outbreak of new catastrophes within France threatening the peace of her neighbors is one of the most solid benefits which we owe to the Congress of Aachen. It was not easy to draw the line between a domineering attitude, which might well have roused and worsened the storms which it was intended to avoid, and a measure of precaution designed solely for future eventualities and yet sufficiently impressive to be effective; but those who are competent to judge will acknowledge that this was done with much prudence and discretion. One may consider the danger which this measure was designed to prevent as more or less probable or imminent, but it is impossible to deny its reality or to refuse to admit that in the present state of affairs France remains, all things considered, the country which is least disposed to respect the general peace and is best situated and best organized to disturb it, and will be able, after a few years, to make such an attempt with most success. So long as the quadruple alliance lasts, reinforced as it now is by the entire mass of military might in Germany, the most audacious party leader, or even a king of France carried along by the ardor of the people, would not lightly decide to give the signal for new battles. Thus, at least one of the clouds which hang dangerously upon our horizon will be held away by an assemblage of substantial forces; and the Congress would have deserved well of mankind had it done no more than to give us this special guarantee, which fits in, as it were, with the general association on which the state of peace rests.

Within every European country, without exception, a burning fever is at work, the accompaniment or the harbinger of the most violent con-

vulsions which the civilized world has known since the fall of the
Roman Empire. It is a struggle, a war to the death between the old and
the new principles, between the old and a new social order. By what
we might call an inevitable mischance, the reaction of 1813, which
checked but did not end the revolutionary movement in France, re-
awakened it in the other states. Everything is in ferment, all the elements of power are menaced by the loss of their equilibrium; the most
solid institutions are shaken to their foundations, like the buildings of
a city feeling the first tremors of an earthquake which will destroy
everything in a few moments. If, in this frightful crisis, the principal
Sovereigns of Europe had been disunited in their principles and their
purposes; if a single one had been capable of seeking in his neighbors'
difficulties the means to advance his own interests or had looked upon
the spectacle about him with blind or criminal indifference; if, finally,
all had not kept their eyes open for the signs of the revolutions which
are being prepared and for the means which they retain to prevent
them or at least to delay their explosion, we would all have been swept
away within a few years. But such, fortunately, are not the dispositions
of the Princes, who are the protectors and the preservers of public
order; their close union, "calm and constant in its action," is the counter-
weight to the disorderly movement of human affairs which is the purpose of so many turbulent spirits who have quit their own proper
sphere; the nucleus of organized forces presented by this union is the
dike which which Providence itself appears to have raised in order to
protect the old order of society, or at least to slow and to soften the
changes which have become indispensable. But this truly sacred
union, of which the Holy Alliance is only an inaccurate and inadequate
symbol, has never been displayed in more reassuring fashion than
during the conference of Aachen. It is not that any of these dangerous
questions, the objects or pretexts of general agitation, was taken up;
neither the form of Governments, nor the representative system, nor
the maintenance of modification of the privileges of the nobility, nor
the freedom of the press, nor anything involving the interests of religion, was discussed. With the deliberate purpose of avoiding a foothold for malevolence and indiscretion, there were excluded from the
formal pronouncements, avowals and assertions which everyone accepted in principle in his soul but which might have aroused troublesome commentary and hostile criticism if stated publicly. What was
done was something better. The Sovereigns and ministers understood
what common safety dictated. They felt strongly the need for mutual
confidence and a closer agreement than can be established by treaty;
they sacrificed secondary interests, which might have divided them in
less serious circumstances, for the sake of the transcendent interest of
defending by concentrated efforts the responsibilities which Provi-

dence has entrusted to them in common, and they silenced all other considerations before the higher duty of preserving authority from shipwreck and saving the peoples from their own aberrations. Without entering into superfluous obligations, they reached a close understanding on the course to follow in the midst of the tempest; and the only title of right which they solemly brought forward in justification and legitimization of this course was that which they asserted in the declaration that *justice, moderation and concord* would constantly preside over their deliberations.

It was in this way that the Congress of Aachen fulfilled its lofty mission. The general impression produced by it in Europe is the first evidence of this. While maintaining a silence wholly befitting its position and dignity, which only a few publications interrupted, it encouraged the friends of order and peace in all countries and gave alarm to innovators and subversives. A diplomatic conference, as such, cannot change the destiny of the world, but it can check and moderate it, it can prevent a host of evils which would make it worse; and if the results which may be reasonably expected from the latest meeting of the Sovereigns were to be paralyzed by events beyond human calculation, it will still retain the glory of having given support and consolation of the virtuous.

57 / NICHOLAS V. RIASANOVSKY: THEORY AND PRACTICE OF TSARISM'S IDEOLOGY

The primary ideology of Russian tsarism was a doctrine called "Official Nationality." It combined specifically Russian theories in support of autocracy with the new conservatism that dominated Europe after the fall of Napoleon. In his study of "Official Nationality" during the reign of Nicholas I, a contemporary American historian of Russia, Nicholas V. Riasanovsky, puts the theory and practice of this doctrine in the balance and finds them wanting. At the same time, he reminds the reader that just as practical needs give much of their meaning and force to ideas, the doctrines in which men believe are—for good or evil—no less the shapers of their needs. The concluding chapter of Riasanov-

sky's book, *"Official Nationality and History,"* is reprinted in its entirety.[2]

The marvel—and the mistake—of Nicholas I's long rule is to be found in its extraordinary doctrinaire rigidity and consistency. The steadfast monarch governed his vast empire and participated in the destinies of the world on the basis of a few simple principles which he held with passionate conviction. The ideology of the reign, known as Official Nationality, deserves more attention that it has hitherto received. Far from being mere propaganda or empty talk, it represented the conscious orientation of the Russian government in the course of thirty eventful years. Its roots lay deep in Russian history, most especially in the creation of the modern Russian state by Peter the Great, as well as in the subsequent development of that state. The doctrine of Official Nationality also faithfully reflected a stage in general European evolution, marked by the defeat of Napoleon and the joint effort of victorious powers to restore something like the old order on the continent. As theory, the Russian teaching constituted a typical philosophy of the age of restoration and reaction. In practice it meant a way of managing the enormous and relatively backward Russian state. And while one can easily criticize Nicholas I's desperate effort personally to set everything straight in his far-flung realm, one should at least try to appreciate the difficulties of his position.

The emperor's stubborn loyalty to his convictions taxed the understanding of many of his contemporaries and of numerous subsequent historians. Time and again they have tried to explain Nicholas I's actions more "realistically," notably on the basis of the immediate interests of Russia rather than of the tsar's professed principles. For example, some specialists have maintained that Russian intervention in Hungary in 1849 resulted from the fear of Polish rebels who took an active part in the Hungarian movement, not from the desire to crush revolution, come to the aid of Austria, or honor the treaty of 1833. Even Schiemann, who is in many ways the leading authority on the reign of Nicholas I, argued that the Russian autocrat wanted to manipulate Austria and Prussia so they would serve as a shield against liberalism and revolution and do his fighting for him—this in spite of the fact that the German scholar also repeatedly pointed out in his work the tsar's eagerness for combat and the reluctance of his allies. In fact, this contrast between the recognition of the extremely rigid and doctrinaire nature of the

[2] Nicholas V. Riasanovsky, *Nicholas I and Official Nationality in Russia, 1825–1855* (Berkeley and Los Angeles: University of California Press, 1959), pp. 266–272. Reprinted by permission of University of California Press.

tsar's policy and the attempts, which nevertheless persist, to ascribe its various manifestations to "practical" reasons, constitutes one of the peculiarities of historical writing dealing with this period. A dismissal of "realistic" interpretations does not indicate, however, that Nicholas I ignored Russian interests. Rather he saw these interests in terms of his fundamental beliefs, not apart from them; the effectiveness of the autocrat's service to his native land depended thus largely on the soundness of the beliefs.

Similarly the extreme regimentation and repression of Nicholas I's reign have to be considered in the light of the emperor's convictions and of the aims which he attempted to achieve. While many specific instances of censorship or police interference must be judged ridiculous and stupid, the system as a whole makes good sense provided one accepts the dogma of Official Nationality and the need to impose it upon Russia. Once more Nicholas I stands vindicated or convicted primarily on the basis of his beliefs.

It is necessary to understand the doctrine of Official Nationality in order to comprehend the reign of Nicholas I. But understanding does not imply endorsement. The government ideology of autocracy and of the absolute control of the life of the country by the monarch represented at best one narrow approach to statecraft. It could be called progressive in the age of Peter the Great, in particular in Russia where the mighty sovereign undertook sweeping reforms in the face of an overwhelming popular opposition and indifference. It became increasingly less forward-looking with the passage of time and the social, political, economic, and intellectual evolution of Europe, turning into something of an anachronism in the ninetenth century. The rigid iron rule of Nicholas I tended to obscure the fact that even during his reign, and perhaps especially during his reign, Russia was undergoing fundamental change. The serf economy of the country steadily declined in favor of freer labor, monetary exchange, distant markets, and, in short, the rise of capitalism. Socially too, in spite of all government efforts, new forces were coming to the fore, the Russian intelligentsia of the 1840's being already much more democratic in origin than that of the 1820's. Russian culture, literature in particular, blossomed out in new splendor which offered infinitely more to the reader than the trite and vulgar pages of *The Northern Bee* and *The Reader's Library*. While, as has been indicated above, a number of leading Russian writers contributed in one way or another to the official doctrine, the main currents of this cultural renaissance ran in other directions. The Russia of Pushkin, of Lermontov, of the young Turgenev and Dostoevskii, or, indeed, of Gogol had little in common with the official version.

Ideas also changed. Educated Russians, from Herzen and Belinskii on one wing to Khomyakov and Samarin on the other, espoused views different from and often antagonistic to the teaching of their government. The Slavophiles, the Westernizers, the members of the Brotherhood of Cyril and Methodius, the Petrashevtsy, all saw visions of their ntaive land and made plans for its future which did not fit the prescribed model. The extremist Bakunin and the moderate Granovskii, religious thinkers of the Slavophile camp and atheists such as Butashevich-Petrashevskii, liberals and socialists, constitutionalists and federalists, found themselves in opposition to the Russia of Nicholas I. The revolutionary ideas of the age, notably romantic nationalism, penetrated the official doctrine itself, contending for allegiance with the older dynastic interpretation. Of still greater significance was the fact that the reign of Nicholas I marked not only the flowering but also the beginning of the waning of romanticism in Russia. The romantic emphasis on religion, authority, uniqueness, history, and tradition gradually gave ground to a secular, materialistic, and positivist outlook which the tsar correctly considered as the deadly foe of his system. It is worth noting that the revolutionary movement of the Decembrists, inspired by the ideas of the Age of Reason and by Jacobin practice, had no militant successor in Russia until the 1870's, after the end of the romantic epoch and the advent of realism and the cult of science.

While the split between government and society in Russia continued to increase during the thirty long years of Nicholas I's reign, the gulf between the empire of the tsars and the West widened even more perceptibly. For the leading countries of the West, propelled by the industrial revolution, were undergoing a still more rapid transformation than the state of the Romanovs. Yet the autocrat's only answer to all the change at home and abroad remained a reaffirmation of his old principles, a heroic effort to turn the clock back. Following the revolutions of 1848, government and life in Russia acquired a certain nightmarish quality which forced even many supporters of the existing regime to cry out in despair. The debacle of the Crimean War came both as logical retribution and as liberation.

The historical significance of the reign of Nicholas I and the system of Official Nationality can be judged in several contexts. In the evolution of Russia it meant an attempt, for three decades, to freeze growth and impose stagnation. The liberal hopes of the time of Alexander I, already betrayed by that monarch himself, gave place to outspoken reaction. Abroad, Russia, the recent liberator of Europe, turned definitely into its gendarme. In fairness to Nicholas I it is right and proper to emphasize that his problems were great and his choices limited. Most critics of the emperor knew less about the condition of Russia than he did, and none of them had the awesome responsibility of translating theory into practice. Still, the sovereign's total refusal to consider any other way but his own led to a dead end, all the more so because the existing system was constantly becoming more obsolete and less workable. Although Russia certainly was not Great Britain or France and although it had to find a solution based on its own capabilities, it seems presumptuous to argue that the great reforms of the 1860's could not have been enacted in the fifties and the forties, or that the liberal hopes of the reign of Alexander I were bound to be doomed even if the successor to that emperor believed in constitutionalism, not autocracy. While numerous circumstances delimited the area within which the government system could operate, the fundamental rigidity lay in the system itself.

In a sense Russia never recovered the thirty years lost under Nicholas I. Alexander II instituted reforms; Alexander III appealed to the nationalist sentiment which his grandfather had spurned; in the reign of Nicholas II the country obtained even a shaky constitutional machinery. But all these new departures remained somehow tentative and incomplete. And it was still largely the old order of Nicholas I, the antiquated *ancien régime,* that went down in the conflagration of 1917. In some ways the willful autocrat proved to be more successful than he could have imagined.

In the broader pageant of European history, Nicholas I and Official Nationality deserve attention on a number of counts. The autocratic rule of the Russian sovereign represented a classic example of its kind, comparable to the reign of Louis XIV in France. "Orthodoxy" and "nationality" too, as indicated repeatedly in this study, reflected beliefs, forces, and problems by no means limited to the empire of the tsars. "Orthodoxy," even more than autocracy, linked Russia to the traditional Christian order on the continent which had been undergoing a profound transformation under the impact of the French Revolution and its aftermath. "Nationality," in its romantic interpretation, acted by contrast as a disintegrator of the established system, as a harbinger of a newer, if not a better, world. Official Nationality offers a fascinating picture of the rise of radical nationalism and of its efforts to supersede the older dynastic orientation. In Russia the attempt never quite succeeded: certainly not under Nicholas I and not even under the last of the Romanovs, when the communist victory in 1917 gave a thoroughly new direction to the history of the country. Still, developments in the tsarist state constituted one instance of that basic process and struggle in modern European history which marked the emergence of integral nationalism out of a traditional and dynastic past. It fell to the lot of Germany, the cradle of romanticism, to explore to the end the implications of radical nationalism, and beyond it racism, unhindered by "Orthodoxy" or other moral principles.

The theory and the practice of Official Nationality have something to tell us in a yet larger context. The system of Emperor Nicholas I demonstrated a remarkable coördination between thought and action, a dedication to a set ideal, a determination to mold reality according to an ideological blueprint. It is true that the government doctrine itself originated and could originate only in a certain historical milieu, conditioned by many circumstances of time and place. It is also true that similar circumstances limited its effectiveness and eventually defeated its aims. But, in the last analysis, the student of Nicholas I and Official Nationality in Russia leaves his subject with a sense of the power, not the weakness, of ideas in history, of the importance, not the insignificance, of man's purpose in the shaping of human destiny.

58 / ABBÉ LAMMENAIS: CATHOLICISM AND THE NEW STATE

In domestic affairs, no more than in international relations, was the Old Regime brought back in its simple totality. This was particularly true of the western countries of Europe. In France the Napoleonic settlement in religion, which made Catholicism the state religion but granted official status to Protestantism and Judaism, with state policy hostile to religious interference, continued largely in force even after the Restoration. The dissatisfaction of ardent Catholics was expressed by Félicité Robert de Lammenais, a notable Catholic thinker, in his work De la religion considérée dans ses rapports avec l'ordre politique et civil *("Religion Considered in Its Relations to the Political and Civil Order," 1825–26), from which the following passages are translated. Lammenais (1782–1854), known as the Abbé Lammenais, was a complex figure; influenced by Rousseau in his youth, he gradually shifted from the rigidly traditional Catholicism expressed in this essay to an advocacy of wide freedom of religion, and ultimately broke with the Roman Church.*[3]

[3] Abbé Félicien Robert de Lammenais, *De la religion considérée dans ses rapports avec l'ordre politique et civil*, 3rd ed. (Paris: Au Bureau du Mémorial Catholique, 1826), pp. 102–6. Translated from the French by the editor.

A despicable materialism has invaded everything: in society men have eyes only for lands, labor and money; in the law, for the proportion of black and white balls; [4] in justice, for the mutable requirements of a deaf and blind law; in crime, for the deed only, which for the safety of the public must be linked with the notion of the executioner.

Moreover, the state knows neither God nor his commandments, neither truth nor duties nor anything pertaining to the moral order. It glories in its indifference toward all dogmas, even in its ignorance of them. In its eyes there exists no higher power than that which directs its activity; it does not rise higher than man and it gives the name of independence to servile submission to his will. It considers all things as good provided that they deny the sovereign authority from which all other powers derive, provided that they give no obedience whatever to the supreme lawgiver. It spurns his very name, which it hears with hatred; it has wiped this name from its laws, so that their only principle is force and their only sanction is death.

The result of this frightful political apostasy is the reduction of religion—which is on the constant verge of banishment, since its spirit and doctrine are in absolute contradiction with the maxims of the state—to a kind of public establishment conceded to the stubborn prejudices of several million Frenchmen. It is tolerated for their sake, much as the theater is protected for the sake of others. It is similarly dependent upon the public administration which pays its salaries. Its expenditures are fixed, its system of bookkeeping is determined, and its positions are filled: that is all. A church is in no wise more sacred than any other building; it is only a building to be erected and kept in repair, just like a jail; and there is no difference between the sanctuary in which rests the Holy of Holies, and a Protestant temple, a synagogue, or even a mosque (if some newcomer should get the idea of establishing one). Bishops, consistories, priests, ministers, rabbis—all are equal in the eyes of the law and, we should add, in the eyes of the administrators, if it were not that the Catholic clergy are for them only too often the objects of special distrust and an aversion which they rarely bother to conceal.

Thus religion, which should be placed in the leadership of society and should entirely permeate it, is relegated among the matters which interest it least, or interest it only in its material relationships. It is permitted because of the danger of suddenly abolishing it; but it is degraded, its operations are interfered with, the circle of its influence is narrowed as much as possible, and no opportunity is let slip to challenge its divine rights. The effort is made to instill in the people hatred and contempt for it, in the hope that in this way it may be gotten rid of

[4] votes against and for bills in the French legislature (ed.)

slowly and without disturbance; or, what would amount to the same thing, the effort is made to enslave its ministers in the performance of their spiritual functions to the civil power, which would become the master in the Church as it is rightfully in the state.

And do not take comfort in the obstacles that the execution of such a plan would face: there is no evil nowadays that we can consider impossible; there will always be people to do anything and to justify anything. For we cannot conceal from ourselves the fact that a new race of men has appeared in our time, a hateful race forever accursed by all who belong to mankind; men of the muck, the vilest of men, except for those who pay them; men who possess reason only in order to prostitute it to the interests to which they are subject, who possess conscience in order to violate it, and who possess a soul in order to sell it; men lower than the lowest, on whom our indignation grows weary and then even our contempt.

Let us repeat: What is being prepared with indefatigable activity is the destruction of Christianity in France by the establishment of a national church subject in all things to the public administration; this is the inevitable goal of the system which has been followed until now; this is, finally, what is wanted by the Revolution. Will it get what it wants? The future will tell.

59 / THE PATTERN OF CONSTITUTIONAL MONARCY

In exceptional cases Roman Catholicism found it advisable and feasible to collaborate with liberals, who emphasized separation of church and state and were often deists in religion. One such case occurred in Belgium, where the hostility of liberals and Catholics to Dutch rule within a unified Kingdom of the Netherlands led to the revolution of 1830 and the expulsion of the Dutch. The constitution adopted by the Belgians on February 17, 1831, expressed this compromise. It is also notable in that it set down the general form of constitutional monarchy which was to become more and more common in Europe during the next century; it has been described by one historian, not too inaccurately, as the unwritten British constitution set down on paper. The following translation of its key passages is based upon the text in the classic history of the Belgian National Congress of 1830–31.[5]

TITLE II

Article 6. No distinction of orders exists in the state.

Belgians are equal before the law; none but Belgians may be appointed to civil or military employment except according to the provisions of a law which may be enacted for special cases.

Art. 7. Personal freedom is guaranteed.

No one may be prosecuted except for causes defined by law and in the manner prescribed by law.

Except in the case of those caught in the act of crime, arrests shall be made only on the authority of a judicial warrant specifying charges, which shall be communicated to the accused upon his arrest or at the latest within the subsequent twenty-four hours.

Art. 8. No one shall be transferred from the court of a judge assigned to him according to law except with his own assent.

Art. 9. No penalty may be established or enforced except as provided by law.

Art. 10. The home is inviolable; no search may be made except in the cases defined by law and in the manner prescribed by law.

Art. 11. No one may be deprived of his property except for the public need in such cases and in such manner as defined by law and subject to the payment of adequate and prior compensation.

Art. 12. No penalty of confiscation of property may be enacted.

Art. 13. The penalty of civil death [deprivation of all civil rights] is abolished and may not be re-established.

Art. 14. Freedom is guaranteed to all religious groups, including public worship; freedom to express opinions on all matters is likewise guaranteed; except that crimes committed on the occasion of the exercise of these freedoms may be punished.

Art. 15. No one may be compelled to participate in any fashion whatsoever in the acts and ceremonies of a religious denomination, nor to observe its day of rest.

Art. 16. The state has no right to intervene in either the nomination or the installation of the ministers of any religious denomination whatever, nor to forbid them to correspond with their superiors or to publish their enactments, except that in this last case they shall be subjected

---

[5] Théodore Juste, *Histoire du Congrès National de Belgique ou de la fondation de la monarchie belge* (Brussels: Librairie Polytechnique d'Aug. Decq, 1850), Vol. II, pp. 410–17, 420. Translated from the French by the editor.

to the ordinary requirements of the law on the press and publications.

Art. 17. Civil marriage shall always precede the nuptial benediction, except for such cases as may be provided by law in event of need.

Public education at the expense of the state is likewise subject to the determinations of law.

Art. 18. The press is free; no censorship may ever be established, and no surety-bond may be required from authors, publishers or printers.

When an author is known and resident in Belgium, no case may be brought against the publisher, printer or distributor.

Art. 19. Belgians have the right to assemble peaceably and without arms, by conforming to the laws which may be enacted to control the exercise of this right, but no requirement of prior authorization may be imposed.

This article does not apply to open-air meetings, which remain wholly under the laws for the maintenance of public order.

Art. 20. Belgians have the right to form associations; this right may not be restricted by any preventive measures.

Art. 21. Anyone has the right to present to the public authorities petitions signed by one or several persons.

Only established authorities have the right to present petitions over the name of a community.

Art. 22. The secrecy of letters may not be violated. . . .

TITLE III

Art. 25. All powers emanate from the nation.

They are exercised in the manner fixed by the Constitution.

Art. 26. The legislative power is exercised collectively by the king, the chamber of representatives and the senate.

Art. 27. Each of the three branches of the legislative powers possesses the initiative.

However, any law concerning the revenues or expenditures of the state, or the size of the army, must be passed first by the chamber of representatives. . . .

Art. 29. The executive power, as determined by the Constitution, belongs to the king.

Art. 30. The judicial power is exercised by courts and tribunals. Sentences and judgments are executed in the name of the king. . . .

Art. 32. The members of the two chambers represent the nation and not solely the province or subdivision of a province by which they were elected. . . .

Art. 47. The chamber of representatives is composed of deputies elected directly by the citizens who pay taxes of an amount determined by the election law; this sum may not be set higher than 100 florins of direct taxation nor lower than 20 florins. . . .

Art. 50. To be eligible, one must be:

i. A Belgian by birth or full naturalization.

ii. In possession of civil and political rights.

iii. At least 25 years of age.

iv. A resident of Belgium.

No other condition for eligibility may be required. . . .

Art. 52. Each member of the chamber of representatives receives a monthly compensation of 200 florins during the entire course of a session. Those who are inhabitants of the city where the session is held do not receive compensation.

Art. 53. The members of the senate are elected in proportion to the population of each province by the citizens who elect the members of the chamber of representatives.

Art. 54. The senate is composed of members to half the number of the deputies of the other chamber. . . .

Art. 56. In order to be eligible as a senator and to remain a senator, one must be:

i. A Belgian by birth or full naturalization.

ii. In possession of civil and political rights.

iii. A resident of Belgium.

iv. At least 40 years of age.

v. A taxpayer in Belgium to the amount of at least 1,000 florins in direct taxes, including business licenses. . . .

Art. 57. Senators receive neither salary nor compensation.

Art. 58. The heir apparent to the throne is a senator by personal right upon reaching the age of eighteen years. He has a deliberative vote only upon reaching the age of 25 years.

Art. 59. Any meeting of the senate held at a different time than the session of the chamber of representatives is legally null and void. . . .

Art. 63. The person of the king is inviolable; his ministers are responsible.

Art. 64. No act of the king may have legal effect unless countersigned by a minister who thereby accepts full responsibility for it.

Art. 65. The king appoints and dismisses ministers.

Art. 66. He grants ranks in the army.

He makes appointments to positions in the general administration and in foreign service, except where otherwise provided by law.

He makes other appointments only upon the authority of explicit provisions of a law.

Art. 67. He issues the regulations and decisions necessary for the execution of the laws, but may never suspend the laws or dispense anyone from the execution thereof. . . .

Art. 69. The king approves and promulgates the laws.

Art. 70. The chambers assemble on their own authority each year on the second Tuesday of November, unless the king has called them into session at an earlier date.

The chambers must remain in session for at least forty days each year.

The king pronounces the cloture of the session.

The king has the right to call the chambers into extraordinary session.

Art. 71. The king has the right to dissolve the chambers, either jointly or separately. The act of dissolution must provide for a new election within forty days and for a new session of the chambers within two months. . . .

Art. 76. He has the right to confer titles of nobility, but may not attach any privileges thereto. . . .

Art. 78. The king has no other powers than those formally endowed upon him by the Constitution and the individual laws passed by the authority of this same Constitution. . . .

Art. 110. No tax on behalf of the state may be established except by law. . . .

Art. 111. Taxes on behalf of the state must be voted annually.

Laws instituting taxation shall run only for one year, unless renewed.

Art. 112. No privileges in the matter of taxation may be established.

Exemptions or reductions of taxes may be established only by a law. . . .

Art. 115. Each year the chambers vote a law of fiscal records and pass the budget.

All revenues and expenditures of the state must be recorded in the budget and in the fiscal records. . . .

60 / JEREMY BENTHAM: UTILITARIANISM AND CONSTITUTIONALISM

Not all advocates of constitutionalism admired the unwritten British constitution, however. The English jurist and ethical philosopher Jeremy Bentham (1784–1832) linked his condemnation of the absence of a written formal constitution to his ethical doctrine of utilitarianism. The doctrine of "the greatest good for the greatest number," already stated by Beccaria at the height of the Enlightenment (see No. 21), was systematized by Bentham with all the furious rigor of a trained jurist. The following passages from Bentham's Constitutional Code for the Use of All Nations, *first published in part in 1827 and 1830, illustrate both Bentham's utilitarianism and his political beliefs.*[6]

When I say the greatest happiness of the whole community, ought to be the end or object of pursuit, in every branch of the law—of the political rule of action, and of the constitutional branch in particular, what is it that I express?—this and no more, namely that it is my wish, my desire, to see it taken for such, by those who, in the community in question, are actually in possession of the powers of government; taken for such, on the occasion of every arrangement made by them in the exercise of such their powers, so that their endeavours shall be, to render such their cause [7] of action contributory to the obtainment of that same end. . . .

In saying, as above, the proper end of government is the greatest happiness of all, or, in case of competition, the greatest happiness of the greatest number, it seems to me that I have made a declaration of peace and good-will to all men.

On the other hand, were I to say, the proper end of government is the greatest happiness of some one, naming him, or of some few, naming them, it seems to me that I should be making a declaration of war against all men, with the exception of that one, or of those few. . . .

This being the basis on which all legislation and all morality rests, these few words written in hopes of clearing away all obscurity and ambiguity, all doubts and difficulties, will not, I hope, be regarded as misapplied, or applied in waste.

FIRST PRINCIPLES ENUMERATED

The right and proper end of government in every political community, is the greatest happiness of all the individuals of which it is composed, say, in other words, the greatest happiness of the greatest number. . . .

The *actual* end of government is, in every political community, the

[6] *The Works of Jeremy Bentham,* ed. John Bowring (Edinburgh: William Tait, 1843), Vol. IX, pp. 4–7, 9–10.

[7] course? (ed. [H. R.])

greatest happiness of those, whether one or many, by whom the powers of government are exercised.

In general terms, the proof of this position may be referred to particular experience, as brought to view by the history of all nations.

This experience may be termed *particular,* inasmuch as the particular class of rulers is the only class concerned in it, to which it bears reference. This may be called the experimental or practical proof.

For further proof, reference may be made to the general, indeed the all-comprehensive principle of human nature. The position which takes this fact for its subject, may be termed an axiom, and may be expressed in the words following.

In the general tenor of life, in every human breast, self-regarding interest is predominant over all other interests put together. More shortly thus,—Self-regard is predominant,—or thus,—Self-preference has place everywhere.

This position may, to some eyes, present itself in the character of an axiom: as such self-evident, and not standing in need of proof. To others, as a position or proposition which, how clearly soever true, still stands in need of proof.

To deliver a position in the character of an axiom, is to deliver it under the expectation that, either it will not be controverted at all, or that he by whom it is controverted, will not, in justification of the denial given by him to it, be able to advance anything by which the unreasonableness of his opinion or pretended opinion, will not be exposed. Of this stamp are the axioms laid down by Euclid. In the axioms so laid down by him, nothing of dogmatism will, it is believed, be found.

By the principle of self-preference, understand that propensity in human nature, by which, on the occasion of every act he exercises, every human being is led to pursue that line of conduct which, according to his view of the case, taken by him at the moment, will be in the highest degree contributory to his own greatest happiness, whatsoever be the effect of it, in relation to the happiness of other similar beings, any or all of them taken together. For the satisfaction of those who may doubt, reference may be made to the *existence* of the species as being of itself a proof, and *that* a conclusive one. For after exception made of the case of children not arrived at the age of which they are capable of going alone, or adults reduced by infirmity to a helpless state; take any two individuals, A and B, and suppose the whole care of the happiness of A confined to the breast of B, A himself not having any part in it; and the whole care of the happiness of B confined to the breast of A, B himself not having any part in it, and this to be the case throughout, it will soon appear that, in this state of things, the species could not continue in existence, and that a few months, not to say weeks or days, would suffice for the annihilation of it. . . .

Note that, if in the situation of ruler, the truth of this position, held good in no more than a bare majority, of the whole number of instances, it would suffice for every practical purpose, in the character of a ground for all political arrangements; in the character of consideration, by which the location of the several portions of the aggregate mass of political power should be determined; for, in the way of induction, it is only by the greater, and not the lesser number of instances, that the general conclusion can reasonably be determined; in a word, mathematically speaking, the probability of a future contingent event, is in the direct ratio of the number of instances in which an event of the same sort has happened, to the number of those in which it has not happened; it is in this direct ratio, and not in the inverse.

If such were the condition of human beings, that the happiness of no one being came in competition with that of any other,—that is to say, if the happiness of each, or of any one, could receive increase to an unlimited amount, without having the effect of producing decrease in the happiness of any other, then the above expressions [8] might serve without limitation or explanation. But on every occasion, the happiness of every individual is liable to come into competition with the happiness of every other. If, for example, in a house containing two individuals for the space of a month, there be a supply of food barely sufficient to continue for that time; not merely the happiness of each, but the existence of each, stands in competition with, and is incompatible with the existence of the other.

Hence it is, that to serve for all occasions, instead of saying the greatest happiness of all, it becomes necessary to use the expression, the greatest happiness of the greatest number.

If, however, instead of the word *happiness,* the word *interest* is employed, the phrase *universal interest* may be employed as corresponding indifferently to the interest of the greatest number or to the interest of all. . . .

A question that now immediately presents itself, is, whether to any individual, supposing him invested by the constitution in question with the supreme power, any inducement can be applied, by that same constitution, of sufficient force to overpower any sinister interest, to the operation of which, by his situation, he stands exposed? Inducements, operating on interest, are all of them reducible to two denominations,—punishment and reward. Punishment in every shape his situation suffices to prevent his standing exposed to; so likewise reward. Being by the supposition invested with supreme power, the matter of reward cannot be applied to him in any shape, in which he has not already at his command, whatever it would be in the power of the constitution,

---

[8] viz., the greatest happiness of *all.* See the ensuing paragraph. (*ed.* [J. B.])

by any particular arrangement, to confer on him. To him who has the whole, it is useless to give this or that part.

To a question to this effect, the only answer that can be given is sufficiently manifest. By reward, an individual so situated cannot be acted upon; for there exists no other individual in the community at whose hands he can receive more than he has in his own. By punishment as little; for there exists no individual at whose hands he is obliged to receive, or will receive any such thing.

The result is, that in a monarchy no such junction of interests can be effected, and that, therefore, by no means can monarchy be rendered conducive to the production of the greatest happiness of the greatest number; nor, therefore, according to the greatest-happiness principle, be susceptible of the denomination of a good form of government.

What, then, is the best *form* of government? . . . My opinion is, that so far as they go, the proposed arrangements which here follow would be in a higher degree conducive to it than any other could be, that could be proposed in a work which was not particularly adapted to the situation of any one country, to the exclusion of all others. . . .

In every community in which a constitutional code, generally acknowledged to be in force, is in existence, a really existing constitutional branch of law, and with it, as the offspring of it, a constitution, is so far in existence. In no community in which no constitutional code thus generally acknowledged to be in force, is in existence, is any such branch of law as a constitutional branch, or any such thing as a constitution, really in existence.

In a community in which, as above, no such thing as a constitution is really to be found, things to each of which the name of a constitution is given, are to be found in endless multitudes. On each occasion, the thing designated by the phrase "the constitution," is a substitute for a constitution,—a substitute framed by the imagination of the person by whom this phrase is uttered, framed by him, and, of course, adapted to that which, in his mind, is the purpose of the moment, whatsoever that purpose be; in so far as the purpose is the promotion, the creation or preservation of an absolutely monarchical form of government, the constitution thus imagined and inverted by him is of the absolutely monarchical cast; in so far as that purpose is the promoting the creation or preservation of a limitedly monarchical form of government, it is of the limitedly monarchical cast; in so far as the purpose is the creation or preservation of a democratical form of government, it is of the democratic cast.

The Anglo-American United States have a constitution. They have a constitutional code; the constitution is the system of arrangements delineated in that code.

It has for its object the greatest happiness of the greatest number, and in pursuit of that object, the powers of government are allotted to it by the greatest number.

The French and Spanish nations have constitutions. The English monarchy has no constitution, for it has no all-comprehensive constitutional code, nor in short, any constitutional code whatsoever generally acknowledged as such; nor by any one individual or the whole community acknowledged as such. Hence, so it is, that of the assertion contained in the phrases, "excellent constitution,"—"matchless constitution," an assertion by which every endeavour to produce the effect of the worst constitution possible is so naturally accompanied, no disproof can be opposed otherwise than by the assertion of a plain and universally notorious matter of fact, viz.—that the English people have no constitution at all belonging to them. England, not having any constitution at all, has no excellent, no matchless constitution; for nothing has no properties. If ever it has a constitution, that constitution will most probably be a democratical one; for nothing less than an insurrection on the part of the greatest number, will suffice to surmount and subdue so vast a power as that which is composed of the conjunct action of force, intimidation, corruption, and delusion. . . .

Under an absolute monarchy, the constitutional branch of the law has, for its sole actual end, the greatest happiness of the one individual, in whose hands without division, the whole of the supreme operative power is lodged.

For decency's sake, the end thus actually and exclusively pursued, is not the end professed and declared to be pursued. For the designation of the end actually pursued, regard for decency and conciseness, substitutes, on each occasion, one or another of a small assortment of phrases: preservation of order, preservation of legitimacy, for example.

Under a limited monarchy, the constitutional branch of law has, for its actual object, a more complex object; viz. the greatest happiness of the monarch, coupled with, and limited by, the greatest happiness of the conjunctly or subordinately ruling few, by whose respective powers the limitations that are applied to the power of the monarch, are applied.

Under a representative democracy, the constitutional branch of law has, for its actual end, the greatest happiness of the greatest number.

61 / GIUSEPPE MAZZINI: NATIONALISM AND LIBERALISM

Far more common in this period than a liberal-Catholic reconciliation was a linkage of the movements of liberalism and nationalism. A free union of European national republics was the ideal of Giuseppe Mazzini, the Italian revolutionary and patriot. He developed further the concept of the nation state that had been taking shape since the period of the French Revolution. His essay, "Nationalité. Quelques idées sur une Constitution Nationale" ("Nationality: Some Ideas on a National Constitution"), the first section of which is translated here, appeared in 1835 in the Swiss revolutionary journal La Jeune Suisse, *and was part of a constitutional debate in progress in Switzerland. Like many other articles by Mazzini, it was written in French. Mazzini (1805–1872) was a fervid republican no less than a patriot seeking Italian national unification, and fought native Italian rulers no less bitterly than the Austrians. He spent most of the period between 1830 and 1870 abroad in France and England, returning to Italy in periods of revolution and national war.*[9]

We often meet the word *nationality* in the pages of writers on politics, but they do not always mean the same thing by it. Like all words that stand for a *principle,* the word *nationality* has various meanings, depending on the place and time of the writer and his particular bias, whether *progressive* or *conservative.* During the middle ages *nationality* was a consequence of the warlike ideal and the general attempt to grow greater in land and riches at the expense of other peoples. Organized warfare was the prevailing condition. Obviously this is not what the nineteenth century means by *nationality.* To be sure, it has been defined in our own time as only passive self-interest by Casimir

---

[9] *Scritti politici editi ed inediti di Giuseppe Mazzini,* Vol. IV (*Edizione nazionale degli scritti di Giuseppe Mazzini,* Vol. VI.) (Imola: Cooperativa Tipografico-editrice Paolo Galeati, 1909), pp. 123–135. Translated from the French by Donald Weinstein and the editor.

Périer,[10] speaking in the French legislature. It is equally obvious that those who inscribe upon their banners the sacred word *Humanity* mean something wholly different by it; we may be sure that when, sooner or later, the Holy Alliance of the Peoples creates its own kind of *nationality,* it will rest upon different principles than those which presided over the Congresses of Westphalia and Vienna.

Since any system of ideas rests upon a definition of terms, let us attempt first of all to determine what we ourselves understand by *nationality.*

The essential characteristics of a nationality are common ideas, common principles and a common purpose. A nation is an association of all those who are brought together by language, by given geographical conditions or by the role assigned them by history, who acknowledge the same principles and who march together to the conquest of a single definite goal under the rule of a uniform body of law.

The *life* of a nation consists in harmonious activity (that is, the employment of all individual abilities and energies comprised within the association) towards this single goal.

Where there is no general uniform body of law, we find castes, privileges, inequality and oppression. Where individual energies are stultified or left unorganized, we find inertia, immobility and obstacles in the way of progress. But where men do not acknowledge a common principle and all its consequences, where all do not share a common purpose, we find not a nation but only a crowd, a mass, a congeries which will fall apart in the very first crisis; it is a chance collection of men which chance events will dissolve sooner or later, and which will give way to anarchy.

To us these principles seem so self-evident, so much a part of the very nature of any association of men, that we see no need to prove them. The very history before our eyes teaches that whenever men lack ties of association and common purpose, nationality is just a meaningless word; it also teaches us that whenever a people does not live by the principles which gave it birth, it perishes.

But nationality means more even than this. Nationality also consists in the share of mankind's labors which God assigns to a people. This mission is the task which a people must perform to the end that the Divine Idea shall be realized in this world; it is the work which gives a people its rights as a member of Mankind; it is the baptismal rite which endows a people with its own character and its rank in the brotherhood of nations.

Life appears to us in a dual aspect. Every living thing has its internal

[10] Casimir Pierre Périer (1777–1832), French statesman, premier during the reign of Louis Philippe.—Editor's note.

and its external life; it lives by its own efforts and by those of the world around it, and hence it lives for itself and for the world around it. Every creature influences other creatures and is in turn influenced by them. This law, which is a law of nature, also holds good for the nations. Countless necessary relationships bind them to all that is alive and active in their surroundings. Only by destroying themselves can they escape these ties. A nation which isolates itself commits suicide. It slays half of its own life. Though it renounces action outside itself, it remains subject to the influence of other nations; though it abdicates its influence, it has no chance to break the chain of interests and relationships which binds the nations to each other. It seeks and achieves *passivity*, that is all.

When this happens, a nation enters a period of more or less rapid decadence which ends only with its death. This is a period of dishonor, shame, suffering, a period of gradually extorted concessions which cause it to lose its nerve, which stifle its conscience and kill its future in the cradle. In consequence, a nation is called upon to answer for every popular disturbance, however minor, for every action which does not please its neighbor. It becomes subject to demands, threats and outrages; when it makes a mistake, its ruthless enemies make it pay for every last consequence. It is forced to bend the knee and drink the cup of humiliation to the last drop. Its protests are met with laughter. To whom can it protest, and how? What guarantees or source of justice can it invoke? The universal law which should control international relations? It does not hold for this nation which renounced its benefits. The peoples? They have no knowledge of this nation, which forsook its own name and has no right to take part in their congresses. Force? It destroyed its force when, by a system of absurdities fatal to progress, it destroyed the conscience and the sense of mission in the hearts of its children. It permitted the mass of its people to stray from the highroad and lose their way, for the banner which should have served to rally them was allowed to drag in the mud. As a result, each individual person lacked any unifying bond, any manly and holy ideal which could rally all the scattered forces of the nation and give them a single goal; instead he set his own goal and found his own route. The virtue of self-sacrifice dies out; individualism invades the land and grows strong. It becomes a giant, a King, God. As some worship fear, others worship individualism. On the one hand, the state begins to tremble before its subjects, feeling that it has lost their respect and looking upon them as enemies. The patriots, on the other hand, realize that there is a vacuum; but they do not know how to fill it, for they have no *faith* to transmit to the people. They fold their arms and abandon hope. The people too lie in the slough of inaction, for they instinctively realize that they have no leaders. Mistrust spreads; heads and hearts turn cold. Bit by bit things change name and words change meaning. Weakness bedecks itself in the name of tactics; cowardice and selfishness are called prudence and philosophy. Patriotic courage is scorned as thoughtless enthusiasm, the spirit of self-sacrifice as madness or calculated self-interest. This is the beginning of the end. When a people reaches this point, it is lost—unless a sudden crisis shakes the earth and unexpectedly opens before it a road by which it can climb out of the abyss; unless new men come up before it succumbs, who tell it of a new life and shout in its ear a mighty slogan such as arouses the human race from the depth of its tomb. Otherwise there is nothing left for a people to do but die. Others will fight over its remains.

There is no need to cite the evidence of history to prove the truth of this picture.

All this happens just because a people, wishing to be alone and failing to comprehend the general law which directs the life of nations, strayed a single time from the right path; because it compromised with its conscience and forsook its mission a single time; because it forgot that a people is responsible to all mankind for its existence and its labors in the world; because, perhaps just once, it bent its knee to diplomacy or some other idol and closed its ear to the voice of God.

When God places a people in the world with the command, "Be a Nation!" he is not saying, "Stay in isolation! Use your life as a miser uses his treasure. Use your freedom as if it were a crime. Listen to my words as if they were a secret which no one else may hear!"

No, he is saying, "March on among the brothers whom I have given you, with head held high, freely and easily, as befits one who carries my words in his bosom. Take your rank among the nations, in obedience to the sign which I placed upon your brow and the words which I whispered in your ear when you were a babe in the cradle. Perform your mission on earth with dignity and courage, for by it you will be judged. Confess aloud the faith of your fathers before the world and its masters; deny not your brothers and help them according to their need and your strength, for you are all made in my image and one day I shall gather you into my bosom. March without fear in the path I have shown you. When you are called upon to justify your acts and your ideas, lift your hand toward heaven and tell those who question you, 'There is my right, there is my law and my assurance.'"

But this name, this assurance, this sign which God places upon the brow of each people—these are part of its *nationality*. So too are the ideas which it is called upon to uphold in the world. They make nationality sacred; they explain why a nation loses its character when it forgets its origin and separates its principle from their source— Humanity. For just as the extent and the safety of the rights of each

citizen consist in the law which defines the duties of all, so the extent
and the safety of the rights of each nation can consist only in the law
of Humanity which defines the duties of all nations.

Nationality depends for its very existence upon its sacredness within
and beyond its frontiers.

If nationality is to be inviolable for all, friends and foes alike, it
must be regarded inside a country as holy, like a religion, and outside
a country as a grave mission. It is necessary too that the ideas arising
within a country grow steadily, as part of the general law of Humanity
which is the source of all nationality. It is necessary that these ideas
be shown to other lands in their beauty and purity, free from any alien
admixture, from any slavish fears, from any skeptical hesitancy, strong
and active, embracing in their evolution every aspect and manifestation of the life of the nation. These ideas, a necessary component in
the order of universal destiny, must retain their originality even as they
enter harmoniously into mankind's general progress.

The people must be the *basis* of nationality; its logically derived and
vigorously applied principles its *means;* the strength of all its *strength;*
the improvement of the life of all and the happiness of the greatest
possible number its *results;* and the accomplishment of the task assigned to it by God its *goal.*

This is what we mean by nationality.

62 / RUSSIA: LEADER OF THE SLAVS?

*Russia's enormous contribution to the defeat of Napoleon
led some Russian intellectuals to see their country as the future
leader of all Slavs. The Pan-Slavism of such writers as Mikhail
Petrovich Pogodin was a new version of that long struggle against
Westernization which had been waged in Russia since before
Peter the Great. His essay,* Letter on Russian History, *from which
the following selection, "The Wealth and Strength of Russia,"* [11]
*is taken (A), was addressed to the heir to the throne when the
future Alexander II visited Moscow in 1837. The prospect of Russian domination under the cloak of Pan-Slavism did not appeal to*

[11] Mikhail Petrovich Pogodin, "The Wealth and Strength of Russia," from *Letter
on Russian History,* translated by Hans Kohn in *The Mind of Modern Russia: Historical and Political Thought of Russia's Great Age* (New Brunswick, N.J.: Rutgers
University Press, 1962), pp. 60–68. Reprinted by permission of the publisher.

other Slavic peoples, particularly to those committed to the new democratic ideas. Poles and Czechs, in the grip of foreign rule for decades and even centuries, were especially sharp in their replies. The leading democratic newspaperman of Bohemia, Karel Havlíček, knew Russia from a long youthful stay. He rebutted the claims of Pan-Slavism in an article, "Czech and Slav," in the newspaper Prague News, *of which he became editor after his return from Russia. Selections from this article are reprinted below (B).*[12] *Both pieces are translated by Hans Kohn, the outstanding modern historian of nationalism.*

A. M. P. POGODIN: THE APPEAL OF PAN-SLAVISM

Russia, what country can compare with her in magnitude? Which one merely by half? . . . A population of sixty million people, that increases by a million every year! Where is there a people as numerous as that? . . . Let us add to it thirty million more of our brothers and cousins, the Slavs . . . in whose veins flows the same blood as ours, who speak the same language as we do, and who feel, therefore, according to the law of nature, as we do. In spite of geographical and political separation, the Slavs form by origin and language a spiritual entity with us. Hence, we may subtract their number from the population of the neighboring countries of Austria and Turkey and of the rest of Europe, and add to it our figure. What will be left to Europe, and what will fall to us? My thinking stops, the spirit seizing me. . . .

The ninth part of the inhabited earth, almost the ninth part of all mankind! . . . Yet the size of the land, the numbers of people, are not the only conditions of strength. Russia is a country that contains all kinds of soil, all climates, from the hottest to the coldest, from the scorched land around Erivan to icy Lapland—a country that even in her present state of development abounds in all products which are indispensable for maintenance, welfare, and enjoyment, a world in itself, self-contained, independent, with no need of supplementation. Many of her products are of a kind that each by itself could in the course of time have been the source of wealth for whole empires. . . .

We possess mountains of gold and silver, metals almost exhausted elsewhere in Europe, and vast untapped deposits in reserve. One might request any amount of iron and copper and it would be delivered to the Fair of Nijnii Novgorod the following year. Grain—we feed all Europe in years of famine. Timber—we could rebuild all the cities of Europe, if they were burnt—which God forbid! Flax, hemp, and hides

[12] Karel Havlíček, "Czech and Slav," translated by Hans Kohn in *The Mind of Modern Russia,* pp. 83–90. Reprinted by permission of Rutgers University Press.

—we give them clothes and shoes. Only yesterday we started to produce sugar, and soon, it is said, we shall not need any more of it from
abroad. And wine—the long-stretched shores of the Black and Caspian
seas, the Crimea, Bessarabia, are waiting for wine growers, and already
the vintners of Burgundy and Champagne are purchasing land in these
regions. Moreover, we export wool—and yet the Novorossiisk Region,
the old domain of nomads, possesses so many fat pastures that countless flocks will thrive there in the future, and we shall not have to envy
the Merinos of Spain and England. Wide regions are fit for silk culture. Shall I speak of cattle, fish, salt, and furs? What do we lack?
What is it that we cannot obtain at home? What is it that we could
not furnish to others? And all this is, as it were, on the outside, on
the surface, near, before our eyes, under our hands, but if we look
further, if we dig deeper, . . . Are there not persistent rumors that
beds of bituminous coal of several versts thickness have been discovered, that marble, diamonds, and other precious stones have been
found?

Those are raw products, but where is there a country more fit for the
establishment of factories, since labor is so cheap and the needs and
demands of workers so moderate? What a short time ago it was that
we started thinking of factories—and yet how well they have developed! Did we not have proof of it at the latest exhibition of our national industry? What about the progress of our spinning, cloth, and
cotton mills, our chemical industry? And where could commerce flour-
ish more briskly than here in this country with its immense turnover,
and its proximity to the seashores, to foreign countries needing our
goods, and to the rich Asian lands of Persia, India, and China? In what
should Russia fear the rivalry of the English, in spite of all their steam-
boats on the Euphrates and the Nile and their railroads at Suez and
Panama?

True, much of what I mention here is not yet in existence, but
everything is within possible reach and, what is more, within easy
reach. And indeed, which of these things could not be realized tomor-
row, if necessary, and if ordered by supreme command? There are
physical resources at our disposition, in quantity and quality as no-
where else in Europe, either in the past or in the present, and there
is unlimited possibility of their future development. . . .

As to the spiritual resources, I wish to point out a peculiar trait of
the Russian people, their *tolk* [insight, good sense, fairness] and their
udal [boldness, courage], for which there are no words in any other
European language—their sensibleness, vitality, patience, devotion,
their stamina in time of emergency, this happy union of qualities of
northern and southern men. Education in Europe is a matter of caste,
although allegedly open to everybody; the lower classes there—with

a few exceptions—are remarkable for a certain dullness of wit, as the traveler finds out at first glance.

But what is the capacity of the Russian man? In order to give some examples, I wish to draw attention to such things as we see before our eyes every day. We see a muzhik with his heavy hands called in for military service: he has just been taken from behind the plow, he cannot look straight at anything. This "bumpkin," this real Russian bear, cannot take a step without knocking against something. He may be thirty, sometimes nearly forty years old. But his hair will be cut, and a year later he cannot be recognized. He marches in the first platoon of the guard, he carries his rifle no worse than any drum major, in an agile, easy, skillful, even elegant manner. And more, a bugle is put in his hand, or a fagot or a flute, and he becomes a regimental musician and plays so well that foreign artists come to listen to him. This soldier when placed in gunfire, will stand and not falter, when sent to death, will go without thinking. He suffers everything possible: he would don a sheepskin in hot summertime and go barefooted in icy cold, he would live off biscuit for weeks, and he is not inferior to a horse in case of forced marches. Charles XII, Frederick the Great, and Napoleon, unbiased judges indeed, preferred him to all soldiers of the world, extended to him the palm of victory.

The Russian peasant himself manufactures everything he needs, with his own hands; his ax and chisel take the place of the machine, and many industrial goods are being made in peasant huts. Look what patterns come from the hands of pupils in drawing or architectural schools! How proficient in physics and chemistry are peasant children in the technical and agricultural schools! How gifted are the youngsters in the Moscow School of Art!

How many remarkable inventions have never been exploited, just because of the lack of communication and publicity? Deep understanding for the Holy Scriptures and original thinking about problems of theology and philosophy are often found among simple people. The young Russian scholars who at the beginning of the reign of the present Tsar went abroad have won the recognition of outstanding European professors; these in admiration of the fast and brilliant success of their Russian students have granted them a place of honor among their rank. All that is proof of the national talents of the Russians. What a spiritual strength in addition to the physical!

All these physical and spiritual forces form a gigantic machine, constructed in a simple, purposeful way, directed by the hand of one single man, the Russian Tsar, who with one motion can start it at any moment, who can give it any direction, any speed he wishes. But let us keep in mind that that machine is moved by more than mechanical function. No, it is all animated by one feeling, an ancient legacy from our ancestors: allegiance, limitless confidence, and devotion to the Tsar, their God on earth.

I ask: who can compare with us? Whom will we not force into submission? Is not the political fate of the world in our hands whenever we want to decide it one way or the other?

The truth of my words will be even more manifest if one considers the conditions in other European countries. . . . In contrast to Russian strength, unity, and harmony, there is nothing but quarrel, division, and weakness, against which our greatness stands out still more —as light against shadow. . . .

I do not know if it is not too hazardous and paradoxical a statement, that those countries [i.e., France and England] were stronger in the past than they are at present, stronger in words than in deeds, that the right of the individual and the constitution, which indisputably may have its good sides too, have developed from their historic roots at the expense of political strength, that the state machinery has become complex and extremely cumbersome, so that every decision, in passing a multitude of stages, persons, and public bodies, loses its natural force and freshness and misses the right time. I do not know what great actions could yet be undertaken even in these two great countries. Must they not admit that Napoleon and Waterloo represented the culminating point of their strength—*ne plus ultra.* . . .

What is impossible to the Russian Emperor? One word, and a whole empire has ceased to exist—one word, and another empire has been wiped out from the earth—one word, and in their place a third empire is rising, stretching from the Eastern Ocean to the Adriatic Sea. One hundred thousand soldiers more, and the Caucasus will be pacified; its savage sons will serve with the Russian cavalry together with Kalmuks and Bashkirs, and yet its new generation will be educated in the Russian Cadet Corps in other customs and in another way of thinking. One thousand soldiers more, and a highway is opened towards the border towns of India, Bokhara, and Persia. The Tsar can reverse even the history of the past according to his will: although we did not participate in the Crusades, did he not liberate Jerusalem by a note to the High Porte, by a mere article of a treaty? [Allusion to the Treaty of Unkiar Skelessi of July 5, 1833.] We did not discover America, although we did discover one-third of Asia; but does not our gold, the output of which increases from year to year, supplement the discovery of Columbus, does it not promise to become a counterpoison against poison?

It is well known that our present Emperor, Your Most August Father, does not think of any conquest of that kind, but I cannot help, I dare not fail to, remark as a historian that the Russian Ruler now, even without such a plan, without such a wish, without any preparation, without any intention, quietly seated in his office at Tsarskoe Selo, is nearer to the universal monarchy than Charles the Fifth and Napoleon ever were in their dreams. Europe itself is well aware of that, although ashamed to admit it. That untiring attention that follows every step of ours in Europe, that incessant suspicion at our slightest moves, that muffled grumbling of jealousy, envy, and malice which issues from newspapers and magazines, are they not the most convincing proof of Russia's strength? Yes, the future of the world depends on Russia— spoken, so God wills. What a glorious prospect!

But, my Lord, there is another glory, a pure, beautiful, sublime, sacred glory, the glory of the good, of love, of knowledge, of right, of happiness. What does power matter? Russia does not admire feats of power, any more than a millionaire is impressed by thousands. She stands calmly and silently—and the world is trembling before her, intriguing and busy about her. Russia can do everything. What more does she want? The other glory is more flattering and more desirable. We can shine forth in that glory, too.

Whoever impassionately contemplates the European countries must admit with all regard for their remarkable constitutions, with all grati- tude for the service they have rendered to mankind, and with all respect for their history that they have outlived their time and spent their best strength, which means that they cannot produce, cannot achieve anything greater than they did before, be it in the field of religion, law, science, or art. But have they really accomplished every- thing? Does not history show, on the contrary, that the development in every single country—as compared with the totality of human life— was merely partial, one-sided, incomplete; that in Germany, for in- stance, the idea prevailed, in religion as well as in other fields; in Italy, feeling; in France, sociability; in England, personality? Yet where is there a full universal development? If we further compare the nations of the entire world, of the old and of the new, we see that each nation has one outstanding quality but is inferior to the rest in other con- cerns. There must be, however, a synthesis.

Let me consider it still from another higher, ethical point of view. Who dares pretend that the goal of humanity has been achieved or kept in sight by any of the states of Europe? In one country we see more knowledge, in another more production, more comfort, in a third more welfare, but where is the "sacred good"? Corruption of morals in France, laziness in Italy, cruelty in Spain, egoism in England, are characteristic of these countries. Are these by any chance compatible with the idea of civic, not merely individual, happiness, with the ideal society, the City of God? It is the Golden Calf, the mammon, to which without exception all Europe pays homage. Should there not be a higher level of a new European civilization, of Christian civilization?

America, on which our contemporaries had pinned their hopes for a time, has meanwhile clearly revealed the vices of her illegitimate birth. She is no state, but rather a trading company, like the East India Company which independently owned territory. America cares solely for profit; to be sure, she has grown rich, but she will hardly ever bring forth anything great of national, let alone of universal, significance. There are no fruits ripening in the countries of the world.

I repeat: where is the "sacred good"? Kollár, the famous Slavic poet of our time, predicts in one of his poetic reflections the coming glory of the Slavs, in particular in the arts. "It is impossible," he exclaims, "that so great a people, so great in numbers, spread over so wide a space, of such talents and qualities, with such language, should accomplish nothing for the good of humanity. Providence does not contradict itself. Everything great is destined for great purposes."

It seems to me one can extend the meaning of Kollár's prophecy and say that the future belongs altogether to the Slavs.

There is in history a succession of nations: one after another steps forth, standing guard, as it were, and does its service to mankind. So far the Slavs have been missing in that illustrious sequence. Their time, therefore, is come to start their course, to begin their noble work for mankind, and to display their highest capacities.

But which of the Slav tribes occupies the first rank today? Which tribe can by its number, its language, and the totality of its qualities be considered the representative of the entire Slav world? Which offers the best pledge for the future goal? Which shows most clearly that it has the conditions for reaching that goal? Which indeed? . . .

My heart trembles with joy, oh Russia, oh my Fatherland! Is it not you? Oh, if it were only you! You, you are chosen to consummate, to crown the development of humanity, to embody all the various human achievements (which hitherto have been accomplished only separately) in one great synthesis, to bring to harmony the ancient and modern civilizations, to reconcile heart with reason, to establish true justice and peace. You alone can prove not only that science, liberty, art, knowledge, industry, and wealth are the goal of mankind, but that there is something higher than scholarship, trade and education, freedom and riches—the true enlightenment in the spirit of Christianity, the Divine Word, which alone can impart to Man earthly and heavenly happiness. . . .

B. KAREL HAVLÍČEK: PAN-SLAVISM DECLINED

Simultaneously with the awakening of the national spirit and some higher activities in our [Austrian-Czech] fatherland, there came also the Slav idea, or rather this idea made itself felt again, but this time with greater strength and greater hope than before. As often happens, this Slav idea, like all other great and new ideas, became fashionable with us, so that some years ago almost everybody called himself a Slav, ashamed, as it were, of something as small as our Czech, Moravian, Silesian, or Slovak. Everybody called the Russians, Poles, Illyrians, and other Slavs his brothers and was concerned for their well-being, at least as much as for the growth of his own nation; and those who were the most practical ones felt in their heart the firm conviction that as time went on all eighty million Slavs (and all the other millions who meanwhile would accrue) would have in common one literary language, the same sympathies and all the other matters, which it is presently not advisable to discuss; in short that they all would become a single nation in the same sense in which the French and others were single nations. . . .

The purpose of this article is to correct these errors as far as possible in the minds of my countrymen, to remove the harmful, and thereby to strengthen the useful, aspects of the Slav idea. I consider that my words will become more acceptable if I prove them from my own life experience: if we wish to combat prejudices we can do it best if we acknowledge that we shared them formerly. One always believes an experienced man more.

In my student days at the university in Prague, when a young man is most inclined to wax enthusiastic for a new idea, when most youth fall in love with girls and a few with ideas, I too was struck by the Slav idea. . . . We recited with low and high voices sonnets from *Slávy Dcera*, we even wrote (but didn't print) sonnets, we got hold of the grammars of various Slav tongues, and regarded it as a great honor to be able to sing two Polish songs, one Russian, and two Illyrian ones. In this blessed time, having as far as possible learned from books the languages, history, and customs of the Slav peoples, I firmly decided to travel in their lands and to get acquainted with all our Slav brothers personally in their countries.

I learned to know Poland and I did not like it. With a feeling of hostility and pride I left the Sarmatian country, and in the worst cold season I arrived in a sleigh in Moscow, being warmed mostly by the Slav feeling in my heart. The freezing temperature in Russia and other aspects of Russian life extinguished the last spark of Pan-Slav love in me. Cosmopolitanism was always completely alien to me, and so I returned to Prague as a Czech, a simple determined Czech, even with some secret sour feeling against the name Slav, which a better knowledge of Russia and Poland had made suspect to me. After some time, when I had somewhat forgotten the unpleasant impression, I again quieted down, and I was able . . . to balance my unpleasant personal experiences and my former poetic enthusiasm. In short, I formed for myself principles about Slavdom and Czechdom, and these I now wish to put before my readers for their consideration.

Above all, I express my firm and unchangeable conviction that the Slavs, that is the Russians, the Poles, the Czechs, the Illyrians, and so on, are not one nation. These words are like a declaration of war and so strong that they need further explanation. . . . Just as Spaniards, Portuguese, Frenchmen, and Italians are together Romance nations, and Germans, Danes, Swedes, Norwegians, and Dutch are Teutonic nations, so we, the Poles, the Illyrians, the Russians, and so on, are Slav nations; and the name Slav is and should forever remain a purely geographical and scientific name, in no way however a name implying the heart and the sympathy with which every nation pronounces its name.

No decent man should be a cosmopolitan (who says that he loves everybody, loves nobody), and it would be ridiculous to feel Indo-European patriotism and to write enthusiastic poetry about it; equally invalid, though to a lesser degree, is a Pan-Slav patriotism. Should somebody object that the differences among the Slav nations are not so great as among the Romance or the Teutonic nations, then we must simply disagree. Even if there be slighter differences among the various Slav languages than among the various Teutonic and Romance languages (though the Dutch tongue is nearer to German than Russian is to Czech, and between French and Italian there is no greater difference than between Russian and Czech), we must not forget that nationality is determined not only by language but also by customs, religion, form of government, state of education, sympathies, and so on, and that the differences among the different nations are based upon these characters. If we take all that in due consideration, then we cannot say that Russians and Czechs, Poles and Russians, Illyrians and Poles, show a greater affinity than any two Teutonic or Romance nations. . . .

We cannot expect unity even among closely related Slav nations. On the contrary, the closer they live together the more disunity we may expect. Let us take the world as it is, and expect friendship and unity among people and nations only when this is advantageous for both sides. . . .

We hold it to be our sacred duty to declare clearly that a Czech who accepts another Slav nationality sins as much against his fatherland as he would if he were to become a Frenchman or a German. . . .

If the whole Slav world were our fatherland, if all Slavs were one nation, then we should long have accepted the Russian language as literary language, which so far certainly no wise man among us has suggested. It must be the first principle of our nationality that we shall never wish to abandon our language and shall never exchange it voluntarily for another, even the most closely related language. Whoever thinks differently is not with us but against us. . . .

I turn now to the most important part of my discussion, to the condition which really decides the whole future of Pan-Slavism. That is the relationship among Russians, Ukrainians, and Poles. . . . If we survey briefly the history of the Eastern Slavs and the fate of these three great Slav nations, then we shall see how each in turn tried to establish its primacy over the two others, which can perhaps be explained geographically by the fact that no natural frontiers exist between them. First Kiev and the Ukrainians ruled; there the first great power rose, so that it seemed that Poland and present-day Russia would be incorporated in it. Soon, however, the great empire of Vladimir [Monomakh] fell and with it the prospects of independence for the Ukrainians. Now Poland and Russia simultaneously began to rise. At first, because their centers, Cracow and Moscow, were very remote from each other, they paid no attention to each other's activities. Later, however, they expanded towards each other until finally two very similar and yet very dissimilar giants met: similar in the anarchy and injustice of their domestic constitutions, different in their faith, the one an autocracy, the other an aristocracy. Soon . . . such national enmity grew between them that each one began to try to destroy the other, and thus even today the two nations stand one against the other. . . .

At the beginning, I sided with the Poles against the Russians. As soon as I recognized the true state of affairs in Poland, as soon as the veil which poetically hid from me the prosaic misery and corruption of the nation (that is, the Polish nobility) dropped from my eyes, my affection changed to dislike, and for a psychologically understandable reason the Russians appeared to me to be better than the Poles. This, however, did not last long. I soon recognized that Peter is like Paul, Russia like Poland. My Slav sympathy disappeared, and I learned to regard the Russians and the Poles, in spite of the affinity of language, origin, and customs, as nations alien to us Czechs. . . . We must not look on the Russian-Polish relations with such a blind eye as the greater part of Europe does; we should not think of an innocent lamb and a wolf, but know that there wolf meets wolf, and we shall say later that the lamb among them is the Ukrainian. The Poles themselves formerly tried to destroy Russia, and the Russians now try the opposite. . . . The Ukraine is the apple of discord which fate threw between these two nations. . . . Thus the suppression of Ukrainian liberty revenges itself on Poland and Russia. . . . The Poles and the Russians buried the national spirit of the Ukraine and began to divide the great body, and, as generally happens in such cases, they began to fight and have not yet ceased. Both the Russians and the Poles regard the Ukrainian language as a dialect of their own language. . . . Thus we have seen three great Eastern Slav nations, each one of which hates the other two, and also has a just reason for it. Nobody can speak reasonably of brotherhood there. Nevertheless, the Pan-Slav idea has been accepted even by these nations. That might seem to contradict me: in reality the way in which Poles and Russians understood and accepted Pan-Slavism will prove that they don't deserve our sympathy.

The Russians (and I do not speak here of the government, because I cannot know its trend of thought) have taken up the idea of Pan-Slavism. In the whole world, but above all in Europe, the Russians are either disliked or rejected (and that almost always for good reasons): it was therefore surprising but most agreeable to them to find at least some friends in the West. Thus they declared immediately their friendship and brotherhood with us and the Illyrians but regarded themselves as the older brother, as our commander. The Russian Pan-Slavs believe that we and the Illyrians would like to be under their domination!! They are firmly convinced that they will one day control all Slav lands!!! They now look forward with joy to their future vineyards in Dalmatia. These gentlemen have started everywhere to say and write Slav instead of Russian, so that later they will again be able to say Russian instead of Slav. . . .

I cannot describe here in detail everything that I heard in Russia about the Slav world: I can, however, testify that the Russians think of the other Slavs in no brotherly fashion, but dishonestly and egoistically. . . . I admit that I prefer the Magyars, who are open enemies of the Czechs and Illyrians, to the Russians, who approach us with a Judas embrace—to put us into their pockets. We are Czechs, and we wish to remain Czechs forever, and we do not wish to become either Germans, or Magyars, or Russians, and therefore we shall be cool to the Russians, if we do not wish to be hostile to them.

But let us be equally cool towards the Poles. They are like the Russians, but with tied hands. It is well known that formerly the Poles did not wish to know anything of the Slavs. Only when the Polish democrats and emigrants in France came upon the happy thought that perhaps the other Slavs could jointly with the Poles make light-hearted revolutions and thus serve them in their poorly calculated plans, did they begin to fraternize with us, and in their easy and sanguine temper they began to imagine how they would be the leaders among the Western liberal Slavs and how we should fight for them against everyone they hate! . . .

Finally, it is also significant that the Russians and the Poles exclude each other from the ranks of the Slavs: Russian scholars have proved that the Poles descend from the non-Slav Sarmatians (and be it said quietly, the Polish nobility thought so too, believing its blood superior to the Slav peasant blood), and the Poles on their part have proved that the Russians are of Mongol origin. . . .

I am very happy that I can proudly say that we Czechs, although insignificant in numbers and power compared to the Russians and Poles, are more highly esteemed by all reasonable and educated men. . . . The Russians are hated everywhere, the Poles are merely pitied everywhere . . . but the world looks on us Czechs with respect seeing . . . how manfully we fight for our preservation, for our life, for nationality! Should we perhaps be afraid of the great and many obstacles, should we perhaps become downhearted before the hard and unpleasant road which we must tread? Should we perhaps rely in a childish and unmanly way upon others? A Czech is not afraid of hard work and obstacles, he is not downhearted, and he does not rely on others: a Czech sets out to do his work and will overcome everything. For the very reason that people work harder among us, there is no doubt that on the better historical foundation we have, and with our better general education, we Czechs will advance in the arts, in literature, and generally in national happiness beyond the Russians and the Poles. . . .

What I wrote here stems from the reading of almost the whole literature on Pan-Slavism and from personal experiences . . . and everything written here is my full conviction. The plain principles, once more summarized, are: the Slavs are not one nation but four nations as independent and unconnected as any other European nations. Each of these Slav nations stands for itself, and none is responsible for another; they share neither national honor nor national infamy. As the result of the great similarity of the Slav languages, it is useful and necessary for each Slav nation to pay as much attention to the literature of the others as possible, and to profit from their literature and languages and nationality. Only between the Czechs and the Illyrians can there be more far-reaching sympathies, because under present conditions one cannot be dangerous to the other but on the contrary useful. The Austrian monarchy is the best guarantee for the preservation of our and the Illyrian nationality, and the greater the power of the Austrian empire grows, the more secure our nationalities will be. It is impossible then for all Slavs to use one literary language, and therefore all efforts in this direction are meaningless and, as a waste of time, harmful.

63 / FRIEDRICH LIST: NATIONALISM AND ECONOMIC UNITY

In Germany economic nationalism gained a foothold while political nationalism remained strictly verboten *("forbidden"). A "tariff union"* (Zollverein) *of North German states was established beginning in 1828 under Prussian leadership; it formed a large part of Germany into a common market without internal barriers to trade and industry. For the German economist Friedrich List, economic unity of Germany was only the prelude to political unity. In his major work,* Das nationale System der politischen Ökonomie *("The National System of Political Economy," 1841), from which the following passages are taken, List drew heavily from his experiences in the United States, where he was an exile from 1825 to 1832. List (1789–1846) had been twice imprisoned in Württemberg for revolutionary activity before his flight to the United States; he returned to Germany in 1832 as a United States consul and continued his theoretical work. He committed suicide in 1846, but his ideas were largely adopted after his death.[13]*

"What is prudence in the conduct of every private family," says Adam Smith, "can scarce be folly in that of a great kingdom." Every individual in pursuing his own interests necessarily promotes thereby also the interests of the community. . . .

How? Is the wisdom of private economy, also wisdom in national economy? Is it in the nature of individuals to take into consideration the wants of future centuries, as those concern the nature of the nation and the State? . . .

No; that may be wisdom in national economy which would be folly in private economy, and *vice versâ;* and owing to the very simple reason, that a tailor is no nation and a nation no tailor, that one family is something very different from a community of millions of families, that one house is something very different from a large national terri-

[13] Friedrich List, *The National System of Political Economy,* translated from the German by Sampson S. Lloyd, rev. ed. (London: Longmans, Green, & Co. Ltd., 1904), pp. 132–6, 141–2. Reprinted by permission of the publisher.

tory. Nor does the individual merely by understanding his own interests best, and by striving to further them, if left to his own devices, always further the interests of the community. We ask those who occupy the benches of justice, whether they do not frequently have to send individuals to the tread-mill on account of their excess of inventive power, and of their all too great industry. Robbers, thieves, smugglers, and cheats know their own local and personal circumstances and conditions extremely well, and pay the most active attention to their business; but it by no means follows therefrom, that society is in the best condition where such individuals are least restrained in the exercise of their private industry.

In a thousand cases the power of the State is compelled to impose restrictions on private industry. It prevents the shipowner from taking on board slaves on the west coast of Africa, and taking them over to America. It imposes regulations as to the building of steamers and the rules of navigation at sea, in order that passengers and sailors may not be sacrificed to the avarice and caprice of the captains. In England certain rules have recently been enacted with regard to shipbuilding, because an infernal union between assurance companies and shipowners has been brought to light, whereby yearly thousands of human lives and millions in value were sacrificed to the avarice of a few persons. In North America millers are bound under a penalty to pack into each cask not less than 198 lbs. of good flour, and for all market goods market inspectors are appointed, although in no other country is individual liberty more highly prized. Everywhere does the State consider it to be its duty to guard the public against danger and loss, as in the sale of necessaries of life, so also in the sale of medicines, &c. . . .

For similar reasons the State is not merely justified in imposing, but bound to impose, certain regulations and restrictions on commerce (which is in itself harmless) for the best interests of the nation. By prohibitions and protective duties it does not give directions to individuals how to employ their productive powers and capital (as the popular school sophistically alleges); it does not tell the one, "You must invest your money in the building of a ship, or in the erection of a manufactory"; or the other, "You must be a naval captain or a civil engineer"; it leaves it to the judgment of every individual how and where to invest his capital, or to what vocation he will devote himself. It merely says, "It is to the advantage of our nation that we manufacture these or the other goods ourselves; but as by free competition with foreign countries we can never obtain possession of this advantage, we have imposed restrictions on that competition, so far as in our opinion is necessary, to give those among us who invest their capital in these new branches of industry, and those who devote their bodily and mental powers to them, the requisite guarantees that they shall not lose their capital and shall not miss their vocation in life; and further to stimulate foreigners to come over to our side with their productive powers." In this manner, it does not in the least degree restrain private industry; on the contrary, it secures to the personal, natural, and moneyed powers of the nation a greater and wider field of activity. It does not thereby do something which its individual citizens could understand better and do better than it; on the contrary, it does something which the individuals, even if they understood it, would not be able to do for themselves. . . .

The system of the school suffers, as we have already shown . . . , from three main defects: firstly, from boundless *cosmopolitanism,* which neither recognises the principle of nationality, nor takes into consideration the satisfaction of its interests; secondly, from a dead *materialism,* which everywhere regards chiefly the mere exchangeable value of things without taking into consideration the mental and political, the present and the future interests, and the productive powers of the nation; thirdly, from *a disorganising particularism* and *individualism,* which, ignoring the nature and character of social labour and the operation of the union of powers in their higher consequences, considers private industry only as it would develop itself under a state of free interchange with society (i.e. with the whole human race) were that race not divided into separate national societies.

Between each individual and entire humanity, however, stands THE NATION, with its special language and literature, with its peculiar origin and history, with its special manners and customs, laws and institutions, with the claims of all these for existence, independence, perfection, and continuance for the future, and with its separate territory; a society which, united by a thousand ties of mind and of interests, combines itself into one independent whole, which recognises the law of right for and within itself, and in its united character is still opposed to other societies of a similar kind in their national liberty, and consequently can only under the existing conditions of the world maintain self-existence and independence by its own power and resources. As the individual chiefly obtains by means of the nation and in the nation mental culture, power of production, security, and prosperity, so is the civilisation of the human race only conceivable and possible by means of the civilisation and development of the individual nations.

Meanwhile, however, an infinite difference exists in the condition and circumstances of the various nations: we observe among them giants and dwarfs, well-formed bodies and cripples, civilised, half-civilised, and barbarous nations; but in all of them, as in the individual human being, exists the impulse of self-preservation, the striving for improvement which is implanted by nature. It is the task of politics to civilise the barbarous nationalities, to make the small and weak ones great and strong, but above all, to secure to them existence and continuance. It is the task of national economy to accomplish *the economical development of the nation,* and to prepare it for admission into the universal society of the future.

A nation in its normal state possesses one common language and literature, a territory endowed with manifold natural resources, extensive, and with convenient frontiers and a numerous population. Agriculture, manufactures, commerce, and navigation must be all developed in it proportionately; arts and sciences, educational establishments, and universal cultivation must stand in it on an equal footing with material production. Its constitution, laws, and institutions must afford to those who belong to it a high degree of security and liberty, and must promote religion, morality, and prosperity; in a word, must have the well-being of its citizens as their object. It must possess sufficient power on land and at sea to defend its independence and to protect its foreign commerce. It will possess the power of beneficially affecting the civilisation of less advanced nations, and by means of its own surplus population and of their mental and material capital to found colonies and beget new nations.

A large population, and an extensive territory endowed with manifold national resources, are essential requirements of the normal nationality; they are the fundamental conditions of mental cultivation as well as of material development and political power. A nation restricted in the number of its population and in territory, especially if it has a separate language, can only possess a crippled literature, crippled institutions for promoting art and science. A small State can never bring to complete perfection within its territory the various branches of production. In it all protection becomes mere private monopoly. Only through alliances with more powerful nations, by partly sacrificing the advantages of nationality, and by excessive energy, can it maintain with difficulty its independence.

A nation which possesses no coasts, mercantile marine, or naval power, or has not under its dominion and control the mouths of its rivers, is in its foreign commerce dependent on other countries; it can neither establish colonies of its own nor form new nations; all surplus population, mental and material means, which flows from such a nation to uncultivated countries, is lost to its own literature, civilisation and industry, and goes to the benefit of other nationalities.

64 / KARL VON CLAUSEWITZ: WAR AND POLITICS

Apart from the general trend of political debate, although vastly significant for the understanding of politics, was the contribution of Karl von Clausewitz, the German military philosopher and historian, to the theory of the relationship between the state and its military arm. The great treatise Vom Kriege *("On War," 1832) concludes with a famous section, "War as an Instrument of Policy," from which the following passages are selected. In writing this work, Clausewitz combined his voluminous studies of earlier wars, particularly those of Frederick the Great, with his knowledge of the revolutionary and Napoleonic wars, which had so largely transformed the military art.*[14]

Up to this point we have had to consider, now from this side, now from that, the state of antagonism in which the nature of war stands with relation to the other interests of men individually and in a social group, in order not to neglect any of the opposing elements—an antagonism which is founded in our own nature, and which, therefore, no philosophy can unravel. We shall now look for that unity to which, in practical life, these antagonistic elements attach themselves by partly neutralizing each other. We would have brought forward this unity at the very beginning if it had not been necessary to emphasize these very contradictions, and also to look at the different elements separately. Now this unity is *the conception that war is only a part of political intercourse, therefore by no means an independent thing in itself.*

We know, of course, that war is only caused through the political intercourse of governments and nations; but in general it is supposed that such intercourse is broken off by war, and that a totally different state of things ensues, subject to no laws but its own.

We maintain, on the contrary, that war is nothing but a continuation of political intercourse with an admixture of other means. We

[14] Karl von Clausewitz, *On War*, translated from the German by O. J. Matthijs Jolles (New York: The Modern Library, n.d.), pp. 596–601. Reprinted by permission of Random House.

say "with an admixture of other means," in order thereby to maintain at the same time that this political intercourse does not cease through the war itself, is not changed into something quite different, but that, in its essence, it continues to exist, whatever may be the means which it uses, and that the main lines along which the events of the war proceed and to which they are bound are only the general features of policy which run on all through the war until peace takes place. And how can we conceive it to be otherwise? Does the cessation of diplomatic notes stop the political relations between different nations and governments? Is not war merely another kind of writing and language for their thought? It has, to be sure, its own grammar, but not its own logic.

Accordingly, war can never be separated from political intercourse, and if, in the consideration of the matter, this occurs anywhere, all the threads of the different relations are, in a certain sense, broken, and we have before us a senseless thing without an object.

This way of looking at the matter would be indispensable even if war were entirely war, entirely the unbridled element of hostility. All the circumstances on which it rests, and which determine its leading features, viz., our own power, the enemy's power, allies on both sides, the characteristics of the people and the governments respectively, etc., . . . —are they not of a political nature, and are they not so intimately connected with the whole political intercourse that it is impossible to separate them from it? But this view is doubly indispensable if we reflect that real war is no such consistent effort tending to the last extreme, as it should be according to abstract theory, but a half-hearted thing, a contradiction in itself; that, as such, it cannot follow its own laws, but must be looked upon as part of another whole—and this whole is policy. . . .

If war belongs to policy, it will naturally take on its character. If policy is grand and powerful, so also will be war, and this may be carried to the height at which war attains *its absolute form.*

In this way of conceiving it, therefore, we need not lose sight of the absolute form of war, rather its image must constantly hover in the background.

Only through this way of conceiving it does war once more become a unity; only thus can we regard all wars as things of *one* kind; and only thus can judgment obtain the true and exact basis and point of view from which great plans are to be made and judged.

It is true the political element does not penetrate deeply into the details of war. Vedettes are not planted, patrols are not sent round on political considerations. But its influence is all the more decisive in regard to the plan of a whole war, or campaign, and often even for a battle. . . .

If, therefore, in drawing up a plan of war, it is not permissible to have two or three points of view, from which things might be regarded, now with a soldier's eye, now with an administrator's, now with a politician's, and so on, then the next question is whether *policy* is necessarily paramount and everything else subordinate to it.

It is assumed that policy unites and reconciles within itself all the interests of internal administration and also those of humanity and of whatever else the philosophical mind might bring up, for it is nothing in itself but a mere representative of all these interests toward other states. That policy may take a wrong direction, and prefer to promote ambitious ends, private interests or the vanity of rulers, does not concern us here, for under no circumstances can the art of war be considered as its tutor, and we can only regard policy here as the representative of all the interests of the whole community.

The only question, therefore, is whether in forming plans for a war the political point of view should give way to the purely military (if such a point of view were conceivable), that is to say, should disappear altogether, or subordinate itself to it, or whether the political must remain the ruling point of view and the military be subordinated to it.

That the political point of view should end completely when war begins would only be conceivable if wars were struggles of life or death, from pure hatred. As wars are in reality, they are, as we said before, only the manifestations of policy itself. The subordination of the political point of view to the military would be unreasonable, for policy has created the war; policy is the intelligent faculty, war only the instrument, and not the reverse. The subordination of the military point of view to the political is, therefore, the only thing which is possible.

If we reflect on the nature of real war, and call to mind what has been said in the third chapter of this book, that *every war should be understood according to the probability of its character and its leading features as they are to be deduced from the political forces and conditions,* and that often—indeed we may safely affirm, in our days *almost always*—war is to be regarded as an organic whole, from which the single members cannot be separated, in which therefore every individual activity flows into the whole and also has its origin in the idea of this whole, then it becomes perfectly certain and clear that the highest standpoint for the conduct of war, from which its leading features proceed, can be no other than that policy. . . .

According to this view, it is an unpermissible and even harmful distinction, according to which a great military event or the plan for such an event should admit a *purely military judgment;* indeed, it is an unreasonable procedure to consult professional soldiers on the plan of war, that they may give a *purely military* opinion, as is frequently done by cabinets; but still more absurd is the demand of theorists that a statement of the available means of war should be laid before the general, that he may draw up a purely military plan for the war or for the campaign in accordance with them. . . .

This is perfectly natural. None of the principal plans which are necessary for a war can be made without insight into the political conditions, and when people speak, as they often do, of the harmful influence of policy on the conduct of the war, they really say something very different from what they intend. It is not this influence, but the policy itself, which should be found fault with. If the policy is right, that is, if it achieves its end, it can only affect the war favorably—in the sense of that policy. Where this influence deviates from the end, the cause is to be sought only in a mistaken policy.

It is only when policy promises itself a wrong effect from certain military means and measures, an effect opposed to their nature, that it can exercise a harmful effect on war by the course it prescribes. Just as a person in a language which he has not entirely mastered sometimes says what he does not intend, so policy will often order things which do not correspond to its own intentions.

This has very often happened and shows that a certain knowledge of military affairs is essential to the management of political intercourse.

But before going further, we must guard ourselves against a wrong interpretation, which readily suggests itself. We are far from holding the opinion that a war minister, buried in official papers, a learned engineer or even a soldier who has been well tried in the field would, any of them, necessarily make the best minister of state in a country where the sovereign does not act for himself. In other words, we do not mean to say that this acquaintance with military affairs is the principal qualification for a minister of state; a remarkable, superior mind and strength of character—these are the principal qualifications which he must possess; a knowledge of war may be supplied one way or another. . . .

We shall now conclude with some reflections derived from history.

In the last decade of the past century, when that remarkable change in the art of war in Europe took place by which the best armies saw a part of their method of war become ineffective, and military successes occurred on a scale of which no one had up to then had any conception, it certainly seemed that all wrong calculations were to be laid to the charge of the art of war. It was plain that, while confined by habit within a narrow circle of conceptions, Europe had been surprised by possibilities which lay outside of this circle, but, certainly, not outside of the nature of things.

Those observers who took the most comprehensive view ascribed the circumstance to the general influence which policy had exercised for centuries on the art of war, to its very great disadvantage, and as a result of which it had sunk into a half-hearted affair, often into mere sham-fighting. They were right as to the fact, but wrong in regarding it as an avoidable condition arising by chance.

Others thought that everything was to be explained by the momentary influence of the particular policy of Austria, Prussia, England, etc.

But is it true that the real surprise by which men's minds were seized was due to something in the conduct of war, and not rather to something in policy itself? That is: did the misfortune proceed from the influence of policy on the war or from an intrinsically wrong policy?

The tremendous effects of the French Revolution abroad were evidently brought about much less through new methods and views introduced by the French in the conduct of war than through the change in statecraft and civil administration, in the character of government, in the condition of the people, and so forth. That other governments took a mistaken view of all these things, that they endeavored, with their ordinary means, to hold their own against forces of a novel kind and overwhelming strength—all that was a blunder of policy.

Would it have been possible to perceive and correct these errors from the standpoint of a purely military conception of war? Impossible. For if there had been a philosophical strategist, who merely from the nature of the hostile elements had foreseen all the consequences, and prophesied remote possibilities, still it would have been quite impossible for such a wholly theoretical argument to produce the least result.

Only if policy had risen to a just appreciation of the forces which had been awakened in France, and of the new relations in the political state of Europe, could it have foreseen the consequences which were bound to follow in respect to the great features of war, and only in this way could it be led to a correct view of the extent of the means required, and the best use to make of them.

We may, therefore, say that the twenty years' victories of the Revolution are chiefly to be ascribed to the faulty policy of the governments by which it was opposed.

It is true that these faults were first displayed in the war, and the events of war completely disappointed the expectations which policy entertained. But this did not take place because policy neglected to consult its military advisers. The art of war in which the politician of the day could believe, namely, that derived from the reality of that time, that which belonged to the policy of the day, that familiar instrument which had been hitherto used—*that* art of war, I say, was naturally involved in the same error as policy, and therefore could not teach it better. It is true that war itself has undergone important alterations, both in its nature and forms, which have brought it nearer to its absolute form; but these changes were not brought about by the French government having, so to speak, freed itself from the leading-strings of policy; they arose from an altered policy which proceeded from the French Revolution not only in France but in the rest of Europe as well. This policy had called forth other means and other forces by which it became possible to conduct war with a degree of energy which could not have been thought of before.

Also the actual changes in the art of war are a consequence of alterations in policy, and, far from being an argument for the possible separation of the two, they are, on the contrary, very strong evidence of the intimacy of their connection.

Therefore, once more: war is an instrument of policy; it must necessarily bear the character of policy; it must measure with policy's measure. The conduct of war, in its great outlines, is, therefore, policy itself, which takes up the sword in place of the pen, but does not on that account cease to think according to its own laws.

65 / INDUSTRIALISM AND CHILD LABOR

By the early nineteenth century, the industrialization of Britain had proceeded so far that the effects of the factory system upon the nation were a matter of central political concern. Child labor in the factories was one of the earliest questions to be debated, and in 1818 a bill was introduced into the British House of Commons to limit the hours of children in the cotton factories. Sir Robert Peel, himself a factory owner, introduced the debate on February 19, 1818; the following excerpts are taken from Hansard's, the official record of parliamentary debate in Britain, which employs the method of indirect quotation. Peel (1750–1830) was the author of the first "Factory Act for the Preservation of the Health and Morals of Apprentices and others, employed in cotton and other mills, and Cotton and other Factories," adopted in 1802. The 1818 bill was designed to overcome the shortcomings of the earlier measure.[15]

[15] T. C. Hansard, *The Parliamentary Debates from the Year 1803 to the Present Time,* Vol. XXXVII (London: T. C. Hansard, 1818), cols. 559–66.

Sir *Robert Peel* rose to make his promised motion on a subject, the importance of which increased more and more on every consideration of it. About fifteen years ago he had brought in a bill for the Regulation of Apprentices in Cotton Manufactories. At that time they were the description of persons most employed in those manufactories. He himself had a thousand of them, and felt the necessity of some regulation with respect to them. Since that time, however, the business had been much extended. Manufactories were established in large towns, and the proprietors availed themselves of all the poor population of those towns. In Manchester alone 20,000 persons were employed in the cotton manufactories, and in the whole of England about three times that number. The business was of a peculiar nature, requiring of necessity that adults and children should work in the same rooms and at the same hours. It was notorious that children of a very tender age were dragged from their beds some hours before day light, and confined in the factories not less than fifteen hours; and it was also notoriously the opinion of the faculty, that no children of eight or nine years of age could bear that degree of hardship with impunity to their health and constitution. It had been urged by the humane, that there might be two sets of young labourers for one set of adults. He was afraid this would produce more harm than good. The better way would be to shorten the time of working for adults as well as for children; and to prevent the introduction of the latter at a very early age. Those who were employers of the children, seeing them from day to day, were not so sensible of the injury that they sustained from this practice as strangers, who were strongly impressed by it. In fact, they were prevented from growing to their full size. In consequence, Manchester, which used to furnish numerous recruits for the army, was now wholly unproductive in that respect. . . .

Lord *Lascelles* said, he felt considerable difficulty on the present subject, which was of the highest importance to the manufacturing districts. It was not all evils that were fit subjects for legislative interference; for instance, he highly applauded the bill of an hon. friend of his, respecting chimney-sweepers. But in the present case it should be recollected, that the individuals who were the objects of the hon. gentleman's proposition were free labourers. This excited his jealousy; for, were the principle of interference with free labourers once admitted, it was difficult to say how far it might not be carried. . . .

Mr. *Philips* strongly objected to the adoption of any measure of this description, and denied that the employment of children in the cotton factories operated, as had been described, to stint their growth, impair their comfort, or scatter disease amongst them. If he conceived that the establishment with which he was connected, though he was only what was called a sleeping partner in it, scattered disease and death in the manner which had been described, he should take shame to himself if he did not immediately attempt to remedy the evil. The fact was, however, that that establishment had been conducted in such a manner that it was an important benefit to the poor, and an example to other factories. In this, however, he himself had no merit, for the whole was done independently of him. During the twenty-seven years which that establishment had existed, no contagious disease had ever been known in it; and during eleven of those years returns of the state of health had regularly been made, and the sickness amounted only to a small fraction per cent. Out of a thousand persons employed, the whole sum paid to them in poors-rates did not exceed £5 per annum—a fortieth part of the sum which the factory contributed to the poor. If such was the fact, could any man say that the employment was unhealthy? There was no manufactory in the country, from which, if the same means were taken which had been resorted to in this case, numerous petitions and complaints might not be got. About four or five persons had been very active in looking out for complaints; they had dispatched their emissaries secretly about the country, and had circulated papers among the people in the different factories for their signature. The hon. baronet had said, the petitioners, in order to have the number of hours reduced, would willingly submit to a reduction of wages; but the petitioners did not say one word about reduction of wages; and if they said they would consent to such reduction, he would not believe them. The habits of these people led them to combine together; and it required great delicacy on the part of their employers to prevent much mischief being done in this way. Small factories were often ill ventilated, and from that circumstance the health of a person might suffer more in six hours in one of these factories, than in fifteen hours in a factory which was well ventilated and properly constructed in other respects. But how could this evil be cured by any bill? The small factories generally went to ruin, and that was the cure for the evil. From the returns made to the House, out of 31,117, the number of persons employed in these returns, 1717, or 5½ per cent, were of the age of 10 and under, 13,203 from 10 to 18, and 16,197 of the age of 18 and upwards. Out of 27,827 persons, there were 1830 only who could not read. Out of 25,000 the number of persons returned sick was 163, very little more than ⅝ths per cent. For these and other reasons, he felt it to be his duty to oppose the hon. baronet's measure.

Mr. *Wilberforce* was desirous that the discussion should be reserved till the whole subject should be fully before them. If different systems of management prevailed in the conduct of different factories, that was a sufficient reason for inducing the House to require farther information. His hope and belief was, that a fair inquiry would prove that the interests of the manufacturers and those of humanity were not at variance. Whatever might be the result of the measure, he was sure the House must feel obliged to the hon. baronet. Discussion must lead to useful results. He was convinced that whatever originated with the hon. baronet was the result of experience, prudence, and humanity.

Mr. *Finlay* said, that excepting in one instance, in the county of Lancaster, there was no proof of the existence of any evils which could justify legislative interference. In that case indeed, evils existed of the highest description. But this was a factory conducted under the provisions of an act of parliament—a proof that no law could prevent bad men from doing wicked things. Even in this factory, however, it was proved, that though children were employed fourteen hours, they were notwithstanding in exceeding good health. He warned the House against entertaining any measure, which went, like the present, to interfere with a manufacture of such vital importance. It was the most important ever established in this country; indeed, he believed, it employed more people than all the other manufactures of the country taken together. The exports from it exceeded 20 millions a year; and what was exported was not equal to what the home consumption was. The whole amount of the manufactures was little short of 40 millions a year. The bill should extend to the linen and woollen manufactures, as the hours of confinement were in them equally long. The medical men, whose opinion had been quoted, had never been in the cotton factories, and a medical man had told a friend of his, six months ago, that within six months he would be a dead man. He mentioned that, to show that medical men were not infallible. . . .

Mr. *Curwen* observed, that at the passing of the bill in 1802, the manufactories were conducted most infamously, but he could now state, from actual observation, that they were much better managed. The present measure did not appear to him to have been well digested; for instead of weighing the whole of the matters it was intended to embrace, the hon. baronet appeared contented with weighing parts. He thought he might be allowed to put the question, whether it was possible that individuals in the situation of parents, who, it must be generally admitted, had some portion of the milk of human nature where their offspring was concerned, should seek to wear away the health and spirits of their children by over exertion. Dr. Blane, previous to his examining some of the factories, had expected to find a great degree of sickness, and was greatly astonished at finding the very reverse. What, then, could have produced effects so striking, but that improvement in the system of preserving health which had been found so efficacious in many of his majesty's goals? In fact, no set of persons could be more healthy than the children so employed, and he could have wished, before the House had been called upon to legislate, that a committee had been appointed to examine into the real state of the case. Before he sat down, he thought it right to remark upon the propriety of legislating between the parent and the child: it went to say, that those of the poorer order were not fit to be trusted with the management of their own children. Let the House not disguise from itself, that the moment it was ascertained that the hours of labour were to be reduced, that moment there would be an outcry for an increase of wages. It had been said, that the parties themselves would consent to a diminution of wages, and farther, that the measure would be the means of calling a greater number of persons into employment. But then the consequences must be, that if the earnings of persons were lessened in point of hours, there must be some means found for increasing their wages. In that case it must be ruinous to the individuals and hurtful to the country: for the well-being of the cotton manufacture must depend on our foreign relations, and the ultimate effect must be, that the trade would be destroyed, and a number of persons thrown out of employment. On a former occasion, he concurred in opinion with those who thought an alteration in the system not only proper, but necessary; but since then he had had many opportunities of becoming more practically acquainted with the details and with the real facts; and he now felt confident, that to legislate at all upon the subject, would be ruinous to the trade, and injurious to the parties who were intended to be relieved.

Sir *John Jackson* thought, as the House had given their attention to the amelioration of the situation of slaves abroad, that they could not in reason neglect their fellow-subjects at home. It was totally impossible that children kept at work for so many hours could be brought up with a due impression of their moral duties. He had had much conversation upon the subject with many persons connected with cotton mills, and particularly with the conductor of the establishment at New Lanark, and the general opinion was, that something was necessary to be done. He hoped, therefore, that the bill would be carried through the House. It came from an excellent quarter, for it was impossible to select a person more experienced in the business than the hon. baronet.

66 / FRIEDRICH ENGELS: INDUSTRIALISM AND SLUMS

The Industrial Revolution transformed the living as well as the working conditions of the new factory hands. Instead of dwelling in farm cottages or in tiny towns, they were massed into the slums of big cities. The impact of the industrial and commercial cities of England, with their dramatic contrast of productivity and penury, upon a sensitive and thoughtful visitor is shown in the following excerpt from Friedrich Engels' Die Lage des arbeitenden Klasse in England in 1844 ("The Condition of the Working Class in England in 1844," 1845). Other sections of this book have been criticized by modern scholars as faulty in the use of evidence, but this chapter, "The Great Towns," reflects primarily direct experience and personal judgment. Engels (1820–1895), the son of a German textile manufacturer, was sent in 1842 to Manchester, England, to help manage a factory in which his father was part owner. Engels came under the influence of early socialist groups, met Karl Marx in Paris, and became his lifelong collaborator. He took part in the unsuccessful revolution of 1848 in Germany, then returned to England to escape arrest and to become manager of the Manchester factory. For two decades Engels maintained the dual roles—so apparently incompatible in spirit—of capitalist manager and socialist theoretician.[16]

A town, such as London, where a man may wander for hours together without reaching the beginning of the end, without meeting the slightest hint which could lead to the inference that there is open country within reach, is a strange thing. This colossal centralisation, this heaping together of two and a half millions of human beings at one point, has multiplied the power of this two and a half millions a hundredfold; has raised London to the commercial capital of the world, created the

[16] Frederick Engels, *The Condition of the Working Class in England in 1844*, translated from the German by Florence Kelley Wischenewetzky (London: Swan Sonnenschein & Co., 1892), pp. 23–7.

giant docks and assembled the thousand vessels that continually cover the Thames. I know nothing more imposing than the view which the Thames offers during the ascent from the sea to London Bridge. The masses of buildings, the wharves on both sides, especially from Woolwich upwards, the countless ships along both shores, crowding ever closer and closer together, until, at last, only a narrow passage remains in the middle of the river, a passage through which hundreds of steamers shoot by one another; all this is so vast, so impressive, that a man cannot collect himself, but is lost in the marvel of England's greatness before he sets foot upon English soil.

But the sacrifices which all this has cost become apparent later. After roaming the streets of the capital a day or two, making headway with difficulty through the human turmoil and the endless lines of vehicles, after visiting the slums of the metropolis, one realises for the first time that these Londoners have been forced to sacrifice the best qualities of their human nature, to bring to pass all the marvels of civilisation which crowd their city; that a hundred powers which slumbered within them have remained inactive, have been suppressed in order that a few might be developed more fully and multiply through union with those of others. The very turmoil of the streets has something repulsive, something against which human nature rebels. The hundreds of thousands of all classes and ranks crowding past each other, are they not all human beings with the same qualities and powers, and with the same interest in being happy? And have they not, in the end, to seek happiness in the same way, by the same means? And still they crowd by one another as though they had nothing in common, nothing to do with one another, and their only agreement is the tacit one, that each keep to his own side of the pavement, so as not to delay the opposing streams of the crowd, while it occurs to no man to honour another with so much as a glance. The brutal indifference, the unfeeling isolation of each in his private interest becomes the more repellant and offensive, the more these individuals are crowded together, within a limited space. And, however much one may be aware that this isolation of the individual, this narrow self-seeking is the fundamental principle of our society everywhere, it is nowhere so shamelessly barefaced, so self-conscious as just here in the crowding of the great city. The dissolution of mankind into monads, of which each one has a separate principle, the world of atoms, is here carried out to its utmost extreme.

Hence it comes, too, that the social war, the war of each against all, is here openly declared. Just as in Stirner's recent book, people regard each other only as useful objects; each exploits the other, and the end of it all is, that the stronger treads the weaker under foot, and that the powerful few, the capitalists, seize everything for themselves, while to the weak many, the poor, scarcely a bare existence remains.

What is true of London, is true of Manchester, Birmingham, Leeds, is true of all great towns. Everywhere barbarous indifference, hard egotism on one hand, and nameless misery on the other, everywhere social warfare, every man's house in a state of siege, everywhere reciprocal plundering under the protection of the law, and all so shameless, so openly avowed that one shrinks before the consequences of our social state as they manifest themselves here undisguised, and can only wonder that the whole crazy fabric still hangs together.

Since capital, the direct or indirect control of the means of sub-sistence and production, is the weapon with which this social warfare is carried on, it is clear that all the disadvantages of such a state must fall upon the poor. For him no man has the slightest concern. Cast into the whirlpool, he must struggle through as well as he can. If he is so happy as to find work, *i.e.*, if the bourgeoisie does him the favour to enrich itself by means of him, wages await him which scarcely suf-fice to keep body and soul together; if he can get no work he may steal, if he is not afraid of the police, or starve, in which case the police will take care that he does so in a quiet and inoffensive manner. During my residence in England, at least twenty or thirty persons have died of simple starvation under the most revolting circumstances, and a jury has rarely been found possessed of the courage to speak the plain truth in the matter. Let the testimony of the witnesses be never so clear and unequivocal, the bourgeoisie, from which the jury is selected, always finds some backdoor through which to escape the fruitful ver-dict, death from starvation. The bourgeoisie dare not speak the truth in these cases, for it would speak its own condemnation. But indirectly, far more than directly, many have died of starvation, where long con-tinued want of proper nourishment has called forth fatal illness, when it has produced such debility that causes which might otherwise have remained inoperative, brought on severe illness and death. The English working-men call this "social murder," and accuse our whole society of perpetrating this crime perpetually. Are they wrong?

True, it is only individuals who starve, but what security has the working-man that it may not be his turn to-morrow? Who assures him employment, who vouches for it that, if for any reason or no reason his lord and master discharges him to-morrow, he can struggle along with those dependent upon him, until he may find some one else "to give him bread?" Who guarantees that willingness to work shall suffice to obtain work, that uprightness, industry, thrift, and the rest of the virtues recommended by the bourgeoisie, are really his road to happi-ness? No one. He knows that he has something to-day, and that it does not depend upon himself whether he shall have something to-morrow. He knows that every breeze that blows, every whim of his employer, every bad turn of trade may hurl him back into the fierce whirlpool from which he has temporarily saved himself, and in which it is hard and often impossible to keep his head above water. He knows that, though he may have the means of living to-day, it is very uncertain whether he shall to-morrow.

Meanwhile, let us proceed to a more detailed investigation of the position, in which the social war has placed the non-possessing class. Let us see what pay for his work society does give the working-man in the form of dwelling, clothing, food, what sort of subsistence it grants those who contribute most to the maintenance of society; and, first, let us consider the dwellings.

Every great city has one or more slums, where the working-class is crowded together. True, poverty often dwells in hidden alleys close to the palaces of the rich; but, in general, a separate territory has been assigned to it, where, removed from the sight of the happier classes, it may struggle along as it can. These slums are pretty equally arranged in all the great towns of England, the worst houses in the worst quarters of the towns; usually one or two-storied cottages in long rows, perhaps with cellars used as dwellings, almost always irregularly built. These houses of three or four rooms and a kitchen form, throughout England, some parts of London excepted, the general dwellings of the working-class. The streets are generally unpaved, rough, dirty, filled with vegetable and animal refuse, without sewers or gutters, but supplied with foul, stagnant pools instead. Moreover, ventilation is impeded by the bad, confused method of building of the whole quarter, and since many human beings here live crowded into a small space, the atmosphere that prevails in these working-men's quarters may readily be imagined. Further, the streets serve as drying grounds in fine weather; lines are stretched across from house to house, and hung with wet clothing.

Let us investigate some of the slums in their order. London comes first, and in London the famous rookery of St. Giles which is now, at last, about to be penetrated by a couple of broad streets. St. Giles is in the midst of the most populous part of the town, surrounded by broad, splendid avenues in which the gay world of London idles about, in the immediate neighbourhood of Oxford Street, Regent Street, of Trafalgar Square and the Strand. It is a disorderly collection of tall, three or four-storied houses, with narrow, crooked, filthy streets, in which there is quite as much life as in the great thoroughfares of the town, except that, here, people of the working-class only are to be seen. A vegetable market is held in the street, baskets with vegetables and fruits, naturally all bad and hardly fit to use, obstruct the sidewalk still further, and from these, as well as from the fish-dealers' stalls, arises a horrible smell. The houses are occupied from cellar to garret, filthy within and without, and their appearance is such that no human being could possibly wish to live in them. But all this is nothing in comparison with the dwellings in the narrow courts and alleys between the streets, entered by covered passages between the houses, in which the filth and tottering ruin surpass all description. Scarcely a whole window-pane can be found, the walls are crumbling, doorposts and window-frames loose and broken, doors of old boards nailed together, or altogether wanting in this thieves' quarter, where no doors are needed, there being nothing to steal. Heaps of garbage and ashes lie in all directions, and the foul liquids emptied before the doors gather in stinking pools. Here live the poorest of the poor, the worst paid workers with thieves and the victims of prostitution indiscriminately huddled together, the majority Irish, or of Irish extraction, and those who have not yet sunk in the whirlpool of moral ruin which surrounds them, sinking daily deeper, losing daily more and more of their power to resist the demoralising influence of want, filth, and evil surroundings.

67 / GOVERNMENT BY ALL THE PEOPLE?

The conviction that an industrial economy and an urban society could be made to produce a good life for the majority of the population became the driving force of various movements, large and small, during the first half of the nineteenth century. In England, where the industrial revolution was by far most advanced, but where representative parliamentary government was also most firmly established, the pattern of reform was modeled not on the French Revolution but on the English Reform Act of 1832, which extended suffrage and eliminated many of the "rotten" boroughs. The focus of reform activity among workingmen and their middle-class sympathizers became the People's Charter of 1832. Presented in 1839 with more than a million signatures, it was rejected by the House of Commons. In 1842 it was reintroduced with the following petition (A), which sums up both the charter and the arguments of its supporters.[17]

The debate in the House of Commons on the new petition for the People's Charter was highlighted by the speech of Thomas Babington Macaulay in opposition. He raised the argument to the

[17] *Hansard's Parliamentary Debates*, 3rd series, Vol. LXII (London: Thomas Curson Hansard *et al.*, 1842), cols. 1376–1381.

level of very high principle and so caused his opponents to do likewise. Most of the arguments during the next century for and against the "welfare state"—a state accepting responsibility for the welfare and prosperity of its subjects in considerable detail— were foreshadowed in this discussion (B). Macaulay (1800–1859) was one of the most eminent lawyers, historians, and essayists of nineteenth century England. He served as an English adminis- trator in India and was a member of the House of Lords before being made a peer two years before his death. His masterpiece was the unfinished History of England from the Accession of James the Second *(1848–1861). John Arthur Roebuck (1801–1879), whose reply to Macaulay is also excerpted here, was, like him, a Whig.*[18]

A. THE PEOPLE'S CHARTER

To the Honourable the Commons of Great Britain and Ireland, in Parliament Assembled

The Petition of the undersigned people of the United Kingdom,

Sheweth—That Government originated from, was designed to protect the freedom and promote the happiness of, and ought to be responsible to, the whole people.

That the only authority on which any body of men can make laws and govern society, is delegation from the people.

That as Government was designed for the benefit and protection of, and must be obeyed and supported by all, therefore all should be equally represented.

That any form of Government which fails to effect the purposes for which it was designed, and does not fully and completely represent the whole people, who are compelled to pay taxes to its support and obey the laws resolved upon by it, is unconstitutional, tyrannical, and ought to be amended or resisted.

That your honourable House, as at present constituted, has not been elected by, and acts irresponsibly of, the people; and hitherto has only represented parties, and benefitted the few, regardless of the miseries, grievances, and petitions of the many. Your honourable House has en- acted laws contrary to the expressed wishes of the people, and by unconstitutional means enforced obedience to them, thereby creating an unbearable despotism on the one hand, and degrading slavery on the other.

[18] *Hansard's Parliamentary Debates,* 3rd series, Vol. LXIII (London: Thomas Curson Hansard *et al.,* 1842), cols. 45–58.

That if your honourable House is of opinion that the people of Great Britain and Ireland ought not to be fully represented, your petitioners pray that such opinion may be unequivocally made known, that the people may fully understand what they can or cannot expect from your honourable House; because if such be the decision of your honourable House, your petitioners are of opinion that where representation is denied, taxation ought to be resisted.

That your petitioners instance, in proof of their assertion, that your honourable House has not been elected by the people; that the population of Great Britain and Ireland is at the present time about twenty-six millions of persons; and that yet, out of this number, little more than nine hundred thousand have been permitted to vote in the recent election of representatives to make laws to govern the whole.

That the existing state of representation is not only extremely limited and unjust, but unequally divided, and gives preponderating influence to the landed and monied interests, to the utter ruin of the small-trading and labouring classes.

That the borough of Guildford, with a population of 3,920 returns to Parliament as many members as the Tower Hamlets, with a population of 300,000; Evesham, with a population of 3,998, elects as many representatives as Manchester, with a population of 200,000; and Buckingham, Evesham, Totness, Guildford, Honiton, and Bridport, with a total population of 23,000, return as many representatives as Manchester, Finsbury, Tower Hamlets, Liverpool, Marylebone, and Lambeth, with a population of 1,400,000: these being but a very few instances of the enormous inequalities existing in what is called the representation of this country.

That bribery, intimidation, corruption, perjury, and riot, prevail at all parliamentary elections, to an extent best understood by the Members of your Honourable House.

That your petitioners complain that they are enormously taxed to pay the interest of what is termed the national debt, a debt amounting at present to £800,000,000, being only a portion of the enormous amount expended in cruel and expensive wars for the suppression of all liberty, by men not authorised by the people, and who, consequently, had no right to tax posterity for the outrages committed by them upon mankind. And your petitioners loudly complain of the augmentation of that debt, after twenty-six years of almost uninterrupted peace, and whilst poverty and discontent rage over the land.

That taxation, both general and local, is at this time too enormous to be borne; and in the opinion of your petitioners is contrary to the spirit of the Bill of Rights, wherein it is clearly expressed that no subject shall be compelled to contribute to any tax, talliage, or aid, unless imposed by common consent in Parliament.

That in England, Ireland, Scotland, and Wales, thousands of people are dying from actual want; and your petitioners, whilst sensible that poverty is the great exciting cause of crime, view with mingled astonishment and alarm the ill provision made for the poor, the aged, and infirm; and likewise perceive, with feelings and indignation, the determination of your honourable House to continue the Poor-law Bill in operation, notwithstanding the many proofs which have been afforded by sad experience of the unconstitutional principle of that bill, of its unchristian character, and of the cruel and murderous effects produced upon the wages of working men, and the lives of the subjects of this realm.

That your petitioners conceive that bill to be contrary to all previous statutes, opposed to the spirit of the constitution, and an actual violation of the precepts of the Christian religion; and, therefore, your petitioners look with apprehension to the results which may flow from its continuance.

That your petitioners would direct the attention of your honourable House to the great disparity existing between the wages of the producing millions, and the salaries of those whose comparative usefulness ought to be questioned, where riches and luxury prevail amongst the rulers, and poverty and starvation amongst the ruled.

That your petitioners, with all due respect and loyalty, would compare the daily income of the Sovereign Majesty with that of thousands of the working men of this nation; and whilst your petitioners have learned that her Majesty receives daily for her private use of the sum of £164. 17s. 10d., they have also ascertained that many thousands of the families of the labourers are only in the receipt of 3¾d. per head per day.

That your petitioners have also learned that his royal Highness Prince Albert receives each day the sum of £104. 2s., whilst thousands have to exist upon 3d. per head per day.

That your petitioners have also heard with astonishment, that the King of Hanover daily receives £57. 10s. whilst thousands of the taxpayers of this empire live upon 2¾d. per head per day.

That your petitioners have, with pain and regret, also learned that the Archbishop of Canterbury is daily in the receipt of £52. 10s. per day, whilst thousands of the poor have to maintain their families upon an income not exceeding 2d. per head per day.

That notwithstanding the wretched and unparalleled condition of the people, your honourable House has manifested no disposition to curtail the expenses of the State, to diminish taxation, or promote general prosperity.

That unless immediate remedial measures be adopted, your petitioners fear the increasing distress of the people will lead to results fearful to contemplate; because your petitioners can produce evidence of the gradual decline of wages, at the same time that the constant increase of the national burdens must be apparent to all.

That your petitioners know that it is the undoubted constitutional right of the people, to meet freely, when, how, and where they choose, in public places, peaceably, in the day, to discuss their grievances, and political or other subjects, or for the purpose of framing, discussing, or passing any vote, petition, or remonstrance, upon any subject whatsoever.

That your petitioners complain that the right has unconstitutionally been infringed; and 500 well disposed persons have been arrested, excessive bail demanded, tried by packed juries, sentenced to imprisonment, and treated as felons of the worst description.

That an unconstitutional police force is distributed all over the country, at enormous cost, to prevent the due exercise of the people's rights. And your petitioners are of opinion that the Poor-law Bastiles and the police stations, being co-existent, have originated from the same cause, *viz.*, the increased desire on the part of the irresponsible few to oppress and starve the many.

That a vast and unconstitutional army is upheld at the public expense, for the purpose of repressing public opinion in the three kingdoms, and likewise to intimidate the millions in the due exercise of those rights and privileges which ought to belong to them.

That your petitioners complain that the hours of labour, particularly of the factory workers, are protracted beyond the limits of human endurance, and that the wages earned, after unnatural application to toil in heated and unhealthy workshops, are inadequate to sustain the bodily strength, and supply those comforts which are so imperative after an excessive waste of physical energy.

That your petitioners also direct the attention of your honourable House to the starvation wages of the agricultural labourer, and view with horror and indignation the paltry income of those whose toil gives being to the staple food of this people.

That your petitioners deeply deplore the existence of any kind of monopoly in this nation, and whilst they unequivocally condemn the levying of any tax upon the necessaries of life, and upon those articles principally required by the labouring classes, they are also sensible that the abolition of any one monopoly will never unshackle labour from its misery until the people possess that power under which all monopoly and oppression must cease; and your petitioners respectfully mention the existing monopolies of the suffrage, of paper money, of machinery, of land, of the public press, of religious privileges, of the means of travelling and transit, and of a host of other evils too numerous to mention, all arising from class legislation, but which your honourable House has always consistently endeavoured to increase instead of diminish.

That your petitioners are sensible, from the numerous petitions presented to your honourable House, that your honourable House is fully acquainted with the grievances of the working men; and your petitioners pray that the rights and wrongs of labour may be considered, with a view to the protection of the one, and to the removal of the other; because your petitioners are of opinion that it is the worst species of legislation which leaves the grievances of society to be removed only by violence or revolution, both of which may be apprehended if complaints are unattended to and petitions despised.

That your petitioners complain that upwards of nine millions of pounds per annum are unjustly abstracted from them to maintain a church establishment, from which they principally dissent; and beg to call the attention of your honourable House to the fact, that this enormous sum is equal to, if it does not exceed, the cost of upholding Christianity in all parts of the world beside. Your petitioners complain that it is unjust, and not in accordance with the Christian religion, to enforce compulsory support of religious creeds, and expensive church establishments, with which the people do not agree.

That your petitioners believe all men have a right to worship God as may appear best to their consciences, and that no legislative enactments should interfere between man and his Creator.

That your petitioners direct the attention of your honourable House to the enormous revenue annually swallowed up by the bishops and the clergy, and entreat you to contrast their deeds with the conduct of the founder of the Christian religion, who denounced worshippers of Mammon, and taught charity, meekness, and brotherly love.

That your petitioners strongly complain that the people of this kingdom are subject to the rule of irresponsible law-makers, to whom they have given no authority, and are enormously taxed to uphold a corrupt system, to which they have never in person or by representation given their assent.

That your petitioners maintain that it is the inherent, indubitable, and constitutional right, founded upon the ancient practice of the realm of England, and supported by well approved statutes, of every male inhabitant of the United Kingdom, he being of age and of sound mind, non-convict of crime, and not confined under any judicial process, to exercise the elective franchise in the choice of Members to serve in the Commons House of Parliament.

That your petitioners can prove, that by the ancient customs and statutes of this realm, Parliament should be held once in each year.

That your petitioners maintain that Members elected to serve in Parliament ought to be the servants of the people, and should, at short and stated intervals, return to their constituencies, to ascertain if their conduct is approved of, and to give the people power to reject all who have not acted honestly and justly.

That your petitioners complain that possession of property is made the test of men's qualification to sit in Parliament.

That your petitioners can give proof that such qualifications is irrational, unnecessary, and not in accordance with the ancient usages of England.

That your petitioners complain, that by influence, patronage, and intimidation, there is at present no purity of election; and your petitioners contend for the right of voting by ballot.

That your petitioners complain that seats in your honourable House are sought for at a most extravagant rate of expense; which proves an enormous degree of fraud and corruption.

That your petitioners, therefore, contend, that to put an end to secret political traffic, all representatives should be paid a limited amount for their services.

That your petitioners complain of the inequality of representation; and contend for the division of the country into equal electoral districts.

That your petitioners complain of the many grievances borne by the people of Ireland, and contend that they are fully entitled to a repeal of the legislative union.

That your petitioners have viewed with great indignation the partiality shown to the aristocracy in the courts of justice, and the cruelty of that system of law which deprived Frost, Williams, and Jones, of the benefit of their objection offered by Sir Frederick Pollock during the trial at Monmouth, and which was approved by a large majority of the judges.

That your petitioners beg to assure your honourable House that they cannot, within the limits of this their petition, set forth even a tithe of the many grievances of which they may justly complain; but should your honourable House be pleased to grant your petitioners a hearing by representatives at the Bar of your honourable House, your petitioners will be enabled to unfold a tale of wrong and suffering—of intolerable injustice—which will create utter astonishment in the minds of all benevolent and good men, that the people of Great Britain and Ireland have so long quietly endured their wretched condition, brought upon them as it has been by unjust exclusion from political authority, and by the manifold corruptions of class-legislation.

That your petitioners, therefore, exercising their just constitutional right, demand that your honourable House do remedy the many gross and manifest evils of which your petitioners complain, do immediately, without alteration, deduction, or addition, pass into a law the documents entitled "The People's Charter," which embraces the representation of male adults, vote by ballot, annual Parliaments, no property qualification, payment of Members, and equal electoral districts.

And that your petitioners, desiring to promote the peace of the United Kingdom, security of property, and prosperity of commerce, seriously and earnestly press this, their petition, on the attention of your honourable House.

B. T. B. MACAULAY AND J. A. ROEBUCK: DEBATE ON THE CHARTER

Mr. *Macaulay*: . . . There are parts of the charter to which I am favourable—for which I have voted, which I would always support; and in truth of all the six points of the charter there is only one to which I entertain extreme and unmitigated hostility. . . . But I do not go the length of the Charter, because there is one point which is its essence, which is so important, that if you withhold it, nothing can produce the smallest effect in taking away the agitation which prevails, but which, if you grant, it matters not what else you grant, and that is, universal suffrage, or suffrage without any qualification of property at all. Considering that as by far the most important part of the Charter, and having a most decided opinion, that such a change would be utterly fatal to the country, I feel it my duty to say, that I cannot hold out the least hope that I shall ever, under any circumstances, support that change. The reasons for this opinion, I will state as shortly as I can. And, in the first place, I beg to say, that I entertain this view upon no ground of finality; indeed, the remarks which I have already made preclude such a supposition, but I do admit my belief, that violent and frequent changes in the Government of a country, are not desirable. Every great change, I think, should be judged by its own merits. I am bound by no tie to oppose any legislative reform which I really believe will conduce to the public benefit; but I think that that which has been brought forward as an undoubted and conclusive argument against a change of this sort, that it is perfectly inconsistent with the continuance of the Monarchy or of the House of Lords, has been much over-stated. And this I say, though I profess myself a most faithful subject to her Majesty, and by no means anxious to destroy the connection which exists between the Monarchy, the aristocracy, and the constitution, that I cannot consider either the Monarchy or the aristocracy as the end of Government, but only as its means. I know instances of governments with neither a hereditary monarchy or aristocracy, yet flourishing and successful, and, therefore, I conceive this argument to have been over-stated. But I believe that universal suffrage would be fatal to all purposes for which government exists, and for which aristocracies and all other things exist, and that it is utterly incompatible with the very existence of civilisation. I conceive that civilisation rests on the security of property, but I think, that it is not necessary for me, in a discussion of this kind, to go through the arguments, and through the vast experience which necessarily leads to this result; but I will assert, that while property is insecure, it is not in the power of the finest soil, or of the moral or intellectual constitution of any country, to prevent the country sinking into barbarism, while, on the other hand, while property is secure, it is not possible to prevent a country from advancing in prosperity. Whatever progress this country has made, in spite of all the misgovernment which can possibly be imputed to it, it cannot but be seen how irresistible is the power of the great principle of security of property. Whatever may have been the state of war in which we were engaged, men were still found labouring to supply the deficiencies of the State; and if it be the fact, that all classes have the deepest interest in the security of property, I conceive, that this principle follows, that we never can, without absolute danger, entrust the supreme Government of the country to any class which would, to a moral certainty, be induced to commit great and systematic inroads against the security of property. I assume, that this will be the result of this motion—and I ask, whether the Government, being placed at the head of the majority of the people of this country, without any pecuniary qualification, they would continue to maintain the principle of the security of property? I think not. . . .

I believe, that it is hardly necessary for me to go into any further explanation, but if I understand this petition rightly, I believe it to contain a declaration, that the remedies for the evils of which it complains, and under which this country suffers, are to be found in a great and sweeping confiscation of property, and I am firmly convinced, that the effect of any such measure would be not merely to overturn those institutions which now exist, and to ruin those who are rich, but to make the poor poorer, and the amount of the misery of the country even greater, than it is now represented to be. I am far from bringing any charge against the great body of those who have signed this petition. As far am I from approving of the conduct of those who, in procuring the petition to be signed, have put the sentiments which it embodies into a bad and pernicious form. I ask, however, are we to go out of the ordinary course of Parliamentary proceedings, for the purpose of giving it reception. I believe, that nothing is more natural than that the feelings of the people should be such as they are described to be. Even we, ourselves, with all our advantages of education, when we are tried by the temporary pressure of circumstances, are too ready to catch at everything which may hold out the hope of relief—to incur a greater evil in future, which may afford the means of present indulgence; and I cannot but see, that a man having a wife at home to whom he is attached, growing thinner every day, children whose wants become every day more pressing, whose mind is principally employed in mechanical toil, may have been driven to entertain such views as are here expressed, partly from his own position, and partly from the culpable neglect of the Government in omitting to supply him with the means and the power of forming a better judgment. Let us grant that education would remedy these things, shall we not wait until it has done so, before we agree to such a motion as this; shall we, before such a change is wanted, give them the power and the means of ruining not only the rich, but themselves? I have no more unkind feeling towards these petitioners than I have towards the sick man, who calls for a draught of cold water, although he is satisfied that it would be death to him; nor than I have for the poor Indians, whom I have seen collected round the granaries in India at a time of scarcity, praying that the doors might be thrown open, and the grain distributed; but I would not in the one case give the draught of water, nor would I in the other give the key of the granary; because I know that by doing so I shall only make a scarcity a famine, and by giving such relief, enormously increase the evil. No one can say that such a spoliation of property as these petitioners point at would be a relief to the evils of which they complain, and I believe that no one will deny, that it would be a great addition to the mischief which is proposed to be removed. . . . There has been a constant and systematic attempt for years to represent the Government as being able to do, and as bound to attempt that which no Government ever attempted; and instead of the Government being represented, as is the truth, as being supported by the people, it has been treated as if the Government supported the people: it has been treated as if the Government possessed some mine of wealth—some extraordinary means of supplying the wants of the people; as if they could give them bread from the clouds—water from the rocks—to increase the bread and the fishes five thousandfold. Is it possible to believe that the moment you give them absolute, supreme, irresistible power, they will forget all this? You propose to give them supreme power; in every constituent body throughout the empire capital and accumulated property is to be placed absolutely at the foot of labour. How is it possible to doubt what the result will be? Suppose such men as the hon. Members for Bath and Rochdale being returned to sit in this House, who would, I believe, oppose such measures of extreme change as would involve a national bankruptcy. What would be the effect if their first answer to their constituents should be, "Justice and the public good demand that this thirty millions a-year should be paid?" Then, with regard to land, supposing it should be determined that there should be no partition of land, and it is hardly possible to conceive that there are men to be found who would destroy all the means of creating and increasing wages, and of creating and increasing the trade and commerce of this country, which gives employment to so many! Is it possible that the three millions of people who have petitioned this House should insist on the prayer of their petition? I do not wish to say all that forces itself on my mind with regard to what might be the result of our granting the Charter. Let us, if we can, picture to ourselves the consequences of such a spoliation as it is proposed should take place. Would it end with one spoliation? How could it? That distress which is the motive now for calling on this House to interfere would be only doubled and trebled by the act; the measure of distress would become greater after that spoliation, and the bulwarks by which fresh acts of the same character would have been removed. The Government would rest upon spoliation—all the property which any man possessed would be supported by it, and is it possible to suppose that a new state of things would exist wherein every thing that was done would be right? What must be the effect of such a sweeping confiscation of property? No experience enables us to guess at it. All I can say is, that it seems to me to be something more horrid than can be imagined. A great community of human beings—a vast people would be called into exist-ence in a new position; there would be a depression, if not an utter stoppage, of trade, and of all those vast engagements of the country by which our people were supported, and how is it possible to doubt that famine and pestilence would come before long to wind up the effects of such a system. The best thing which I can expect, and which I think every one must see as the result, is, that in some of the desperate struggles which must take place in such a state of things, some strong military despot must arise, and give some sort of protection—some security to the property which may remain. But if you flatter yourselves that after such an occurrence you would ever see again those institu-tions under which you have lived, you deceive yourselves: you would never see them again, and you would never deserve to see them. By all neighbouring nations you would be viewed with utter contempt, and that glory and prosperity which has been so envied would be sneered at, and your fate would thus be told: "England," it would be said, "had her institutions, imperfect though they were, but which contained within themselves the means of remedying all imperfection. Those in-stitutions were wantonly thrown away for no purpose whatever, but because she was asked to do so by persons who sought her ruin; her ruin was the consequence, and she deserves it." Believing this, I will oppose with every faculty which I possess the proposition for universal suffrage. . . .

Mr. *Roebuck* said, that the speech of the right hon. Gentleman who had just sat down, plainly indicated to him, that in spite of the right hon. Gentleman's declaration, he had little of kindly feeling for the persons who had petitioned that House. . . . There was a natural desire in every man to profit by another's labour. The object of Government was to prevent that desire from breaking out into action. In a state of nature, if he was wrong, he obtained that which he desired; as men advanced, they met together, and formed societies. In this country, the people had hit upon the principle of deputation to a few to do that which in former times was done in the market-place by the whole body of the people. The House of Commons then sat there to prevent the desire that each man has of profiting by another's labour from coming into action; they were put over the people to watch for them; but then, that being the case, who was to watch them—to watch the watchers? That could only be done with effect by making the House of Commons responsible to the people, and the charge against the House of Commons on the part of the people was, that there had been delegated to a small section of the people, the power of enforcing this responsibility, and that that small section had joined with the House of Commons to oppress the remainder of the people; and that they did oppress the remainder of the people. . . . But were those who signed this petition really unfit to govern themselves? Separate the people of this country into classes, and they would see which of them were against property; the classes who had a share in education—the enlightened mechanics, were not against property. The right hon. Gentleman had said, that if any one class was dependent upon property and the security of property, that class was the labouring class, and yet he wished to make out that this class was so blind to their real interests and to all that prudence would dictate, that it was that class of all others which would be willing to reduce the country to the condition of a desert. Now, he judged the people of England otherwise; he did not judge by the words of the foolish, malignant, cowardly demagogue who had written that petition. He knew where to put his finger on the man, and he was convinced it was not that man who was entitled to stand forward as the representative of the labouring classes. He would ask those hon. Members who had borne witness to the long-suffering of the industrious classes, amidst the privations and distresses to which they had been exposed, and which they were yet daily suffering, what was the character of his fellow-countrymen? Yes, it was from these sufferings that he judged of his fellow-countrymen, and not from the trashy doctrine contained in the petition, which would be of itself ridiculous but for the grandeur of the multitude of names appended to it. What they asked was, for the power which they saw their fellow-citizens enjoying. What they complained of was, that their fellow-citizens, whom they knew to be made by nature no better than themselves, were selected as the repositories of political power. That was a distinction which was peculiarly galling to them. But he did not believe, speaking from the knowledge which he had of his fellow-citizens, and it had been his fortune to mix much with them, that the belief was general that the great accidents which regulate the happiness of their lives were within the power of the Government. In fact, he believed that the class to which he referred was as enlightened as the present electoral body. Well then, if they were as enlightened as the present electoral body, let the House consider that this country had wealth, and had security for property under the present electoral body. Why then should the country not have the same under the labouring classes? If they were as worthy to be electors as the present body, why was he to conclude that under them the country would be involved in that anarchy which had been painted by the somewhat terrific pencil of the right hon. Gentleman. That was not his judgment of the people of England. If he were wrong, what kept them from displaying their real character? He affirmed that the Government had not physical force adequate to keep them down. If they were to rise as one man, as they might do, the Executive had nothing but what was as a rush to keep them down with. What then kept them down? They kept quiet from knowing that the advantages which they and their ancestors had derived from obedience to the law were not to be thrown away slightly and that was their only feeling in the matter. And if he were to be asked by what his countrymen were peculiarly distinguished from the other nations of Europe and from the people of all other countries that he knew of, he should say that the distinguishing feature in their character was obedience to the law. It had happened to himself and many other hon. Members to travel in other countries; he asked those hon. Members what was the case there? On the continent it was said *la force* was everywhere—here it was obedience to the law. The feeble constable without any question took the offender into custody solely from the moral feeling of the people. It was not physical force, but law, that bore sway here, and this it was that made him believe that if the whole body of the people ruled the country he should walk home just as quietly as he should that evening. Such was his confidence in his fellow-countrymen. He believed that if ever there had been a libel spoken,—he did not desire to say so in any sense that could be painful to the right hon. Gentleman,—but if ever there was a libel spoken upon his patient, forbearing, his industrious fellow-countrymen, it was that idle declaiming which said that they were unable to govern themselves. Why, it was they who had done everything for this country—upon them rested the whole fabric of English prosperity and greatness; and now, the very fact of this peaceful organisation for the attainment of what they believed to be their natural political rights, was a lesson which the world had never seen before. . . . He should vote for the Charter, because he believed that the people ought to be admitted into the pale of the Constitution, and because, from what study he had been able to give to the history of mankind, and from what consideration he had had of man's nature, he believed that the best government that could be got for any people, whether looking to the necessities of instruction, the interests of wealth, or to any of the peculiar circumstances affecting particular nations—that the best government that could be got was that which proceeded from the whole; and it did strike him, that if to-morrow they could transform, by legislative means, not by any violent revolution, that House into a complete representation of the people of England, there would not be one iota of difference as to all the interests and tendencies of property in this country—with this simple, peculiar, and advantageous exception, that every man in that case would have the proceeds of his own labour, with only so much taken from it as would form his fair share of contribution to the State.

68 / THE SOCIALIST DREAM

During the decades from the Restoration of 1815 to the revolution of 1848, much of the dissatisfaction with the existing social order found vent in the imaginative creations of totally reconstructed societies—"Utopias," as they have been called since Sir Thomas More's masterpiece. The Utopia-makers of the period of triumphing industrialism reflected the specific problems and possibilities of the new technology. This was especially true of Claude Henri, comte de Saint-Simon, who embraced the system of industrialism instead of rejecting it like earlier social critics. The following letter (A) was appended by Saint-Simon to his work, Du système industriel *("On the Industrial System," 1821). Saint-Simon (1760–1825) begin life as a member of a great aristocratic family in France, made and lost a fortune during and after the revolution, and then became the inventor and chief propagandist for a theory of socialism which he called the "New Christianity." [19]*

Where most of Saint-Simon's followers came to emphasize industrial activity as businessmen and engineers, rather than his dream of a socialist society, Charles Fourier was able to spur men to attempt immediate reorganization of society on a small scale.

[19] Henri de Saint-Simon, *Du système industriel* (Paris: Antoine-Augustin Renouard, 1821), pp. 262–7. Translated from the French by the editor.

Fourierist "phalanxes," as his proposed cooperative colonies were called, were founded in several countries. The most numerous and, for a while, the most successful were established in the United States. Fourier (1772–1837) saw his proposals not as the limited practical solutions to specific problems, but as the culminating phase of a vast theory of history and society. His ideas are set forth in his Théorie de l'unité universelle *("Theory of Universal Unity"), first published in 1822 under the title* Traité de l'association domestique-agricole, ou Attraction industrielle *("Treatise on the domestic-agricultural association, or Industrial attraction") from which the following passages (B) are taken.*[20]

A. SAINT-SIMON

To the Farmers, Manufacturers, Merchants, Bankers and other Industrialists, as well as to the Scientists practising the physical and mathematical sciences and the Artists practising the fine arts.

GENTLEMEN:

I hereby give you notice that I shall publish the Letters which it has been my honor to write to you until now, including the present letter. In publishing them it is my intention to attract the attention of all scientists, artists and scholars, not only in France but throughout Europe and indeed the whole world.

It is my intention to persuade all scientists and artists whose minds are capable of rising to the level of philosophical reason, to suspend their work in advancing the special sciences and arts in order to devote themselves to the organization of a system of morality and politics so clear and positive that the rulers, like the ruled, will be forced to follow it.

It is also my intention to show the industrialists that the theoretical labor which they need for the establishment of the social regime most advantageous to industry, requires financial sacrifices on their part, in view of the fact that it cannot be instituted until they give guarantees to the scientists who will devote themselves to this labor and thereby remove them from their present absolute dependence upon the existing governments, which desire to prolong the present order, or rather disorder.

It is my intention, finally, to open the eyes of the industrialists to another important point: that it is they who produce all wealth and who consequently meet all expenses, and that it is necessary as a consequence of these two facts that it is they who should draft the budget,

[20] Charles Fourier, *Theory of Social Organization: Theory of Universal Unity*, translated from the French (New York: C. P. Somerby, 1876), pp. 22–5, 76–7.

especially because they form the class of citizens whose administration is most economical.

Gentlemen: The great moral movement which must bring about the transformation of society from the modified regime of arbitrary rule to the regime most advantageous to the majority of society cannot be a purely national movement; it cannot be accomplished except as the joint work of the most enlightened peoples. This transformation must occur in the same way and by the same means as the passage from polytheism to theism.

The French cannot participate in this great task by themselves; for the success of this enterprise it is necessary that all the peoples who comprise the great Western nation of Europe cooperate in it—the French, English, Belgians, Portuguese, Spaniards and Italians. These peoples were all subject to Roman rule; they all adopted feudal government at about the same period; they must all raise the level of their civilization to the industrial regime at about the same time. These peoples all have similar and almost equal means; they must work with equal zeal in establishing the industrial regime which will be the final form of the organization of the human race, because this form, or more exactly this kind of association, is the only one which is fundamentally moral, that is, the most advantageous to the majority of the members of society.

Gentlemen: The immediate purpose of my enterprise is to improve as much as possible the conditions of the class which has no means of livelihood but the labor of its hands; my purpose is to improve the conditions of this class not only in France, but also in England, Belgium, Portugal, Spain, Italy, in the rest of Europe and throughout the world. This class, despite the immense progress of civilization (since the liberation of the commons), is still the most numerous one in the most civilized countries; it forms the majority in a greater or lesser proportion in all nations of the globe. Thus it is the class to which the governments should give their principal attention, but whose interests, on the contrary, receive their least concern; for they consider it fundamentally as the group which has to pay taxes and be ruled, and their only important concern for it is to keep it as passively obedient as possible.

What way is there to improve the condition of the people as promptly and surely as possible? This is the great political problem which requires solution. I believe that I have found the solution and shall present it to you. Gentlemen: I ask your undivided attention. Keep in mind that you will be deciding the fate, if not of the human race, at least of the present generation.

The common people, like the rich, have needs of two kinds: they have physical needs and moral needs; they need subsistence and they also need education.

What is the way to provide to the common people as a whole the fullest possible subsistence with the greatest possible speed?

I observe first of all that the only general way of providing subsistence for the people consists in providing them with jobs. The question is therefore transformed into the following:

What is the way to provide the people with the greatest possible number of jobs?

To this question I reply:

The best way is to entrust to the leaders of industrial enterprises the task of preparing the budget and hence of directing the administration of the state; for, in the nature of things, the leaders of industrial enterprises (who are the true leaders of the people, since it is they who command the people in their daily work) will always tend, in their own interest and in the most direct fashion, to expand their enterprises as much as possible, and there will result from their efforts to this end the greatest possible increase in the number of jobs which will be performed by the common people.

I now pass to the next question:

What kind of education should be given to the people? How should it be given?

The education which the people most need is that which will enable them to perform most capably the jobs they are given. Now it is incontestable that some notion of geometry, physics, chemistry and hygiene is the knowledge which will be most useful to them in their usual lives, and it is evident that the scientists practising the physical and mathematical sciences are the only persons qualified to provide them with a good system of education.

The system of education in the primary schools must therefore be organized by the scientists engaged in the positive sciences.

As for the method of instruction, mutual teaching by students has the advantage of being fastest and assuring the greatest uniformity of doctrine; it should therefore receive preference.

Gentlemen: The opinions which I have just put before you do not require proof, they are not subject to discussion, because common sense is sufficient for judging them and they are a direct consequence of the great principle of morality which serves as the foundation of the Christian religion: *Love thy neighbor as thyself.* All truly pious men will eagerly adopt these principles—they need only to be disseminated. Therefore, gentlemen, disseminate them as actively as possible; it is your duty and your advantage to do so.

I have the honor to be,

> Gentlemen,
> Your most humble and obedient
> servant.

B. CHARLES FOURIER

In studying the problem of social development and progress, we must rise to the conception that the Human Race, considered as a whole, must pass, like the individual, through a regular career, subject to the four phases of Infancy, Youth, Manhood, and Old Age; I shall show that it is now in the first of these phases.

The social Infancy of the Race is much shorter in proportion than that of the individual man; but the effects in both cases are the same; that is, a social world in the phase of Infancy may be compared to a child that at the age of six or eight, wholly absorbed in childish sports, has not yet any knowledge of the career of manhood. In like manner the Human Race on an infant globe, or a globe in the first phase of its career, does not rise to the conception of a future state of Harmony, in which the social world will pass from indigence to opulence; from falseness to truth and justice; from a state of social discord to social unity.

If Association can be demonstrated to be practicable, it is certain that the existing societies—the Civilized, Barbaric, and Savage—will disappear before it, and that the social world will pass from the phase of Infancy to that of Adolescence,—to the essential and happy destiny which awaits mankind,—the duration of which is seven times that of the ages of social chaos and misfortune.

I shall endeavor to prepare the mind to conceive the possibility of this great social change, which will absorb all party contentions and all conflicting interests in the grandeur of new hopes and interests. The prospect of such a vast social transformation should rouse the minds of men from their present lethargy, from their apathetic resignation to misfortune, and especially from the discouragement diffused by our moral and political sciences which proclaim the impossibility of the reign of social unity and happiness on earth, and assert the incompetency of human reason to determine our future social destiny. If the calculation of future events is beyond the reach of the human mind, whence comes that longing common to all mankind to fathom the secret of human destiny, at the very mention of which the most passive natures experience a thrill of impatience, so impossible is it to extirpate from the human heart the desire to penetrate the future. Why should God, who does nothing without a purpose, have given to us this intense longing, if he had not reserved the means of some day satisfying it? At last that day has arrived, and mortals are about to rise to the prescience of future events. I shall give, in the chapters on Cosmogony, an outline of universal Analogy, which will reveal to us these mysteries, and open to us the book of eternal decrees. Philosophy, unable to explain them, would deter us from their research by declaring that they are impenetrable. But if Nature is really impenetrable, as the philosophers assert, why has she permitted Newton to explain the fourth branch of her general system? This was an indication that she would not refuse us a knowledge of the other branches. Why, then, have our men of science been so timid in pursuing the secrets of Nature, who has encouraged them by allowing a corner of the veil that covers her mysteries to be raised? With their brilliant paradoxes, they communicate the scepticism and doubt with which they are filled, and persuade the human race that nothing can be discovered where their sciences have been unable to discover anything.

Meanwhile, they delude us with the idea that civilized society is progressing rapidly, when it is evident that it moves only in a vicious circle, and that there can be no great improvement but in the discovery and establishment of a new Social Order, higher in the scale than the present; and that human reason, under the influence of existing prejudices, is incapable of conceiving and executing any radical good. Twenty scientific centuries elapsed before any amelioration was proposed in the condition of the slaves; whence it would seem that thousands of years are necessary to suggest to the civilized mind an act of justice and social progress.

Thus our scientific guides are utterly ignorant of the means of promoting the real welfare of mankind. Their efforts at political reforms produce only commotions and disasters. The sluggish progress of our societies may be compared to that of the sloth, whose every step is attended with a groan; like it, civilization advances with an inconceivable slowness through political storms and revolutions. In each generation it gives birth to new schemes and experiments, which serve only to bring disasters upon those who try them.

At length the end of our social miseries, the term of the Political Infancy of the globe, is at hand. We are on the verge of a great social transformation, which a universal commotion seems to announce. Now, indeed, is the present big with the future, and the excess of human suffering must bring on the crisis of a new birth. Judging from the continual violence of political convulsions, it would seem as if Nature were making an effort to throw off a burden that oppresses her. Wars and revolutions devastate every part of the globe. Political storms, for a moment lulled, burst forth anew, and party conflicts and hatreds are becoming more and more intense, with no hope or prospect of reconciliation; the policy of nations has become more tortuous and crafty than ever, and diplomacy is familiar with every variety of political turpitude and crime; the revenues of States fall a prey to the vampires of the stock exchange; Industry, by its monopolies and excesses, has become a scourge to the laboring classes, who are reduced to the fate of Tantalus—starving in the midst of wealth and luxury; the ambition of colonial possession has opened a new volcano; the implacable fury of the negro race threatens to convert whole regions of the New World into a vast charnel-house, and avenge the exterminated aborigines, by the destruction of their conquerors; commerce, with a cannibal cruelty, has refined the atrocities of the slave trade, and treads under foot the decrees for its abolition; the mercantile spirit has extended the sphere of crime, and at every war carries devastation into both hemispheres; our ships circumnavigate the globe only to initiate Barbarians and Savages into our vices and excesses; the earth exhibits the spectacle of a frightful chaos of immorality, and Civilization is becoming more and more odious as it approaches its end.

It is at this crisis, when the social world seems to have reached the bottom of the abyss, that a fortunate discovery brings to it a guide out of the labyrinth—Association, based on the laws of universal harmony, which the age, but for its want of real faith in the universality of Providence, might have discovered a hundred times over. Let it know, and it cannot be too often repeated, that Providence must before all things have determined upon the plan of a Social Mechanism for man, since the social is the most noble branch of Universal Movement, the direction of which belongs to God alone.

Instead of comprehending this truth—instead of seeking what were the designs of God in respect to the organization of human society, and by what means he must have revealed them to us, the age has rejected every principle which admitted the UNIVERSALITY OF PROVIDENCE, and a plan of social organization devised by God for man. Passional Attraction, the eternal interpreter of his decrees, has been defamed; the social world has confided itself to the guidance of human legislators and philosophers, who have arrogated to themselves the highest function of Deity—the direction of the Social Movement. To their disgrace, humanity has, under their auspices, bathed itself in blood for twenty-five sophistical centuries, and exhausted the career of misery, ignorance and crime.

But Fortune has at length become propitious; Fate is disarmed, and the discovery of the associative theory opens to us the means of escape from that social prison called Civilization. . . .

The Civilized Order is based on the smallest possible domestic and industrial combination, that of one man and one woman,—a single couple in a separate household. The Combined Order would, on the contrary, be based on the largest combination possible, say about fifteen hundred persons, who would substitute in the place of domestic monotony, conjugal apathy and industrial indifference, active emulation, general enthusiasm and ardor in labor.

The Civilized Order secures for the most part fortune and honor to intrigue and falseness, while ruin is the result of generous devotion and the practice of truth; the Combined Order on the other hand would insure success only to the practice of strict veracity and justice, and the exercise of the nobler sentiments.

Such is the true basis of integral or compound convergent Liberty. It is, then, a very different thing from that superficial liberty, limited to the political sphere, which has been the subject of such interminable controversies in Civilization.

Without doubt Liberty is a very precious boon, since every party wishes to secure it for itself, deprive all others of it, monopolize every thing, and concentrate all privileges, all honors, all power in the hands of a limited number. In Civilization, this is the only kind of liberty known; I will point out the conditions of a liberty of a character entirely different.

Liberty, unless enjoyed by all, is unreal and illusory. Whenever the free action of the Passions is restricted to a small minority, there is only oppression; as for example in Civilization, where it is limited to an eighth, while even this favored few do not enjoy a fourth of the passional development they will possess in the Combined Order.

To secure liberty, that is full scope for the action and development of the Passions to all, a Social Order is necessary which shall fulfill the following conditions:

1. Discover and organize a system of Attractive Industry.

2. Guarantee to every individual the equivalent of the seven natural rights.

3. Associate the interests of all classes, rich and poor, since the latter would be envious of the former, if they did not participate with them in their welfare and social enjoyments.

It is only on these three conditions that the masses can be assured a *minimum*—that is, a comfortable subsistence, together with the enjoyment of all social pleasure; for the agreeable is as necessary to man as the useful. Deprived of pleasures, he would remain discontented, and would not give a cordial assent and adherence to the established order of things; he would be deprived of the seventh natural right, namely, freedom from care. He can enjoy this fully only by being insured a *compound minimum*—that is, the means of satisfying the wants of both the body and the soul.

69 / FRANÇOIS GUIZOT: CONSTITUTIONAL MONARCHY AT BAY

At the beginning of the Restoration epoch, constitutional monarchy on the British model had seemed the solution of moderation to those who wished neither a total restoration of the Old Regime nor a revolutionary new order. The monarchy of Louis Philippe, established by the revolution of 1830, became the first full-fledged government of this type in France. It was overthrown in 1848 when it proved unable to hold the loyalty of the bourgeoisie, far less of the laboring classes of the towns. How Louis Philippe and his great minister, the historian François Guizot, looked upon their regime is indicated in the following passages from Guizot's Mémoires pour servir à l'histoire de mon temps *("Memoirs to Serve The History of My Own Time," 1858–1868). Guizot (1787–1874) was a professor of modern history at the University of Paris before becoming a member and finally the leader of the government after 1830.*[21]

. . . The opposition . . . erected into a constitutional maxim the celebrated phrase, "The King reigns but does not govern." This was to pervert equally, in right, the true principle of constitutional monarchy, in fact, its natural consequences and the examples of its history wherever it had founded itself. "Although it has often been implied," I said in the debate in the Chamber of Deputies, at the sitting of the 29th of May, 1846, "the throne is not an arm-chair on which a key has been placed to prevent anyone from sitting there, and solely to prevent usurpation. An intelligent and free person, with his own ideas, sentiments, desires, and wishes, sits in that arm-chair. The duty of that royal personage—for there are duties for all, equally elevated and sacred—his duty, I say, and his mission is to govern in accordance with the other great powers instituted by the charter, with their consent, adhesion, and support. The duty of the advisers of the crown is to influence it with the same ideas, measures, and policy with which they

[21] François Guizot, *The Last Days of the Reign of Louis Philippe,* translated from the French (London: Richard Bentley, 1867), pp. 77–8, 81, 471–3.

desire and are able to influence the Chambers. Such is constitutional government: not only its sole, true, and legitimate form, but its only dignified one; for we ought to entertain for the crown, as we require the crown to entertain for us, the respect of believing that it is worn by an intelligent and free being with whom we *treat*, and not by a mere inert machine, made to occupy a place others would seize if it were not there."

Such is the rational principle of constitutional monarchy, the principle on which the two essential inseparable conditions of that form of government rest—the inviolability of the monarch, and the responsibility of his advisers. That people may not wish constitutional monarchy, that they may think the responsibility of power and the just influence of the country in its own government better assured by the institutions of the American republic—this I perfectly understand, although quite opposed to the opinion; but when the partisans of constitutional monarchy assume that the maxim, *the King can do no wrong,* signifies *the King can do nothing,* and that royal inviolability leads to royal nullity—this appears to me a strange oblivion of the dignity and moral liberty of a human being, even though placed upon a throne and surrounded by advisers responsible for his acts, whether suggested by them or accepted from his will. . . .

The philanthropic ideas of the eighteenth century, the principles of 1789, the first impulse and social progress of the French Revolution, had no adherent more sincerely convinced and constant than this prince, entirely unswayed by personal interest or calculation.

Moreover, as King and in his government, he was firmly resolved never to emerge from the constitutional circle, and always to accept, definitively, the thought and sentiment of the country manifested after free discussion and trials legally authorized. No sovereign ever more frankly adopted the principle of a contract between the people and himself. . . .

The cabinet and its political friends had one determined thought and design. They aspired to close, in France, the era of revolutions by founding the free government which in 1789 France had promised herself as the consequence and the political guarantee of the social revolution which she had accomplished.

We looked upon the policy which, with the exception of a few passing difficulties, had prevailed in France since the ministry of M. Casimir Périer, as the only efficacious one, and sure to attain the desired end. This policy was, in fact, at the same time liberal and anti-revolutionary. Anti-revolutionary without as within, for outside it sought the maintenance of the peace of Europe, within that of the constitutional monarchy. Liberal, because it accepted and respected the essential conditions of free government, the positive interference of the country in its affairs, constant and earnest discussion among the public as in the Chambers, of the ideas and acts of those in authority. In fact, from 1830 to 1848 this double aim was attained. Exteriorly peace was maintained, and I think even now, as I thought twenty years ago, that neither the influence nor the high standing of France in Europe was lowered. Internally, from 1830 to 1848, political liberty had been very great; from 1840 to 1848 especially, it extended itself without any new legal limits being imposed on it. If I were to utter my thoughts without reserve, I would say that, not only the impartial spectators, but the greater portion of the former adversaries of our policy, admit now, in their own minds, the truth of this assertion. The policy which we thus adopted and adhered to was principally supported by the preponderating influence of the middle classes; an influence recognized and accepted in the general interest of the country, and subjected to all the tests and all the influences of the general liberty. I am not here discussing the system. I only record the fact, and I will not dwell on either its importance or its character. The middle classes, without any privilege or limit in civil affairs, and constantly open, in political affairs, to the ascending movement of the whole nation, were, in our eyes, the best organs for, and guardians of, the principles of 1789, of social order as well as of constitutional government, of liberty as of order, civil as well as political liberty, and of progress as well as stability.

At the end of several general elections of which the liberty and legality could not be seriously questioned, and under the weight of important debates incessantly repeated, the preponderating influence of the middle classes had caused, in the Chambers and in the country, the formation of a majority which approved the policy the characteristics of which I have just retraced, wished it to be maintained, and did support it through the difficulties and trials, interior and exterior, which events imposed on it: this majority was successively renewed, recruited, strengthened, exercised in public life, and from day to day more intimately united to the government, as the government was to it. According to the natural inclination of the free and representative government, it had become the conservative party, on the anti-revolutionary and liberal policy of which it had, since 1831, wished and promoted the success.

Parliamentary government, the practical form of free government under a constitutional monarchy; the preponderant influence of the middle classes, an efficacious guarantee of the constitutional monarchy and of political liberties under this form of government; the conservative party, the natural representative of the influence of the middle classes, and the necessary instrument of parliamentary government: such were, it is our firm conviction, the means of action and the conditions of duration for the liberal and anti-revolutionary policy which we had at heart to practise and maintain.

70 / VICTOR HUGO: ROMANTICISM AND LIBERAL POLITICS

The connection between the literary and artistic movement of Romanticism and the social and political worlds was complex. The franker emotionalism so characteristic of Romanticism made its appeal both to doctrinal conservatives, with their growing suspicion of rationalism, and to doctrinal liberals, to whom it appeared as a release from old bonds of form and style. Typical of the way that politics and art were deliberately tied together is the preface written by the French writer Victor Hugo to his play Hernani *in 1830. The innovations of the play, which seem mild indeed to modern literary students, aroused a riot at the first performance. Hugo (1802–1885), the leader of French literary Romanticism, was the outstanding French poet of his century, and was also productive as a playwright and novelist. He abandoned his early royalism to become a liberal, even going into exile during the reign of Napoleon III but becoming a national hero under the Third Republic.*[22]

Some weeks ago the author of this play wrote these words about a poet who died before his time:

"In this hour of literary strife and storm, whom shall we pity—the dying or those who still fight? It is surely sad to see a poet who leaves us at the age of twenty, a lyre shattered, a future that will not be. But should we not also give sleep its due? Why may not they have their rest too, those upon whom calumny and insult, hatred, envy, secret intrigues and foul treason are ceaselessly heaped; the loyal men against

---

[22] Victor Hugo, "Preface to *Hernani*," *Édition nationale: Hernani—Marion de Lorme—Le Roi s'amuse* (Paris: Émile Testard, 1887), pp. 3–6. Translated from the French by the editor.

whom disloyal war is waged; the dedicated men who wish only to give their country one more freedom—the freedom of art and the intellect; the toiling men who peaceably perform the tasks which conscience assigns them, but who are on the one hand the prey of the vile schemes of censors and policemen and on the other only too frequently the victims of the ingratitude of the very people for whom they toil? Have they no right to turn envious eyes now and then upon those who have already fallen and rest now in the tomb? '*Invideo,*' said Luther in the cemetery at Worms, '*invideo, quia quiescunt.*' [23]

"Yet what does it matter? Be of good heart, you who are young! Harsh as our present may be made, the future will be good. In the final analysis, romanticism (to which so many false definitions have been given) is, considered as a combatant, nothing but *liberalism* in literature. That is its true definition. Almost all right-thinking people —and their number is great—already understand the truth of this definition, and soon liberalism in literature will have no less popularity than liberalism in politics: for the work is already far advanced. Freedom in art, freedom in society—these are the double goal toward which all consistent and logical minds should march in single step; these are the double banner around which rally all the youth, who today are so strong and so patient (a very few excepted, and even these will be enlightened); and then, with this youth and at its head, will come the élite of the generation which came before us, all those wise old men who recognized after a first moment of mistrust and inquiry that the deeds of their sons were the consequence of their own deeds and that freedom of literature is the daughter of political freedom. In vain will the Ultras [24] of every species, classicists and monarchists, lend each other aid in the endeavor to rebuild the Old Regime in its entirety, in society and in literature. Their whole shaky edifice will topple under the blows of every advance made by the country, every development of intellectual life, every gain of liberty. Their reactionary endeavors will serve a purpose after all is done. In revolutions every change results in progress. It is one of the merits of truth and freedom that they are served equally by what is done for them and against them. Now we have witnessed all the great accomplishments of our fathers and leave the old social order behind: is it possible that we shall not also leave the old form of poetry behind? For a new people—a new art. Although they will admire the literature of the age of Louis XIV, which befitted his monarchy so well, France—the France of our own day, the nineteenth century, which received its freedom from Mirabeau and

---

[23] "I envy those who are at rest."

[24] the "ultra-royalists" after the Bourbon Restoration, who were even more conservative than the king, Louis XVIII (ed.)

its power from Napoleon—will be able to produce its own individual and national literature."—*Letter to the Publishers of the Poems of M. Dovalle.*

May the author of this play be pardoned for quoting himself. His weak words are not such as to engrave themselves on men's memories and so he must repeat them often. In any case, it may well be fitting at this moment to place before his readers the two pages I have just transcribed. Not that this play of mine can deserve in any way the fine name of *new art* or *new poetry;* far from it. But it is true that the principle of freedom in literature has made a step forward, that progress has been made not in the field of art—this play is too slight a thing—but in the public, and that at least in one respect some portion of the predictions which I have ventured has come true.

There was certainly some danger in changing one's audience in this way, in risking upon the stage trial efforts which hitherto had been entrusted only to paper, *which puts up with no matter what;* the book-reading public is quite different from the playgoing public and there was reason to fear that the latter would reject what the former had accepted. This has not happened. The principle of literary freedom, which the public which reads and thinks has already understood, has also been adopted with equal completeness by the immense crowd which thirsts for pure artistic experience and nightly floods the theaters of Paris. The people's voice, loud and strong like the voice of God, proclaims that henceforth poetry shall bear the same device as politics:

TOLERANCE AND FREEDOM!

Now the poet may come, for he has a public!

And the public desires freedom in its proper form, harmonized with order in the state and with art in literature. Freedom has a wisdom of its own, without which it is not complete. It is well that D'Aubignac's old rule book of dramatic art should perish along with Cujas's old book of customary law; it is still better that a people's literature should succeed a court literature; but it is best that an inner purpose should be at work within all these innovations. Let freedom do what it wills, but let it do it well. In literature as in society, we need neither ceremonials nor anarchy but laws, neither red-heeled aristocrats nor red-capped revolutionaries.

This is what the public wants, and rightly. As for us, in deference to that public which has so indulgently welcomed a trial effort which deserved so little indulgence, we now offer it this play as it has been staged. The day may come to publish it as it was first conceived by the author, indicating and discussing the changes required by the stage. Such critical details may not be without their interest and their lessons, but today they would look like minutiae. Freedom of art has been accepted and the principal question is decided: why tarry on secondary problems? In any event, we shall return to them some day, and we shall also discuss then in great detail, in order to destroy it by argument and fact, that censorship of the stage which is the sole obstacle to freedom of the theater now that the public is not an obstacle. At our own risk and peril (because we are dedicated to art and its works), we shall attempt to depict the myriad misdeeds of this petty inquisition of the intellect, which, like that other Holy Office, possesses its secret judges, its masked executioners, its tortures, mutilations and penalties of death. We shall rip off, if we can, the swaddling clothes in which the police have shamefully swathed the theater even today, in the nineteenth century.

Now my duty is only to express gratitude and thanks. From the bottom of his heart the author of this play expresses his gratitude and thanks to the public. The public has given this work generous protection against numerous enmities, not because the play displays talent but because it is dedicated to honesty and liberty, to which the public is also dedicated. Thanks be then to the public, and to that mighty generation of our youth which has given aid and favor to the work of a young man who has the same sincerity and independence as they! It is for them above all that he works, because the applause of this élite of intelligent, logical and consistent youth, true liberals in literature as in politics—a noble generation which does not balk at opening its eyes wide to look upon truth and to receive light from either side— would be a very great glory indeed.

71 / HEINRICH HEINE: ROMANTICISM IN GERMANY

The Romantic movement in France was a model of disciplined deportment compared to the passionate turbulence that marked it in Germany. The character of German Romanticism was analyzed with withering insight by one of its greatest figures, the poet and essayist Heinrich Heine. But the Jewish-born Heine was a Romantic with a difference: he expressed the Romantic's vibrant feelings with classical control and grace, and he despised the conservative obscurantism of so many German Romantics. These attitudes can be seen in the following selections, "The Character of the Romantic School in Germany" and "Why Did the

Germans Take to the Romantic School?" taken from his The Romantic School, *published in 1836.*[25]

THE CHARACTER OF THE ROMANTIC SCHOOL IN GERMANY

But what was the Romantic School in Germany?

It was nothing else but the reawakening of the poety of the Middle Ages, as it had manifested itself in song, painting, architecture, art and life. But this poetry had its origin in Christianity; it was a passion-flower which had sprung from the blood of Christ.

I do not know whether the melancholy flower which in Germany is called the passion-flower is known by that name in France, and whether popular legend attributes to it the same mystical origin. It is a strange flower of a repulsive color, in the chalice of which we find replicas of the implements of martyrdom used in the crucifixion of Christ, such as the hammer, pincers, nails, etc.,—a flower which is not so much ugly, as eerie, and the sight of which awakens in us a horrible kind of pleasure, like those agreeable paroxysms of feeling we experience in pain itself. For this reason, the flower would indeed be the fittest symbol for Christianity itself, whose most gruesome appeal is to be found in that very same voluptuous pain.

Though in France the word Christianity is used only in the sense of Roman Catholicism, I must here specifically remark that I am speaking only of the latter. I speak of that religion in whose first dogmas is to be found damnation of all flesh, and which not only extends to the spirit supremacy over the flesh, but would also destroy the flesh in order to glorify the spirit. I speak of that religion whose unnatural demands brought sin and hypocrisy into the world; for condemnation of the flesh made the most innocent sensual pleasures a sin, and the impossibility of ever attaining a perfect spiritual state brought forth hypocrisy. I speak of that religion which, because it teaches rejection of all earthly goods, abject, hang-dog humility and angelic patience, became the most reliable pillar of despotism. Men have now come to see clearly the true nature of this religion; they will not be contented merely with Barmecide celestial suppers. They know that matter also has its virtues, and does not wholly belong to the devil. They vindicate the pleasures of this world, this beautiful garden of the Lord, and our inalienable inheritance. And because we so thoroughly understand the

[25] Frederic Ewen, ed., *The Poetry and Prose of Heinrich Heine* (New York: The Citadel Press, 1948), pp. 721–727. Translated by Frederic Ewen. Reprinted by permission of The Citadel Press.

consequences of that absolute spirituality, we may now be sure that the Christian-Catholic world-view has come to an end. For every age is a sphinx, which hurls itself into the abyss when man has solved its riddle.

Yes, we would by no means deny the benefits which the Christian-Catholic view of the world conferred on Europe. It was necessary as a salutary reaction against that horrible and colossal materialism which had developed within the Roman Empire, and which threatened to destroy the spiritual grandeur of humanity. Just as the prurient memoirs of the last century form the *pièces justificatives* [26] of the French Revolution, just as the terrorism of a *comité du salut public* [27] appears as a necessary physic, when we read the confessions of the French aristocracy since the time of the Regency, so we understand the wholesomeness of ascetic spirituality when we read Petronius or Apuleius—books which may in turn be regarded as the *pièces justificatives* of Christianity. The flesh became so arrogant in that Roman world that it needed the chastening rod of Christian discipline. After Trimalchio's banquet, one needed the hunger-cure of Christianity.

Perhaps Rome had herself scourged in her old age so that she might experience the more exquisite delights of torture and voluptuous raptures of pain, like those lechers who seek through whippings to rouse the palsied flesh to new pleasures?

Evil excess of stimulants! It robbed the Roman body politic of its last remnants of strength. Not because of the division into two realms did Rome perish. On the Bosphorus as well as by the Tiber it was Jewish spirituality that devoured it; and in both places Roman history is but a long death-bed agony, lasting for centuries. Did murdered Judea, when it bequeathed its spiritualism to the Romans, wish to avenge itself on its victorious foe, like the dying centaur who craftily transmitted the fatal garment, poisoned with his own blood, to the son of Jupiter? For Rome, the Hercules among nations, was so thoroughly consumed by Judea's poison that helm and harness fell from her withered limbs, and her imperial battle-cries died away in the wailing cadences of monkish prayers and the trilling of castrates.

But that which weakens old age, strengthens youth. Spirituality had a healthy influence on the all-too-sound races of the North. The barbarians, with their excessively full-blooded bodies, became spiritualized by Christianity, and European civilization commenced. This is the creditable, sacred aspect of Christianity. The Catholic Church has in this regard the strongest claims upon our reverence and admiration. By its great and inspired institutions it succeeded in subduing the

[26] documentary proofs
[27] committee of public safety

bestiality of the Nordic barbarians and in gaining mastery over brute matter.

WHY DID THE GERMANS TAKE TO THE ROMANTIC SCHOOL?

The political conditions in Germany were then especially favorable to the Christian Old-German movement. "Poverty teaches us to pray," says the proverb, and as a matter of fact, never was Germany in greater distress; hence people were more inclined to prayer, religion, and Christianity. There are no people more devoted to their princes than the Germans. What grieved them even more deeply than the sad condition to which their country had been reduced by war and foreign domination was the melancholy sight of their vanquished princes grovelling at the feet of Napoleon. The whole country resembled those faithful old servants of great houses we often see on the stage, who feel the humiliations of their masters more profoundly than the masters themselves; who secretly weep bitter tears when the family plate is to be sold, and even buy aristocratic wax-tapers with their own savings, so that the plebeian tallow candles may not be seen on the gentlefolk's tables.

This general depression found relief in religion, and there arose a pietistic surrender to the will of God, from whom alone help could be expected. For indeed, what other help could avail against Napoleon? No longer was reliance placed on earthly armies. All eyes turned expectantly toward heaven.

We could have made our peace with Napoleon. But our princes, though they were hopeful that God would free them, thought that the united strength of their people could also be of great help. With this in view, they sought to arouse a feeling of solidarity among them, and even the most eminent personages now spoke of a German nation, of a common German Fatherland, of the union of Christian-German races, of a united Germany. We were commanded to become patriots—and patriots we became; for we do as our princes command.

But one must not confuse the term patriotism as here used with what it implies for the French. The patriotism of the Frenchman consists in the fact that his heart is warmed by it; as a result, it expands, spreads, and with its love no longer embraces only his next of kin, but also all of France, the land of civilization. The patriotism of the German, on the other hand, makes his heart narrower, so that it contracts like leather in the cold—he hates whatever is foreign, and does not wish to be a citizen of the world, or of Europe, but only a cabined and cribbed German. Hence that idealized churlishness which was erected into a system by Herr Jahn, and thus commenced that shabby, crude, unwashed opposition to the holiest and most glorious sentiment ever felt in Germany—that humanitarianism, that universal brotherhood of man, that cosmopolitanism to which our greatest spirits, Lessing, Herder, Schiller, Goethe, Jean Paul and all the learned men of Germany, did homage.

What happened soon thereafter in Germany is too well known. When God, snow, and the Cossacks destroyed the best of Napoleon's forces, we Germans received the all-highest order to liberate ourselves from the foreign yoke; we became enflamed with manly rage at the servitude we had so long endured; and we were filled with an inspiration drawn from the good tunes and bad lines of Körner's songs, and we won our freedom. For we do as our princes command.

At the time we were preparing for this struggle, a school of thought, most inimical to all that was French and glorifying all that was German in art and life, naturally prospered. The Romantic School then worked hand in hand with the efforts of the governments and secret societies, and A. W. von Schlegel conspired against Racine with the same end in view as Minister Stein against Napoleon. The Romantic School followed the current of the time—that is, the current which was reverting to its source. When at last German patriotism and German nationalism triumphed, the German-Christian Romantic School also triumphed, with equal decisiveness, and "Neo-German-Religious-Patriotic Art" as well. Napoleon, that great classicist—as classical as Alexander and Caesar—succumbed, and Messrs. August Wilhelm von Schlegel and Friedrich Schlegel, the little Romantics, as romantic as Tom Thumb and Puss-in-Boots, were victorious. But here too as everywhere else reaction followed on the heels of excess. Just as spiritual Christianity represented a reaction against the brutal sway of the materialism of Imperial Rome; as the renewed love of joyous Greek art and learning was a reaction against Christian spiritualism which had degenerated into imbecile asceticism; as the reawakening of medieval romance was a reaction against the prosaic imitation of ancient, classical art—so we now witness a recoil against the restoration of Catholic-Feudal thought and that knighthood and priesthood which had been preached in word and image under the most amazing forms. When the highly-praised models—the masters of the Middle Ages—were extolled and admired, their excellence was attributed to the fact that they believed in the subjects they were portraying. It was said that in their artless simplicity they were capable of greater achievements than their successors who lacked faith, although they possessed more advanced techniques; —and that it was this very faith which had wrought miracles in their souls. And indeed, how else could one explain the glories of Fra Angelico da Fiesole or the poetry of Brother Ottfried? Hence it followed that those artists who took art seriously, and hoped to reproduce

the divine distortions of these wonder-paintings, and the saintly awk-
wardness of those wonder-poems—in short, to capture the ineffable
mysticism of the ancient works of art—decided to repair to the same
Hippocrene from which the old masters had drawn their miraculous
inspiration. They made pilgrimages to Rome, where the vicar of Christ
was to strengthen consumptive German art with the milk of the she-ass.
They betook themselves to the bosom of the only soul-saving Roman
Catholic Apostolic Church. Many of the adherents of the Romantic
School needed no formal conversion. Herr Görres and Herr Klemens
Brentano, for example, were born Catholics, and they merely renounced
their former free thinking. Others like Friedrich Schlegel, Herr Ludwig
Tieck, Novalis, Werner, Schütz, Carové, Adam Müller, etc., had been
brought up in the bosom of the Protestant Church—and their conversion to Catholicism required a public declaration. Here I have only
named the writers; the number of painters who abjured their evangel-
ical faith in droves—and along with it, reason—was much greater.

When the German world saw these young people waiting in line for
tickets of admission to the Roman Catholic Church, and again crowding into the old prisonhouse of the spirit, from which their fathers had
with so much labor succeeded in delivering themselves, they shook
their heads with concern. But when they discovered that the propaganda of priests and Junkers which had conspired against the religious
and political freedom of Europe had a hand in this game too, and that
it was really Jesuitism which was enticing German youth to destruction
with the dulcet notes of romance—like the Pied Piper of Hamelin—then
great disaffection and burning indignation took hold of the friends of
Protestantism and of freedom of thought.

I have named freedom of thought and Protestantism in one breath;
and I hope that even though I belong in Germany to the Protestant
Church, I shall not be charged with partisanship in her favor. Without
partiality I have classed freedom of thought and Protestantism; for
there is, in very fact, a friendly relation between them in Germany.
They are closely allied, like mother and daughter. Though we may
reproach the Protestant Church with many instances of frightful narrowness, we must still grant, to her immortal credit, that she allowed
free inquiry into the Christian religion, and liberated our minds from
the yoke of authority, so that bold investigation could take root, and
learning and science develop independently. German philosophy,
though it would at the present time rank itself by the side of, even
above, the Protestant Church—is nevertheless always her daughter;
and as such, obliged to retain an indulgent reverence for her mother—
and the interests of her family require an alliance between them when
both are threatened by a common enemy, Jesuitism. All friends of free
thought and Protestantism, sceptics and believers, rose at once against

the restorers of Catholicism, and, it goes without saying, that the liberals too, who were more interested in defending bourgeois political freedom than philosophy or Protestantism, made common cause with them. In Germany, the liberals have always been at the same time professors of philosophy and theologians, and they always fight for the idea of freedom, no matter whether it takes a purely political, philosophical, or theological form.

DATE DUE